S0-AKV-930

English Structure in Focus

Book Two

Second Edition

POLLY DAVIS

Newbury House Publishers, New York
A DIVISION OF HARPER & ROW, PUBLISHERS, INC.
Philadelphia, San Francisco, Washington, D.C.
London, Mexico City, São Paulo, Singapore, Sydney

Director: Laurie E. Likoff
Production Coordinator: Cynthia Funkhouser
Text Design Adaptation and Cover Design: Suzanne Bennett Associates
Text Illustrations: Kathie Kelleher and Elisabeth Clark
Photo Research: Mira Schachne
Compositor: Waldman Graphics
Printer and Binder: Malloy Lithographing, Inc.
Cover Printer: Phoenix Color

Photo Credits: Laurie H. MacIvor, Dept. of Forestry and Wildlife, University of Massachusetts, Amherst: p. 2. New York Zoological Society Photo: p. 18. Acid Rain Monitoring Project, Water Resources Research Center, University of Massachusetts, p. 22. Gans/© The Image Works: pp. 40, 202, 240. © Morrow/Stock, Boston: 54. AP/Wide World: pp. 80, 352, 460, 478. Deborah Snow, photographer: p. 98. © Antman/The Image Works: p. 118. Whitley/Taurus: p. 136. Monkmeyer Press Photo: p. 152. © Daemmrich/The Image Works: p. 170. Polly Davis: p. 188. Herwig/Taurus: p. 224. Browne/Stock, Boston: p. 240. By permission of the Folger Shakespeare Library: p. 280. Alford S. Peckham/Huskywood Kennels: p. 294. Grant/Photo Researchers: p. 314. © Time Magazine, Time-Life, Inc.: p. 332. Roberts/Photo Researchers: p. 352. Invent America!: p 370. Forsyth/Monkmeyer: p. 386. Smith College Museum of Art, Northampton, Massachusetts: p. 418, gift of Mr. and Mrs. Richard Lyman (Charlotte Cabot '32), 1970, p. 452, purchased with funds given by the estate of Mrs. Chapin Riley (Mary Alexander '30), 1965. Courtesy of the Art Institute of Chicago: p. 435. The Baltimore Museum of Art: p. 442 (bequest of Mabel Garrison Siemonn in memory of her husband George Siemonn).

NEWBURY HOUSE PUBLISHERS
A division of Harper & Row, Publishers, Inc.

Language Science
Language Teaching
Language Learning

English Structure in Focus, Book Two, Second Edition

Copyright ©1989 by Newbury House Publishers, a division of Harper & Row, Publishers, Inc. All rights reserved. Printed in the United States of America. No part of this book may be used or reproduced in any manner whatsoever without written permission, except in the case of brief quotations embodied in critical articles and reviews. For information address Harper & Row, Publishers, Inc., 10 East 53d Street, New York, NY 10022.

Library of Congress Cataloging in Publication Data

Davis, Polly, 1930–
English structure in focus.

1. English language—Text-books for foreign speakers.
2. English language—Programmed instruction. I. Title.
PE1128.D35 1987 428.2'4 86-12623
ISBN 0-06-632138-7

92 91 90 89 9 8 7 6 5 4 3 2

Contents

Introduction to the Second Edition—Book Two

English Structure in Focus is a contextual grammar text for students of English as a second language. The second edition consists of two volumes: *Book One* for intermediate students and *Book Two* for high-intermediate to advanced learners.

Book Two can be used both as a continuation of *Book One* and as an independent text for students entering a program at the high-intermediate/advanced level. After a review of tenses and modals, the main focus of *Book One,* this text places major emphasis on expanding the sentence through the use of verbals and clauses. Topics of relevance to university and adult students are carried through the exercises in order to present the structures in real contexts, as well as to stimulate interest in and provide the vocabulary for discussion.

The grammatical sequence of the text proceeds from smaller to larger structural units; however, it is not rigid and may easily be altered to suit the needs of a particular curriculum or class. For example, a teacher might skip over the initial review sections in order to devote an entire course to work with verbals and clauses. Similarly, the order of units may be changed according to the needs of particular classes.

Lesson Format and Suggestions for Teachers

Each lesson in the text is divided into four main sections, which teachers will want to use differently according to their general approach and their teaching situation. Some of the possibilities are pointed out in the following outline.

1. The **structural focus** in each lesson is presented in two, three, or occasionally four parts, each with accompanying exercises. The presentation includes a chart with examples and a brief explanation. These may be presented in a number of ways. For example, you might write the examples on the blackboard and ask the class to participate in formulating the rules. In many cases it is also possible to begin with oral practice and allow students to arrive at the rules inductively; the explanation in the text can then be used as follow-up.

The exercises give controlled practice of the new structures in contexts related to a central theme. They include the following types, among others:

(a) Fill-in-the-blank exercises focus sharply on particular grammatical choices.

(b) Transformation and combining exercises teach not only a grammatical structure, but also editing techniques which the student can apply in writing compositions. Besides leading to greater sentence variety, these techniques enable the student to summarize and paraphrase—essential skills in academic writing.

(c) Completion exercises are a half-way point between controlled and free use of the language.

There are both oral and written exercises, exercises specifically designed for pair and group work, and many exercises which can be used in a variety of ways.

Vary the pace by alternating pair and group work with exercises for the whole class. Besides exercises specifically designated for pair work, those which begin, "Ask a classmate . . ." are often most productive and interesting when done in pairs. In addition, students benefit from working with a partner on particularly challenging written exercises. After they have completed an exercise in pairs, it is often valuable to have them report some of the answers to the whole class both for interest's sake and as a check on correctness.

2. In the **Transfer Exercises,** students apply what they have learned to their own experience or to a new context. Most of the exercises are suitable for oral practice in pairs, in groups, or as a whole class. They may all be taught together as a follow-up after the other exercises have been worked through, or they may be used out of sequence. For example, some are easy and can be used as oral practice before students start the written exercises in the lesson. Others require thought and an integration of several structures; they are best taught at the end, as a transition between controlled practice and independent use of the structures in discussion.

3. The **Discussion Topics** invite students to share their own ideas and experiences using vocabulary, structures, and information already presented. Students generally enjoy answering the questions in pairs or small groups because this allows each group of individuals to exchange more information. In some cases, input from the whole class will enrich the discussion.

At this point in the lesson, concern for grammatical accuracy can be relaxed. The questions help students use the structures taught for their own purposes; however, the emphasis should now be more on content than grammar, and the teacher's role can be minimized. Pair and group work help create a relaxed atmosphere in which students are willing to experiment with the language in genuine communication.

Instead of a discussion period at the end of the lesson, you may wish to raise questions for discussion at various points, injecting an exchange of opinions into an exercise done in class or following up the previous night's homework assignment with an exchange of cultural information.

4. The **Composition Topics** guide students in using the structures of the lesson in independent writing on the themes and issues raised in the lesson. The text is not designed to teach paragraph development, but of course such instruction can be introduced at this point if desired. Because the topics involve issues already read about and discussed in earlier sections, students will find it easier to decide what to write about, what to say, and how to say it, and will be motivated to communicate their experiences and viewpoints as effectively as possible.

Acknowledgments

I wish to thank those who reviewed the text at different stages of completion. Their insightful comments have helped immeasurably to clarify murky sections and eliminate snags. My thanks to Rebecca Dauer for her comments on the units on clauses, to David Veleta for looking at two lessons with an expert eye, and to the anonymous reviewers, who gave valuable perspective as well as concrete suggestions. I especially thank Robert Rainsbury, who field-tested the material in his classes at the American Language Institute at New York University. His comments led to the correction of many details, and his personal reactions were a barometer of enthusiasm pointing to needed improvements and lending encouragement at the same time.

I am grateful to Elaine Klein for permission to use her version of the Mark Twain story and to Eleanor Lander, whose creative use of the original edition gave direction to this revision.

Lastly, I thank Laurie Likoff, Director, and Cindy Funkhouser, Production Coordinator, at Newbury House for their patient attention to every detail throughout the stages of review and production.

English Structure in Focus

UNIT I

THE PRESENT TENSES

1. A Whale in the Sacramento River

2. Acid Rain: A Problem That Crosses Borders

Lesson 1

A Whale in the Sacramento River

1.1 Review of Question Patterns

Exercise 1. Pretest: First Auxiliaries

A. Fill in a different word in each space on the left and complete the answers.

1. can ______ ______	John drive to school?	Yes, he	can. ______. ______.
2. ______	you need some help?	Yes, I	______.
3. ______	I open a window?	Yes, please do.	
4. ______	I bothering you?	Yes, you	______.
5. ______ ______	the dog sleeping?	Yes, he	______. ______.
6. ______ ______	the children playing?	Yes, they	______. ______.
7. ______ ______	you seen that movie?	Yes, I	______. ______.
8. ______	John seen that movie?	Yes, he	______.

B. Working together with your classmates, can you find seven additional words which can begin sentence 1? These twenty auxiliaries are the only words that begin yes–no questions in English.

YES–NO QUESTIONS

FIRST AUXILIARY	SUBJECT	MIDDLE ADVERB	VERB	
Does	John	usually	drive	to school?
Did	he		walk	yesterday?
Have	you	ever	written	a poem?
Are	the children		eating	breakfast?
Is	Maria			from Bogota?
Are	the men	often		late?

PREDICATE QUESTIONS

INTER-ROGATIVE	FIRST AUXILIARY	SUBJECT	MIDDLE ADVERB	VERB		
Where	does	Ahmed	usually	eat	dinner?	At home.
When	will	you		help	me?	Tomorrow morning.
Who / Whom	did	the boss		choose	for the job?	He chose Jim.
To whom	were	you		speaking	just now?	To Bob.
Who	were	you		speaking	to just now?	
How	can	I		get	a job?	
Why	are	you		laughing?		
What	are	you		thinking	about?	
What color	is	your hair?			It's brown.	
How tall	are	you?			I'm five feet seven inches.	

Word Order: Notice that **be (is, am, are, was, were)** precedes the subject in questions, even when it is the only verb.

Formal and Informal Usage: **Whom** is more formal than **who** in predicate questions. In conversation, most people use **who** except after a preposition. After a preposition, we must use **whom.**

SUBJECT QUESTIONS

INTERROGATIVE SUBJECT	FIRST AUXILIARY	MIDDLE ADVERB	VERB		
How many students	are		taking	this course?	About ten. (a)
Who		usually	washes	the dishes?	My sisters do. (b)
Who	is		sitting	at this table?	Ana and Joe are. (b)
Who	has		been using	this room?	The students have. (b)
What			started	that fire?	A cigarette did.

Agreement: a. When the subject of a subject question is clearly marked as plural, the verb is plural.
b. In other subject questions, the verb is singular, even when the answer is plural.

Exercise 2. Interrogatives (pair work)

Fill in an appropriate interrogative from the list. Then ask a classmate the questions.

How	What	Where
How long	What kind of	Who
How many	When	Why

1. What __________ is your name?
2. __________ do you spell it?
3. __________ do you come from?
   or: __________ are you from?
4. __________ did you come to this country? (Ask two or three questions.)
5. __________ have you been studying English?
6. __________ other courses are you taking besides English?
7. __________ brothers and sisters do you have?
8. __________ are they living?
9. __________ are they doing now?

10. Are you working?
    If so: ________________ job do you have?
    If not: ________________ job did you have in your country?
    Or: ________________ job do you want to get eventually?
11. ________________ do you like life in this country?
12. ________________ do you like to do in your spare time?*

Exercise 3. Yes–No Questions

Read each sentence and then write a similar yes–no question using the expression in parentheses. Complete the answers where indicated.

1. Whales are mammals.* (land mammals)
   Are they land mammals? No, they are marine mammals.*
2. They live in the ocean. (lakes and rivers)
   Do they... No, they *don't*.
3. They can survive in salt water. (fresh water)
   ________________? Yes, but only for short periods.
4. A humpback whale has been seen in the Sacramento River recently. (for a long time)
   ________________? No, only for about three weeks now.
5. It is swimming up and down the river. (very fast)
   ________________? No, it is swimming slowly.
6. It likes something about the river. (the warm water in the river)
   ________________? Perhaps. Scientists are not sure.
7. It will be all right if it returns to the ocean soon. (if it stays much longer in the river)
   ________________? No, it will get sick.

**Spare time:* free time.

**Mammal:* an animal which gives milk to its young. A marine mammal is a mammal which lives in the ocean.

8. There are scientists who are concerned about saving whales. (who are concerned about this humpback whale)
_______________? Yes, there _______________.

9. They want to save its life. (capture it)
_______________? No, they _______________.

10. They have been trying to get it back to the ocean. (to pull it)
_______________? No, they _______________.

11. They have** several ideas about how to help it. (any good ideas)
_______________? They aren't sure yet.

12. They played a recording of humpback whale songs yesterday. (under water)
_______________? Yes, they _______________.

13. They wanted the whale to swim toward the sound. (downstream toward the sea)
_______________? Yes, they _______________.

14. Everybody was interested in the experiment. (the whale—*use as the subject*)
_______________? No, it _______________.

15. The rescue workers will not try whale songs again tomorrow. (a different strategy***)
_______________? Yes, they _______________.
They are not giving up yet.

When **have is a main verb, Americans generally use **do, does,** and **did** to form questions. The British often ask **Have you got...?**

American: **Do you have a car?**

British: **Have you got a car?**

Rare: **Have you a car?**

When **have** is a first auxiliary (as in items 4 and 10), it precedes the subject in questions.

Have you seen that movie?

****Strategy:* plan for solving a problem.

1.2 The Simple Present and the Present Progressive

Action Verbs

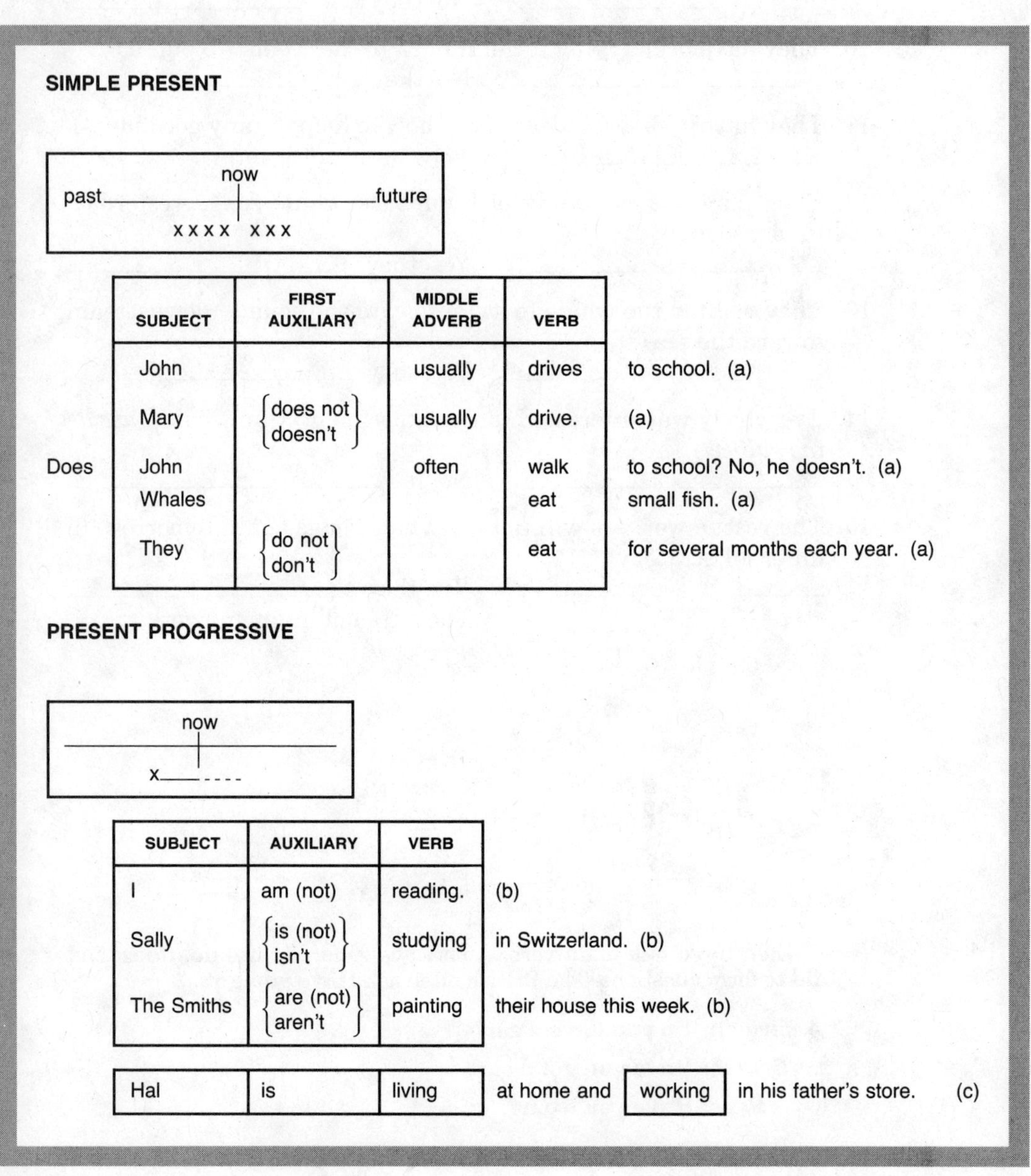

SIMPLE PRESENT

	SUBJECT	FIRST AUXILIARY	MIDDLE ADVERB	VERB	
	John		usually	drives	to school. (a)
	Mary	does not / doesn't	usually	drive.	(a)
Does	John		often	walk	to school? No, he doesn't. (a)
	Whales			eat	small fish. (a)
	They	do not / don't		eat	for several months each year. (a)

PRESENT PROGRESSIVE

SUBJECT	AUXILIARY	VERB	
I	am (not)	reading.	(b)
Sally	is (not) / isn't	studying	in Switzerland. (b)
The Smiths	are (not) / aren't	painting	their house this week. (b)
Hal	is	living	at home and working in his father's store. (c)

Spelling: Appendix 1 gives the spelling rules for adding **-s, -es,** and **-ing.**

Word Order: Middle adverbs (**always, usually, often, never,** etc.) usually occur directly after the first auxiliary or the verb **be.** They occur before the verb.

Exception: A few middle adverbs precede negative auxiliaries. **Generally, sometimes, occasionally, still,** and **probably** are among the most common.

Sally probably doesn't know many people here.

Jim {sometimes / occasionally} doesn't come home until late.

Meaning: a. The *simple present* tense refers to action which is *repeated* or which is generally or always true in the past, present, and future.

b. The *present progressive* refers to action which is *in progress now*—either at the moment of speaking or in the period surrounding the moment of speaking. For example, *painting* is in progress *this week,* but not necessarily at this moment.

Deletion: c. When two verbs in the same tense are connected by **and,** the auxiliary is not usually repeated.

Note: The *present progressive* is also used for action in progress at a repeated moment of focus:

Sandra is often watching TV when I call her in the evening.

Stative Verbs

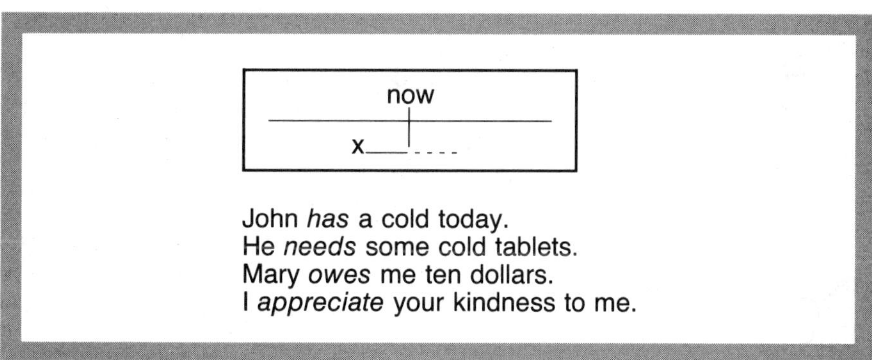

now
x
John *has* a cold today.
He *needs* some cold tablets.
Mary *owes* me ten dollars.
I *appreciate* your kindness to me.

Vocabulary: The following verbs, which refer to states (not actions), are not usually used in the progressive tenses. They fall into several categories:

Knowledge and Belief

agree/disagree with	mean
believe	recognize
doubt	remember
feel (*meaning:* believe)	suppose
imagine (believe)	think (believe)
know	understand

Possession	*Attitude*	
belong to	appreciate	need
have (possess)	dislike	prefer
owe	hate	want
own	like	
possess	love	

Appearance	*Perception*	*Other*
appear	hear	consist of
look	see	contain
seem		depend on
smell		weigh (have a weight)
sound		
taste		

Note: Some of the verbs above have more than one meaning. When they refer to action, they can occur in a progressive tense. Some examples:

State	*Action*
I see you clearly.	**John is seeing (consulting with) a lawyer.**
He looks tired.	**He is looking at the blackboard.**
I think he is here.	**I'm thinking about our problem.**
This bread tastes sour.	**Mary is tasting the stew to find out if it needs salt.**
Joe has a car.	**He is having a good time in this country.**

Exercise 4. Action Verbs

Fill in the *simple present* or the *present progressive* in the following news item.

SACRAMENTO, Calif., Nov. 3—Humphrey, a forty-foot long humpback whale, left the Pacific Ocean and entered the Sacramento River a little over three weeks ago. He (1) is now swimming
(now, swim)

near the point where the San Joaquin River joins the Sacramento, about forty miles inland.

Humphrey (2) ________________ (carry) two small radio transmitters on his back. How can scientists attach a transmitter to a whale? The director of rescue efforts explained the procedure this way: They (3) attach (attach) a small transmitter to an arrow and (4) "________________ (shoot) it with a crossbow. The arrow (5) ________________ (stick) in the whale's blubber* and the radio (6) ________________ (send) out signals.[1]" Humphrey's transmitters (7) ________________ (send) out signals, and scientists (8) ________________ (monitor**) his movements up and down the river.

Although whales (9) ________________ (breathe) air, like other mammals, they (10) ________________ (normally, live) in the ocean and cannot survive indefinitely in fresh water. At present several dozen experts (11) ________________ (try) to direct Humphrey back to the Pacific Ocean. Using thirty-three small boats, they (12) ________________ (bang) on metal pipes under water to make a lot of noise. They (13) ________________ (also, use) guns that discharge compressed air into the water. They hope that these unpleasant sensations will make Humphrey swim downstream.

The National Oceanic and Atmospheric Administration (14) ________________ (coordinate) rescue efforts, but a number of other private, state, and federal agencies (15) ________________ (be) also involved. The federal government (16) ________________ (pick)

CROSSBOW

**Blubber:* fat.
***Monitor:* observe and check systematically.
[1]"Transmitters attached to wandering whale," *New York Times,* November 3, 1985, Section I, page 29

up the tab,*** which (17) ____________ (be) already up to $50,000.

Exercise 5. Action Verbs and Stative Verbs

Fill in the *simple present* or the *present progressive.*

1. Humphrey ___belongs___ (belong) to the species of whale which is known as the *humpback* whale.
2. During the mating season, humpbacks ____________ (make) very complicated musical sounds or "songs."
3. Whales cannot survive indefinitely in fresh water, and Humphrey's black skin ____________ (already, turn) gray.
4. Scientists ____________ (work) to save the whale.
5. They ____________ (try) to direct him back to the ocean.
6. This is not easy, because Humphrey ____________ (weigh) forty-five tons.
7. He ____________ (resist) all efforts to save him.
8. He apparently ____________ (like) the warm water in the river.
9. Some scientists ____________ (now, believe) that Humphrey is a *she.*
10. Pregnant females ____________ (usually, go) to warm waters to give birth.
11. However, other experts ____________ (disagree).

***_Pick up the tab:_ pay the bill.

12. They ______________ sure that Humphrey is a male.
(feel)

13. Meanwhile, Humphrey ______________ lazily up and
(swim)
down the Sacramento River.

14. Some days he/she ______________ a few miles down-
(swim)
stream, but other days, he/she ______________ back
(swim)
upstream.

15. Whale watchers everywhere ______________ to see
(wait)
what will happen.

Exercise 6. Negative Sentences

Fill in the negative of an appropriate verb from the list. Use the *simple present* or the *present progressive*. Use each verb on the list at least once.

√be	have	realize
chew	√nourish	swim
eat		

1. Fish __are not__ mammals; that is, they __do not nourish__ their young with milk.
2. Humpback whales ______________ teeth so they ______________ large fish.
3. They ______________ their food but swallow it whole.
4. There ______________ any bones in a whale's tail.
5. Unlike most mammals, Humphrey ______________ any hair, and his nose is on top of his head.
6. Humphrey ______________ in the San Francisco Bay. He is in the Sacramento River.
7. He ______________ the largest whale in the world, but he is quite large: forty feet long.
8. He probably ______________ that he has two transmitters on his back.

Transfer Exercises

1. Asking About Now

Ask a classmate these questions using the *simple present* or the *present progressive.*

1. Are you listening to me?
   (you, listen)
   Do you hear the (traffic/wind/birds) outside?
   (you, hear)
2. Who or what ________________ at right now?
   (the teacher, look)
   ________________ tired, in your opinion?
   (the teacher, look)
3. ________________ to you?
   (this English book, belong)
   How many lessons ________________ of?
   (consist)
   ________________ explanations in another language?
   (contain)
   What lesson ________________ today?
   (we, study)
4. I think that this lesson is (not too) difficult.
   ________________ with me?
   (you, agree)
5. ________________ a course in Spanish this term?
   (you, take)
   ________________ any Spanish?
   (you, know)
   ________________ this Spanish phrase: "¡Hasta la vista!"?
   (you, understand)
   What ________________?
   (mean)
6. ________________ marine biology this term?
   (you, study)
   ________________ interested in whales?
   (you, be)
   ________________ it is important to save Humphrey?
   (you, think)
   ________________ about Humphrey right this minute?
   (you, think)

2. Life Situations (pair work)

Ask a classmate these questions, using the *simple present* or the *present progressive*. In some sentences, either tense is possible.

1. Where are you living now?
   (live)
   ______ a house (here or in your country)?
   (own)
2. ______ now?
   (work)
   If so, ______ to work every day after class?
   (go)
3. How ______ life in this country?
   (like)
   ______ along all right?
   (get)
4. ______ married?
   (be)
   If so, ______ any children?
   (have)
   How old ______ they?
   (be)
5. How many languages ______?
   (speak)
   What ______ they?
   (be)
6. How ______ to school in the morning?
   (come)
   How much time ______ (on the bus) every day?
   (spend)
7. ______ your own meals?
   (usually, cook)
   What kind of food ______?
   (like)
8. ______ money to buy something special? If so,
   (save)
   what?
   ______ money to anybody?
   (owe)

9. ______________________ about your family right now?
(think)

______________________ that your friends in (Brazil) miss you?*
(think)

3. The Extended Present (pair work)

Tell a classmate about something you are doing these days outside of class. Then answer his or her questions about your project. Choose one of the topics below or a topic of your own. The questions may be in the *present progressive* or in the *simple present.*

1. save money to buy

Example: **—I'm saving money to buy a new car.**
—How much do you save every week?
—Usually about thirty dollars.
—Do you have a car now?
—Yes, but it's old.

2. look for (a job/an apartment, etc.)
3. study (computer science)
4. keep a diary
5. fix up* (my apartment)
6. make (a dress)
7. read (name of a book)
8. ______________________

4. Prepositions

Fill in the correct preposition or particle according to the word or words before the blank. These preposition combinations and two-word verbs occur in this lesson.

1. Captain, that ship is sending __out__ distress signals. It must be in trouble.
2. This car is old, but we can fix it ______ so it looks like new.
3. That will be very expensive. Who will pick ______ the tab?
4. Bob is lonely. He is looking ______ a girlfriend.

**Miss you:* feel sad because you are not there with them.

**Fix up:* decorate, redecorate, or repair.

5. Samantha belongs _______ an environmental group.
6. Her group is concerned _______ whales and other sea mammals which are in danger of extinction.
7. Samantha is especially interested _______ the songs of the humpback whales.
8. Yesterday she listened _______ an interesting record at the music library.
9. It consisted _______ underwater recordings of humpback whale music.

Discussion Topics

Working as a class or in small groups, discuss the following questions.

A. Have you ever seen whales or photographs of whales? Do you find them interesting animals, and if so, why?

B. Perhaps you wonder why scientists and others want to save Humphrey's life. One reason is that Humphrey belongs to an "endangered species." Whales are hunted for their meat, oil, and whalebone, and today there are only about a thousand humpback whales left. If we are not careful, the species may become extinct.

Do you agree that it is important to protect humpback whales? Why, or why not? Should we continue to hunt whales, in your opinion? Is the government wasting its money trying to save Humphrey? Do we need to protect all species that are endangered? Are all of them important or only some of them? Are there right and wrong ways to treat wild animals?

C. In your country, are people concerned about endangered species or other wild animals? If so, which species are they particularly concerned about? How do they show their concern? For example, do people wear "Save-the-whales" T-shirts? Are there private organizations or government agencies which protect animals, fish, and birds? What are they doing to help endangered or other species?

D. What wild animals are common in your country? Where do they live? What special habits do they have? What wild animal interests you particularly and why?

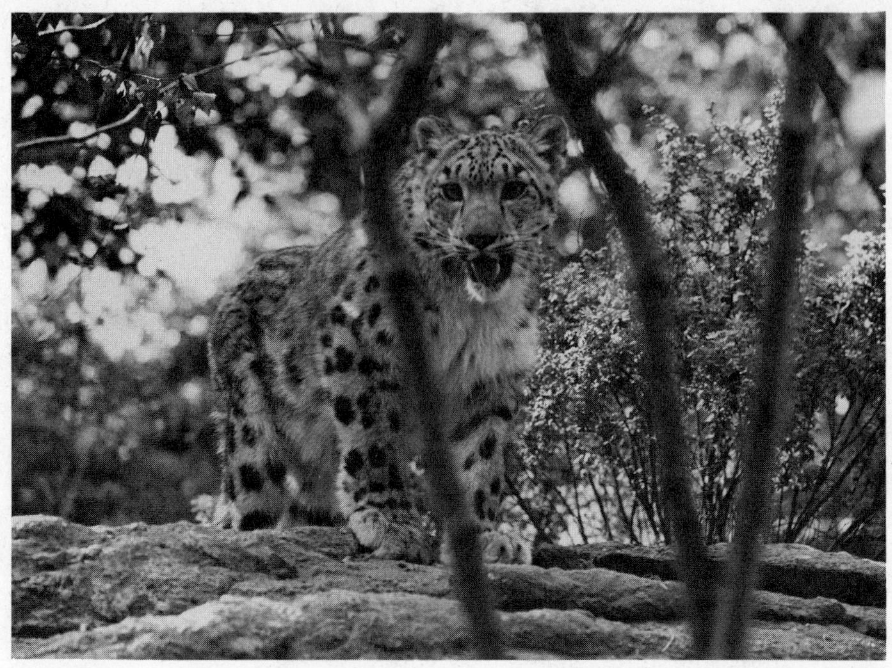

Model Composition

Fill in the *simple present* or the *present progressive*. In some cases, either tense is correct.

Studying the Snow Leopard

The animal in this picture is participating (participate) in an experiment. Although she doesn't know (negative: know) it, she ________ (take) her own picture. She is a snow leopard, one of the rarest and most beautiful of the big cats.

Snow leopards ________ (live) high in the Himalayan Mountains of Central Asia. They ________ (have) silvery coats with black spots which ________ (make) them difficult to spot among the snow and rocks. Few people have seen a snow leopard in the wild.

Now a team of researchers ________ (track) several snow leopards' movements and ________ (photograph) them as they go about their solitary

lives. How can they do this? One tool they ____________ is the radio
(use)
collar. Here is how it works: First, they ____________ a trap and
(set)
____________ a leopard. Then they ____________ it with a tranquil-
(capture) (inject)
izer, and while the animal is immobile, they ____________ a collar
(fasten)
around its neck. A small radio transmitter which is attached to the collar ____________ out radio signals to tell them where the animal is
(send)
at any moment. At present, the team ____________ four leopards'
(track)
movements by means of these radio signals.

The snow leopard's coloring ____________ it so well that the re-
(camouflage)
searchers ____________ one, even when they know from the radio sig-
(seldom, see)
nals that one is close at hand. Nevertheless, they ____________ some
(obtain)
excellent photographs of the animals as they move about at night. They ____________ a hidden camera which is connected to a pressure
(use)
pad. The pressure pad is buried under a wild animal path which the leopards ____________ frequently. When a leopard ____________ on
(use) (step)
the pad, the camera ____________ its picture. The team has obtained
(take)
three "self-portraits" of snow leopards so far and one of a surprised villager.

The snow leopard ____________ an endangered species for two
(be)
reasons: first, because in the past it was hunted for its beautiful coat (this is now prohibited), and second, because human settlers ____________ into its high mountain habitat, bringing their live-
(gradually, move)
stock* with them. The grazing** of their animals ____________ out
(crowd)
the snow leopard's wild prey.*** In studies like the present one, researchers ____________ against time to protect this magnificent cat
(work)
from extinction.

**Livestock:* domesticated food animals.
***Graze:* eat grass and leaves.
****Prey:* animals that the leopard kills and eats.

Notice these points:

1. The title is in the center of the first line, and every word except **the** is capitalized.
   Rules for capitalizing titles:

   Capitalize the first and last words of the title.
   Capitalize all the other words, except:
   a, an, the
   short prepositions such as **in, on, at, for,** etc.

2. The composition is divided into five paragraphs. The first word of each paragraph is indented (written several spaces to the right). The composition looks like this:

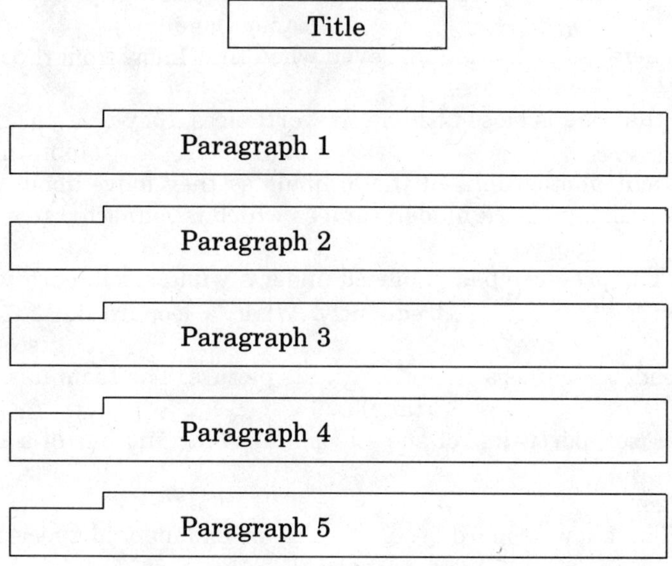

Use this form when you write a composition.

Composition Topics

Write a short composition about one of the following topics. Use the *simple present* and *present progressive* tenses.

1. Find a snapshot* of someone you know, and write about that person. First, describe what is happening in the photograph. Then

**Snapshot:* informal photograph.

give some information about what the person is doing now and about his or her daily life. Bring the snapshot to class with your composition.

If you don't have a snapshot, you can draw a picture or cut a picture from a newspaper or magazine. Describe what you know or imagine about the person's life.

2. Find or draw a picture of an animal, and write about it. First, describe what is happening in the picture. Then tell something about the animal's habits. If it is a wild animal, where and how does it live?

3. Write a composition about an endangered species. For example, you might write about:
   a. a species which people in your country are concerned about,
   b. a species which interests you particularly,
   c. endangered species in general.

   Answer some of the questions in section B and C of the Discussion Topics.

Postscript

Humphrey finally swam out to sea on November 4, 1985. Although recordings of humpback whale "music" did not interest him, he was very interested in recorded sounds of a group of whales *eating*. He was not hungry, but perhaps he was lonely! A boat played the recording as it went out through the Golden Gate to the Pacific, and Humphrey swam close behind.

A year later Humphrey was spotted again, so apparently his adventure in the river did not do him any harm.

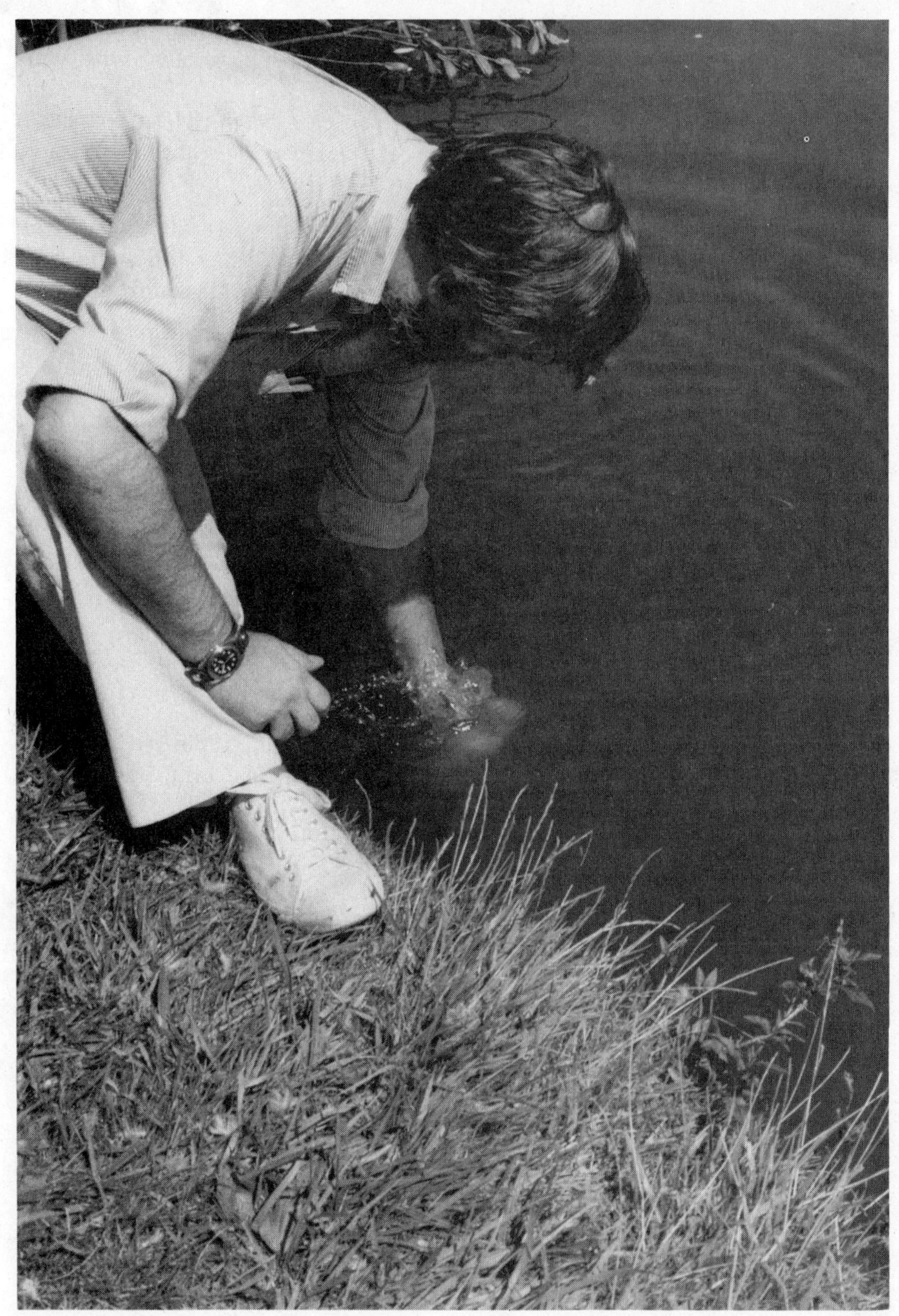

Lesson 2

Acid Rain: A Problem That Crosses Borders

2.1 The Present Perfect: Completion before Now

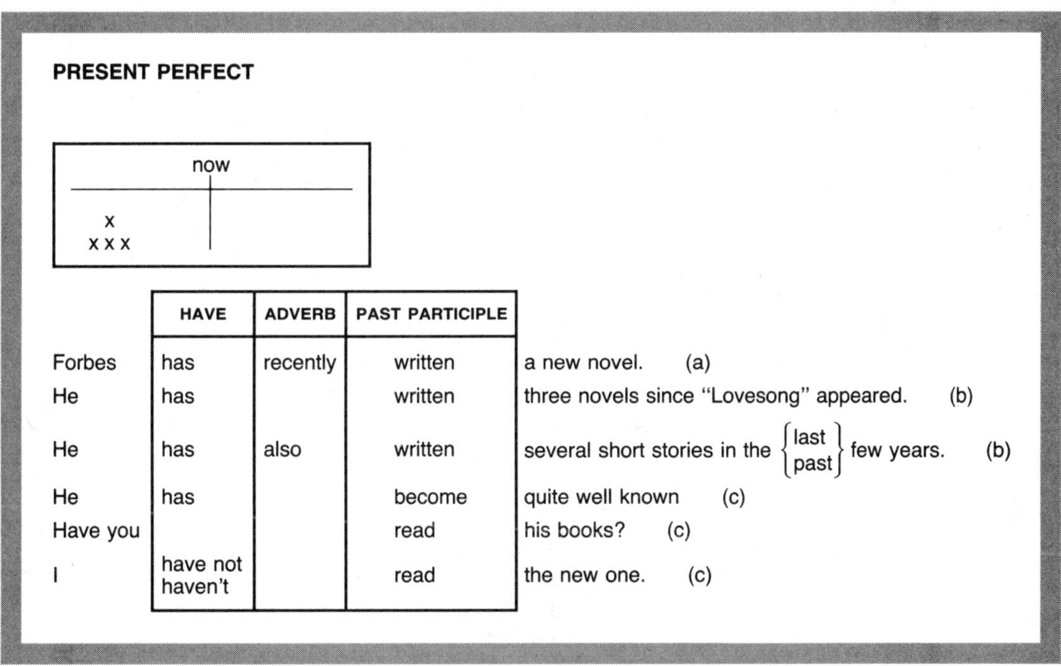

PRESENT PERFECT

	HAVE	ADVERB	PAST PARTICIPLE	
Forbes	has	recently	written	a new novel. (a)
He	has		written	three novels since "Lovesong" appeared. (b)
He	has	also	written	several short stories in the {last / past} few years. (b)
He	has		become	quite well known (c)
Have you			read	his books? (c)
I	have not haven't		read	the new one. (c)

Spelling: Appendix 1 gives the spelling rules for adding **-ed** to form the regular past participle.
Appendix 2 lists the irregular past participles.

Meaning: The *present perfect* is used to talk about an action which has been *completed before now.* A definite past time expression is not used.

a. Indefinite time expressions (**recently, lately, already, yet,** etc.) are often used with the present perfect.

b. A past period which includes the present (**this week, today, since 1948,** etc.) is often indicated.

c. The *present perfect* is often used without any time expression.

Time Expressions: The following time expressions are used only with the perfect tenses.

(I have taken three tests) { **lately.** / **up to now.** / **in the** { **last** / **past** } **(three)(weeks).** / **since** { **Monday.** / **classes began.** } }

The following time expressions are often used with the *present perfect* when it means *completion before now.*

(I have taken three tests) { **so far.** / **today.** / **this (week).** / **in the past.** / **recently.*** / **already.*** }

In the negative:

I haven't written my paper *yet.*
I *still* haven't written my paper.
I have *never* written a long paper.

In questions:

Have you *ever* written a paper?

Note: When a definite past time or period is mentioned, we use the simple past tense. See Lesson 5.

**Recently* and *already* also occur after the first auxiliary:

I have { **recently** / **already** } **taken three tests.**

Already is used in affirmative sentences only. *Yet* is used in the negative.

Exercise 1. Questions and Answers with Irregular Verbs

a. Fill in the past participle for each verb in the list.

b. Complete each question with an appropriate verb from the list. Use each verb only once.

c. Ask a classmate the questions. If your answer to a question is negative, add another sentence with more information on the topic.

be *been*	fall ______	give ______	meet ______	√spend ______
buy ______	fly ______	go* ______	read ______	take ______
do ______	get ______	have ______	see ______	write ______

1. How much money *have you spent* for bus fare this week?

   I've spent about $1.50 (a dollar fifty).

   or: **None. I haven't spent any money for bus fare since I bought my car.**

2. How many letters ______________ to your folks** this month?
3. ______________ any letters from home recently?
4. ______________ any good books lately?
5. How many tests ______________ the teacher ______________ us so far this term?
6. ______________ your homework every night up to now?
7. ______________ ever ______________ asleep in class?
8. ______________ ever ______________ a class that was too difficult for you?
9. ______________ ever ______________ bored in an English class?
10. ______________ difficulty with your courses this semester?

*In the *present perfect,* the past participle **been** is sometimes used instead of **gone,** to indicate that someone has *gone and returned.*

Example: **I have been to Europe three times.**

***Folks:* parents.

11. How many movies ______________ in the past few weeks?

12. ______________ many American students since you came to this (university)?

13. ______________ ever ______________ in a helicopter?

14. How many parties ______________ to this week?

15. ______________ any new clothes lately?

Exercise 2. Statements

Complete each sentence using the *present perfect* tense.

Example: **Up to now, my professors** { **have not given any tests.** / ***or:*** **have given very easy assignments.** }

1. Up to now, my roommate and I ______________.
2. Since the semester began, he/she ______________ a few times.
3. We have never ______________.
4. My roommate ______________ already ______________.
5. I ______________ yet.
6. So far this year, my parents ______________.
7. In the last few weeks, they ______________.
8. My mother ______________ letters since I left home.

2.2 The Present Perfect and the Present Perfect Progressive: Duration Up to Now

Action Verbs

PRESENT PERFECT/PRESENT PERFECT PROGRESSIVE

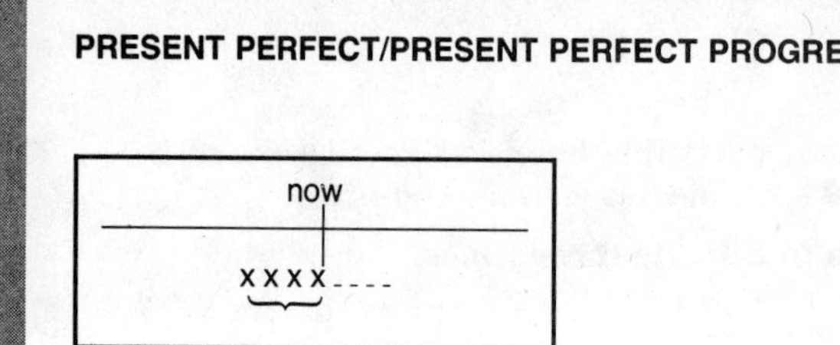

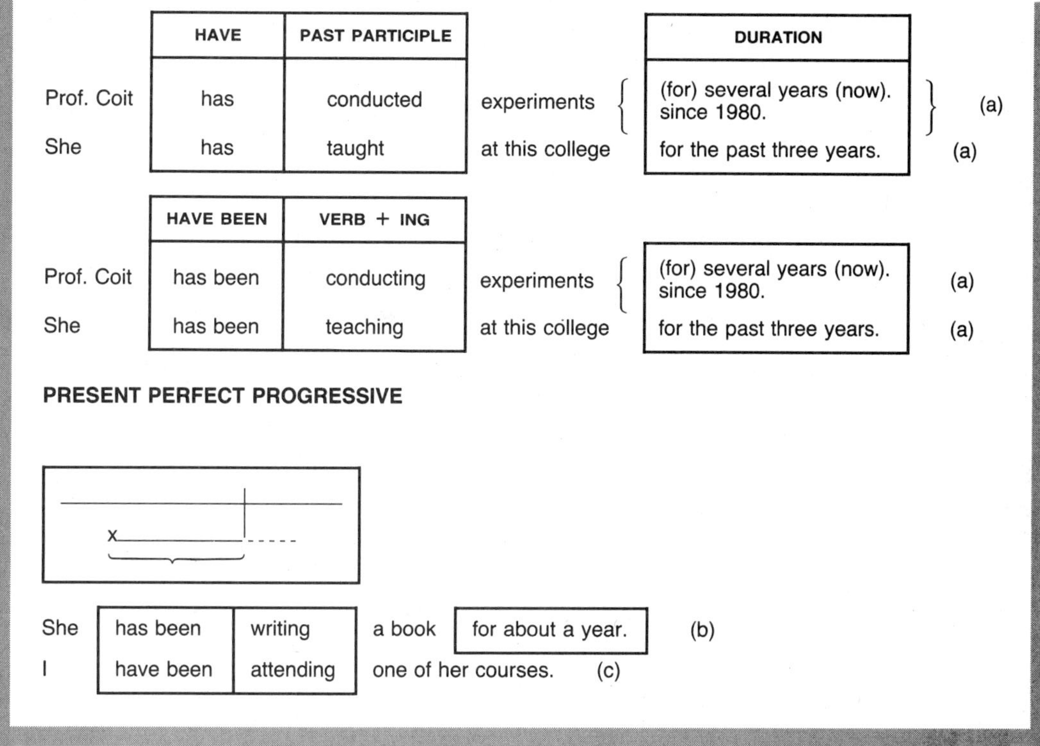

	HAVE	PAST PARTICIPLE		DURATION	
Prof. Coit	has	conducted	experiments	(for) several years (now). since 1980.	(a)
She	has	taught	at this college	for the past three years.	(a)

	HAVE BEEN	VERB + ING			
Prof. Coit	has been	conducting	experiments	(for) several years (now). since 1980.	(a)
She	has been	teaching	at this college	for the past three years.	(a)

PRESENT PERFECT PROGRESSIVE

She	has been	writing	a book	for about a year.	(b)
I	have been	attending	one of her courses.		(c)

Tense Choice: When an expression (with **for, since,** etc.*) is used to give *duration up to now,* the *present perfect* or the *present perfect progressive* must be used.

a. Either the *present perfect* or the *present perfect progressive* may be used for *repeated action* when the duration up to now is given. The *present perfect progressive* emphasizes that the action is still continuing in the present.

b. For a single uncompleted action, only the *present perfect progressive* may be used when the duration is stated.

c. When the *present perfect progressive* is used without an expression of duration, it emphasizes the idea that the situation has been con-

*Other expressions which give duration up to now include

all my life
all (this) week

for the {last / past} (three) weeks

so far
up to now

tinuing *for a while,* whereas the *present progressive* emphasizes the idea of *now.* Compare:

Sue is feeling sick. (*Emphasis:* now)
Sue has been feeling sick. (*Emphasis:* for a while)

The following chart summarizes the uses of the *present perfect* and the *present perfect progressive.*

PRESENT PERFECT	PRESENT PERFECT PROGRESSIVE
DIFFERENT MEANINGS	
1. *A single completed action*	*A single action not completed (still continuing)*
I have written a letter to my folks.	I have been writing a letter to my brother.
2. *Repeated action: The number of times is mentioned.*	*Repeated action continuing to the present: The number of times is not mentioned.*
I have read his letter ten times.	I have been reading his letter (over and over) all morning.
DIFFERENT EMPHASIS	
	Emphasis that the action is still continuing now
I have taught English for twenty-five years.	I have been teaching English for twenty-five years.
I have gone home frequently this semester.	I have been going home frequently this semester.

Notes: 1. When the action of the verb is very short or instantaneous, the idea of duration is not logical and the *present perfect progressive* is not used unless the action is repeated. Compare:

The plane has arrived. (completed short action)

The plane is arriving. (uncompleted short action)

More and more planes have been arriving late. (repeated short action)

The plane has been circling the field for ten minutes. (longer action with duration)

2. **For long** or **long** after a negative indicates that the action is occurring but has only been occurring for a short time.

   John hasn't {been working / worked} there (for) long.

   (He started to work there a short time ago.)

   For a long time after a negative means that the action is *not* occurring.

   John hasn't {been working / worked} there for a long time. (He stopped working there a long time ago.)

Stative Verbs

PRESENT PERFECT

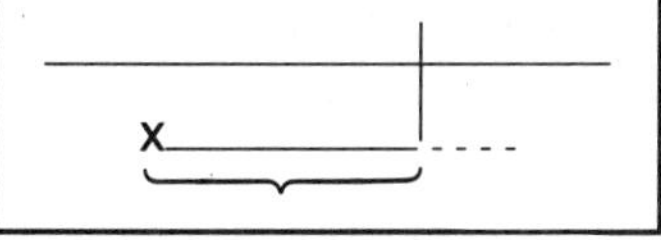

Professor Coit *has had* a Ph.D. for several years (now).
She *has loved* science since she was a child.
She *has been* at this university for three years.

Tense Choice: Use the *present perfect* of stative verbs when you give the *duration* of a state *up to now.*

Vocabulary: See page 10 for a list of stative verbs.

Exercise 3. Action Verbs (pair work)

Working with a partner, make short dialogues consisting of a statement, a question, and an answer. Use an expression with **for** or **since** (or **all (my) life**) in each dialogue.

1. living

   Examples:

   a. **—I'm living on 87th Street.**

   —Have you been living there since you came to Chicago?

   —Yes, I've been living there since last May.

   or:

   b. **—President (   ) is living in the White House.**

   —How long has he been living there?

   —For three years. (He's been living there for three years.)

2. studying
3. hoping to
4. working for (name of company)
5. trying to find (a good used car)
6. saving money for

Exercise 4. Stative Verbs (pair work)

Working with a partner, make short dialogues consisting of a statement, a question, and an answer. Use the *simple present* and the *present perfect.*

1. appreciate

   Example:

   —I really appreciate my parents' kindness.

   —Have you always appreciated it?

   —Well yes, but I've appreciated it more since I left home.

2. have
3. know
4. be worried about
5. owe (somebody) a letter
6. need
7. want
8. dislike
9. own
10. believe
11. be married (single, engaged, divorced)
12. be in love with

Exercise 5. The Present Perfect versus the Present Perfect Progressive

Fill in the blanks with the *present perfect* or the *present perfect progressive.* In which sentences is either tense correct? Is there a difference in meaning?

Marcia Beloit is a documentary filmmaker. She is currently making a documentary on the problem of acid rain* for a public television station. She (1) {has worked / has been working} (work) on the project for the last six months. This week she (2) ________ (visit) the Adirondack Mountain region, where she will be filming for about two more weeks. In this region, acid rain (3) ________ (damage) lakes and forests for several decades. Beloit (4) ________ (interview) some residents of the area, as well as scientists who are doing research on acid rain. She (5) ________ (also, see) three lakes in the region. One of them is a "dead" lake because its water (6) ________ (become) so acidic that it cannot support life, and all the fish in it (7) ________ (die). In the second lake, the water is slightly acidic, but the acidity (8) ________ (*negative;* kill) any fish yet. In the third lake, the acidity is normal. Why (9) ________ (*negative*) acid rain ________ (affect) this lake? This is the question that geologist Richard Tilson is trying to answer.

Tilson (10) ________ (investigate) the effects of acid rain on lakes and fish since 1982. For the last few months he (11) ________ (develop) a computer model which will help scientists understand the processes of lake acidification. He (12) ________ (receive) a number of grants to support his research.

Beloit (13) ________ (make) documentary films since she joined the television station seven years ago. She (14) ________ (always,** enjoy) work-

**Acid rain:* rain which is polluted with sulfuric acid or other acids.
We use the present perfect, not the progressive, with **always.

ing outdoors and (15) __________ interested in environmental prob-
(be)
lems for some time. So far she (16) __________ five short documen-
(complete)
taries concerned with the environment.

Exercise 6. Understanding the Present Tenses

When we speak or write, we choose the tenses which best express our meaning. Many sentences have no time expression restricting our choice of tense. Instead, the tense carries the meaning by itself.

In the following passage, there are some cases where only one tense is possible and other cases where more than one choice is grammatically correct.

Fill in the blanks with the *simple present, present progressive, present perfect,* or *present perfect progressive.* Then discuss your choices with your classmates. Try to decide whether one tense conveys a more appropriate meaning than another. In some cases, several meanings are appropriate.

Examples: (1) and (2) **Canada and the United States *have been* friendly neighbors for as long as the two countries *have existed.*** (The *present perfect* is required because the duration is given. These are stative verbs, so the *present perfect progressive* is not used.)

(3) and (4) *Possible:* **Whenever disagreements *arise* between them, they *always settle* them peacefully.** (The *simple present* implies that the situation is always true in the past, present, and future. It leads us to believe that the passage will emphasize the peaceful relations between the two countries.)

Better: **Whenever disagreements *have arisen,* they *have always settled* them peacefully.** (The *present perfect* tells only about what has happened up to now. It implies that the passage will emphasize a new disagreement between the two countries.)

Canada and the United States (1) ________________ friend-
(be)
ly neighbors for as long as the two countries (2) ________________ .
(exist)
Whenever disagreements (3) ______________ between them, they (4)
(arise)
________________ them peacefully. They (5) ______________ to war.
(always, settle) (never, resort)

In recent years, the problem of acid rain (6) ______________ (be) a source of friction* between the two countries. Acid rain (7) ______________ (form) when sulfur emissions from the smoke-stacks of the industrial midwestern United States enter rain clouds. These clouds (8) ______________ (drift) northeastward and eventually (9) ______________ (fall) as rain in New York State, the New England states, and eastern Canada. Acid rain (10) ______________ (damage) trees and lakes in these regions for several decades, and the Canadian government (11) ______________ (pressure) the United States to do something about it.

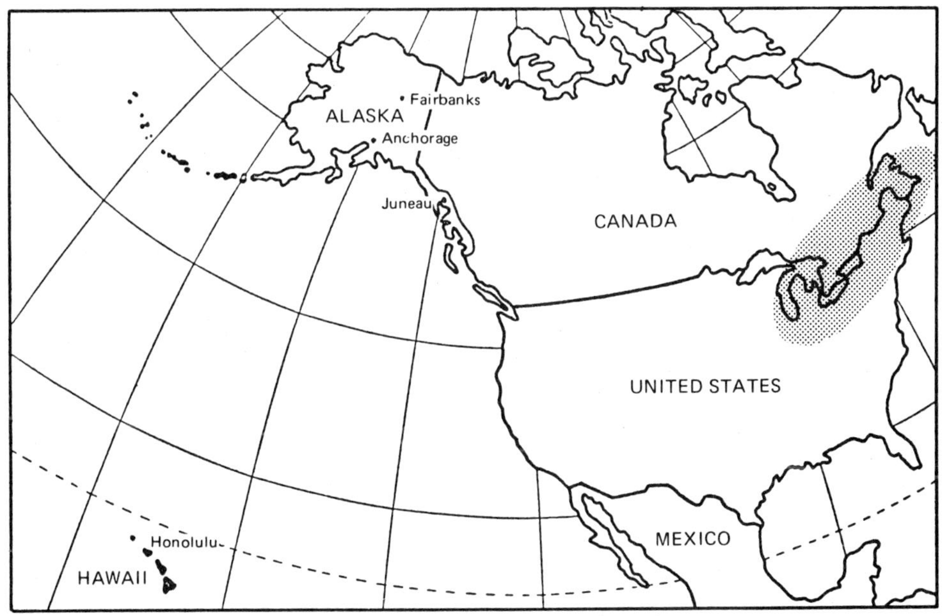

*Friction: disagreement.

This year,** officials in the two governments (12) __________ (release) a report on the problem, and both the Prime Minister and the President (13) __________ (already, endorse) it. The United States (14) __________ (agree) to spend five billion dollars to develop technology to control sulfur emissions. Canada will spend about half that amount. Environmental groups (15) __________ (react) to this news in various ways. Some (16) __________ (believe) that it is a step in the right direction, since the President (17) __________ (finally, acknowledge) that acid rain is a problem. But other groups (18) __________ (express) disappointment because the report does not call for reductions in emissions. They (19) __________ (say) that we (20) __________ (need) stricter controls, not new technology.

**1986

Transfer Exercises

1. Pictures

A. Answer these questions about the picture:

1. What are the two people and the dog doing?
2. How long have they been doing it?
3. What have they already done?
4. What haven't they done yet?
5. How often do they do these things?

Vocabulary:

Nouns	*Verbs*
hose	give . . . a bath
paw	rinse off
tub	scrub

B. Cut a picture out of a magazine and bring it to class. Ask a classmate about your picture using the questions in A (or write the answers to the questions for homework).

2. Life Situations (pair work)

Tell a partner about the life situation of somebody you know. Begin with a statement, and then answer your partner's questions. Your partner should include some questions with **how long, how many (times), yet,** and **ever.**

Example: **A: My brother is living in Boston now.**

B: What's he doing there?

A: He's an electronics engineer. He's working for a robotics company. He designs robots.

B: How long has he been working with robots?

A: Since he got this job. For about five years, I guess.

B: How many robots has he developed?

A: Only one so far, but he's developed several variations on it.

B: Have people used the robot yet?

A: Sure. They've sold it to lots of companies.

B: Have you ever seen it?

A: No, but I've seen pictures.

B: Does he enjoy his job?

A: Yes, I think so.

B: Is he married?
etc.

3. Current Events

What is happening in the news right now? Have a short conversation with a classmate about it. Use the *present progressive* and the *present perfect progressive* (and if you can, add a sentence in the *present perfect* as well).

Example: **A. Teachers are striking in (name of city).**

B. How long have they been striking?

A. For three weeks. They have been negotiating with the school board, but they haven't reached a settlement yet.

Some verbs you may need: campaigning, fighting, suffering from (hunger), trying to negotiate

4. Prepositions

Fill in the correct preposition according to the word which precedes the blank (in #8, according to the word **reacted**). These preposition combinations occur in this lesson.

1. My uncle works ______ a big international corporation.
2. The company is interested ______ the problem of acid rain because it affects them directly.

3. Our city government has recently issued a report _______ its financial crisis.
4. The city is suffering _______ heavy debts and a lack of income.
5. Some city employees are worried _______ losing their jobs.
6. They want higher pay, but in this situation they will not resort _______ a strike.
7. The mayor has called _______ higher taxes.
8. The citizens have reacted negatively _______ this proposal.
9. The mayor and a committee of citizens are working _______ the problem, and they hope to come up with a solution.

Discussion Topics

A. Is acid rain a problem in your country? Are there other forms of pollution that are creating problems? Choose one form of pollution to talk about, and answer these questions:

What kind of damage has the pollution caused? Has it damaged lakes? forests? ancient buildings and monuments? crops? Has it affected people's health or the quality of life? What is the cause of the problem? Does it involve another country? Do you know how long it has been occurring? How long have you been aware of the problem?

Is the government trying to solve the problem? What have they done about it? Have they issued reports or passed laws about it? Have there been international meetings and/or agreements about it?

In your opinion, has your government done enough to solve the problem? If not, what else do they need to do?

B. Has the government of your country been negotiating with another country to solve a problem or resolve a disagreement? If so, how long have the negotiations been going on? What is your government trying to achieve? Have they made progress in the negotiations?

Composition Topics

Write a short composition about one of the following topics. Use the *simple present, present progressive, present perfect,* and *present perfect progressive.*

1. Write about something that is happening in the news. Tell how long it has been going on and what has taken place up to now. (See Transfer Exercise 3 for examples.)

2. Find a picture of an activity and describe what is happening, how long it has been happening, and what has happened so far. Be sure to hand in your picture with your composition.
3. Describe the life situation of someone you know. The example in Transfer Exercise 2 shows the type of information you might include.
4. Write about a form of pollution that is affecting your country. Answer some of the questions in Discussion Topic A.
5. Write about negotiations that your country is involved in at present. (See Discussion Topic B.)

UNIT

II

■

THE PASSIVE

Lesson 3

Housing Starts and Smart Houses

3.1 The Passive

Compare:

ACTIVE

	SUBJECT	VERB PHRASE: FIRST AUXILIARY	VERB PHRASE: ADVERB	VERB PHRASE: VERB	DIRECT OBJECT	
Simple present	Pollution		sometimes	damages	buildings.	
Present progressive	Scientists	are		doing	research	on the problem.
Present perfect	The President	has		endorsed	a report on acid rain.	

PASSIVE

SUBJECT	VERB PHRASE: FIRST AUXILIARY	VERB PHRASE: ADVERB	VERB PHRASE: BE	VERB PHRASE: PAST PARTICIPLE		BY PHRASE	
Buildings	are	sometimes		damaged		by pollution.	(a)
Research	is		being	done	on the problem.		(b)
The report on acid rain	has		been	endorsed		by the President.	(a)

Form: A passive verb phrase always includes a form of **be** plus the *past participle* of the verb. **Be** takes the same form as the verb in the active sentence.

Sentence Structure: The *subject* of a passive verb is the same as the *direct object* of the active verb. It tells *who* or *what* received the action.

a. When a phrase with **by** is included, the *object* of **by** is the same as the *subject* of the active sentence. It tells *who* or *what* performed the action.

Deletion: We usually omit the **by** phrase

1. if we don't know exactly who performed the action.
2. if it is not important to say who performed the action—for example, if the performer is "someone," "people," or the type of person who always does that action. In example (b), since scientists are the people who do research on pollution, we say:

    Research is being done on the problem (of pollution). We omit **by scientists.**

3. The performer of the action has been mentioned in a previous sentence.

    A bomb exploded in a restaurant last night. Three people were killed. We omit **by the bomb** because it is repetitious.

Transitive and Intransitive Verbs: In general, only verbs which can have a direct object *(transitive verbs)* occur in the passive.

Some English verbs can be either *transitive* or *intransitive,* with a slight change in meaning.

Transitive:

active: **The phone company has changed our phone number.**
passive: **Our phone number has been changed.**

Intransitive:

active: **The world has changed a lot since I was a child.** (No passive is possible.)

Note: Sometimes the object of a preposition can become the subject of a passive sentence. This happens only with certain intransitive verb-preposition combinations.

We can always depend on Stuart.
→ **Stuart can always be depended on.**
How do they deal with that problem in your country?
→ **How is that problem dealt with in your country?**

Exercise 1. The Simple Present Passive

Fill in the blanks with a verb from the list. Use the *simple present passive.* Use each verb once.

√build	lay off*	require	use
influence	report	start	

Every year from 1.5 to 2 million homes (1) are built in the United States and Canada, and about 5 million workers are employed in building them. The housing industry is thus very important in the economics of these countries. When "housing starts" are up, more workers (2) ____________ to build them. When fewer houses (3) ____________, workers (4) ____________ and unemployment rises.

However, the number of housing starts varies greatly from year to year, and even from month to month. The industry (5) ____________ (strongly) by other factors in the economy (such as interest rates), and in its turn, it has a strong effect on the economy. Therefore, housing starts (6) ____________ as an important economic indicator, and the number of housing starts (7) ____________ regularly in the business news.

Exercise 2. The Present Progressive Passive

Fill in the blanks with a verb from the list. This time, use the *present progressive passive.*

build	issue	replace	tear
√construct	put	sell	

This month, housing starts in the United States are up by 15 percent to an annual rate of 2.09 million units. This means that approximately 170,000 new homes (1) are being constructed right now. Building permits (2) ____________ (also, issue) at a higher rate, which is a good sign for future construction, and more houses (3) ____________ (sell) than last month.

Not all these new homes (4) ____________ up on newly developed land, however. In some cases, existing buildings (5) ____________ down to make room for them. For exam-

**Lay off:* dismiss temporarily from a job.

ple, one-family houses (6) ______________________ by apartment houses. Fewer families can afford the high cost of a house, so proportionately more apartment houses (7) ______________________ than in previous years.

Exercise 3. The Present Progressive Passive and the Present Perfect Passive

Describe the houses in the illustration.

What has already been done?
What is being done now?
What hasn't been done?

A. *The house on the corner.* Use these verbs:

√complete	plant
connect	put on the market
install	sell
paint	

1. The major construction **has been completed.**
2. Some bushes ______________________ .
3. A tree ______________________ now.
4. Five solar panels ______________________ on the roof.
5. (Continue)

B. *The house in the middle.* Use these verbs:

lay	put on
put in (install)	put up

1. The frame of the house
2. The roof
3. The walls
4. The windows
5. The front walk
6. The electrical wiring
7. The partition walls*
8. The fireplace and chimney
9. (Continue, using some of the vocabulary from A.)

C. *The house on the right.* Use these verbs in addition to verbs from A and B:

dig
draw

1. The plans ______________________ .
2. The foundation hole ______________________ .
3. A temporary fence ______________________ around the lot.
4. (Continue, using ideas from A and B.)

Exercise 4. Transitive and Intransitive Verbs

Fill in the *active* or *passive* form of the verb in parentheses. More sentences will be active than passive.

Transitive Verbs	*Intransitive Verbs*
lower / reduce / cut } = decrease	fall / drop / go down } = decrease
raise = increase	rise / go up } = increase
change	change
affect	
develop	develop

**Partition walls:* walls which divide the rooms.

A. Use the *present perfect.*

1. (drop) The price of oil has dropped this year.
2. (reduce) The Arab states ____________________ the price of oil.
3. (fall) The rate of inflation ____________________ also ____________________ .
4. (go down) The prime interest rate ____________________ .
5. (lower) Mortgage rates have also been lowered .
6. (cut) Taxes ____________________ .
7. (rise) Therefore the number of housing starts __________ .
8. (increase) This ____________________ employment.
9. (affect) The economy of the country ____________________ by these developments.

B. Use the *present progressive.*

10. (change) Our economy is changing .
11. (develop) New land ____________________ for housing.
12. (change) The landscape ____________________ by this development.
13. (develop) Optimism ____________________ in the country.
14. (buy) More houses ____________________ .
15. (rise) However, the price of houses ____________________ .
16. (increase) Therefore, the number of people who live in apartments ____________________ .

3.2 Past Participles Used as Adjectives (the stative passive)

Compare:

PASSIVE

Most houses	are constructed	in the warmer seasons.	(a)
My house	was constructed	in 1960.	(a)

ADJECTIVE

This house	is constructed	of modern materials.	(b)
It	is located	on good land.	(b)

Meaning: a. The passive of action verbs describes action.
b. Sometimes we use the past participle after **be** to indicate a condition, not an action. In this case, the past participle is like an adjective and there is no **by** phrase.

Exercise 5. Past Participles Used as Adjectives

Fill in the blanks with **is/are** plus a past participle. Use each verb on the list once.

begin	√equip	make
connect	finish	surround
construct	insulate	
design	locate	

1. The house on the corner _is equipped_ with five solar panels.
2. The solar panels __________ to collect heat from the sun to heat the house.
3. They __________ of glass.
4. They __________ to the heating system in the basement.
5. The house itself __________ of wood.

6. The walls __________ with six inches of fiberglass (to keep the house warm in the winter).
7. The house __________ on the corner of Lakeview Drive and Grant Avenue.
8. The second and third houses __________ not __________ yet.
9. In fact, construction on the third house __________ barely* __________ .
10. This housing development __________ by open fields and a lake.

3.3 Present Participles Used as Adjectives

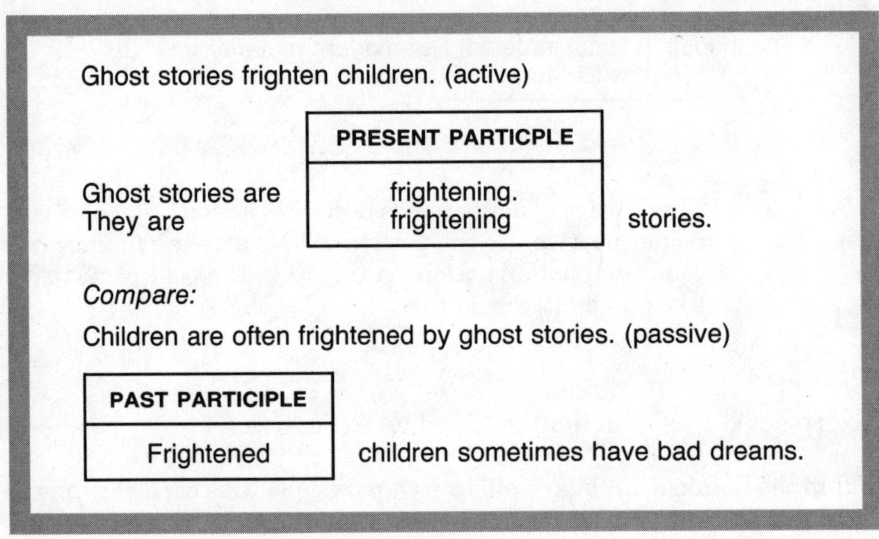

Ghost stories frighten children. (active)
PRESENT PARTICPLE
Ghost stories are frightening.
They are frightening stories.
Compare:
Children are often frightened by ghost stories. (passive)
PAST PARTICIPLE
Frightened children sometimes have bad dreams.

Exercise 6. Present and Past Participles

Fill in the present or past participle of the verb.

1. Today's rain has disappointed the children.
   a. The children are *disappointed* in the weather.
   b. The rainy weather is *disappointing* .

*Barely: almost not.

2. This small bowl of soup is not enough to satisfy my appetite.
   a. A small bowl of soup is not a ____________ meal.
   b. I am not a ____________ customer.
   c. I am not ____________ with such a small meal.

3. My mistakes in English sometimes embarrass me.
   a. I make ____________ mistakes sometimes.
   b. I am ____________ about my mistakes.

4. This grammar point often confuses students.
   a. Students are often ____________ about the **-ed** and **-ing** forms.
   b. This is a ____________ point of grammar.

5. Mrs. Adams's nine-to-five job exhausts her.
   a. She is ____________ from working nine to five every day.
   b. It's an ____________ job.
   c. An ____________ mother can not take good care of her children.

6. Tonight's speaker interests me a great deal.
   a. He is an ____________ speaker.
   b. He has picked an ____________ topic for his talk.
   c. The audience is always ____________ in his ideas.

7. He can usually convince his audience that his position is correct.
   a. He presents ____________ arguments to support his position.
   b. I am ____________ that he knows what he is talking about.

Exercise 7. Present and Past Participles

Fill in the blanks with the present or past participle. Use each verb in the list once.

automate	fall	interest
connect	fascinate	leak
convince	√insulate	prefabricate
equip	insure	rise

1. Fiber glass is an important insulating material.
2. Most houses in the United States are ____________ against fire and burglary.
3. Housing starts have been stimulated by ____________ (fall) interest rates.
4. But houses are becoming more and more expensive because of ____________ costs.

5. Houses which are built in a factory are called __________ houses.
6. A __________ new development in housing is the __________ house, which is sometimes called the "smart" house.
7. In this kind of house, all the electrical systems are __________ to the telephone so that the owner can turn them on or off from the office, or even from a pay phone.
8. Smart houses are also __________ with sensors which detect __________ gas, smoke, and trespassers.
9. Developers of the smart house are __________ that many people will be __________ in buying these homes.

Transfer Exercises

1. Personal Situations

Describe the situations using the past participles of the verbs on the list. Use **not** if you need it.

bend	crowd	marry	take (= occupy)
close	locate	paint	tire
confuse	make	schedule (for 2:00 P.M.)	

1. Your family house
   a. **Our house is located (in a suburb of Bangkok).**
   b. **It . . .**
   c.
2. Your brothers and sisters

   Two of my brothers . . .
3. The buses at rush hour
   a.
   b.
4. Your next exam
5. When you get out of class every day
   a.
   b.
6. The campus bookstore (on Sunday)
7. Your fingers when you write

2. Construction

Have you noticed any construction in your city recently? If so, describe it to a classmate, answering the questions.

A. Informal style: Use the active form of the verb with **they.** Notice that **they** does not refer to any particular noun. This style is appropriate only for informal conversation.

Example: **They're building a three-story parking lot across the street from the library.**

Questions: 1. How much have they done? (Be specific.)

They've dug the foundation and put up a steel framework.

2. What are they doing right now?
3. What haven't they done yet?

B. Formal style: State the information again, using the passive and eliminating the unclear **they.** This style is appropriate for writing and for formal classroom discussion.

Example: **A three-story parking lot is being built across the street from the library. The foundation has been dug and . . .**

3. Disasters

Describe what happens (or often happens) in the following situations. Use the active or passive of the verbs on the list. (You can also use other verbs if you wish.)

burn	disrupt	√increase	shut down
bury	drop	kill	wound
destroy	evacuate	lay off	
die	hire	shoot down	

A. An economic depression

1. workers

In an economic depression, workers are laid off.

2. factories

Factories . . .

3. unemployment

Unemployment increases.

B. A war

4. airplanes
5. bombs
6. people
7. crops
8. towns and cities
9. normal life
10. the economy
11. black market activity

C. An earthquake

D. A forest fire

4. Current Events

Talk about events which are in the news right now. What has happened? What is happening?

Some possibilities:

1. the war in ______
2. the drought in ______
3. the economic crisis in ______
4. pollution
5. a strike
6. other: ______

5. Preposition Combinations

Ask a classmate these questions, filling in the prepositions. You can find these combinations in Exercises 1, 5, and 6.

1. Are you satisfied ______ your progress in English, or are you disappointed ______ it?
2. Are you confused ______ the passive in English?
3. When you go to bed at night, are you exhausted ______ studying (or working)?
4. Are you excited ______ your next vacation?
5. Are you interested ______ American architecture?
6. Is brick used ______ a building material in your country?
7. Are some houses made ______ wood?
8. Are houses in your country usually equipped ______ air conditioning? How about cars?
9. Is the garage usually connected ______ the house, or is it a separate building?
10. Has American culture had an effect ______ life in your country?

Discussion Topics

A. What are houses usually made of in your country? Are most houses traditional in style, or have new styles been introduced? Are there prefabricated houses in your country? Are solar houses popular? Are there many mobile homes? Have you seen any "smart" homes? Would you like to live in any of these kinds of homes? Give reasons for your answer.

B. Are there any special houses that are found only in your country? If so, describe them: What are they made of? What shape are they? How big are they? What is special about them? Are they traditional or modern?

C. In the cities in your country, do most people live in single-family homes or in apartments? How many families usually live in one apartment building?

D. Are many new houses being built in your country or in your region right now? Are "housing starts" an important economic indicator in your country? Do you hear or read about them in the news?

E. Have many bridges, highways, subway systems, or airports been built in your country in the last five or ten years? Is an important construction project going on now? If so, what stage is it in (i.e., what is being done, what has been done, and what hasn't been done yet)?

F. Is construction or land development changing the landscape or the lifestyle in your country? If so, what changes are taking place? Are you happy to see these changes, or are they causing some problems?

Composition Topics

Write a short composition about one of the following topics. Make some of your sentences passive.

1. Write about a style of house that is popular in your country today. Tell what the house is made of and what features it is usually equipped with. If you can, tell how the house is built, step by step.
2. Write about a particular construction project that is going on in your neighborhood or in your city. Tell what has been done up to now, what is being done, and what hasn't been done yet. In your opinion, is this a useful project or not? Why?
3. Write about an important economic indicator that you know about (such as housing starts or the unemployment rate). How is the economy affected by changes in this indicator?
4. Is development changing the landscape of your city or country? Write about the changes that are taking place.

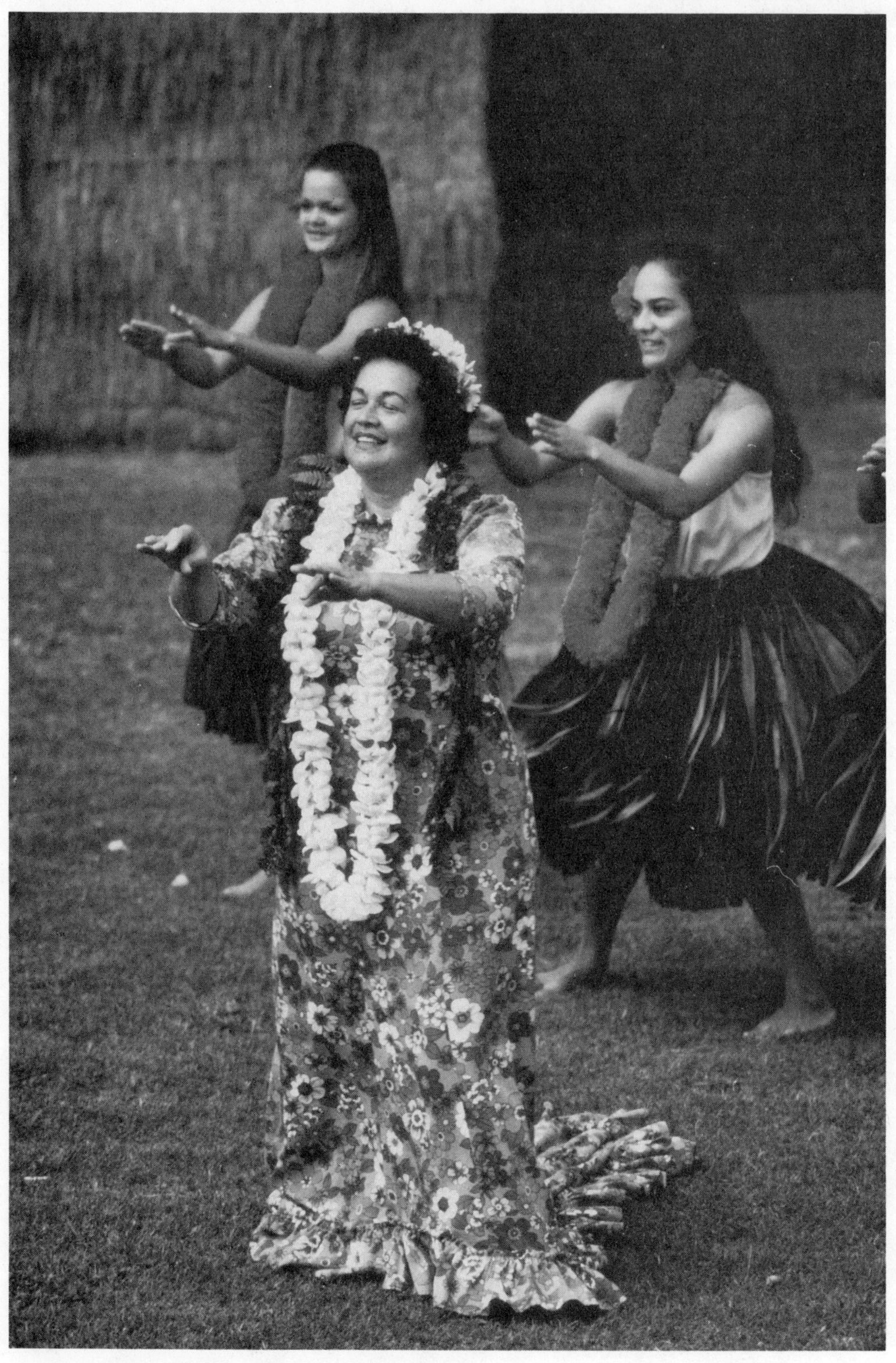

Lesson 4

The Garden Isle and the Forbidden Island of Hawaii

4.1 Quantifiers in Affirmative Statements

Without a Definite Determiner

COUNT NOUNS

Singular

QUANTIFIER	COUNT NOUN	
A One Each Every	boy	is here.

NON-COUNT NOUNS

COUNT NOUNS

Plural

QUANTIFIER	OF	COUNT NOUN
A few	—	
Several	—	
Some	—	
A number	of	
Quite a few	—	
Many	—	boys
A great many	—	
A lot	of	
Lots	of	
Most	—	
All	—	
Two	—	
A dozen	—	

NON-COUNT NOUNS

Singular

QUANTIFIER	OF	NON-COUNT NOUN
A little	—	
—		
Some	—	
A certain amount	of	
Quite a little	—	
Quite a bit	of	
Much	—	coffee
A great deal	of	
A good deal	of	
A lot	of	
Lots	of	
Most	—	
All	—	

With a Definite Determiner

COUNT NOUNS

Singular

QUANTIFIER	OF	DEFINITE DETERMINER	COUNT NOUN	
		The / That / Sue's	boy	is ready.
One / Each	of	the / those / Sue's / my	boy(s)	is ready.

Plural

QUANTIFIER	OF	DEFINITE DETERMINER	COUNT NOUN
A few / Several / Some / A number / Quite a few / Many / A great many / A lot / Lots / Most / Two / A dozen / Two dozen	of	the / these / those / Sue's / my / your / its / his / her / our / their	boys
All / Half / Both	(of)	the / my / etc.	boys
Both			boys

NON-COUNT NOUNS

Singular

QUANTIFIER	OF	DEFINITE DETERMINER	NON-COUNT NOUN
A little / Some / A certain amount / Quite a little / Quite a bit / Much / A great deal / A lot / Lots / Most / Two (bags) / A dozen (bags)	of	the / this / that / Sue's / my / your / etc.	coffee
All / Half	(of)	the / my / etc.	coffee

Before a Personal Pronoun

COUNT NOUNS

Singular

QUANTIFIER	OF	PRONOUN	
One Each	of	us you them	is here.

Plural

QUANTIFIER	OF	PRONOUN	
A few Several Both Half etc.	of	us you them	are ready.

NON-COUNT NOUNS

Singular

QUANTIFIER	OF	PRONOUN	
A little Some Half etc.	of	it	is ready.

Both and All: We use **both** when there are only two. These alternate forms have the same meaning:

both boys = both the boys = both of the boys

We use **all** when there are three or more. **All** clarifies that there are no exceptions:

Cats are mammals = All cats are mammals. (general)
My cats are gray = All my cats are gray. (specific)

Formal and Informal Usage: **A lot of** and **lots of** are common in informal conversation. In most writing it is better to use **many, a great many, much,** and **a great deal of.**

Much is used in affirmative sentences in formal language. In conversation it is better to use **a lot of, lots of,** and **a great deal of.**

Vocabulary: Appendix 3 lists the categories of non-count nouns, along with some examples.

Exercise 1. Subject–Verb Agreement (oral—books closed)

Say **is** when you hear a singular subject and **are** when you hear a plural subject.

1. A friend . . . **is**
2. A few books . . . **are**
3. Every book
4. Some books
5. Some of my money
6. A certain amount of trouble
7. A little of the food
8. One of them
9. Each of us
10. Most of the students
11. Half of my time
12. Half of the students
13. Several students
14. A dozen of my cousins
15. A great deal of fun
16. A great many of the new students
17. All my money
18. All my friends
19. A number of people

Exercise 2. Quantifiers with and without *of*

If you want to get married in a romantic setting, how about Hawaii, the "Island Paradise of the Pacific"? A travel agent will give you brochures which tell you all about it.

Circle the correct choice in parentheses and fill in **of** if it is needed.

1. One brochure contains (quite a few/quite a bit) ______ information about a chapel* at Coco Palms Resort on the island of Kauai.
2. (A great many/A gread deal) ______ marriage ceremonies (is/are) performed there every year—about 350.
3. (Many/Much) ______ them (is/are) scheduled for Valentine's Day.**
4. In fact, there are so (many/much) ______ requests for Valentine's Day weddings that only about half ______ them can actually be scheduled on that day.
5. But make your reservation early, and with (a few/a little) ______ luck, you can have a Valentine's Day wedding in a beautiful chapel that was built as part of a movie set.
6. (Quite a few/Quite a little) ______ films (have/has) been made on Kauai, several ______ them at Coco Palms.

**Chapel:* a small building like a church.

***Valentine's Day:* February 14—a day when lovers send cards or give each other presents.

7. You will find (a great many/a great deal) ______ wonderful things to do on your honeymoon, including swimming, hiking, boating, and horseback riding.
8. In fact, there (is/are) so (many/much) ______ variety on Kauai that you will need to stay a while to see it all.
9. There (is/are) (many/much) ______ varieties of exotic flowers on the island, as well as waterfalls, mountains, and the rainiest spot on earth.
10. Here (is/are) (a few/a little) ______ facts about the State of Hawaii.
11. Five large companies own most ______ the land in the state.
12. Although almost anything will grow in the islands, the state imports most ______ its food.
13. Most ______ the traditional ways are disappearing from the Hawaiian Islands, but there (is/are) a number ______ people who are working to preserve them.
14. For example, a certain amount ______ taro*** (is/are) still raised in the traditional way.
15. (Many/much) ______ full-length movies (has/have) been made in Hawaii, most ______ them on Kauai.
16. However, most ______ filming for television series (is/are) done on another island, Oahu.
17. Some ______ film sites (welcome/welcomes) visitors.
18. You will find a great variety of people in Hawaii. All ______ Hawaii's ethnic groups (is/are) minorities. They include native Hawaiians, Filipinos, Chinese, Japanese, and Caucasians (whites).

****Taro:* a root vegetable something like a potato.

4.2 Quantifiers in Negative Statements

Either/neither

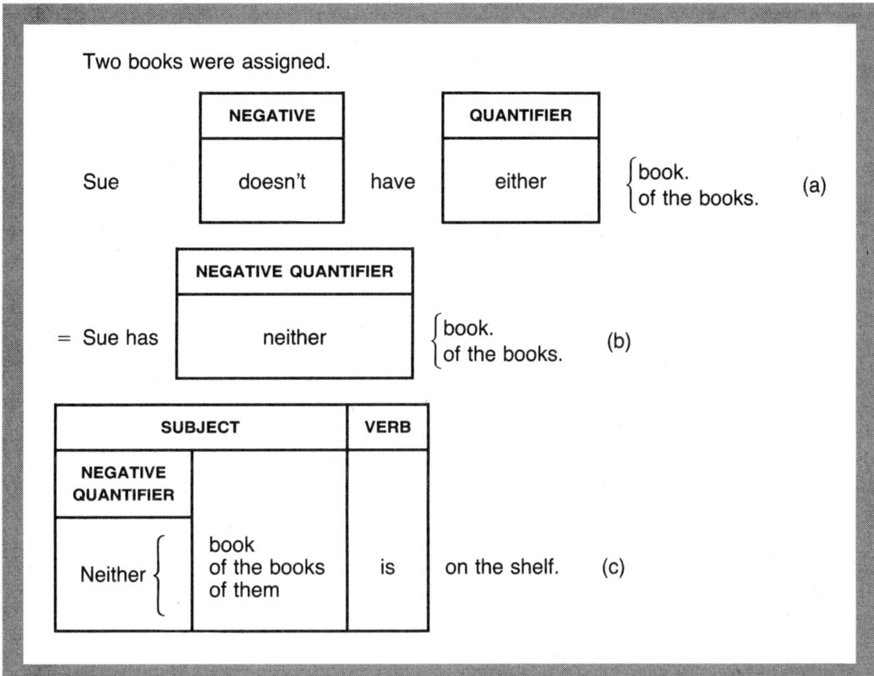

Two books were assigned.
NEGATIVE
QUANTIFIER
Sue
doesn't
have
either
book.
of the books.
(a)
NEGATIVE QUANTIFIER
= Sue has
neither
book.
of the books.
(b)
SUBJECT
VERB
NEGATIVE QUANTIFIER
Neither
book
of the books
of them
is
on the shelf.
(c)

All/any/no/none

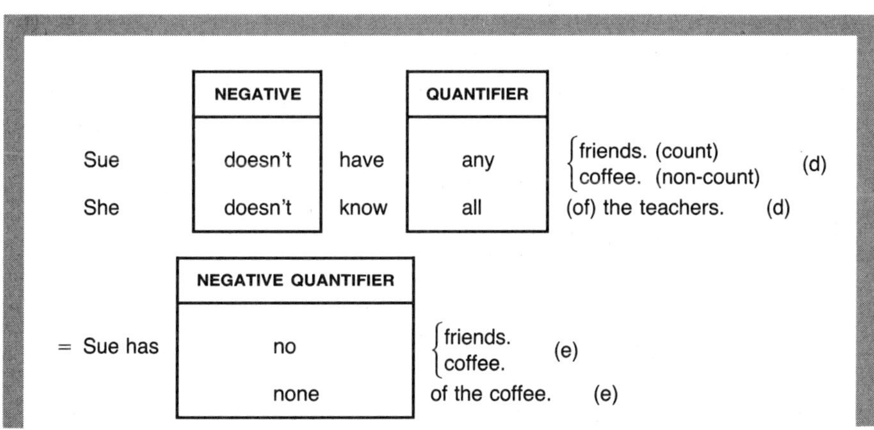

NEGATIVE
QUANTIFIER
Sue
doesn't
have
any
friends. (count)
coffee. (non-count)
(d)
She
doesn't
know
all
(of) the teachers.
(d)
NEGATIVE QUANTIFIER
= Sue has
no
friends.
coffee.
(e)
none
of the coffee.
(e)

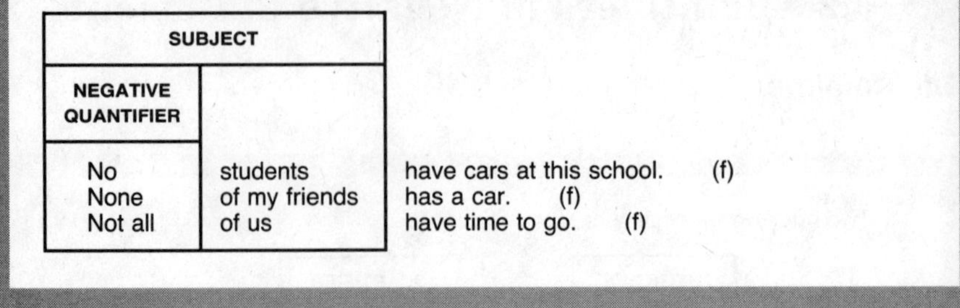

SUBJECT		
NEGATIVE QUANTIFIER		
No	students	have cars at this school. (f)
None	of my friends	has a car. (f)
Not all	of us	have time to go. (f)

Word Choice: **Either** and **neither** refer to *two.*

a. **Either** is used after a negative, but not before.

b. **Neither** can be used instead of **not . . . either.**

c. **Neither** is also used in the subject of a negative statement. (We cannot use **both** or **either** before a negative.)

All, any, no, and **none** refer to more than two and also to non-count nouns.

d. **Any** and **all** may be used after a negative, but not before.

e. **No** and **none** can be used instead of **not . . . any. No** is the adjective form, and **none** is the pronoun form.

f. We use **no, none,** and **not all** in the subject of negative statements. (We cannot use **any** or **all** before a negative.)

Agreement: After **neither** and **none,** the singular form of the verb is traditionally considered correct, even when a plural count noun is referred to. In informal conversation, however, the plural is often heard.

> *Note:* **Either** and **any** may also be used in affirmative statements to mean that it doesn't matter which one.
>
> 1. **A: Do you want to meet on Saturday or Sunday?**
>   **B: *Either* day is all right with me. You decide.**
>
> 2. **A: What day do you want to meet next week?**
>   **B: *Any* day is all right with me. You decide.**

Quantifier + *not*

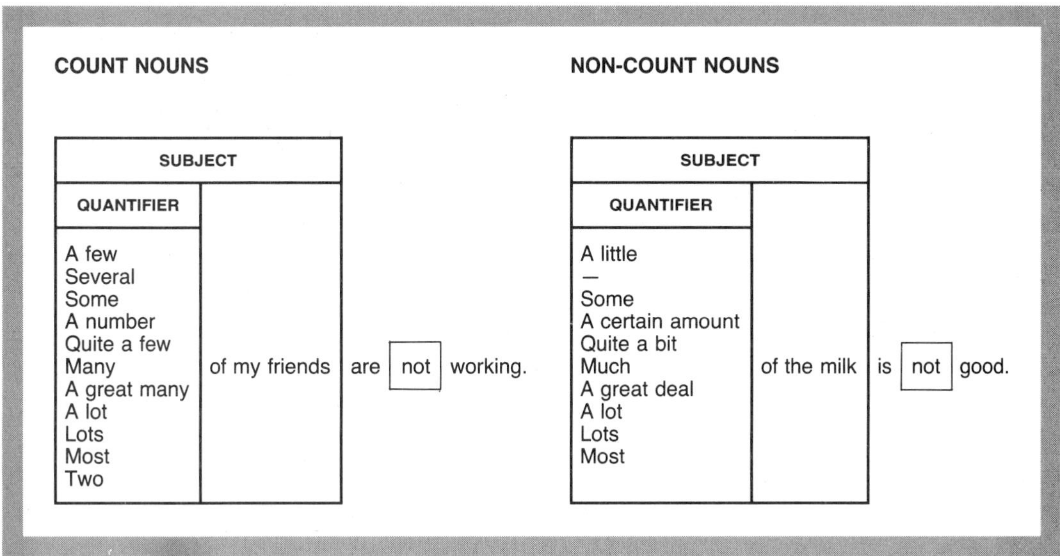

COUNT NOUNS

SUBJECT				
QUANTIFIER				
A few Several Some A number Quite a few Many A great many A lot Lots Most Two	of my friends	are	not	working.

NON-COUNT NOUNS

SUBJECT				
QUANTIFIER				
A little — Some A certain amount Quite a bit Much A great deal A lot Lots Most	of the milk	is	not	good.

Not + quantifier

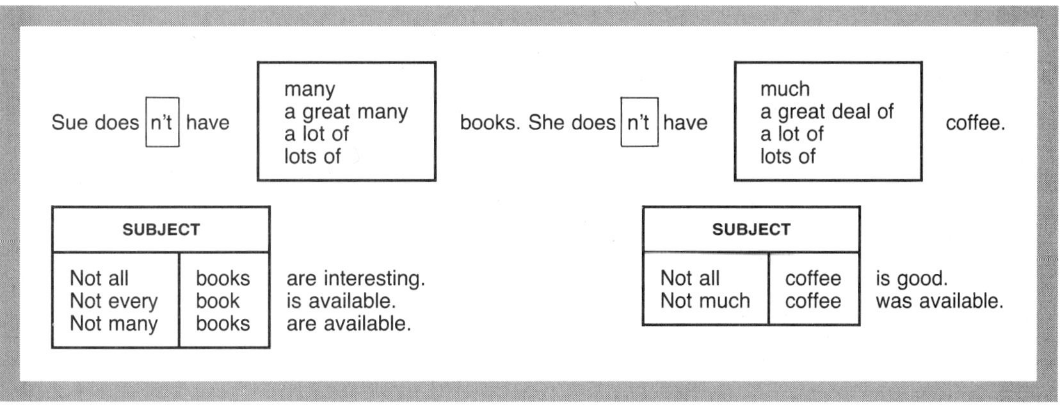

Sue does [n't] have [many / a great many / a lot of / lots of] books. She does [n't] have [much / a great deal of / a lot of / lots of] coffee.

SUBJECT		
Not all	books	are interesting.
Not every	book	is available.
Not many	books	are available.

SUBJECT		
Not all	coffee	is good.
Not much	coffee	was available.

Word Order: Quantifiers which mean *many* or *much* can occur before or after **not,** but with different meanings. Compare:

> **Many cars don't have air conditioning.** (But many others have it.)
> **Not many cars have air conditioning.** (Most do *not* have it.)

Quantifiers with Negative Force

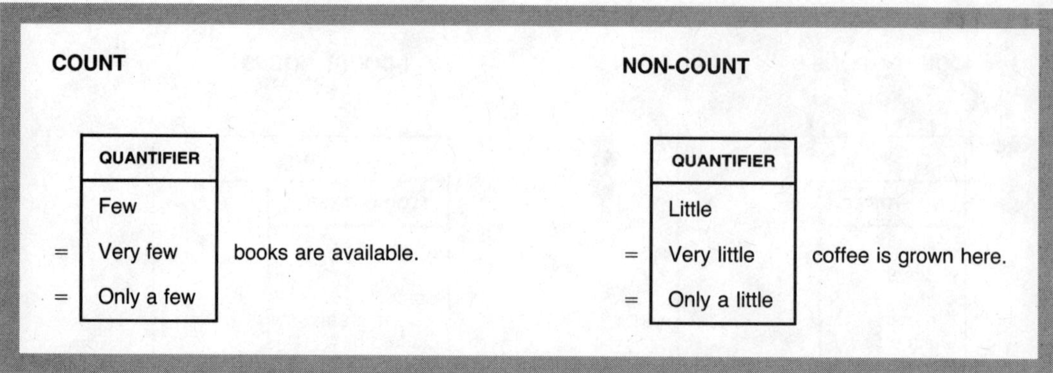

COUNT			NON-COUNT		
	QUANTIFIER			QUANTIFIER	
	Few			Little	
=	Very few	books are available.	=	Very little	coffee is grown here.
=	Only a few		=	Only a little	

Word Choice: Notice that **a few** and **a little** have a positive meaning, but **few** and **little** have a negative meaning.

Few
Very few } = **not many**
Only a few

Little
Very little } = **not much**
Only a little

Exercise 3. *Either/neither/both; all/any/no/none*

This year, the Coco Palms Resort has received several dozen inquiries from couples who want to get married at the chapel on Valentine's Day. One of them was from Betsy Cape and her fiancé Russ, who will fly to Hawaii from Oregon for the wedding.

Answer the questions. In each of your answers include one of the following expressions:

all	no	both
not all	none	either
any		neither

1. Has the Coco Palms Resort turned down some of the applications this year? (no)

    No, they haven't turned down any of { **the applications.** / **them.** }

    or: **No, they have turned down none of the applications.**

2. Have some applications been turned down?

   No, $\left\{\begin{array}{l}\textbf{no applications}\\ \textbf{none of them}\end{array}\right\}$ **have been turned down.**

3. Are the couples enthusiastic about their wedding plans? (yes)
4. Do they want rain on Valentine's Day? (no)
5. Are all the couples residents of Hawaii? (no)
6. Have Russ and Betsy been to Hawaii before? (no) (Use **them**.)
7. Do they know some of the other couples? (no)
8. Can all of them get married in the chapel on Valentine's Day? (no)
9. Does it upset Russ and Betsy that their wedding will be the day *after* Valentine's Day? (not really) (Use **them**.)
10. Do film crews interrupt the wedding ceremonies on Valentine's Day? (no)
11. Do all the newlyweds plan to hike to Koholela Falls? (no)
12. Do Betsy and Russ want to do some hiking? (yes)
13. Do the prehistoric temples on the island interest Russ and Betsy? (yes)
14. Do the tennis courts and golf courses interest them? (no)
15. Do Betsy and Russ want to spend their honeymoon at the Coco Palms Resort? (no) (Use **them**.)
16. Do they want to visit at least one other island in Hawaii besides Kauai? (yes)

Exercise 4. Passive Sentences with Negative Subjects

Below are some facts about Hawaii.

a. Change the underlined clauses to the passive. Each clause will begin with a negative. Omit the **by** phrase when possible. (The rules for omitting the **by** phrase are given on page 42.)

b. In which sentences can you use **few** or **little** in place of **not** + quantifier?

Note to the Student: In transforming sentences from the active to the passive, you are not only learning a point of grammar but are also practicing one of the skills involved in *paraphrasing*. In most of your academic writing, you will be required to report material that you have read *in your own words,* that is, to paraphrase. Many of the exercises in this book (those which involve tranforming, combining, and reducing) will help you to learn this important skill.

1. Although the 124 islands of the Hawaiian chain stretch for 1,600 miles (2,500 kilometers), people do not inhabit many of them.
   a. **(Although the 124 islands of the Hawaiian chain stretch for 1,600 miles,) not many of them are inhabited.** (It is not important to say **by people** because we know that "people" is the intended meaning.)
   b. **. . . , few of them are inhabited.**
2. Although Hawaii is surrounded by water, the islanders don't realize* much income from fishing.
   a. **(Although Hawaii is surrounded by water,) not much income . . .**
3. Hawaii was once famous for its sugar plantations, but farmers don't export much sugar now.
4. Hawaii does not produce many pineapples now, compared to former times.

5. The state has never produced any tea. (Use **ever.**)
6. Because the original inhabitants have intermarried with the white and Asian immigrants, tourists don't see many full-blooded Hawaiians** in the islands now.
7. Tourists do not visit every island, however.
8. The owners of Niihau do not permit any tourists to visit that island. (Use **the island of Niihau.**)
9. Moreover, they do not permit any non-Hawaiians to live there.
10. Although the 250 residents of Niihau know English, they don't speak much English outside of school. (They prefer to speak Hawaiian.)

**Realize:* get.

***Hawaiians:* In this case, we don't mean the residents of the state, but the original Polynesian people who lived in the islands before Europeans went there.

4.3 Some Rules for Singular and Plural

Singular Nouns Ending in *-s*

COUNT

SUBJECT	VERB	
A new means	has been found	for preventing colds. (a)
A new series	is starting	on television next week. (a)
Our species	is called	*homo sapiens.* (a)

NON-COUNT

Mathematics	is	a required subject at my school. (b)
Statistics	is	a difficult subject. (b)
Physics	is	hard, too. (b)
The good news	is spreading	fast. (b)

PROPER

The United States	is	in North America.

Form: a. The count nouns listed above have the same form in the singular and in the plural.

b. Nouns which end in **-ics** are singular non-count when they refer to a field of study.

Collective Nouns

The committee	has issued	its decision.
My family	is not	wealthy.
The government	has passed	the new law. Now *they* have to enforce it.

Agreement: Nouns which refer to groups take the singular form of the verb. However, **they** (not **it**) is generally used to refer to these nouns after the first sentence.

Notes: 1. One exception to the rule is **faculty,** which usually takes a plural verb.

The faculty are meeting in Green Hall.

2. The plural may be used after a collective noun when characteristics of the individuals in the group are being discussed.

The committee are all very intelligent. (Each member is intelligent.)

Irregular Plurals

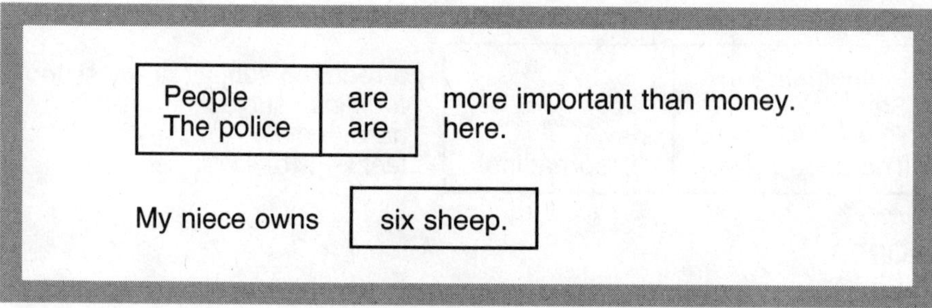

Vocabulary: Appendix 4 gives a list of irregular noun plurals.

The + Adjective

	ADJECTIVE		
The	sick	need	our care.
The	young	have	fresh ideas.

Agreement: Certain adjectives which describe people are used with **the** as plural nouns. These adjectives have no **-s** but take the plural form of the verb. **The sick** means *sick people in general.*

Nationalities and Languages

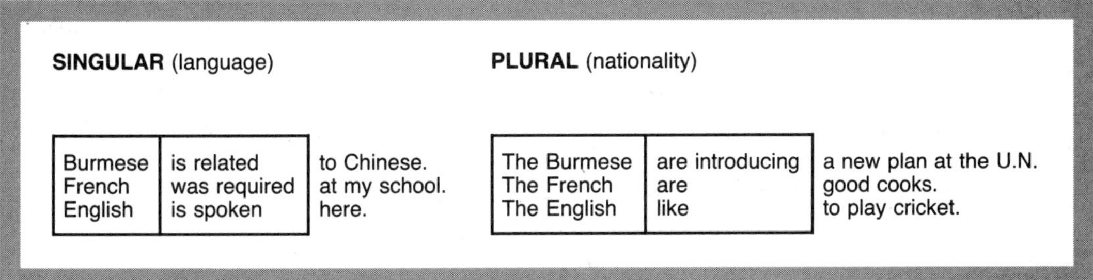

SINGULAR (language)

Burmese	is related	to Chinese.
French	was required	at my school.
English	is spoken	here.

PLURAL (nationality)

The Burmese	are introducing	a new plan at the U.N.
The French	are	good cooks.
The English	like	to play cricket.

Form: Nouns of nationality which end in **-ch, -sh,** and **-ese** do not change in the plural.

When the noun refers to a language, do not use **the.** However, we do use **the** before *adjective* + **language.**

Burmese is related to Chinese.

but: **The Burmese language is related to Chinese.**

Numbers, Fractions, and Percentages

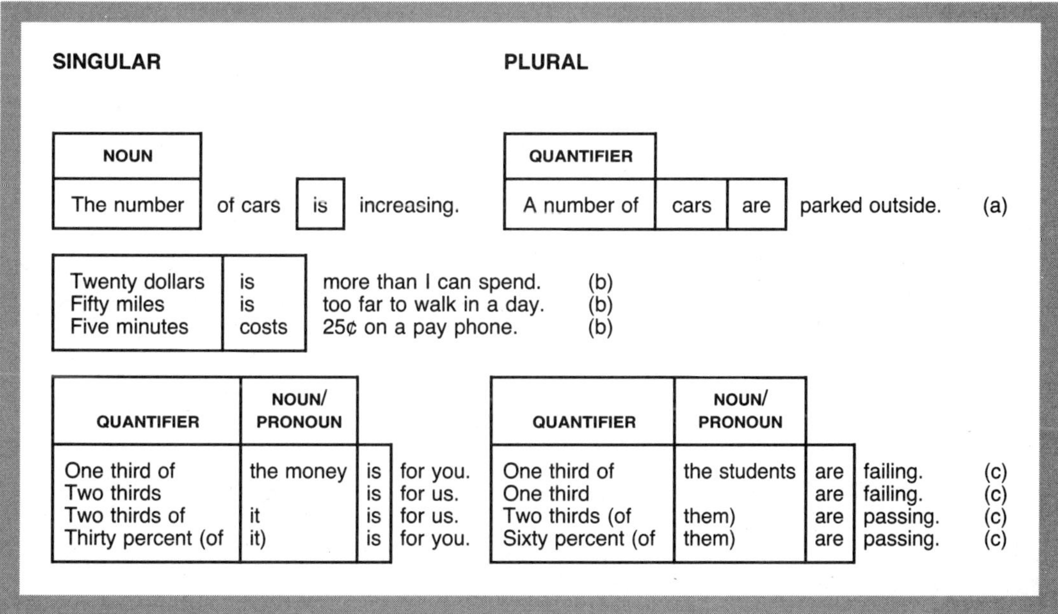

SINGULAR

NOUN				
The number	of cars	is	increasing.	

PLURAL

QUANTIFIER				
A number of	cars	are	parked outside.	(a)

Twenty dollars	is	more than I can spend.	(b)
Fifty miles	is	too far to walk in a day.	(b)
Five minutes	costs	25¢ on a pay phone.	(b)

QUANTIFIER	NOUN/ PRONOUN		
One third of	the money	is	for you.
Two thirds		is	for us.
Two thirds of	it	is	for us.
Thirty percent (of	it)	is	for you.

QUANTIFIER	NOUN/ PRONOUN			
One third of	the students	are	failing.	(c)
One third		are	failing.	(c)
Two thirds (of	them)	are	passing.	(c)
Sixty percent (of	them)	are	passing.	(c)

Agreement: a. **The number** takes a singular verb. **A number** is a quantifier and takes a plural verb.

b. When we speak of an amount of money, distance, or time, the verb is often singular even though the subject is plural in form. The verb refers to the total amount, not the units of measurement.

c. After a fraction or percentage, the verb agrees with the noun, not the quantifier. Sometimes the noun is not stated but is understood from a previous sentence.

Nouns Followed by Phrases and Clauses

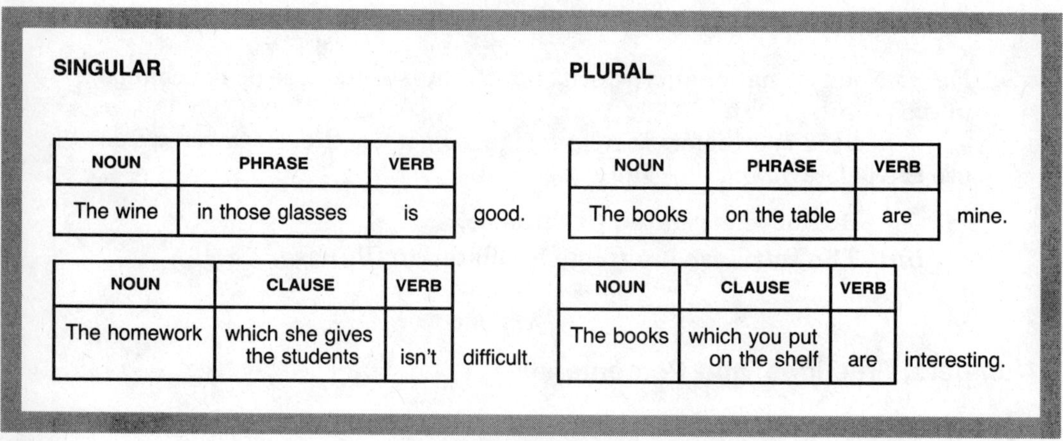

SINGULAR

NOUN	PHRASE	VERB	
The wine	in those glasses	is	good.

NOUN	CLAUSE	VERB	
The homework	which she gives the students	isn't	difficult.

PLURAL

NOUN	PHRASE	VERB	
The books	on the table	are	mine.

NOUN	CLAUSE	VERB	
The books	which you put on the shelf	are	interesting.

Agreement: Notice that the verb agrees with the noun that it tells about.

Compound Subjects

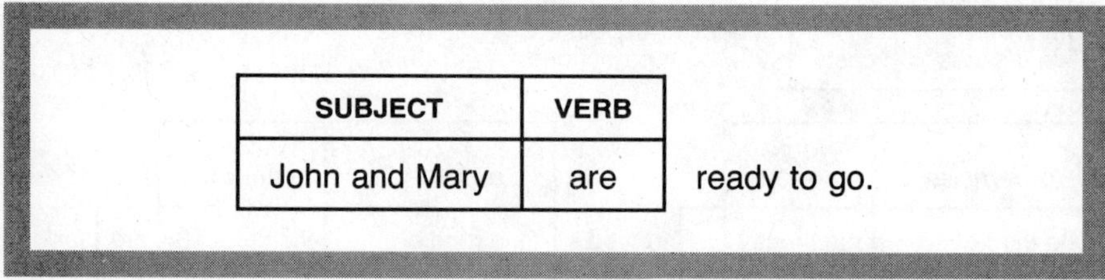

SUBJECT	VERB	
John and Mary	are	ready to go.

Agreement: When two or more subjects are connected by **and,** the verb is plural.

Exercise 5. Changing from the Active to the Passive

Underline the direct object in the following sentences. Then change the sentences to the passive. Omit the **by** phrase whenever possible.

1. Nobody inhabits most of the islands in the State of Hawaii.

   Most of the islands in the State of Hawaii are not inhabited.

2. Many people in Hawaii speak Chinese.
3. The population also includes many Japanese. (Use **in the population.**)
4. People in Hawaii don't use the words *north, south, east,* and *west.*
5. Instead, they use *mauka* and *makai* to mean "toward the mountains" and "toward the sea." **(Instead, . . .)**
6. On Niihau, the Forbidden Island, people speak the language of the original Hawaiians.
7. There, the people are preserving the way of life of the original Hawaiians.
8. The owners don't admit visitors from the outside.
9. They don't admit anyone except guests of the residents.
10. The owners employ the people who live there on their ranch.
11. The ranch raises sheep. (Use **on the ranch.**)
12. It also exports honey.
13. The owners have built an elementary school and a small store.
14. They take the sick to the island of Kauai for treatment.
15. At present, the county government is holding a series of hearings* about Niihau (because the owners want to buy a helicopter).
16. The owners feel that the ranch needs a means of providing for medical emergencies. **(The owners feel that . . .)**
17. (They also plan to bring tourists to the island in the helicopter.) Newspapers and television and radio newscasters have reported this news throughout the state.

**Hearings:* meetings where people can give evidence and opinions.

18. According to some, the plan threatens the way of life of the islanders.

Exercise 6. Changing from the Passive to the Active

Change the sentences to the active voice.

1. When a young person on Niihau decides to go to college, his or her expenses are paid by the owners of the island.

   When a young person on Niihau decides to go to college, the owners of the island pay his or her expenses.

2. Niihau is separated from Kauai by seventeen miles (twenty-seven kilometers).
3. The island is owned by one family.
4. Niihau is not patrolled by police because there is no crime there.
5. The Hawaiian language is spoken by everybody who lives there.

Exercise 7. Subject–Verb Agreement

Fill in the correct present form of the verb or auxiliary.

1. Less than half of the people in Hawaii _are_ Caucasian. (be)
2. About one third of the people ______ of Japanese descent. (be)
3. Nearly 15 percent ______ from other Asian countries. (be)
4. The number of native Hawaiians ______ only about 9,000. (be)
5. But two fifths of the unemployed ______ (be) Hawaiian or part Hawaiian.
6. The number of sugar plantations ______ (have) decreased from forty to thirteen in recent years.
7. A number of factors ______ (have) caused this decline in sugar production.

8. More than four fifths of Hawaii's food _______ imported.
(be)

9. About $4 billion _______ brought into the Hawaiian economy annually by tourism.
(be)

10. About four fifths of the population _______ on the island of Oahu, the most highly developed island.
(live)

11. The government _______ trying to limit development on the other islands so that Hawaii's natural beauty and wildlife will be preserved.
(be)

12. Many native species of birds _______ threatened with extinction.
(be)

13. (For example, the *nene,* or Hawaiian goose, is one of seventy species of birds which lived on the island before the Polynesians arrived.) This species _______ now on the endangered list.
(be)

Transfer Exercises

1. Commonalities

A. Pair off with a classmate and find out what you have *in common.* Use **both, either,** and **neither.**

1. What languages do you speak?

Example: **Both of us speak some English, but neither of us speaks it perfectly.**

or: **Both of us speak Spanish and English, but neither of us writes in English very well.**

2. What do you like to do in your leisure time?* What leisure activities don't interest you?

3. What are some things that you want to do in your lives? What don't you want to do?

**Leisure time:* free time.

4. What interesting places have you visited? What places would you like to visit sometime?

5. Which of these things bother or upset you? Which do not?

loud rock music	being away from home
the food in the cafeteria	walking in the rain
hard work	walking on an icy sidewalk
having a lot of homework	horror movies
being alone	

6. Who are your favorite movie stars and singers? What stars and singers don't appeal to you?

7. What else do you have in common?

B. Work with a partner from another country. What do your two countries have in common? Discuss some or all of the following.

holidays	government
food and drink	exports and imports
climate	types of music
	etc.

Examples: **Both our countries celebrate Christmas.**
People in both countries eat rice.
Neither of our countries has snow in the winter.

2. Polling Your Classmates

A. Working in groups of four or more, ask the questions in 1A again. Keep notes for your group.

B. Working from your notes, tell the class about your group. Use these expressions:

one, two
some, any
all
none
half
most } of us

Examples: **In our group, only one of us speaks French.**
None of us speaks Spanish.
Half of us speak Vietnamese.

3. Marriage

Answer the questions using one of these quantifiers in each answer.

Count	*Non-count*
a few	a little
several	
some/any	some/any
a number of	a certain amount of
quite a few	quite a bit of
many	much
a great many	a great deal of
most	most

1. Does it take courage to get married?

   Yes, it takes a certain amount of courage.
   or: **No, it doesn't take any courage.**

2. Do a husband and wife need patience?
3. Can you* expect to make mistakes when you get married?
4. Do married couples have quarrels from time to time? Even happy couples?
5. Does understanding help at such times?
6. Are the problems of married couples caused by a lack of communication?**
7. Do you need money to have a happy marriage?
8. Is it helpful if a husband and wife have interests in common?
9. Are intercultural marriages usually successful? Why or why not?

4. Miscellaneous (oral or written)

a. Say (or write) **is** or **are** after each expression below.

b. Choose ten items and complete the sentences, using the *simple present, present progressive, present perfect,* or *present perfect progressive* tense.

**You:* anybody, people in general.

***Lack of communication:* not having communication.

1. a. Our class . . . **is**
   b. **Our class has twelve students.**
   or: **Our class has been meeting for three weeks.**
2. Some of the students in our class . . . **are**
3. The number of students . . .
4. When we do our homework, spelling and punctuation . . .
5. In our classroom, about one (fifth) of the chairs . . .
6. The other (four fifths) of them . . .
7. The color of the chairs . . .
8. At our school, a number of teachers . . .
9. Economics . . .
10. History and geography . . .
11. English . . .
12. Our government . . .
13. The people who run the government . . .
14. The public . . .
15. Young people . . .
16. The old . . .
17. The unemployed . . .
18. Much of the population . . .
19. Right now, the news . . .
20. The United States . . .
21. The President and his wife . . .
22. French . . .
23. The French . . .
24. The Chinese language . . .

Discussion Topics

A. What is the most perfect spot in your country for a wedding or a honeymoon? What makes it so perfect? What is the climate like? What is the scenery like? Is it a sacred* place?

B. In your country, do people usually get married at the bride's home? At the bridegroom's home? Is the ceremony in a church, synagogue, mosque, shrine, or temple?** Do many couples marry somewhere besides the city where their parents live?

**Sacred:* important to a religion.

***Church, etc:* These are buildings for religious practice.
church—the Christian religion
synagogue—the Jewish religion
mosque—Islam, the Mohammedan religion
shrine, temple—other religions

C. When the honeymoon is over, what is needed for a happy marriage? What qualities should a husband have? A wife? Both spouses?

D. Hawaii's economy has changed a great deal since it became a state in 1959. Has the economy of your country been changing? What is the most important industry in your country? What items are manufactured? What crops are raised for export? Is much of your food imported? Is tourism an important industry in your country? If so, what features are tourists attracted by?

E. Would you like to live on Niihau? Why or why not?

Composition Topics

Write a short composition about one of the following topics. Use quantifiers in some of your sentences.

1. Write about a beautiful place in your country. What makes the place beautiful? Is it a favorite spot for vacationers? For honeymooners? What is the climate like? Include some information about how people live in the area. What crops are raised there, and what items are produced?
2. Write about two people who have a lot in common. You might choose yourself as one of the people. Answer some of the questions in Transfer Exercise 1A.
3. Write about the ethnic composition (different nationalities, races, or cultures) of the population of your country. Approximately what proportion of the population belongs to each group? How do the different groups live? What work do they do? Do they live together peacefully, or are there disagreements and divisions? (Do not choose this topic if the people in your country all belong to the same ethnic group.)
4. Write about the composition of your class. Do the students in the class have a lot in common, or are you very different from each other? Do you all get along well together? (See Transfer Exercises 1 and 2.)
5. What are the necessary ingredients of a good marriage, in your opinion? (See Transfer Exercise 3 and Discussion Topic C.)
6. Write about the economy of your country. Answer the questions in Discussion Topic D.

UNIT III

THE PAST AND THE FUTURE TENSES

Kentucky
Fried Chicken

Lesson 5

Floods

5.1 The Simple Past and the Past Progressive

Exercise 1. Pretest: Irregular Verb Forms (oral/written)

With your books closed, practice giving the *past* and *past participle* forms of these irregular verbs. (Your teacher or a partner can read the base forms to you.) Then write the irregular forms and check your spelling in Appendix 2.

Base Form	*Past*	*Past Participle*	*Base Form*	*Past*	*Past Participle*
1. be	was/were	been	14. hold	______	______
2. begin	______	______	15. leave	______	______
3. build	______	______	16. lose	______	______
4. come	______	______	17. make	______	______
5. drive	______	______	18. rise	______	______
6. fall	______	______	19. run	______	______
7. fight	______	______	20. say	______	______
8. find	______	______	21. see	______	______
9. get	______	______	22. speak	______	______
10. give	______	______	23. sweep	______	______
11. go	______	______	24. take	______	______
12. have	______	______	25. wear	______	______
13. hear	______	______	26. write	______	______

Active

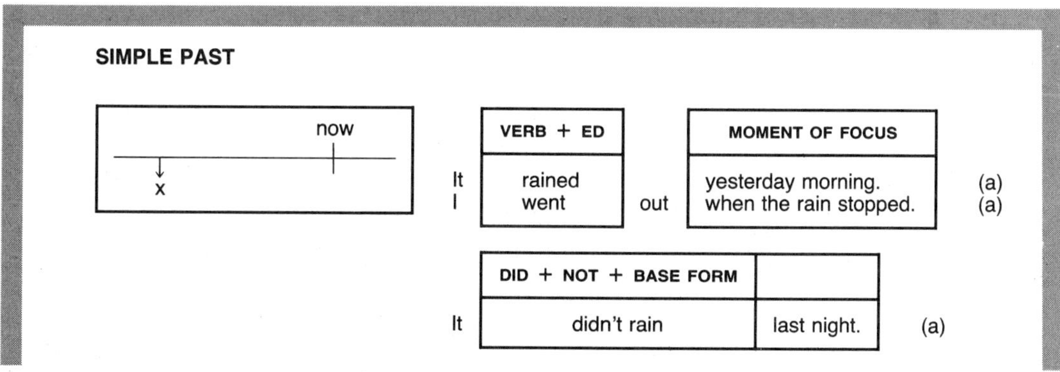

PAST PROGRESSIVE

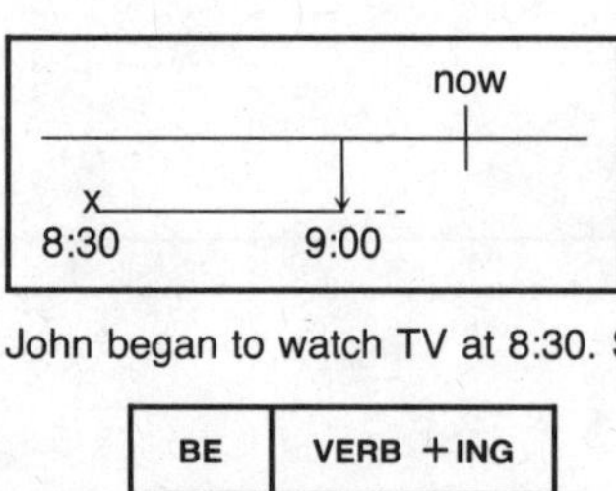

John began to watch TV at 8:30. Susan called at 9:00.

	BE	VERB +ING		MOMENT OF FOCUS	
John	was	watching	TV	at 9:00.	(b)
John	was	watching	TV	when Susan called.	(b)

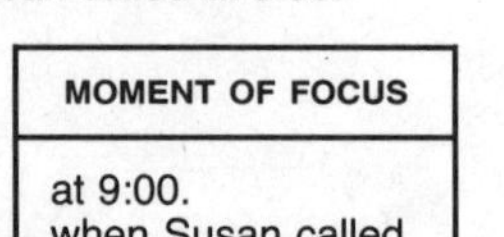

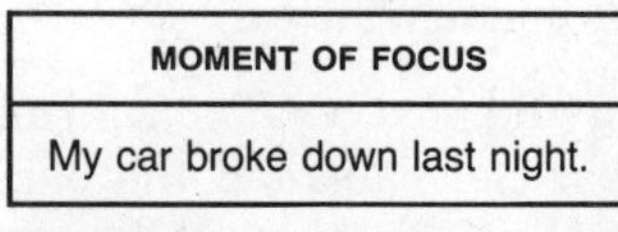

My car broke down last night. A man who was passing by took me to town. (b)

Susan called while John *was watching* TV. (c)
Margaret *was working* last year. (She's not working now.) (d)

SIMPLE PAST OR PAST PROGRESSIVE

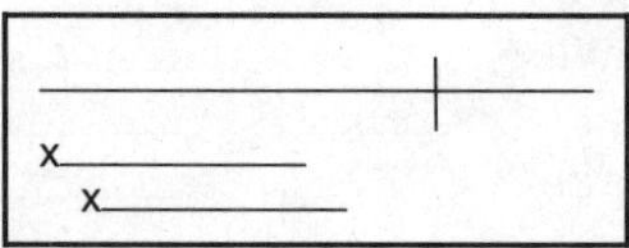

While John watched TV, Tom washed the dishes. (e)
While John was watching TV, Tom was washing the dishes. (e)

Spelling: Appendix 1 gives the spelling rules for adding **-ing** and **-ed** to regular verbs. Irregular past forms are given in Appendix 2.

Meaning: a. The *simple past* means that an action occurred or a condition existed at a stated or known time in the past. Sometimes the exact time is not known, but we know that the event occurred during a certain past period, such as a person's lifetime.

Shakespeare wrote several plays about kings.

b. The *past progressive* is used for an action that was already *in progress* at a particular moment of focus in the past. The action *began before* the moment of focus and continued past it or was interrupted at that moment.

c. The **past progressive** is used in clauses with **while** to indicate a period of time during which another action occurred.

Period: **while Tom was watching TV**
Other action: **Susan called**

d. The *past progressive* is also used to emphasize that an action continued during a given period.
e. When **while** connects two verbs in the same tense (both *simple past* or both *past progressive*), we mean that two actions were *in progress* at the same time.

Passive

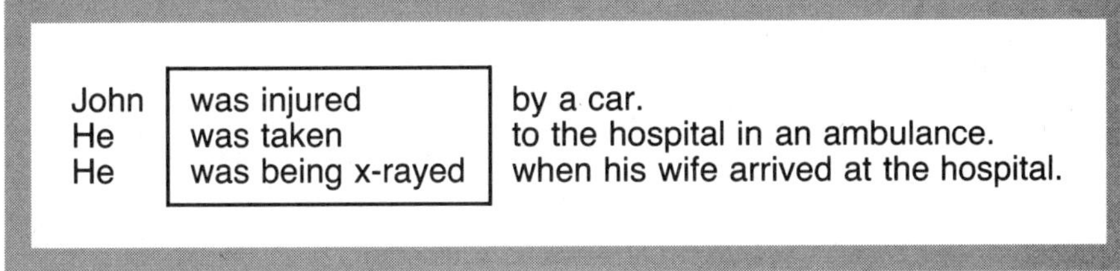

John	was injured	by a car.
He	was taken	to the hospital in an ambulance.
He	was being x-rayed	when his wife arrived at the hospital.

Exercise 2. The Simple Past versus the Past Progressive (active)

In November 1985, a devastating flood occurred in the Middle Atlantic States in the United States. The town of Weston, West Virginia, was saved from complete destruction by a new dam on the West Fork River. For a while, however, residents thought that the town was lost. A reporter interviewed some of them and reported these stories.

Fill in the blanks with the *simple past* or the *past progressive*. In a few cases, either tense is possible.

At the town lunch counter, the cook (1) was cooking (cook) up an order of scrambled eggs when a volunteer fireman (2) came (come) in and (3) ______ (say) that the dam had broken. The people who (4) ______ (eat) in the restaurant (5) ______ (run) out. "They (6) ______ (yell) and (7) ______ (scream)," she (8) ______ (say).

James Kratovil (9) ______ (relax) at home when a National Guard truck (10) ______ (drive) down his street broadcasting the news over a loudspeaker. He (11) ______ (*negative:* wear) his shoes at the time and he (12) ______ (*negative:* take) time to put them on. He just

(13) __________ out in his stocking feet. A few hours later, when he
(run)
(14) __________ back to his house, he (15) __________ his base-
(go) (find)
ment full of water. He (16) __________ his furnace and hot water
(lose)
heater and also some books and papers which he (17) __________ in
(store)
the basement.

Robert Ramsey (18) __________ the flood warning on the radio,
(hear)
and he (19) __________ to move some equipment from his garage
(decide)
into his house. While he (20) __________ , the first wave of water,
(work)
about five inches high, (21) __________ in. The next time he
(wash)
(22) __________ out the window, a chair (23) __________ by.
(look) (float)

While people in the temporary shelter (24) __________ for the
(wait)
water to recede, the volunteer fire department, which owns five boats,
(25) __________ people who were stranded.* All over the region, res-
(rescue)
cue workers (26) __________ people by boat and helicopter.
(evacuate)

Exercise 3. Understanding the Simple Past and the Past Progressive (books closed)

Answer these questions about the information in Exercise 2. Whenever the answer is *no,* your teacher will ask a second question.

1. Did the cook cook some scrambled eggs when she heard that the dam had broken?

    No, she didn't. (She *was* cooking scrambled eggs.)
    What did she do?
    She ran outside.

2. Were the people in the restaurant running when they heard the news?

**Stranded:* unable to get out.

3. Did they run out of the restaurant when they heard the news?
4. Did Kratovil relax when he heard the news?
5. Was he wearing socks?
6. Did he put on his shoes?

Exercise 4. The Past Progressive: Active and Passive

When the reporter wrote his story about Weston, West Virginia, this is what was happening. Fill in the blanks with the correct form of the *past progressive*.

1. The flood waters were receding (recede), but several streets and bridges were still under water.
2. The state hospital was still completely surrounded by water, and patients and supplies were being taken (take) in by boat.
3. People who had lost their homes ________ (house) in temporary shelters.
4. The cook at the lunch counter ________ (make) box meals for the homeless people in the shelters.
5. Robert Ramsey ________ (pull) up the wet carpeting in his house and ________ (use) fans to dry the floors.
6. He ________ (help) by some neighbors whose homes were not flooded.
7. Elsewhere in the state, dairies ________ (provide) fresh water in cartons.
8. Stranded people ________ (rescue) from rooftops by boat and helicopter.
9. National Guardsmen ________ (help) to evacuate them and ________ (guard) damaged property.

Exercise 5. The Simple Past: Changing to the Passive

Here are some facts about the 1985 flood. Change each sentence to the passive if it is possible to do so. Omit the **by** phrase. In some sentences, the passive is not possible.

1. Rescue workers evacuated 20,000 people from their homes.

   20,000 people were evacuated from their homes.
2. Twenty inches of rain fell in some places.

   (Do not change. No passive is possible.)
3. The storm killed forty-two people.
4. Creeks and rivers overflowed.
5. Tides rose five to seven feet above normal.
6. The flood waters destroyed thousands of homes.
7. They completely swept away some small towns.
8. Nothing remained except the foundations.
9. The swollen rivers washed out bridges.
10. The water blocked highways.
11. The President declared a state of emergency in Virginia, West Virginia, and western Pennsylvania.
12. The governors of these states called out the National Guard.

Exercise 6. The Present Perfect and the Simple Past

Review the uses of the *present perfect* given in Lesson 2. Then fill in the *present perfect* or the *simple past* in the dialogue below.

Remember: 1. Use the *simple past* for a definite past time.

2. Use the *present perfect* for an indefinite past time.

3. Use the *present perfect* or the *present perfect progressive* when a duration up to the present is given.

Reporter: (1) Have you lived (live) in this area long?

Resident: Well, my family (2) moved (move) here in 1935, so I (3) ______ (be) here for fifty years.

Reporter: (4) ______________ there ______________ (be) many floods in Weston?

Resident: Oh yes. Up to now, we (5) ______________ (average) about one a year. Now that the dam (6) ______________ (construct), we shouldn't have so many.

Reporter: (7) ______________ you ever ______________ (see) a flood worse than this one?

Resident: Yes, the 1950 flood (8) ______________ (be) worse, but not by much. That time, the water (9) ______________ (reach) a depth of 25′ 6″. Of course we (10) ______________ (*negative:* have) the dam then. That dam (11) ______________ (save) us this time.

Reporter: (12) ______________ all the residents ______________ (go) back to their homes?

Resident: Yes, most of them (13) ______________ (go) back yesterday, but some of them (14) ______________ (lose) their homes. They have nowhere to go back to.

5.2 The Past Perfect and the Past Perfect Progressive

Exercise 7. Pretest: Forming the Past Perfect Tenses

A. Change the sentences to the *past perfect* or *past perfect progressive.*

On-the-Spot Report	*Later Summary of the Report*
On November 7, 1985, a reporter in Washington, D.C., filed this report:	
1. "The Potomac (River) has flooded parts of Washington."	1. At the time the reporter filed his report, the Potomac <u>had flooded</u> parts of Washington.

On-the-Spot Report	*Later Summary of the Report*
2. "The National Parks Service has closed several monuments."	2. ______________________ ______________________
3. "The flooding has tied up traffic."	3. ______________________
4. "It has not contaminated the drinking water."	4. ______________________ ______________________
5. "Store owners have been preparing for the flood for two days."	5. ______________________ ______________________
6. "They have been moving goods to upper floors."	6. ______________________ ______________________
7. "They have been placing sandbags around their shops."	7. ______________________ ______________________

B. Now change your past sentences to the passive. Omit #5. In #6 and #7, use the *past perfect passive* (the perfect progressive is not used in the passive).

1. Parts of Washington ______ ______ ______ .
   etc.

PAST PERFECT

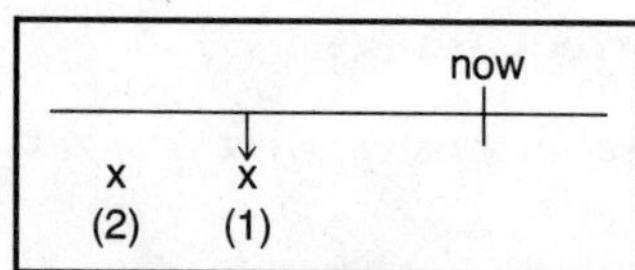

The flood reached Washington on Thursday. (later event)

It **had struck** West Virginia two days earlier. (earlier event) (a)

It **had already devastated** parts of three states when it reached Washington. (b)

Parts of three states **had already been devastated** when it reached Washington. (b)

Compare:

SIMPLE PAST

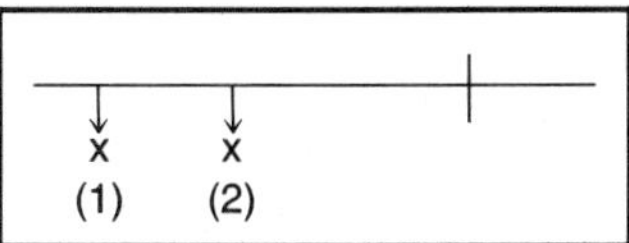

The flood struck West Virginia on Tuesday. (earlier event)
It reached Washington, D.C., two days later. (later event)

Meaning: The *past perfect* means that an action was *completed before* a moment of focus in the past.

Tense Choice: We use the *past perfect* to show the order of events when the order is not clear; for example:

a. when the actions are mentioned in reverse order and no other words indicate the order

b. when two clauses are joined by a word which does not indicate the order (such as **when** or **because**).

With time expressions which show sequence, such as **before** and **after,** the *past perfect* is often used for the earlier event for added clarity, especially in writing.

The flood {devastated / had devastated} parts of three states before it reached Washington.

PAST PERFECT PROGRESSIVE AND THE PAST PERFECT OF STATIVE VERBS

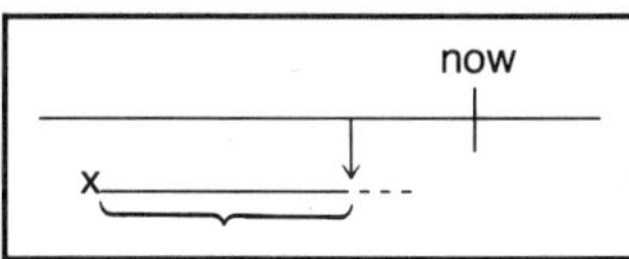

			DURATION	MOMENT OF FOCUS	
Residents	had been preparing	for the flood	for two days	when it reached Washington.	(c)

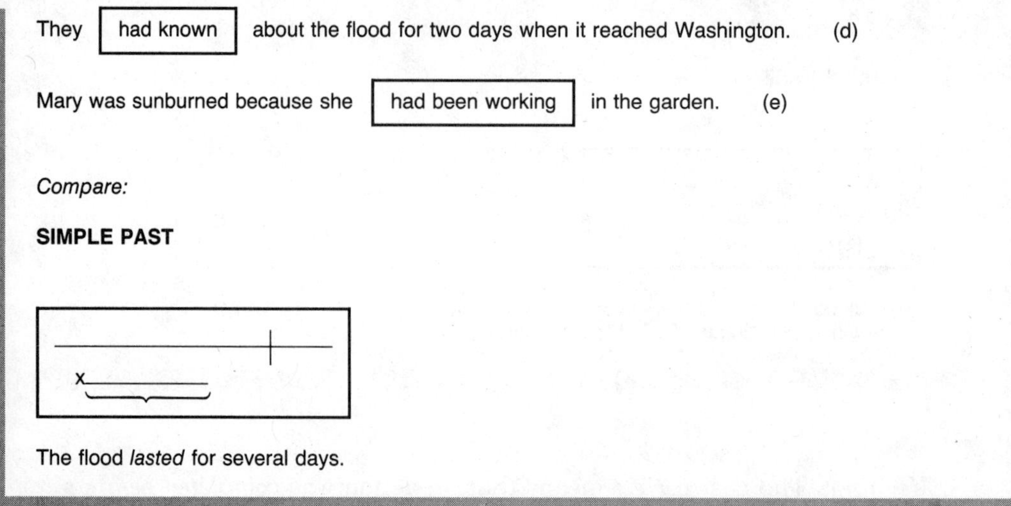

They had known about the flood for two days when it reached Washington. (d)
Mary was sunburned because she had been working in the garden. (e)
Compare:
SIMPLE PAST
x
The flood lasted for several days.

Meaning: c. The *past perfect progressive* means that an action had been *in progress* for a given *duration* up to a moment of focus in the past.

d. With stative verbs, the *past perfect* is used for duration up to a past moment of focus.

e. The *past perfect progressive* is also used to emphasize the recency of an activity before the moment of focus. Whereas the *past perfect* emphasizes *completion before* that moment, the *past perfect progressive* emphasizes the idea of *recent* activity.

Notes: 1. The *past perfect* of action verbs may also be used with expressions of duration:

Professor Jones {had taught / had been teaching} at the college for ten years when he was appointed Dean of Students.

2. The *past perfect progressive* is not used in the passive.

Choice of Tense with already, yet, and by (the time): The following expressions mean that something was true *before a moment of focus:*

already/yet (adverbs)
by + *noun* (prepositional phrase)
by the time + *clause* (adverb clause)

The choice of tense with these expressions depends on the meaning of the verb and the verb type.

Action Verbs

1. *Past perfect:* The action *finished before* the moment of focus.

   By the time I went to bed, I *had* (already) *written* the exercise.
   I *hadn't written* the composition yet.

2. *Past progressive:* The action *started before* the moment of focus.

   I *was* already *sleeping* when you called last night.
   By ten last night, I *was sleeping* soundly.

3. *Past perfect progressive:* The action *started before* and had been *in progress for a given duration* at the moment of focus.

   By ten last night, I *had been sleeping* for half an hour.

Stative Verbs

4. *Simple past:* The situation *started before* the moment of focus.

   When I came here, I already *knew* the irregular verbs.

5. *Past perfect:* The situation *started before* and had been *in progress for a given duration* at the moment of focus.

   I *had* already *known* my roommate for a year when we decided to share an apartment.

Exercise 8. The Past Perfect and the Past Perfect Progressive

A. Combine the sentences using **when** or **by the time.** Use the *past perfect* to talk about the earlier event.

1. Joe woke up at 8:50 this morning. His roommate left for class at 8:45.

   {By the time / When} Joe woke up this morning, his roommate had already left for class.

2. The cafeteria closed at 9:00. Joe got there at five past.
3. He got to class at 9:15. The class started at 9:10.
4. The professor gave out the assignment at the beginning of the class. Joe came in after that.
5. Joe got out his notebook, put his bookbag under his seat, and found his pen. He missed quite a bit of the lecture.
6. He started to take notes. Some important points were presented before that.

B. Restate each sentence using the *past perfect progressive* and an expression of duration with **for.** (Refer to the times in A.)

7. When Joe woke up, the birds were singing. They had started at six.

   When Joe woke up, the birds had been singing for almost three hours.

8. When he got to the cafeteria, the workers were cleaning up.
9. When he got to class, the professor was talking.
10. When the class ended at 10:00, he was listening intently and taking notes.
11. When he went to the cafeteria for lunch at 12:00, he was very hungry. He started to feel very hungry at about 10:00.

Exercise 9. Using the Past Tenses

Fill in the blanks with the *simple past, past progressive, past perfect,* or *past perfect progressive* (active or passive). Where more than one answer is possible, explain the difference in meaning.

1. The town of Weston, West Virginia, was saved (save) by a dam which had been built (build) the year before.
2. At the time of the flood, however, the dam ________ (*negative:* complete).
3. A temporary structure which ________ (erect) gave way during the flood.
4. When this ________ (happen), an engineer at the dam ________ (call) the Fire Department and the Fire Department ________ (call) the National Guard.
5. At about 2:00 P.M., a fireman ________ (run) into the luncheonette where several townspeople ________ (eat) to say that the dam ________ (give) way.

6. The cook ______________ (serve) customers at the lunch counter since 6:30 that morning.
7. She and the customers ______________ (discuss) the possibility of a flood when the fireman ______________ (give) the warning.
8. They all ______________ (run) for higher ground.
9. By the time three feet of water ______________ (rush) down the main street of the town, the townspeople ______________ (escape) because they ______________ (warn) in time.

Transfer Exercises

1. Recent Events

A. What was happening in your country or in the world when you left to come to this country? (*Or:* What was happening when your classes began this year?) Here are some possibilities:

1. Politicians/campaign for election

   Politicians were campaigning for election.

2. hold/an election

   They were holding an election for president when I left.

   or: **A presidential election was being held when I left.**

3. build/a new dam (bridge, tunnel, airport, nuclear power plant, etc.)
4. people/worry about
5. workers/strike
6. fight/a war

B. What season was it when you left your country? (*Or:* What season was it when you graduated from high school?) Describe what was happening in the countryside. Here are some possibilities:

7. snow/melt
8. plow/fields
9. plant/(rice)
10. harvest/crops
11. people/go on summer vacation

2. Personal Experiences

A. The sentences below describe a day when Roger Fields flew to Chicago for a business meeting. Combine the sentences with **when, by the time,** and **and.** Use the *simple past, past progressive, past perfect,* and *past perfect progressive* to show the time relationships. (Remember that we do not use the *past perfect progressive* in the passive.) You do not need to mention clock time in your sentences.

1. Roger left the house at 7:30. It snowed from 7:00 A.M. to 3:00 P.M. Driving conditions were bad.

   When Roger left the house, it was snowing, and driving conditions were bad.

   or: **When Roger left the house, it had been snowing for half an hour, and driving conditions were bad.**

2. The plane left at 8:30. He got to the airport at 8:40.

   The plane had already left by the time he got to the airport. (Roger had to wait for the next flight.)

3. He got to the meeting at 10:30. It started at 10:00. His project was discussed from 10:15 to 10:45. Important decisions were made between 10:15 and 10:30.

4. Roger got back to Kansas City at 4:00. The snow was twelve inches deep.

5. The streets were plowed earlier that day. Roger got back at 4:00. Traffic moved well (after the streets were plowed).

B. Talk about some events in your life. Tell what was happening at the time and what had happened before. When appropriate, tell how long something had been happening.

1. When I got on the plane to come to this country, . . .
2. By the time I arrived at (Miami) Airport, . . .
3. When (   ) phoned me (last week), . . .
4. By the time I graduated from high school, . . .

5. By the time I got my first job, . . .

6. When my husband/wife proposed* to me, . . .
or: When I proposed to my wife/husband, . . .

3. History

A. Fill in the correct verb forms. (In some cases, more than one tense is possible.) Then ask a classmate these questions about the region of the world which is now his or her native country. Write down a few brief notes for use in B.

1. ____________ your country ever ____________ invaded, colonized, or settled by outsiders?

   Example: **Has England ever been invaded by outsiders?**

   Oh, yes. England has been invaded at least five times: by the Celts, the Romans, the Anglo-Saxons, the Danes, and the Normans.

   If so:

2. When ____________ it happen? (Choose just one event.)
3. What people ____________ there at that time?
   (live)
4. How long ____________ they ____________ there then?
   (live)
5. What language ____________ there then?
   (speak)
6. What ____________ the official language in your country now?
   (be)
7. How long ____________ that language ____________ in your country?
   (speak)
8. ____________ other languages ____________ there also?
9. What alphabet or writing system ____________ to write your language?
   (use)
10. How long ____________ that system ____________?
    (use)

**(He) proposed to me:* (He) asked me to marry (him).

11. Had your language ever ________ before the present writing
(write)
system was introduced? If so, how?

12. ________ your country ever ________ from invaders or
(liberate)
from colonial rule?

13. If so, when ________ it ________?
(liberate)

14. Who ________ it ________ by until that time?
(rule)

15. How long ________ it ________ by them?
(rule)

16. ________ your people ________ a war of liberation?
(fight)

17. If so, how long ________ they ________ when liberation
(fight)
________?
(achieve)

B. Prepare a short report for the class on some of the facts your classmate gave you in A. Your teacher may ask you to speak from your notes or to prepare the report in writing.

Discussion Topics

A. Have you ever been in a flood, earthquake, or other natural disaster? If so, what can you remember about it? Did you have any warning? What were you doing when it happened? What did you do? Did you have to leave your home? Did everybody in your city escape safely, or were some people injured?

B. Have you ever been evacuated from your home for any reason? If so, why? Who evacuated you? Where were you taken, or where did you go? Did you stay there long? How did you get food and water? Were you able to return to your home afterwards?

C. Are there some areas in your country where there are frequent floods? If so, have dams been built for flood control? Have trees been planted? Have any other measures* been taken to alleviate** the situation?

**Measures:* actions to solve a problem.

***Alleviate:* make better.

D. Has there ever been a severe drought*** in your country? If so, what were some of the problems? Did crops or animals die? How did people get water? Has anything been done to prevent future water shortages? For example, have reservoirs and dams been built? Have trees been planted?

E. Have there been other serious weather conditions in your country that you can remember? What were some of the problems connected with these conditions? How did people cope with the situation?

Composition Topics

Write a short composition about one of the following topics. Try to use the four past tenses (but remember that the *simple past* is used more frequently than the others.)

1. Write about an emergency situation (such as a flood or drought) that you experienced or know about. See Discussion Topics A, B, D, and E for examples and questions.
2. Write about something that was happening in your country at the time you left to come to this country. (See Transfer Exercise 1.)
3. Write about your trip to this country. You might focus especially on two moments:
   a. when you got on the plane and
   b. when you got off the plane.
   For each of those moments, tell what had happened, what was happening, and what happened after that.
4. Write about another important moment in your life. (See Transfer Exercise 2B for some ideas.)
5. Write about an important event in the history of your country. (See Transfer Exercise 3.)

****Drought:* lack of rain.

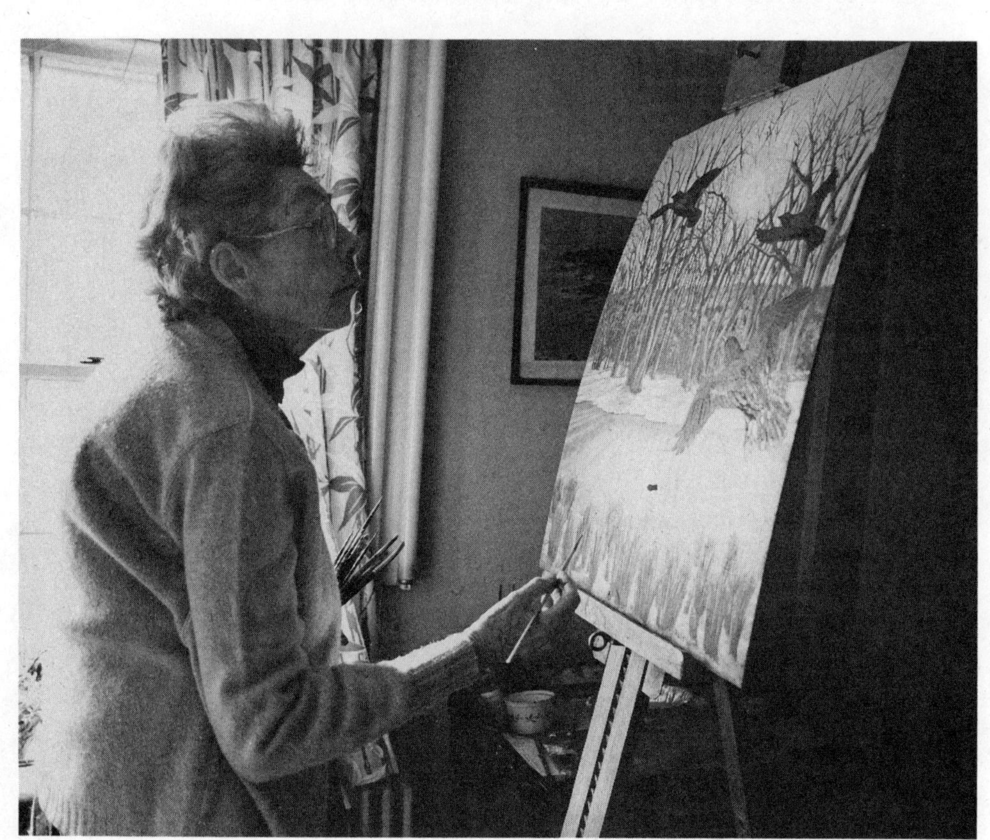

Lesson 6

Life Styles in Retirement

6.1 The Future: *be going to, will,* and the Present Tenses

Will

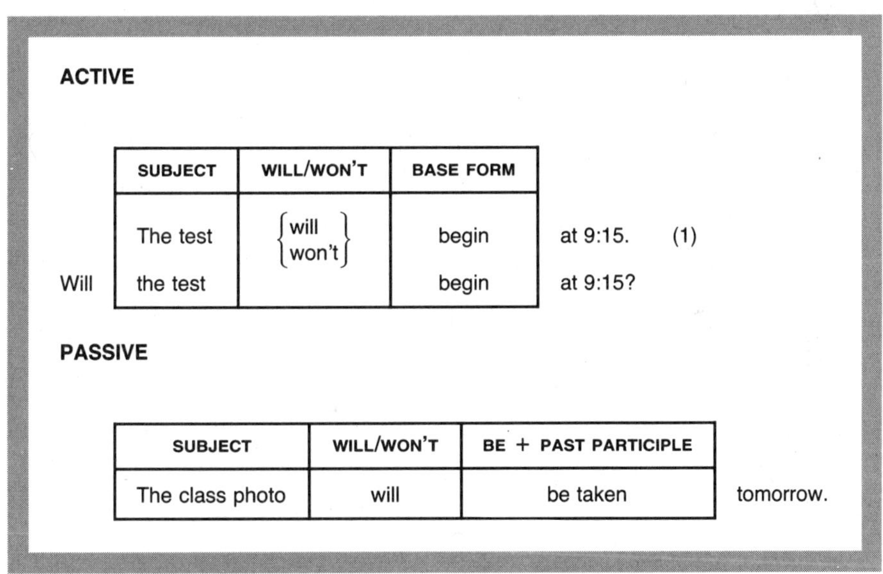

ACTIVE

	SUBJECT	WILL/WON'T	BASE FORM		
	The test	will / won't	begin	at 9:15.	(1)
Will	the test		begin	at 9:15?	

PASSIVE

SUBJECT	WILL/WON'T	BE + PAST PARTICIPLE	
The class photo	will	be taken	tomorrow.

Be going to

ACTIVE

BE	SUBJECT	BE	GOING	TO + BASE FORM	
	The teacher	is(n't)	going	to give	a test tomorrow.
Is	it		going	to rain	today?

PASSIVE

			TO + BE + PAST PARTICIPLE	
The exam	is	going	to be given	in Room 318.

Meaning: **Will** and **be going to** are both used to talk about a *future* event.

Formal and Informal Usage: a. *In formal speech and writing,* **will** and **be going to** can be used with the same meaning. **Will** is more frequent, however. **Going to** is not used repeatedly in a series of sentences.

b. *In conversation,* **will** often means *willingness, helpfulness, promise,* (or their opposites).

The teacher will help us review for the test.

She won't help us during the test.

Going to is used for the future. It is often pronounced "gonna."

Note: **Will** can be used in conversation to mean future as long as it is clear that willingness is not the intended meaning. Some examples:

1. With an inanimate subject.

Will the test cover all the tenses?

2. With **be.**

   Will you be in class tomorrow?

3. With qualifiers such as **probably, maybe, I think.**

   Alice and John will probably go to Florida for their vacation.

The Present Progressive

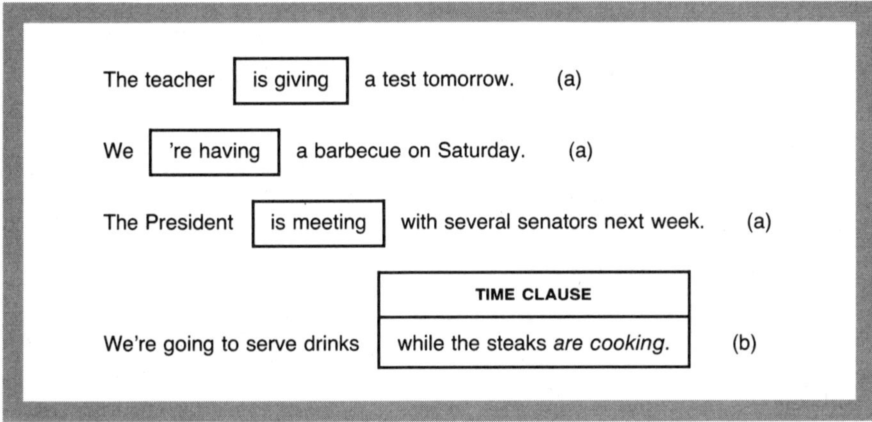

Meaning: a. The *present progressive* may be used to talk about a *definite future plan.* Of course, **going to** and **will** may also be used:

The teacher is going to give a test tomorrow.
We are going to have a barbecue on Saturday.
The President will meet with several senators next week.

For events that cannot be planned ahead, do not use the present progressive:

***Incorrect:* I ~~am getting~~ a good grade on the test tomorrow.**

b. The *present progressive* is used in time clauses to express future meaning. We do not use **will** or **going to** in time clauses. (Time clauses begin with **before, after, when, until, as soon as,** etc. See Lesson 17.)

The Simple Present

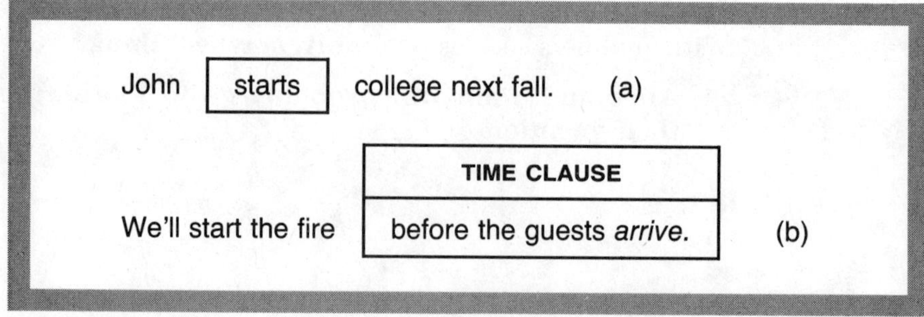

John starts college next fall. (a)
TIME CLAUSE
We'll start the fire before the guests *arrive.* (b)

Meaning: a. The *simple present* may be used to talk about an event that is *officially scheduled* for a future time. The *present progressive,* **going to** and **will** may also be used:

John is starting college next fall.
John is going to start college next fall.
John will start college next fall.

b. In time clauses, we use the *simple present* to express future meaning.

Exercise 1. *Be going to* versus the Simple Present

When Americans retire, they usually plan to lead independent, active lives for as long as they can. In fact, 75 percent of Americans aged 65 and over live independently—not with their children or in nursing homes. Many make careful plans for their retirement. In this lesson, you will read about the retirement plans of four couples. Ray and Sue West are perhaps typical of those who move to a warmer climate when they retire.

Fill in the blanks with the *simple present* or the **be going to** *future.*

1. When the Wests retire next year, they <u>are going to move</u> (move) to Florida.

2. They ______________ (sell) their house before they <u>leave</u> (leave) and* ______________ (use) the

*When two verbs are joined by **and,** we do not repeat **going to.** Which two verbs are joined by **and** in this sentence?

money to buy a new house in a retirement community called Sun City Center.

3. Sun City Center now ______________ a population of
(have)
about 9,000, and almost all its residents ______________
(be)
over sixty. No children under eighteen ______________ to
(*passive:* permit)
live there.

4. The community ______________ many recreational
(offer)
activities for its residents, and Ray and Sue
______________ to lead active lives.
(plan)

5. As soon as Ray ______________ his clubs, he
(unpack)
______________ an electric golf cart and ______________
(buy) (join)
the golf club. He ______________ to play golf almost
(expect)
every day.

6. Sue ______________ classes in painting, shell jewelry,
(take)
and other arts and crafts.

7. They ______________ in volunteer activities: Ray
(also, participate)
______________ with the "meals-on-wheels" program,
(help)
which brings cooked meals to people who can't cook for themselves, and Sue ______________ at the hospital.
(volunteer)

8. Of course, they ______________ their daughter and
(not, see)
granddaughter as often as they do now, and they
______________ them.
(miss)

9. When their granddaughter ______________ them during school vacations, they ______________ her to Disney World and to the beach.
   (visit) (take)

10. ______________ their new life in Sun City? They certainly expect to. They are looking forward to living a life of leisure in a warm climate.
   (they, enjoy)

Exercise 2. The Simple Future with *will* versus the Simple Present

Walt Hinslow is a retired reporter who worked in Asia for a number of years. Now he puts that experience to work lecturing on cruise ships that tour the Far East. In that way, he and his wife can enjoy luxury travel without putting a strain on their income.

Fill in the blanks with the *simple future* with **will** or the *simple present.*

1. Next month, Walt and his wife Wanda will take (take) a three-week cruise to the Orient.
2. When the ship visits (visit) Japan, Hinslow ______________ (give) two lectures on Japan's culture and economy.
3. After it ______________ (leave) Japan, the ship ______________ (stop) in China and Hong Kong.
4. Hinslow ______________ (give) another lecture before they ______________ (reach) China.
5. He ______________ (not, lecture) every night, but altogether he ______________ (give) eight lectures.
6. What compensation ______________ (he, receive) for his services? Free passage and free food for himself and Wanda.

7. Wanda ________________ (not, lecture), but she ________________ (keep) careful notes and ________________ (photograph) the daily life in each country that they visit.

8. She's planning to write an article for a travel magazine. She ________________ (work) on it whenever the ship ________________ (be) at sea (between stops).

9. When the cruise ________________ (end), the Hinslows ________________ (return) to their home in San Diego and ________________ (enjoy) the quiet life of a retired couple—until the next cruise ________________ (take) them on a new adventure.

Exercise 3. The Present Progressive with Future Meaning

In which sentences below can the *present progressive* be used with future meaning? Rewrite those sentences. (*Remember:* We use the *present progressive* to talk about a definite future plan.)

1. Walt and Wanda are going to celebrate their golden wedding anniversary* next month.

   Walt and Wanda are celebrating their golden wedding anniversary next month.

2. All their friends are going to congratulate them. (No change is possible.)
3. Their children are going to have a big party for them.
4. They are going to invite all Walt and Wanda's friends and relatives.
5. About 150 people will be invited all together.
6. A band will be hired.
7. The guests are going to sing and dance.
8. They're going to enjoy themselves.

**Golden wedding anniversary:* the fiftieth anniversary of their marriage.

9. Champagne will be served.
10. Some of the guests will probably make toasts** to Walt and Wanda.
11. They will remember all the years they have known the couple and the good times they have had together.
12. (Some of the family have chipped in*** to get a present.) They are going to give Walt and Wanda a gold bowl with an inscription on it.

Exercise 4. Choosing the Active or the Passive

In October 1986, the United States Congress passed a law which banned* mandatory retirement ages in most jobs. At the time the law was passed, newspapers reported on its provisions and discussed the pros and cons*** of the measure.**

Fill in the active or passive using **will.**

A. What does the law say?

1. From now on, companies with more than twenty employees will not set (not, set) a mandatory retirement age for their employees.
2. This practice will be forbidden (forbid) by the law.
3. However, for the next seven years, college professors, fire fighters, policemen, and some other types of employees __________ (not, include) under the law.
4. Mandatory retirement ages __________ (still, permit) for these jobs until 1993.

**Toast:* a short speech made before drinking in someone's honor.
***Chip in:* When several people buy something together, each person chips in part of the price.

**Ban:* make illegal.
***Mandatory retirement age:* the age at which a company can require an employee to retire.
****Pros and cons:* arguments for and against.

B. What do proponents**** of the law say about it?

5. Representative Claude Pepper, the oldest member of Congress, says, "It ______________ (give) new hope, new courage, and a new feeling of meaningfulness to the elderly people of this country."

6. Age discrimination ______________ (abolish).

7. Older workers ______________ (protect) from losing their jobs.

8. The government ______________ (save) millions of dollars because Social Security and Medicare***** payments ______________ (reduce).

C. What do other analysts say about the law?

9. It ______________ (help) a few people who want to work past age 70, but most people ______________ (not, affect) because most people want to retire at or before age 65.

10. The average age of retirement is now 63, and it ______________ (continue) to go down.

11. Many businesses ______________ (offer) older employees financial incentives****** in order to encourage early retirement.

D. What do opponents of the law believe?

12. Relations between employers and employees ______________ (disrupt).

13. Many more age-discrimination suits ______________ (file) in the courts.

*****Proponents:* people who are in favor of something.
******Social Security and Medicare:* forms of government insurance for retired workers.
*******Incentive:* an act or promise which encourages.

14. If older workers postpone their retirement, fewer younger workers ______________ .
(hire)

What do you think? Will this law be good for older employees? Will it be good for businesses? For the economy?

6.2 The Future Progressive, the Future Perfect, and the Future Perfect Progressive

Action Verbs

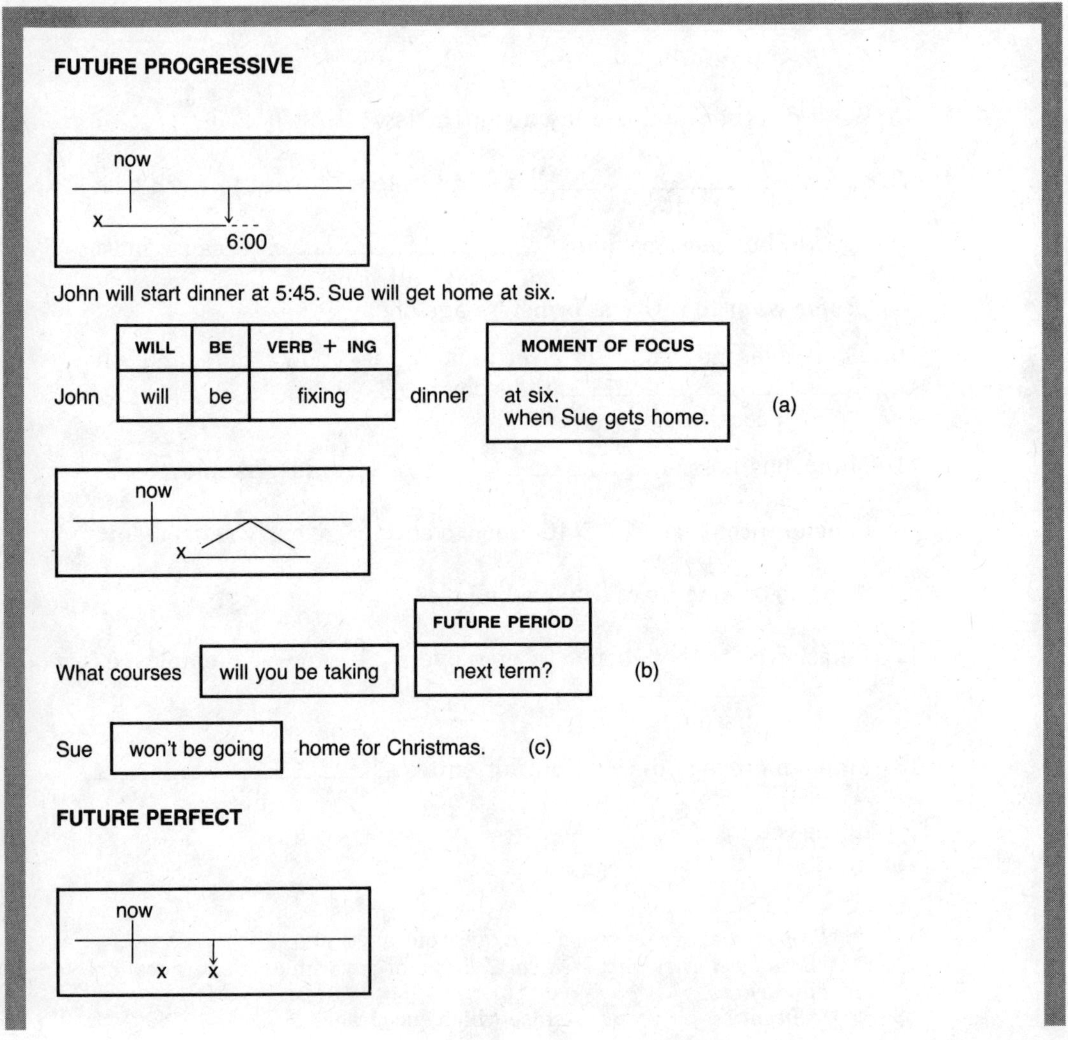

FUTURE PROGRESSIVE
now
x
6:00
John will start dinner at 5:45. Sue will get home at six.
WILL
BE
VERB + ING
MOMENT OF FOCUS
John
will
be
fixing
dinner
at six.
when Sue gets home.
(a)
now
x
FUTURE PERIOD
What courses
will you be taking
next term?
(b)
Sue
won't be going
home for Christmas.
(c)
FUTURE PERFECT
now
x
x

Active:

John and Sue will finish eating dinner at 6:45. Marylou will arrive at 7:00.

	WILL	HAVE	PAST PARTICIPLE		MOMENT OF FOCUS	
John and Sue	will	have	eaten	dinner	when / by the time } Marylou arrives.	(d)

Passive:

	WILL	HAVE	BEEN	PAST PARTICIPLE		
The dishes	will / won't	have	been	washed	by then.	(d)

FUTURE PERFECT PROGRESSIVE

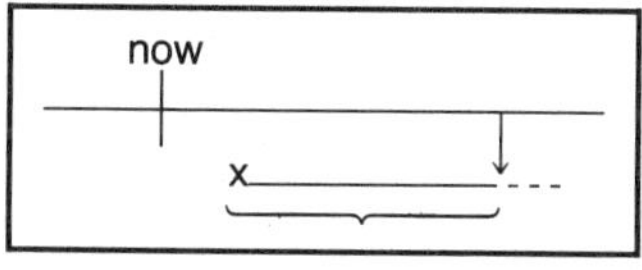

	WILL	HAVE	BEEN	VERB + ING		DURATION	MOMENT OF FOCUS	
José	will	have	been	studying	English	for two years	by the end of this semester.	(e)

Meaning:

a. The *future progressive* is used for an action that will be *in progress* at a particular moment of focus in the future.

b. The *future progressive* is also used for action in progress during a future period.

c. Sometimes the *future progressive* has about the same meaning as the **going to** future.

d. The *future perfect* means that an action will be *completed before* a moment of focus in the future.

e. The *future perfect progressive* means that an action will be *in progress* at a moment of focus in the future. When the *duration up to the moment of focus* is given, we must use the *perfect*. Sometimes, but not always, the *future perfect* is also possible.

Joe will have studied English for two years by the end of this semester.

The *future progressive* and the *future perfect progressive* are not used in the passive.

Note: The *future progressive* and the *future perfect* can also be formed with **going to:**

> **I*'m going to be standing* on the dock when the ship pulls in.**
> **They*'re going to have seen* all the sights by the time they leave Tokyo.**

Stative Verbs

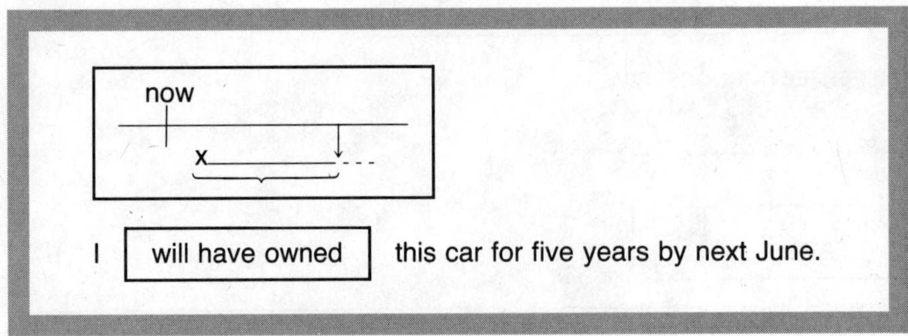

now
x
I
will have owned
this car for five years by next June.

Tense Choice: Use the *future perfect* of stative verbs when you give the duration of a state up to a moment of focus in the future.

Exercise 5. Present and Future Tenses

Fill in the blanks with the correct tenses. In the time clauses, use the *simple present.* In the main clauses, use the *simple future, future progressive, future perfect,* or *future perfect progressive.*

1. Walt and Wanda's cruise leaves for the Far East exactly three and a half weeks from today. By this time next month, they will be getting / will have gotten (get) near the coast of Japan. They will have been living (live) aboard ship for five days.
2. When the cruise ship ______________ (pull) into Tokyo Bay, most of the passengers ______________ (stand) on deck in order to catch sight of land.

3. After the cruise ______________ (leave) Japan, it ______________ (sail) to Shanghai.

4. When Francine Frazier ______________ (retire) in June, she ______________ (work) for the same company for twenty-five years.

5. By the time her husband ______________ (retire) five years from now, they ______________ (own) their present house for eighteen years.

Exercise 6. Present and Future Tenses

Jacob Brewer is only thirty-eight years old, but he is already planning his retirement. He is a doctor and is making good money,* but he wants to devote his time to helping poor people. Therefore, he plans to retire from his city practice in ten years and work in a depressed area in the Appalachian Mountains, giving medical care to the needy people there.

Fill in the blanks. Use the *simple present, present perfect,* or one of the *future* tenses in each blank.

When Dr. Brewer (1) leaves (leave) his city practice, he (2) will still be supporting (still) (support) his two children. They are aged eight and six now, so ten years from now his older child (3) ______________ (be) eighteen years old. She (4) ______________ (graduate) from high school and (5) ______________ (attend) college. His son (6) ______________ (still) (attend) high school. But Dr. Brewer (7) ______________ (already) (save) several hundred thousand dollars now, and by then he (8) ______________ (save) quite a lot more, so he (9) ______________ (not) (have) to worry about income.

**Make good money:* have a high income.

Exercise 7. Present and Future Tenses

Fill in an appropriate *present* or *future* tense. You will need the passive in some places.

When Mark Frazier (1) ____________ (retire) five years from now, he (2) ____________ (be) seventy years old and (3) ____________ (work) as a lawyer for over forty years. His law practice is very demanding, and he is looking forward to living a quiet life. According to the Fraziers' current plan, they (4) ____________ (sell) their house in Atlanta, Georgia, as soon as Mark (5) ____________ (retire), and they (6) ____________ (move) into their summer house by the ocean. By then, the house (7) ____________ (winterize) so that it will be comfortable all year round. A new wing (8) ____________ (also) (add) by that time, so there (9) ____________ (be) room for their children and grandchildren to visit.

Mark is building a sailboat in his free time. He (10) ____________ (finish) it by the time he (11) ____________ (move), so he (12) ____________ (plan) to spend a lot of time sailing.

The Fraziers' present plan may not work out, however, because Mark's wife, Francine, has always been interested in local politics, and as soon as she (13) ____________ (leave) her job in June, she (14) ____________ (become) more active in that area. Perhaps she (15) ____________ (run) for the state legislature in the election three years from now. If she (16) ____________ (elect), she (17) ____________ (serve) in the legislature when Mark (18) ____________ (retire), and it (19) ____________ (not) (be) easy for the couple to move away from Atlanta. They (20) ____________ (have) to reconsider their plans when the time (21) ____________ (come).

Transfer Exercises

1. Ten Years from Now.

Imagine your life ten years from now. Imagine that your plans for the future all work out and that your hopes for yourself, your family, and your friends are fulfilled.

Complete the questions and then ask a classmate.

1. Where will you ______ living ten years from now? How long will you ______ ______ living there?
2. Will you be married? How many children ______ you have?
3. Will you ______ working? If so, what kind of work ______ you ______ doing? How long ______ ______ ______ ______ doing that kind of work?
4. Will you have finished college? graduate school? What degrees ______ ______ ______ received? (For example, will you have received your B.A., B.S., M.A., Ph.D., or M.D.?)
5. How about your parents? ______ they have retired by then? Where ______ they ______ living?
6. What ______ your brothers and sisters ______ doing at that time? (You can talk about each one separately.) What ______ they ______ accomplished?
7. How about your best friends? Talk about one or two of them.

2. An Important Date in the Future

What is an important date in the future for you or someone you know? Answer these questions about it.

1. What will happen and when?
2. What will have happened?
3. What else will be happening at that time?

Example: **In May 199__ , I'm going to graduate from college. I will have survived four cold winters in Minnesota by then. I will have taken all the required courses in my major, and I will have completed all the required English courses. My English will have improved a lot. I will be applying for jobs at that time. Perhaps I will already have gotten some job offers, or perhaps not. My girlfriend is going back to Peru next spring, so she will be living in Peru and will not be at my graduation, but perhaps my parents will be there.**

Discussion Topics

A. At what age do people usually retire in your country? Is retirement mandatory at that age, or is it optional? Do men or women sometimes start a new job after they retire officially? Do they often take up hobbies or other kinds of activities?

B. When a man retires in your country, do he and his wife usually continue to live in the same city and the same house? If they move, where do they go? Do they move to a smaller house? To a warmer climate? In the United States, there are "retirement communities" where only older people can live. Are there similar communities in your country, and if so, are they popular?

C. If your father has already retired, answer these questions: What kind of changes took place in his life when he retired? Did he move? Did he take up new activities? Did he feel good about retiring and enjoy his new life from the start, or did he feel bored or restless in the beginning?

If your mother has retired from a job outside the home, answer the same questions about her (changing *he/his* to *she/her.*)

D. If your parents haven't retired yet, talk about what will happen, as far as you know, when they do retire. Are both your parents working? At what age will they retire? What changes will they make when they retire? Will they move? If so, where? Do they have specific plans for their retirement? Are they looking forward to retiring, or do they want to work as long as possible?

E. Have you ever thought about your own retirement? How old do you think you will be when you retire? What would you like to do after you retire?

If you have already retired, answer the questions in C about yourself. In what ways has your retired life been different from your father's or mother's?

Composition Topics

Write a short composition about one of the following topics.

1. Imagine your life twenty or twenty-five years from now. Imagine that your plans and hopes all work out and that you will be living a good life. Where will you be living, and what will you be doing? What will your wife or husband be doing at that time? Your children? What will your lifestyle be like? Also mention some things that you will have done or some events that will already have happened to create your situation at that time.

2. Write about the year 2100. How will people live in that year? What will have happened to change people's life styles? For example, what political changes or medical advances will have taken place to change life on earth? Use your imagination.

3. Interview an older working person about his or her plans for retirement, and write about what you learned in the interview.

   How long will the person have been working by the time he or she retires? Where will the children and grandchildren be living by then? What changes does the person plan to make in his or her life? Is the person going to move, and if so, where? Does the person plan to take on new responsibilities, learn new hobbies, or participate in other activities?

UNIT IV

MODAL AUXILIARIES

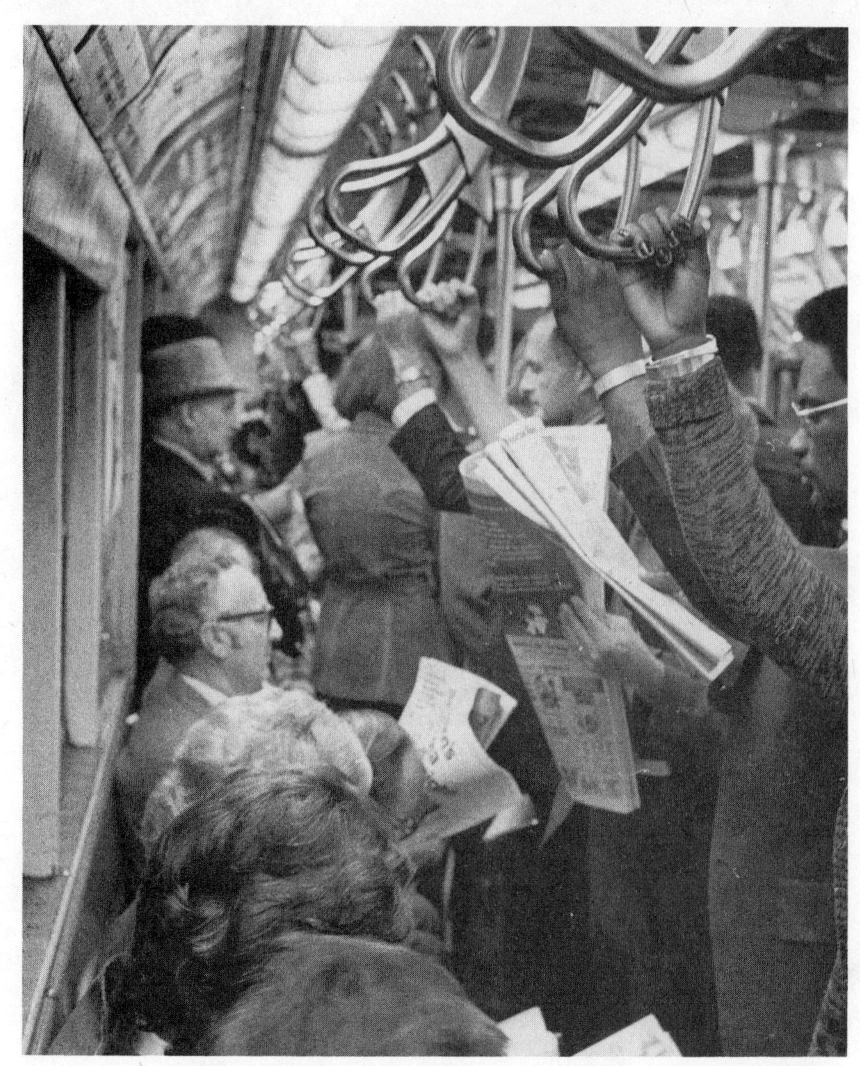

Lesson 7

Urban Transportation

7.1 Introduction to Modal Auxiliaries

Exercise 1. Pretest

The following conversation takes place on a crowded city bus. Add the word **to** where it is needed.

A: (1) There is so much traffic the buses can _______ hardly move. It's faster to walk.

B: (2) You're right. We ought _______ have special bus lanes. (3) Then the buses would be able _______ move faster. (4) As a result, more people would _______ ride them instead of driving their cars.

A: (5) Let's _______ write to the mayor about it.

B: (6) One letter won't _______ help. (7) We have _______ get our friends to write, too.

A: (8) True. A lot of my friends ride the buses and they must _______ care about the situation as much as we do.

B: (9) If he gets enough letters, the mayor might _______ pay attention and do something.

A: (10) I'll write a letter, and you can _______ sign it, if you'd like.

B: (11) No, I'd rather _______ write my own letter. The more letters the better. (12) And could you please _______ phone your friends about it? We've got to get organized.

Simple

ACTIVE

	MODAL	BASE FORM	
We	can could will would must should ought to may might	write	letters.

I	would rather	write	my own letter.

We	cannot / can't could not / couldn't will not / won't must not / mustn't should not / shouldn't ought not to may not might not	waste	time.

I	would rather not	do	it.

Shall Can etc.	we	write	letters?

PASSIVE

	MODAL	BE	PAST PARTICIPLE
Letters	can could will would must should ought to may might	be	written.

I	would rather	be	told	what to do.

Time	cannot / can't could not / couldn't will not / won't must not / mustn't should not / shouldn't ought not to may not might not	be	wasted.

I	would rather not	be	told	what to do.

Should Can etc.	the letters	be	typed?

Progressive

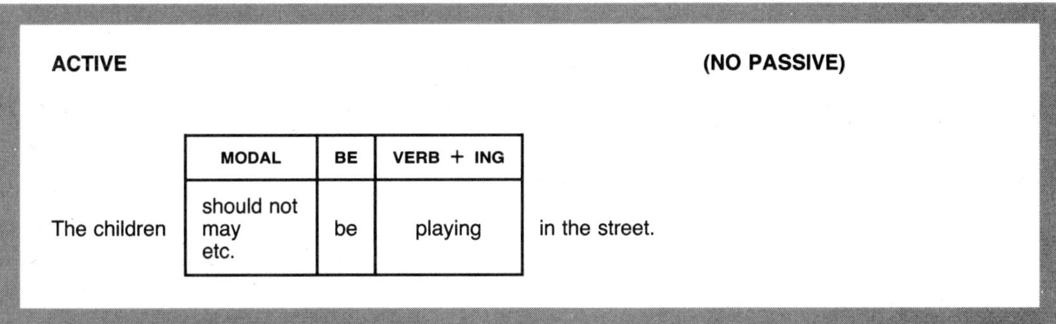

ACTIVE **(NO PASSIVE)**

	MODAL	BE	VERB + ING	
The children	should not may etc.	be	playing	in the street.

Perfect

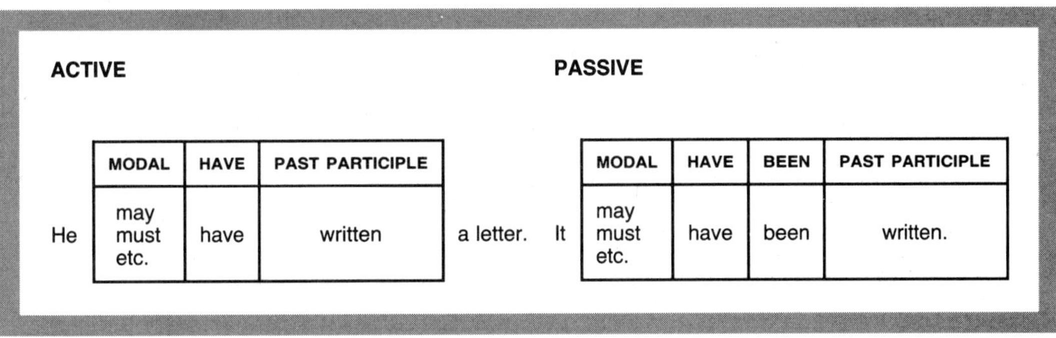

ACTIVE

	MODAL	HAVE	PAST PARTICIPLE	
He	may must etc.	have	written	a letter.

PASSIVE

	MODAL	HAVE	BEEN	PAST PARTICIPLE
It	may must etc.	have	been	written.

Perfect Progressive

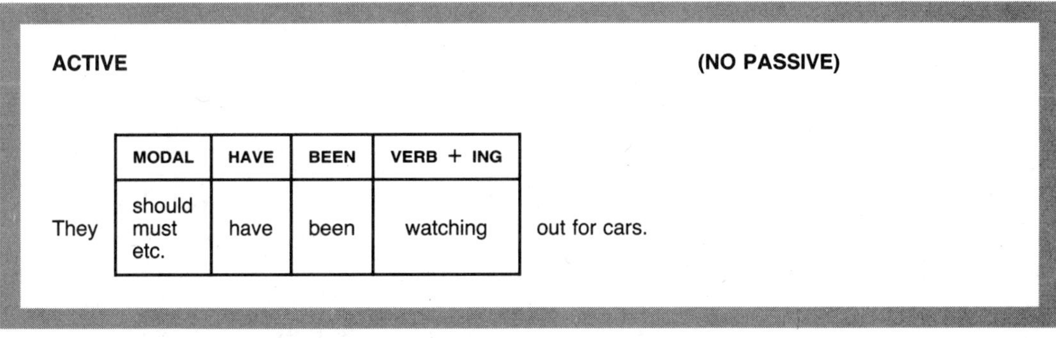

ACTIVE **(NO PASSIVE)**

	MODAL	HAVE	BEEN	VERB + ING	
They	should must etc.	have	been	watching	out for cars.

Form: Modal auxiliaries

1. always occur with a subject,
2. always come *first* in the verb phrase,
3. are always followed by the *base form* of the verb (or of auxiliaries **have** and **be**).

Shall is used mostly in active questions in American English. Notice that

1. **ought** is followed by **to,**
2. **can't** has only one **n,**
3. **may** and **might** have no contracted forms.

Meaning: Modal auxiliaries add meaning to the verb phrases. They tell about *possibility, advisability, necessity,* and so forth. You will study these meanings in the lessons of this unit.

Modal perfects (modal + **have** + past participle) do not have the same meaning as the perfect tenses. Modal perfects may refer either to the future or to the past:

1. They sometimes refer to action completed before a moment of focus in the future.

   My roommate may have already gone to bed by the time I get home tonight.

2. Modal perfects most often refer to past time and mean
   a. that an action did not occur,

   John should have studied last night. (He didn't study.)

   b. or that we are not certain whether an action occurred or not.

   Sara {should have / may have / must have} gotten my letter by now. (I don't know for sure whether she got it.)

Exercise 2. Verb Phrases with Modals

There has been an accident in the subway. A man has fallen onto the tracks and been hit by a train. Other people on the platform are commenting on the situation.

Complete the modal verb phrases by filling in **be, have, have been,** or **Ø** (nothing). Use the charts above to help you. (Notice that **be** and **have**

been may be used to complete either a passive or a progressive verb phrase.)

1. He shouldn't ___have been___ standing so near the edge of the platform.
2. How did he get there? They don't know yet. He might ________ pushed by the crowd or he might ________ jumped.
3. What are they doing down there? I can't ________ see.
4. Some people are trying to help. They must ________ giving him first aid.
5. Here come the police and some ambulance workers. The conductor must ________ called them.
6. They're carrying the man out on a stretcher. He must ________ hurt badly.
7. They must ________ taking him to the hospital.
8. Something should ________ done soon to improve safety in the subway.
9. You're right. They should ________ make the conductors slow down before they come into a station.
10. A lot of accidents could ________ prevented that way.
11. This conductor may ________ going too fast.
12. The accident will ________ investigated, and the conductor may ________ fired if he is found to be at fault.

7.2 Advisability: *should, ought to*

Present-Future Time

We {*should* / *ought to*} *be* kind to animals. (a)

That sick dog {*should* / *ought to*} *be taken* to the vet.* (b)

**Vet:* veterinarian, animal doctor.

Sara {*should* / *ought to*} *study* more. (b)

She {*should not* / *ought not to*} *be watching* TV right now. (b)

She {*should* / *ought to*} *be studying.* (b)

Meaning: **Should** and **ought to** mean that

a. an action is a responsibility or ethical obligation.
b. an action is advisable, a good idea.

Note: **Had better** + *base form* is also used to express advisability, especially when we want to tell someone how to avoid an undesirable consequence.

You had better take your umbrella. (If you don't, you'll get wet.)

You had better not drink that water. (If you drink it, you may get sick.)

Past Time

The conductor {*should* / *ought to*} *have slowed* down before he came into the station.

He {*should* / *ought to*} *have been* more careful.

The victim's family {*should* / *ought to*} *have been notified* immediately.

The man {*should not* / *ought not to*} *have been standing* so near the edge of the platform.

Meaning: **Should have (ought to have)** + *past participle* generally refers to an advisable or desirable action which *did not occur.*

Exercise 3. Present-Future Time: Active and Passive

New York City's subway system is the most extensive (in terms of track mileage) in the world. Its 390 kilometers of track provide a rapid and efficient way of getting around the city. Nevertheless, subway riders often complain about the graffiti,* insufficient lighting, malfunctioning doors, delays, and so forth. They also worry about crime in the subways. Some of them have formed groups such as the "Straphangers' Campaign" and the "A-Train Coalition" to try to improve conditions on the subway. The Transit Authority has also set its own goals for subway improvements.

Complete each modal verb phrase to refer to present-future time. Use the simple active or passive (do not use progressive or perfect forms), and add **to** where you need it. Use each verb on the list once.

allocate (to)	enforce	raise	stay
announce	have	remove	walk
be	install	√run	√wash
behave	open and close	spend (on)	

A. Goals that the Transit Authority has set for subway improvement:

1. The trains ought *to run* on schedule.
2. The trains should *be washed* once a week.
3. The graffiti ought ________________ .
4. The no-smoking regulation ought ________________ .
5. All the doors should ________________ properly.
6. Train crews should ________________ more politely with riders.
7. Whenever there is a delay, the reason for it should ________________ over the public address system.

B. Suggestions that riders have made:

8. The trains should ________________ rubber tires to make them quieter.
9. Air conditioning should ________________ in all the trains.

**Graffiti:* words that people have written (or pictures they have drawn) on the walls of the subway cars.

10. Because of the high crime rate, there ought __________________ more police on the subways.
11. The police ought __________________ through the cars.
12. They shouldn't __________________ in one car.
13. The government ought __________________ more money on improving the subways.
14. However, they ought not __________________ the fare.
15. Instead, less money should __________________ to highway construction so that more is available for mass transit.

Exercise 4. *Should (ought to) have ______-ed*

Almost every New Yorker gets lost or confused in the subway occasionally. Finding one's way around is especially confusing for newcomers. On his way to school one morning, a foreign student named Anthony saw people entering the subway through an open gate.

Read the story and describe Anthony's mistakes using **should (ought to) have** + *past participle.*

1. Anthony didn't notice that the people were all waving subway passes.

   He should have noticed (ought to have noticed) that they were all waving subway passes.

2. Instead of using a token in the turnstile, Anthony went through the gate.

   He should have . . .
   He shouldn't have . . .

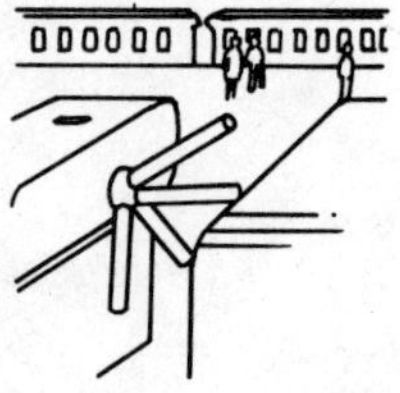

3. When a policeman stopped him, he didn't explain that he was a newcomer. (He couldn't because suddenly he forgot all his English.) The policeman gave him a summons to appear in court.

   Anthony . . .

4. He was so shaken up by the experience that he got on the express train instead of the local.
5. He sat down in the train and tried to read the summons. It was difficult to understand, and he had to use his dictionary. When he looked up several stops later, he was in Brooklyn!
6. Anthony got off the train, jumped down onto the tracks, and walked across them to the other side to catch the local train back. A woman on the platform explained to him that crossing the tracks was very dangerous. She told him to use the stairs next time to cross over.
7. When Anthony finally got to the university, he looked at his watch and realized that he had already missed the first hour of his English class, so he just sat in the park to wait for his afternoon class.

Exercise 5. The Progressive

Form sentences with **should (ought to)** and the *progressive*.

1. Simona has to write a composition this evening. It's due tomorrow. Nevertheless, she isn't thinking about the composition. She's watching TV.

   a. Simona ought to be writing her composition.
   b. She shouldn't ______________ TV.

2. Harry is telling the waiter to bring him sausages and french fries for lunch, even though his doctor told him not to eat fried food.
   a. Harry ______________ french fries or sausages.
   (order)
   b. He ______________ a sandwich or a salad for lunch.

3. On the bus: Look at those women smoking. This bus is too crowded for that. Besides, it's against the law to smoke on city buses. And listen to that loud radio! And do you see those boys hanging onto the back of the bus? They could be killed!
   a. Those women ______________ .
   b. That passenger ______________ his radio out loud.
   c. He ______________ earphones.
   d. Those boys ______________ .

4. Aurora needs to find work. Nevertheless, she is spending her time drinking in bars. She is not looking at the want ads in the paper. She isn't doing anything about getting a job. (Form three or four sentences.)

Exercise 6. The Perfect and the Perfect Progressive

Although most people would rather have a car than rely on public transportation, drivers also have their problems, as the following story shows.

Use **should** or **ought to** and the *perfect* or *perfect progressive.*

Example: **Once Patricia parked in a bus stop because she wasn't paying attention.**

Patricia shouldn't have parked in a bus stop.

She {should have / ought to have} been paying attention.

1. Several times this spring, Patricia left her car too long and got a parking ticket.
2. She didn't pay the tickets right away because she was low on funds.*
3. When her registration expired, she didn't renew it because she hadn't paid the parking tickets.
4. One day a state policeman stopped her on the highway. She was driving without a valid registration.
5. She was driving 75 miles an hour at the time.
6. She was drinking a beer as she drove.
7. She didn't notice the blinking blue light behind her.
8. Finally she heard the police siren and stopped her car. But when the policeman was rude to her, she began to shout at him.

Patricia was fined for speeding, for driving while intoxicated, for driving an unregistered car, and for talking back to a policeman. Moreover, she had to leave her car at the police station until she registered it. She was lucky she didn't lose her license.

**She was low on funds:* She didn't have much money.

7.3 Suggestions: *Let's, Why don't, Shall*

Suggestions for Both Speaker and Listener

	BASE FORM	
Let's	go	out to eat tonight. (a)
Why don't we	eat	at the Mexican Cafe? (a)
Shall we	meet	around 7:00? (b)

Frequent responses: All right.
That sounds good.
No, let's (meet at 8:00).

Meaning: a. **Let's (let us)** and **why don't we** are used to suggest action for both the speaker and the listener.
b. A question with **shall we** suggests an action for both speaker and listener and asks the listener if he/she agrees.

Suggestions with **let's, why don't we,** and **shall** are not as strong as sentences with **should.** The listener is free to disagree or make a different suggestion.

Suggestions for the Listener

Why don't you bring your roommate? (c)

Suggestions for the Speaker

Why don't I phone for a reservation? (d)
Shall I phone for a reservation? (d)

Possible responses: That's a good idea.
No, it's not necessary.

Meaning: c. **Why don't you** suggests action for the listener.
d. **Why don't I** and **shall I** suggest action for the speaker. The speaker wants agreement before going ahead. **Shall I** is more open-ended than **why don't I.** The speaker does not expect either *yes* or *no* for an answer.

Asking for Suggestions

How shall we get there? (Let's take the subway.)
What shall I order? (The tacos are really good.)
How much shall I tip the waiter? (Tip him 15 percent.)

Exercise 7. Suggestions

A. Plan a field trip for your class by making suggestions with the following phrases. Make as many suggestions as necessary until everyone agrees.

Let's (go to) ______________________ .
No, why don't we ______________________ ?
All right. Shall we ______________________ ?
(Jorge), why don't you ______________________ ?
Shall I ______________________ ?
Why don't I ______________________ ?
When / How / etc. } shall we ______________________ ?

B. Imagine that your school has hired your class to redecorate your classroom in any way you wish. Plan the project together. Begin your sentences as in A, making as many suggestions as necessary until everyone agrees.

Transfer Exercises

1. Transportation in Your Area

A. Is there a public transportation system in the city or town where you are living now? If so, suggest possible improvements to the system using **should** and **ought to.** Use the following questions to help you.

1. Do the (buses) run often enough?
2. Are the routes convenient?
3. Is the fare reasonable?
4. Are there free transfers if you need to transfer from one bus to another?
5. Are the bus drivers or conductors polite?
6. Do they drive well?
7. Are the smoking regulations enforced? other regulations?
8. Are the (buses) clean? comfortable?
9. Do the windows, doors, heating system, and air conditioning work?
10. Are there enough seats?
11. Can you suggest other improvements?

B. If there is no public transportation system in your area, do you think one is needed? If so, what kind of system is needed? Who should set it up? Make suggestions about routes, financing, comfort, regulations, etc. (Use **should** and **ought to.**)

C. If you drive a car, can you suggest improvements in the roads or parking facilities? (Use **should** and **ought to.**)

2. Problems with Transportation (pair work)

Have you ever made mistakes while riding public transportation or while driving? With a partner, ask and answer the following questions. Whenever your answer is *yes,* tell your partner what you (or the driver of the car) did, and what you (he/she) should have done.

A. Public transportation

1. Have you ever gotten on the wrong bus, train, streetcar, or subway?

   Example: **Yes, one day I got on the eastbound subway when I should have gotten on the westbound. When I realized my mistake, I was in Queens!**

2. Have you ever gone past your stop?

B. Driving

3. Have you ever taken a wrong turn while driving (or while you were a passenger in someone else's car)?

4. Have you ever run out of gas on the road?
5. Have you ever been stopped for speeding? How fast were you going?
6. Have you ever been stopped for going through a red light or making an illegal left turn?

3. Crime on the Subways

In December 1984, four young men approached Bernhard Goetz on the New York subway and asked him for money. Fearing that they were going to rob him, he shot them. Goetz said that he thought one of them had a gun and that he acted out of fear. In his trial, he was convicted* of carrying a gun illegally, but he was acquitted of the charge of attempted murder. The American people were divided about this decision. Because the youths were black, many saw the verdict*** as unjust and harmful to race relations, but some blacks and many whites felt that Goetz had a right to defend himself.**

Respond appropriately to each item.

1. Take the position of the defense lawyer (the lawyer helping Goetz) in the Goetz case. Say what the four young men should or shouldn't have done from his point of view.
2. Say what Goetz should or shouldn't have done from the point of view of the prosecution lawyer.
3. What do you think? Did the jury make the right decision?
4. Although the maximum sentence for illegal possession of a gun is seven years in prison, Goetz was sentenced to only six months. He was also fined $5,000 and was required to do community service and to get psychiatric help. Do you think this sentence was appropriate? If not, what should have been done, in your opinion?

4. Prepositions

Fill in the correct preposition according to the preceding word or phrase. These preposition combinations occur in this lesson.

1. Bernhard Goetz was convicted ______ illegal gun possession.

**Convicted:* judged guilty.
***Acquitted:* judged not guilty.
****Verdict:* decision.

2. He was fined $5,000 ______ his crime, and he was sentenced ______ six months in jail.

3. He was acquitted ______ attempted murder.

4. In bad weather, we can't rely ______ public transportation to run on schedule.

5. Smoking is prohibited on public transportation because it is harmful ______ the health of the passengers.

6. Bus drivers in New York are sometimes rude ______ passengers.

7. We need to allocate more money ______ mass transit.

8. New Yorkers often complain ______ problems in the subway. Straphangers' Campaign is trying to do something ______ them.

9. In some subway stations there are always beggars asking ______ money.

10. When a policeman stops someone ______ speeding, he always wants to look ______ the driver's license and the car registration.

11. If you run ______ ______ gas on the highway, you may have to walk to the nearest gas station.

12. Robert wants to transfer ______ the state university where he is now ______ a small college.

13. What are his reasons ______ wanting to transfer?

14. He says that the professors at a small college really care ______ individual students.

15. If you want a good grade, never shout ______ your professor!

Discussion Topics

A. There are about fifty subway systems in the world today. Is one of them in your country? If so, what city is it in? How does it compare with what you have read in this lesson about the New York subway system? Do the two systems have any of the same problems? Is there anything that should be done to improve the system in your country?

B. What are the main forms of transportation in the cities of your country? Do they usually function efficiently? If there are weak points in one or more of these forms of transportation, what should be done, in your opinion, to improve them?

Some forms of public transportation:

buses	taxis
streetcars	rickshas
ferries and other ships	subways
commuter trains	other: ______

C. What are the forms of transportation between cities in your country? Are there trains, intercity buses, airports, and highways? Are any improvements needed in intercity transportation?

D. What are the important forms of private transportation in your country? Should anything be done to help people get around more easily, in your opinion? For example, should special bicycle paths be built? Should there be more parking lots? Should the speed limits or other regulations be changed, and if so, how?

Some forms of private transportation:

cars	donkeys
trucks	horses
bicycles	camels
motorcycles	water buffalo
mopeds	other: ______

E. Is there a crime problem in the buses or subways in your city? If so, what should be done about it, in your opinion?

F. Do you think that people should carry and use guns in self-defense, or should there be "gun control" laws? Give reasons for your opinion.

G. Have you ever disagreed with the verdict or sentence in an important court case? What should have been done, in your opinion?

H. Can you think of times when the government of a country made a serious mistake? What did the government do? What should they have done?

Composition Topics

Write a short composition about one of the topics below. Use **should** and **ought to** in some of your sentences.

1. Write a story about someone who made several mistakes and got into trouble. You can write a true story or make one up. Exercises 4 and 6 are examples.

2. Write a letter about a system of transportation which, in your opinion, needs improvement. For example, you might write about the buses or trains in your city, the subway in a city you have visited, or the highways and bridges of your country. Address your letter to the mayor of the city or the president of the country and tell him or her what improvements need to be made. (See Exercise 3, Transfer Exercise 1, and Discussion Topics A through E.)

3. Choose your own topic. Write about mistakes that have been made and/or improvements that are needed. For example, you might write about your school, government decisions and policies, the housing problem in your city, or how to deal with crime.

Lesson 8

Diving for Sunken Treasure

8.1 *Can, could, be able*

Can and *could*

ACTIVE

Can

Cats *can climb* trees, but dogs {*cannot.* / *can't.*} (a)

John *can help* you move your furniture tomorrow. (b)
You *can use* my truck. (c)

Can/could

Don't climb that tree. You {*can* / *could*} *fall* and hurt yourself. (d)

Since we're late, we {*can* / *could*} *take* a taxi. (e)

Could

—Where's John?
—I don't know. He *could be studying* at the library. (f)

I *could walk* to school, but I prefer to take the bus. (g)
Sue *could type* a lot faster if she practiced. (g)
Leah *could speak* Spanish when she was a little girl. (h)

PASSIVE

This book *can be understood* by a ten-year-old child. (a)

Meaning: **Can** and **could** mean that *nothing prevents* an action or event. They have the following specific meanings. Notice that with certain meanings, **could** refers to present-future time. It refers to past time only with meaning (h).

Can:

a. Someone has the skill or *ability* to do something in the present.
b. Someone is free or *available* to do something.
c. The speaker gives *permission* to do something (see Section 8.2).

Can *or* **could:** (In these situations **can** and **could** have approximately the same meaning.)

d. A situation has a *possible consequence.* Sentences of this type are often warnings.

e. The speaker *suggests* a possible action. (But we use **should** if we want to say that it is the best action.)

Could:

f. The speaker is *guessing* about the present. (= **might**)

g. A possible action or ability is *not occurring* or not realized in the present because of certain conditions. (See Lesson 19.)

h. Someone had an ability or was available to do something in the past. (But we use **was/were able** if the event occurred.)

Could have + Past Participle

ACTIVE

John *could have read* the book in French, but he read a translation. (i)
You *could have studied* harder for your exam. (j)

—Where's John? He's thirty minutes late.
—I don't know. He *could have taken* a wrong turn and gotten lost. (k)

PASSIVE

John *could have been stopped* for speeding. (k)

Meaning: **Could have** + *past participle* is used when the action *did not occur* or when we *don't know* what happened. Specifically:

i. Someone had the ability to do something but did not do it.

j. The speaker points out a desirable past action which did not occur. In this meaning, **could have** is like **should have,** but it is softer.

k. The speaker is guessing about the past.

Be able + Infinitive

Leah *was able to speak* Spanish when she was a little girl. (l)
Cats *are able to climb* trees. (l)
John *will be able to help* you move tomorrow. (l)
When you complete the listening comprehension course, you *will be able to understand* academic lectures. (m)
Andrea *was able to pass* her exam. (n)

Form: **Be able** is followed by an active infinitive. It is not generally used with the passive.

Meaning: **Be able (to)** means **can,** but is used only for these specific meanings:

l. **Be able** may be substituted for **can/could** to refer to ability and availability. (a) and (b)

m. For clarity, we generally use **will be able** (not **can**) to refer to a future ability which does not exist now.

n. When talking about a particular event or events in the past, we use **was/were able** to indicate that the subject *succeeded* in doing something. (In the negative, either **couldn't** or **wasn't/weren't able** is possible.)

Exercise 1. *Can/could:* Active or Passive

Fill in **can** or **could** plus the simple active or passive form of the verb. Can you identify the different specific meanings? In which sentences are both **can** and **could** possible?

1. Sea mammals such as whales and seals __can stay__ (a) (stay) under water for long periods (up to two hours in some cases), but human beings don't have this ability. Humans ________ ( ) (only, swim) under water for one or two minutes. Oxygen tanks and diving equipment ________ ( ) (use) to lengthen this time. However, deep sea divers must be careful to follow certain rules to protect their health. For example, they must come up to the surface very slowly. Otherwise, they ________ ( ) (develop) the bends* from the sudden change in pressure.

2. Ruth has always loved the water. She ________ ( ) (swim) when she was just a baby. And she's really fast. She ________ ( ) (make) the Olympic team, I think, but she is not planning to try out for it. I don't know her reasons for not trying out. It ________ ( ) (be) that she doesn't have enough money to train.

3. **A:** What would you like to do this afternoon?
   B: We ________ ( ) (go) swimming at Rocky Point, if you like.
   A: It's dangerous to swim at Rocky Point because of the undercurrent. You ________ ( ) (carry) out to sea and ________ ( ) (drown)!
   B: Then let's go to the public beach.
   A: I don't have a bathing suit.
   B: That's okay. You ________ ( ) (borrow) one of mine.

**The bends:* decompression sickness, caused by a sudden decrease in pressure on the body.

Exercise 2. *Could have . . . -ed*

When Lucia had to write her first term paper in her freshman year at college, she had a lot of trouble with it. She didn't know the best procedures to follow, and in some cases, she made some poor choices.

Working together as a class, suggest some things that Lucia could have done. Try to make more than one suggestion for each item. (Your teacher may be able to give you specific information about how to get help with a paper on your campus.)

1. After Lucia read the books on the bibliography* that her professor gave her, she needed more information, but she didn't know how to get it.
   a. She could have gone to the library.
   b. She ________________ in the subject index for appropriate titles.
   c. She ________________ in the *Readers' Guide to Periodical Literature* for references to journal articles.
   d. She ________________ the librarian for help.
2. She read the books on the bibliography from cover to cover,** although only a few chapters were relevant to*** her topic.
3. She took a lot of information from these books. Her professor accused her of plagiarism because she copied word for word from the books.
4. She took notes in her notebook, but they were not in any order. She had a lot of trouble organizing the information in her paper.
5. When she finished the paper, she wasn't sure if her points were clear.
6. She doesn't have a typewriter, so she wrote the paper longhand.
7. She misspelled a lot of words.
8. She overslept and missed class on the day the paper was due, so she handed it in late at the next class.
9. When she got the paper back, it had a low grade on it. She didn't understand the professor's written comments, so she put the paper away in a drawer and tried to forget about it.

**Bibliography:* list of books.
***From cover to cover:* completely from beginning to end.
****Relevant to:* about.

8.2 Choice/No Choice: *must, have to, may, can*

No Choice

AFFIRMATIVE

	FORMAL		INFORMAL
PRESENT/FUTURE:	must	=	have to has to
PAST:	had to		

Divers {*must* / *have to*} *carry* oxygen tanks in order to explore in deep water. (a)

John *had to leave* the country when his visa expired. (a)

NEGATIVE

PRESENT/FUTURE:	must not mustn't may not	=	cannot can't
PAST:	could not couldn't		

Divers {*must not* / *can't*} *come* to the surface quickly or they get the bends. (b)

Pure oxygen *may not be used* in the tank at depths of more than 35 feet. (c)

Form: **Have to** is a verb followed by an infinitive (it does not have the form of a modal auxiliary). Use **do, does,** and **did** in questions and negatives.

Does John have to take a test tomorrow?

Meaning: a. **Must** and **have to** mean that an action is necessary because of a rule, law, physical condition, or logical necessity. (See Lesson 9 for logical necessity.) We often add an infinitive phrase with **to** or **in order to** when the action is necessary in relation to a particular goal.

b. **Must not, can't,** and **couldn't** mean that an action is impossible or not permitted.

c. **May not** means that an action is not permitted by a person in authority, by regulation, or by the requirements of comfort, safety, custom, etc. Using **may not** or **must not** (instead of **cannot**) makes it clear that a person's ability is not what limits his or her choice. (See Lesson 9 for other meanings of **may.**)

Note: **Have got to** is used in conversation with the same meaning as **must** and **have to.** It is present perfect in form, but refers to present/future time.

I've got to go to the store this afternoon.

In informal speech, **have got to** sounds like "gotta."

Pronunciation: The first *t* in **mustn't** is silent (mus~~t~~n't).

Choice

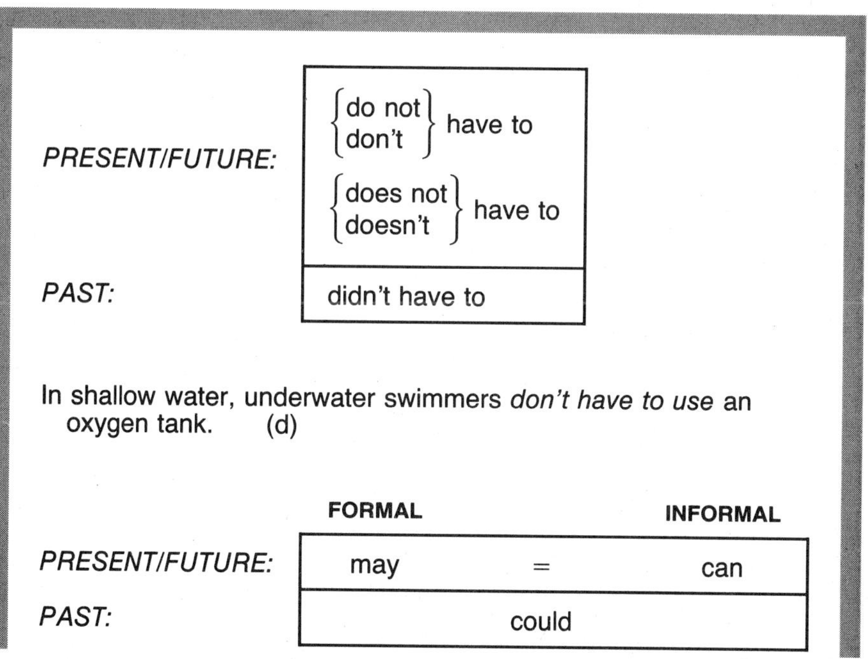

PRESENT/FUTURE:	{do not / don't} have to {does not / doesn't} have to
PAST:	didn't have to

In shallow water, underwater swimmers *don't have to use* an oxygen tank. (d)

	FORMAL		INFORMAL
PRESENT/FUTURE:	may	=	can
PAST:		could	

Instead, a short tube which sticks up out of the water

may / *can* } *be used.* (e)

Meaning: d. **Don't have to** means that an action is not necessary, so the actor may do it or not as he or she chooses.

e. We use **may, can,** and **could** to mean that an action is permitted or is a possible choice among several alternatives.

Exercise 3. *Must not* versus *do not have to*

Scuba diving is a popular sport as well as a technique of underwater exploration. It involves equipment and procedures to protect the safety of the diver.

Form sentences with **must not** (no choice) and **don't have to** (choice) to fit the information given.

1. It is dangerous to go scuba diving alone.

   You must not go scuba diving alone.

2. Divers with no breathing apparatus must come up to the surface to breathe every sixty seconds. With air tanks, this is not necessary.

   A diver with an air tank doesn't have to come up to the surface to breathe.

3. If a diver stays down too long or comes back to the surface too quickly, he or she will get the bends, which can cause death.

4. A protective rubber suit called a wet suit is often worn in cold water. However this is not necessary in warm water. In warm water, divers ________________________ .

5. Oxygen is poisonous under pressure. Therefore oxygen tanks ________________________ at depths greater than 33 feet (10 meters).

6. Compressed air tanks can be used at greater depths. However, beyond 200 feet, the nitrogen in air makes people "drunk" so that they make foolish, often fatal* mistakes. Therefore, ________________________ .

**Fatal:* causing death.

7. If harmless gases such as helium are mixed with oxygen, divers can go deeper. They ______________ stop at 200 feet but can go down as far as 1,000 feet.

8. In fairly shallow water, air is sometimes supplied from the surface through a tube. In that case, air tanks ______________ .

Exercise 4. *May* versus *must*

Supply **may** (choice) or **must** (no choice) plus the active or passive of the verb in parentheses.

1. There are several ways of supplying air to divers underwater. In one method, air *may be breathed* (breathe) through a short tube called a snorkel. In this case, the diver can keep his face in the water but ______________ (stay) close to the surface so that the end of the tube is above the water. Air ______________ (also, pump) from the surface to the diver through a long tube, or tanks of compressed air ______________ (carry) on the diver's back.

2. Divers use different air mixtures at different depths. Pure oxygen ______________ (use) for depths up to 33 feet. Ordinary air ______________ (use) safely up to about 200 feet. After that, oxygen ______________ (mix) with other harmless gases.

3. The bends, or decompression sickness, is a serious problem that can develop when a diver resurfaces too quickly. Below about 35 feet, the water pressure causes the body to absorb gas. The length of time a diver ______________ (remain) below 35 feet without danger depends on the depth. For example, a diver ______________ (remain) at a depth of 100 feet for twenty-five

minutes and then come directly back to the surface. If he stays longer, however, he ______________________ gradually, allowing
(resurface)
time for the gas to pass out of his body through the lungs. A diver who develops the bends after he has reached the surface ______________________ into a special decompression machine in
(put)
which the pressure can be increased and then decreased gradually.

Exercise 5. Past Forms: *had to, could, was/were able*

Among those who use the techniques of deepsea diving are treasure hunters searching for sunken ships that have been lying on the ocean floor for hundreds of years. One such search was Mel Fisher's attempt to find a ship that sank off the coast* of Florida while carrying a treasure of silver and gold to Spain.

Fill in **had to, didn't have to, could, couldn't, was able to,** or **were able to** with the verb in parentheses. Remember that **was/were able** (not **could**) is used for a particular action that succeeded.

1. The *Nuestra Señora de la Atocha* sank in 1622 in a hurricane. Salvage crews were sent to recover her treasure soon afterwards, but they ______________________ it because another storm broke
(not, recover)
the wrecked ship apart and scattered the treasure on the ocean floor. They ______________________ up the search.
(give)
2. Fisher ______________________ for sixteen years before he
(search)
______________________ the main treasure.
(find)
3. For several years he ______________________ anything because
(not, find)
he was searching in the wrong place.
4. After he finally found the general location, he ______________________ for the exact location of the wreck. His
(look)
boats ______________________
(crisscross)

**Off the coast:* in the water near the coast.

hundreds of square miles of ocean floor before he ______________
(find)
it in July 1985.

5. He ______________________ the needed license to search the
(obtain)
area, but in order to keep it he ______________________ several
(fight)
legal battles.

6. He ran short of money and ______________________ more and
(borrow)
more to pay for the search. Sometimes he ____________________
(not, pay)
the divers on time.

7. After he finally ______________________ the main part of the
(locate)
treasure, he ______________________ armed divers, several
(station)
ships, and an underwater camera near it in order to protect his find from unlicensed treasure hunters.

8. The water was only 54 feet deep, so the divers ________________
(not, use)
a special air mix. They __________________________ ordinary
(use)
compressed air. They ______________________ decompression stops
(not, make)
when rising to the surface, either, because they ______________
(not, worry)
about getting the bends. At that depth, they ________________
(stay)
underwater for over an hour and rise directly to the surface without danger.

9. Altogether, Mel Fisher and his crew ______________________
(recover)
about $130 million from the Atocha.

Exercise 6. *Should have* versus *have to*

Write sentences with **should(n't) have, had to,** and **didn't have to** according to the information given. Remember that **should have** refers to action which did not occur, whereas **had to** refers to action about which there was no choice and which therefore occurred.

1. In 1973, Fisher found silver bars at a place quite far from the actual location of the *Atocha*. After that, he searched for years in the wrong area. He didn't stay at the spot indicated by the old Spanish documents.

   Fisher should have stayed at the spot indicated by the old Spanish documents.

2. Fisher got a license to search for the *Atocha.*
3. He fought several legal battles in order to keep his license.
4. As a result of these court cases, the federal court did not revoke* his license but gave him full rights to the wreck. Some people disagreed with the court's decision. In their opinion:
   (a) ________________________ .
   (b) ________________________ .
5. Archeologists were also disturbed because the excavation was not conducted in a scientific way.
   Archeologists felt ________________________ .
6. The archeologist who worked on the *Atocha* planned to record the location of all the finds, but on the first day, the excited divers brought up one hundred bars of silver without making any records.
   The location of the finds ________________________ .
   The divers ________________________ .
7. A percentage of the treasure was paid to the investors and divers.
8. Fisher gave the investors twenty dollars for every one dollar they invested, according to their agreement. He didn't give them all the money.

Transfer Exercises

1. Goals

A. Laura is a junior at the university. She is majoring in archeology and hopes to become an underwater archeologist.
   1. What does she have to do?
      a. good grades in college — **She has to get good grades in college.**
      b. graduate school
      c. experience in the field
      d. a doctoral dissertation
   2. She doesn't have enough money to pay the tuition and living expenses for all those years. What can she do?

**Revoke:* take back.

3. She isn't sure which graduate school to apply to. What should she do, in your opinion?

B. Tell a partner or the class about a goal that you have.
   1. What do you hope to do?
   2. What do you have to do to reach that goal?
   3. What are some problems you may meet in trying to reach your goal? What can you do to overcome them?
   4. What are some uncertainties that you have about it? Ask your classmate(s) for advice or information.

2. Achievements

Tell a partner or the class about something that you achieved in the past. Answer these questions:

1. What were you able to do?

   Examples: **I was able to get into this university.**
   I was able to save enough money to buy a car.

2. What did you have to do to achieve your goal?
3. Were there any problems? If so, what couldn't you do?
4. Did you make any mistakes that slowed you down or made things difficult? If so, what should you have done?
5. Did you do anything in connection with the goal that you didn't have to do? If so, why did you do it?

3. Prepositions

Fill in the correct preposition. These preposition combinations occur in this lesson.

1. When you write a composition, all the information in it should be relevant ______ your main topic.
2. Your grade on a composition depends ______ the grammar, organization, vocabulary level, and content.
3. Before you hand in a composition, always proofread it to look ______ mistakes in spelling, subject–verb agreement, and tense.
4. John had exactly the same mistakes on the test as the student who was sitting next to him. The teacher accused them ______ cheating.
5. Don't throw snowballs near the house! If you break a window, you will have to pay ______ it.

6. Jim doesn't like to wear a hat, but he wears earmuffs in the winter to protect his ears ______ the cold.
7. We searched everywhere ______ a suitable place to live when we moved to this town.
8. According to an old proverb, "Children should be seen and not heard." Do you agree or disagree ______ that idea?
9. —What's your favorite sport?
   —Basketball. I'm going to try ______ ______ the varsity team* next fall.
10. —Did you buy some milk when you went to the store?
    —Oh, I'm sorry. I forgot ______ it completely.

Discussion Topics

A. Do you enjoy diving from a springboard? Can you dive from a high board? What kinds of dives can you do? (If you don't know the English names for the dives, give the names in your language and describe one or more of the dives.) How did you learn how to dive? Did you have to practice a great deal to become proficient?

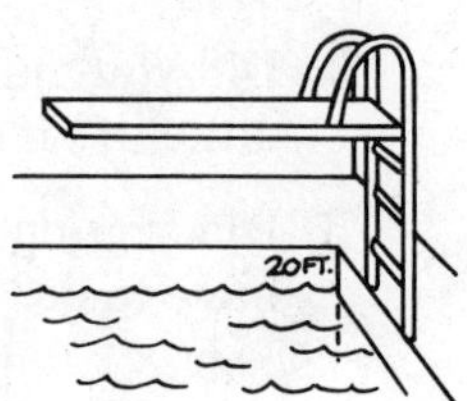

B. Are you a good swimmer? How long can you swim underwater holding your breath? Have you ever used a snorkel (short breathing tube)? What safety procedures would you recommend for swimmers?

C. Have you ever been scuba diving? If so, how deep did you go? What safety procedures did you have to follow? What did you see while diving?

D. Is scuba diving popular in your country? If so, what are the most popular places for diving and why? Are there sunken ships and treasures in the coastal waters of your country? In lakes and rivers? Have scientists or treasure hunters from your country done underwater exploration and excavation? If so, what have they found? What has been done with their finds?

*_Varsity team:_ main college team.

E. The gold and silver on the *Nuestra Señora de la Atocha* originally belonged to the American Indians. When the ship sank in 1622, the treasure was in the possession of the Spanish government. Three hundred years later, Mel Fisher recovered the treasure and his company gained sole rights to it, although many thought it should belong to the U.S. government and be used to benefit the people of the United States. The State of Florida also claimed it. In your opinion, who should have gotten it? Was Fisher entitled to it? In general, how should underwater excavation be regulated? Who should get the treasure?

Composition Topics

Write a short composition about one of the following topics, using modal auxiliaries (and **have to**) in some of your sentences.

1. Write about a goal that you hope to achieve. Answer the questions in Transfer Exercise 1B.
2. Write about something that you have achieved. Answer the questions in Transfer Exercise 2.
3. Imagine that your teacher is planning to go to your country to teach English at a high school or university for a year or more. Write him or her a letter with advice and information.

   Or:

   Imagine that you have a pen friend in the United States who plans to visit your country. Give your friend advice and information which will help him or her enjoy the trip. What can your friend do and see? What should he or she bring? What customs should your friend follow while there, etc.?
4. If you enjoy scuba diving, write about your experiences with that sport. Include information on safety procedures. (See Discussion Topic C.)
5. If you are a springboard diver, write about your training, abilities, and achievements in that sport. (See Discussion Topic A.) (*Note:* In the *Encyclopedia Americana,* under "diving," you can find pictures of different dives, with their English names.)
6. Choose another sport at which you are proficient, and write about your training, abilities, and achievements in that sport.
7. Write about underwater exploration or treasure seeking in your country. Answer some of the questions in Discussion Topic D.
8. Give your opinion about how underwater excavation should be regulated and why. (See Discussion Topic E.)

Lesson 9

Inferring Our Human Beginnings

9.1 Deduction: *must, may/might, can't/couldn't, should*

LOGICAL NECESSITY (certainty)

John works until 5:00 every day. It's only 4:30 now. He *must be working* now. (a)

The dog is whining at the door. He *must want* to come in. (a)

—I tried to call you this afternoon.

—You *must have called* while I was in the shower.
or:—I *must have been taking* a shower when you called. } (a, g)

The child is holding the book upside down. He *must not know* how to read. (b)

LOGICAL IMPOSSIBILITY (certainty)

—Is John playing tennis now?

—He {*can't* / *couldn't*} *be playing* tennis. His racket is here on his bed. (c)

—That man says he knew Abraham Lincoln.

—He {*can't* / *couldn't*} *have known* him. He was born after Lincoln died. (c)

LOGICAL POSSIBILITY (uncertainty)

—Why didn't that woman answer my question?

—She {*may* / *might* / *could*} *be* deaf. (d)

She {*may* / *might*} *not understand* English. (d)

She {*may* / *might*} *not have heard* you, or she {*could* / *may* / *might*} *have been daydreaming*. when you spoke to her. (d)

REASONABLE EXPECTATION

John left at six and it's a four-hour drive from here to New Orleans. It's ten thirty now.

He *should be* there by now. (He probably is.) (e)
He *should have arrived* by now. (He probably has arrived.) (e)

John left at six and it's a four-hour drive from New Orleans to here.

He *should be* here by now. (But he isn't.) (f)
He *should have arrived* by now. (But he hasn't.) (f)

Meaning: We use **must, may/might, can't/couldn't,** and **should** to make logical deductions (inferences) about an event or state. Except for (f) below, these deductions are about situations which we have not directly perceived.

a. **Must** means that we see only one logical possibility. We feel certain.

b. **Must not** means that the speaker is guessing that the negative is true.

c. **Can't** and **couldn't** mean that an event seems logically impossible.

d. **May (not), might (not),** and **could** mean that an event is possible, but not certain.

Should (not) means that it is reasonable to think that an event will occur, is occurring, or has occurred, but

e. we don't feel completely certain, or

f. the event did not occur as expected.

Sequence of Tense: (g) Modals of deduction occur in the main clause, never in the time clause.

Exercise 1. Deductions about the Present (oral—books closed)

Imagine that you are walking around the campus of a college or university in the United States or Canada. You see a number of things happen. Draw conclusions about what you see using **must** or **may/might.**

1. A man is walking back and forth in front of a building and looking frequently at his watch.

   a. He must be waiting for someone.
   b. He might ___________ for his girlfriend.
   c. The other person ___________ late.

2. A man that you don't know comes up to you and speaks to you in a language that you don't understand. What does he think?

   He must think . . .

3. You see two women on their hands and knees. They are looking very closely at the sidewalk. What are they looking for?

4. A group of students playing tubas is marching toward the athletic field. You know that it is football season. What do you conclude?

5. Several students are standing in front of a small table. One person is sitting on the other side of the table. Why are the students standing there? What is the seated person doing?

6. Going closer, you notice a political poster pinned to the front of the table. Now what do you think?

7. Several students are sitting on the grass with large pads of paper. They appear to be drawing one of the older buildings.

8. Looking through the windows of a classroom building, you see that all the students in the room are writing. The professor is sitting silently reading a magazine.

9. In another classroom you can see students looking through microscopes. What subject are they studying?

10. One student has a box of Kleenex next to the microscope on her desk and you see that she is sneezing quite a lot. She ___________ a cold.

11. In the lobby of the classroom building, a student is standing in front of a soda vending machine. She keeps putting coins in at the top and taking them out at the bottom.
    a. She ___________ .
    b. The machine ___________ .

12. Another student asks you if you can give him change for a dollar. Why does he need change?

Exercise 2. Deductions about the Past

Human culture began many thousands of years before the invention of writing. Therefore we have no written records of how these early people lived. Whatever we know about them has to be inferred from the bones, artifacts* and other remains that we find buried in the ground.

A. The facts: Below are some facts about objects which have been found which date from the late Ice Age (from 10,000 to 35,000 years ago). Read the facts and make inferences about them. Use **must have** if you feel certain. Use **may/might have** if you think that more than one explanation is logically possible. Refer to the questions in B if you need suggestions. You may want to work in small groups and discuss your answers with your classmates.

1. Beautiful, realistic paintings of animals (horses, cows, bison, reindeer, and others) have been found in underground caves where there is no daylight. How could the artists see to paint them?

    They may have used oil lamps, or they may have used torches.

    Why did they paint these pictures?

2. Stone bowls have been found which are blackened by fire on the inside.

3. Many of the paintings are high up on the walls or ceilings of the caves. How could the artists reach such high places?

4. Some of the paintings show men with spears in their hands. What does that mean?

5. There are also figures that are half human but have an animal head.

**Artifact:* man-made object.

6. There are symbols scratched on the walls.

7. There is no evidence that people lived in these painted caves. Then how were the caves used?

Besides the caves, all of the following have been found from the same period:

8. Floors paved with stones.

9. Rows of postholes in the sides of cliffs.

10. Harpoon heads and fishhooks made of bone.

11. Fireplaces lined with stones.

12. Needles with eyes.

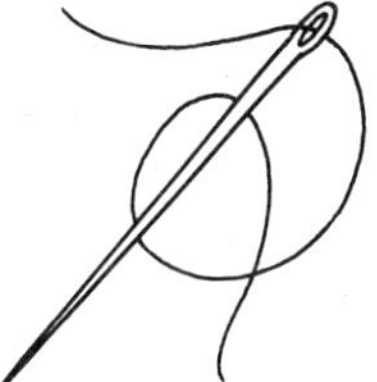

13. Human skeletons with walls around them. Some of them have bracelets on their wrists. Shells with holes in them are arranged in various patterns on their bodies.

14. A bone flute with five holes.

15. Many small statues of pregnant women dating from around 25,000 years ago.

16. Shells have been found far inland. They come from the Mediterranean Sea to the south, the Baltic Sea to the north, and the Atlantic Ocean to the west.

17. No woven materials have been found which date from this period.

18. No ceramic pots have been found, but a baked clay figurine has been found.

B. Questions: Use these questions to help you interpret the facts in A and to summarize your conclusions (inferences from the facts).

1. Where did these early people live? Did they construct houses?

2. What did they eat? How did they get their food? Did they cook it or eat it raw?

3. Did they wear clothes? If so, what kind?

4. Did they know how to weave? Did they know how to make pottery?
5. Did they have language? Writing?
6. Were they intelligent?
7. Did they have a religion? If so, what did they worship?
8. Did they believe in life after death?
9. Was each group isolated from all the others, or was there trade between groups?
10. Did these people have money?
11. Did they know how to sing and dance?
12. Were their feelings similar to ours, or were they very different, in your opinion?

Exercise 3. Deductions, Past and Present

Deduction is a very important part of scientific method. Scientists draw inferences from evidence that they collect, and they use those inferences to build theories. Below are a few examples of scientific inference from a number of different fields.

Read the facts and then draw a conclusion. Use the correct form of **must** or **can't.**

1. *Facts:* a. Light waves appear slightly longer when they come from an object that is moving away from the viewer.
   b. The light waves from the stars appear longer than normal.

   Conclusion: (Is the universe expanding, contracting, or staying the same?) It must be ______ -ing.

2. *Facts:* In 1846, only seven planets were known. Then two astronomers, John Adams and Urbain Le Verrier, observed that the planet Uranus was moving irregularly, as if another planet was pulling it outward.

   Their conclusion: There ____________________ beyond Uranus. (*Note:* Later in 1846, German astronomers observed the planet Neptune for the first time.)

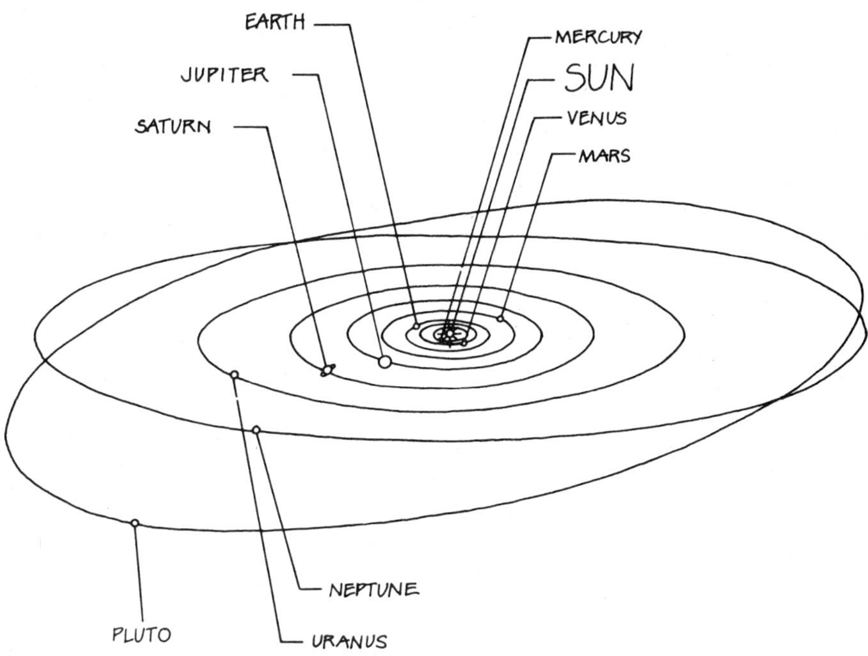

3. *Fact:* The temperature on the planet Venus is 885° F (475° C).
   Conclusion: (Is there life there?)

4. *Fact:* Proportionately more smokers than nonsmokers die of lung cancer.
   Conclusion: Smoking ______________________ .

5. *Fact:* The western coastline of Africa fits exactly the eastern coastline of North and South America, like two pieces of a jigsaw puzzle.
   Conclusion: ______________________ .

6. *Fact:* There are many craters on the moon.
   Conclusion: (How did they get there?)

7. *Facts:* Scientists have planted trees and then after a few years have counted the rings in their trunks. They have found that a tree adds one ring every year. Some redwood trees in California have 2,000 rings.
   Conclusion: Those trees ______________________ .

8. *Fact:* They have also found that in a rainy year, the tree ring is wider than in a dry year.
   Conclusion: If they find a narrow ring for a particular year many centuries ago, what do they conclude? That year ______________________ .

9. *Facts:* These are the numbers from one to ten in four languages.

Japanese	*Tibetan*	*Spanish*	*German*
ichi	chik	uno	eins
ni	nyii	dos	zwei
san	sum	tres	drei
shi	shi	cuatro	vier
go	gna	cinco	fünf
roku	druk	seis	sechs
shichi	dun	siete	sieben
hachi	gye	ocho	acht
kyu	gu	nueve	neun
jyu	chu	diez	zehn

Conclusions:

10. *Facts:* Here are some words in Japanese and English:

Japanese	*English*
kohii	coffee
donatsu	doughnut
hotto dogu	hotdog
terebi	television
kasetto	cassette recorder

Conclusion:

Exercise 4. Deductions with *should*

Complete the sentences. Use **should (not)** and the correct form of the verb to express a reasonable expectation.

1. —When will the new vaccine against flu be on the market?
   —It's being tested now. It ______________________ soon.
2. —Does Sam have to have an operation?
   —He doesn't know yet, but he's going in for tests tomorrow. He ______________________ the results in about a week.
3. —Where's my bicycle?
   —You parked it in the driveway. It ______________________ unless somebody moved it.
4. —Let's go to a movie.
   —Okay. But I only have $5.00.
   —Five dollars ______________________________. The movie ______________________ more than that.

5. —How well does Sarah read Spanish?
—She studied it for five years. She ______________________ .

6. —Where can I find out more about cave art?
—Our town library isn't large, but it's a good one. It ______________________ .

7. —How are you going to do on the next exam?
—I've studied hard up to now, so ______________________ .

8. —May I see the newspaper when you're finished?
—Sure. I ______________________ .

9. I had twenty dollars in my wallet this morning, and I spent $4.50 for lunch. I haven't bought anything else. Why do I only have ten dollars? I ______________________ .

10. We have done a lot of exercises using the passive, so we ______________________ .

11. Juan swam really well during training. I don't understand why he didn't win the race. He ______________________ easily.

12. —I wrote to the state university for some information over a month ago, but I haven't received an answer yet.
—That's strange. ______________________ by now.

Exercise 5. Summary of Deductions

Fill in **must, may/might, could,** or **should** and the correct form, active or passive, of the verb in parentheses. In some cases, more than one answer is possible, but the meanings are different.

It is believed that the human race originated in the Old World* and that the first immigrants to America came during the Ice Age. At that time, much of the earth's water was frozen in glaciers, and therefore, the oceans (1) must have been (be) much lower than now. It seems certain that there (2) ______________________ (be) a land bridge between Siberia and Alaska. Since American Indians resemble Asians in appearance, anthropologists believe that the first settlers (3) ______________________ (walk) across the land bridge from Asia.

When the ice melted and the oceans rose again, supposedly all contact between the two hemispheres was cut off. But were the two

The Old World: Africa, Asia, and Europe.

worlds really completely isolated? If they were, how can we explain the presence of weaving, ceramics, and writing systems in both hemispheres as well as the amazing similarities in the tools and art of the old world and the new?

There are two possible explanations for these similarities: People (4) ______________________ the ocean in ships even in prehistoric
(cross)
times, or the technologies and art forms (5) ______________________
(reinvent)
independently at different times in different places.

For many years, scientists debated this question. One group, the diffusionists, felt certain these similarities (6) ______________
(not, occur)
by chance. There (7) ______________________ contact between the
(be)
old and new worlds. The other group, the independent inventionists, disagreed. They claimed that civilization not only (8) ____________
(develop)
independently, but (9) ______________________ that way because
(develop)
prehistoric people (10) ______________________ the ocean in their
(not, cross)
small boats.

One diffusionist, the anthropologist Thor Heyerdahl, was struck by** the similarities between Polynesian culture in the southwest Pacific islands and the ancient cultures of Peru in South America. He decided to build a raft similar to the rafts made by the ancient Peruvians and to sail west from the coast of Peru. He reasoned as follows: "The raft will be carried west by the ocean current, and eventually I (11) ______________________ able to reach the Polynesian islands."
(be)
He knew that he (12) ______________________ that people really did
(not, prove)
cross the ocean in this way, but he hoped to demonstrate that they (13) ______________________ it. In 1947 Heyerdahl successfully
(cross)
made the 4500-mile trip from Peru to the Polynesian islands on his raft, the *Kon-Tiki*.

Heyerdahl also noticed similarities between the reed boats used in some parts of Africa and those used on Lake Titicaca in Peru and Bolivia. To show that people from the Old World (14) ______________________ across the Atlantic in these boats, he
(sail)
constructed several of them and successfully sailed one from Morocco, in Africa, to Barbados, an island near the coast of South America.

***Was struck by:* noticed with great interest.

Since these adventurous voyages were made, research has made it clear that there really was transoceanic contact in ancient times. As we continue to gather evidence, the story of this contact (15) ______________ clearer and clearer.
(become)

9.2 Substituting *be able* for *can* after an Auxiliary

(Sally can walk). Sally *has been able to walk* since she was eleven months old.

Eric has studied English for a year.
(He can speak it quite well.) He *should be able to speak* it quite well by now.

Cro-Magnon people had needles.
(They could sew.) They *must have been able to sew.*

Word Choice: Since **can** is a modal auxiliary, it is always the first word in the verb phrase. After another auxiliary, therefore, we use **be able to** to express the meaning of **can.**

Exercise 6. *Be able* after the Present Perfect (oral—books closed)

A. Answer the questions. If your answer is *yes,* add a sentence which tells how long.

Can you

1. ride a bicycle?

   Yes, I have been able to ride a bicycle since I was (eight) years old.

2. dive from a springboard?

3. whistle?
4. drive?
5. type?
6. use a personal computer?
7. make (scrambled eggs)?
8. remember the name of every student in the class?
9. spell the teacher's name?
10. understand the teacher?

B. Ask classmates other questions with **can.**

Exercise 7. *Be able* after *will* (oral or written)

Complete the sentences, using **will be able to.**

1. When I finish this English course, . . .
2. When I get my degree in (subject), . . .
3. After I become well-known in my field, . . .
4. After my children grow up and get jobs, . . .
5. When I retire, . . .
6. If I win a million dollars in the lottery, . . .

Exercise 8. *Be able* after Modal Perfects

From what you learned in Exercise 2, what do you think that Ice Age people in Europe knew how to do? Use **must, may/might,** and **be able.** (Refer back to Exercise 2 if you need to.)

Example: **They had needles, so they must have been able to sew.**

Transfer Exercises

1. Time Zones Around the World

Refer to the map and the time chart to find out what time it is now in different cities and countries around the world. Describe what people are doing in these different places using **must, may/might, should,** and **can't/couldn't.**

A. What time is it in (Shanghai) now? What are people doing there? (You can talk about working people, housewives, farmers, children, night watchmen, etc.)

B. What are your relatives and friends back home doing now?

6	7	8	9	10	11	12	1	2	3	4	5	6	7	8	9	10	11	12	1	2	3	4	5
7	8	9	10	11	12	1	2	3	4	5	6	7	8	9	10	11	12	1	2	3	4	5	6
8	9	10	11	12	1	2	3	4	5	6	7	8	9	10	11	12	1	2	3	4	5	6	7
9	10	11	12	1	2	3	4	5	6	7	8	9	10	11	12	1	2	3	4	5	6	7	8
10	11	12	1	2	3	4	5	6	7	8	9	10	11	12	1	2	3	4	5	6	7	8	9
11	12	1	2	3	4	5	6	7	8	9	10	11	12	1	2	3	4	5	6	7	8	9	10
12	1	2	3	4	5	6	7	8	9	10	11	12	1	2	3	4	5	6	7	8	9	10	11
1	2	3	4	5	6	7	8	9	10	11	12	1	2	3	4	5	6	7	8	9	10	11	12
2	3	4	5	6	7	8	9	10	11	12	1	2	3	4	5	6	7	8	9	10	11	12	1
3	4	5	6	7	8	9	10	11	12	1	2	3	4	5	6	7	8	9	10	11	12	1	2
4	5	6	7	8	8	10	11	12	1	2	3	4	5	6	7	8	9	10	11	12	1	2	3
5	6	7	8	9	10	11	12	1	2	3	4	5	6	7	8	9	10	11	12	1	2	3	4

2. What's Wrong?

Give one or more possible explanations for the different problems described below. Use **may/might** or **could.** If you feel certain, use **must.** You might want to disagree with a classmate's answer, as in example (b) below.

Some useful expressions: Sometimes things don't work because

a battery goes dead
a pilot light goes out
the paper jams
the power goes out in the neighborhood

something is broken, dull, worn out, out of (gas)
something needs to be cleaned
someone forgets to wind something
someone blows a fuse (uses too much electric power)
someone doesn't focus a camera
someone runs over a nail or a sharp piece of glass

1. Lucy's watch has stopped. What's wrong with it?

   a. **First student: It {might / may} need to be cleaned.**

   Second student: She {could / may / might} have forgotten to wind it.

   Third student: The battery might be dead.
   Fourth student: Something might be broken.

   or: b. **First student: Something must be broken.**
   Second student: Not necessarily. She might have forgotten to wind it, or it might just need to be cleaned.

2. My car won't start. What's the matter with it?
3. Eric has a flat tire. Why?
4. Last night Tim was ironing his shirts when suddenly the lights went out. What happened?
5. My gas stove doesn't light when I turn the knob.
6. Mark bought a camera recently. He has just gotten his first roll of film back from the developer. The pictures aren't clear—they're fuzzy. He is wondering why.
7. I can't cut my steak. What's wrong with this knife?
8. When Mrs. Jones went down to her garden this morning, she saw that all the tops of her carrots were gone.
9. She also saw holes in the leaves on the plants.
10. The Xerox machine isn't working.
11. Why did Roger fail his chemistry course?
12. I saw Julie talking with her boyfriend a few minutes ago, and now she's crying. I wonder what happened.

3. Prepositions

Fill in the correct preposition. If no preposition is needed, fill in Ø (nothing). These preposition combinations occur in this lesson.

1. Many American children believe _______ Santa Claus, a friendly old man who puts presents in their stockings on the night before Christmas.
2. We think of Santa Claus as a fat, smiling man with a white beard and a red suit. This picture dates _______ the early nineteenth century, when the poem "The Night Before Christmas" described him that way.
3. The custom of the Christmas tree originated _______ Germany.
4. Spruce and fir trees are the most common kinds of Christmas trees. They are similar _______ pine trees but have shorter needles.

5. Some people prefer an artificial tree, which resembles _______ a real tree but is made _______ nonflammable material.*
6. Our tree was tall this year. We could not reach _______ the top of it to put the star on. We had to use a ladder.
7. **A:** Something is the matter _______ our Christmas tree lights. They're not working.
   B: A bulb might have burned out.
   A: No, I checked all the bulbs. They're okay.
   B: Then something must be wrong _______ the wiring.

Discussion Topics

A. Who were the very first people to live in your country? Where do scientists think they must have come from? What do you know about their way of life? Did they have a highly developed culture? Did they make pottery or weave cloth? Have you seen any objects that they made, or pictures of objects? If so, what can you deduce about their food, houses, customs, religion, etc. from these objects?

B. Do you think that spoken language originated in one group and then spread all over the world, or do you think that it could have originated independently in several different places? Give reasons for your opinion.

**Nonflammable material:* material which cannot burn.

C. Do you think that the following originated in one place or in several places? Give your reasons.

writing	the domestication of dogs, cats, cows, horses, and other animals
the use of fire	
religion	the wheel and axle
farming	

Composition Topics

Write a short composition about one of the following topics. Make inferences with **must, may/might,** and **could** in some of your sentences.

1. Write about your great-grandparents (your father's or mother's grandparents). Give the facts that you know about their lives, and also make some guesses. For example:

   How were they raised and educated?
   How did they meet each other?
   What kind of work did each of them do?
   What did they do for entertainment or relaxation?
   Did they travel?
   How many languages did they know?
   etc.

2. Write about one of your earlier ancestors that you have heard about. From what you know, make deductions about his or her life and character.
3. Write about the first people who lived in your country. Use your knowledge to make intelligent guesses about them. (See Discussion Topic A.)
4. Write about the origin of language, or the origin of some other important feature of human culture. Use your knowledge and imagination to describe how it must have originated. (See Discussion Topics B and C.)
5. How did the early people described in Exercise 2 use their painted caves? Use your imagination.
6. Write about a famous person such as the president of your country, the president of the United States, or a well-known athlete, movie star, or singer. From what you have seen on TV or read in the newspaper, what can you imagine about his or her personal life and feelings?

UNIT V

NOUN CLAUSES

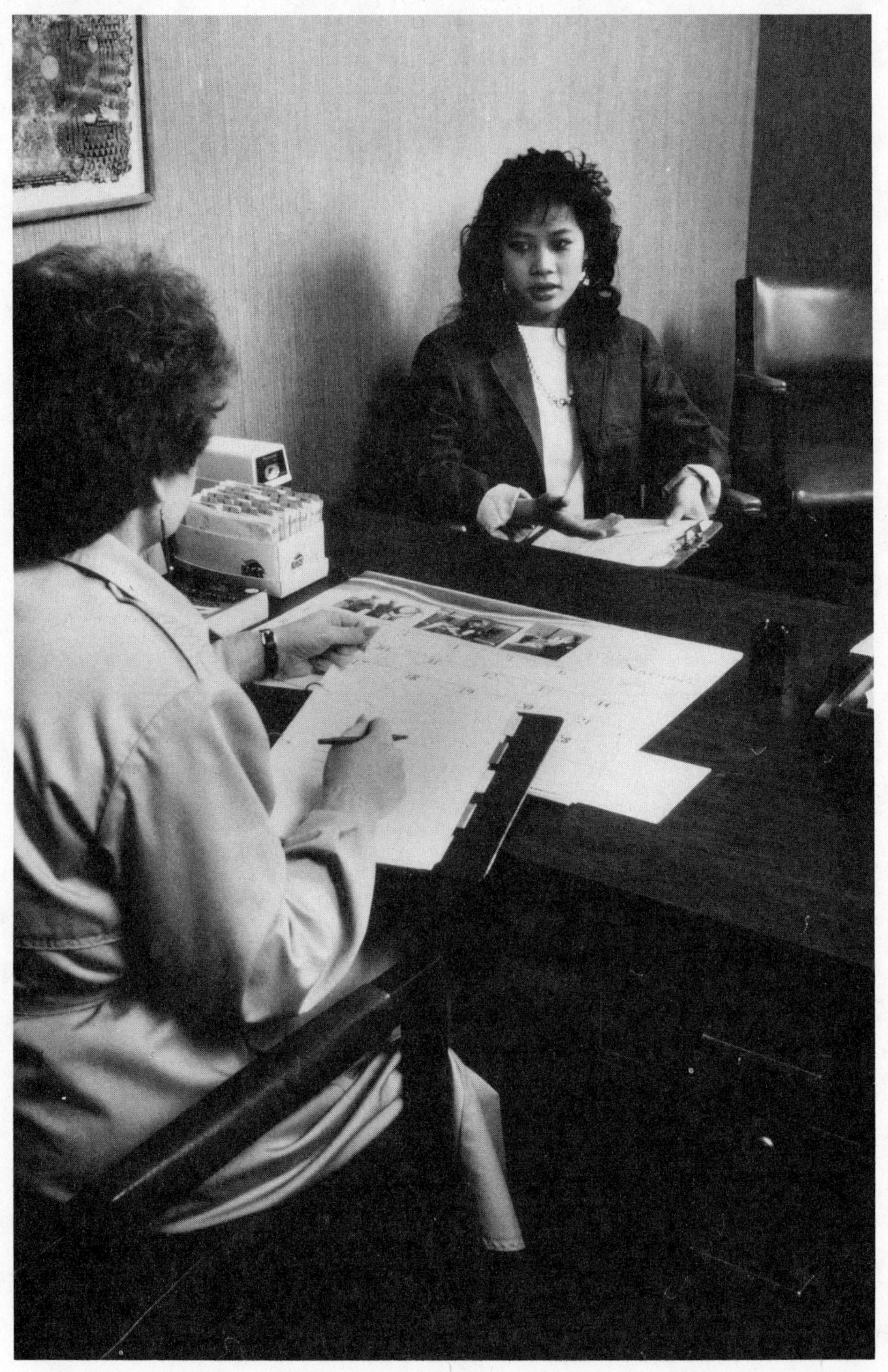

Lesson 10

Hiring an ESL Teacher

10.1 Introduction to Dependent Clauses; Indirect Questions

Introduction

INDEPENDENT CLAUSE (sentence)	DEPENDENT CLAUSE (not a sentence)
He bought the book.	that he bought the book (a)
What did he buy?	what he bought (a)
When did he buy the book?	when he bought the book (a,b)
	which he bought (c)

Sentence Structure: An independent clause can stand alone as a complete sentence. A dependent clause cannot stand alone. It must be part of a longer sentence.

Types of Dependent Clause: a. *Noun clause:* The clause functions as a noun.

I know *that he bought the book.*
I don't know *what he bought.*
I don't know *when he bought the book.*

b. *Adverb clause:* The clause functions as an adverb.

He paid by check *when he bought the book.*

c. *Adjective clause:* The clause functions as an adjective.

The book *which he bought* cost almost $20.

Indirect Questions

DIRECT QUESTION	INDIRECT QUESTION (NOUN CLAUSE)
What is this?	what this is
How can he speak so fast?	how he can speak so fast
Who laughed?	who laughed
Did John finish the test?	whether / if } John finished the test

Indirect question (noun clause) = direct object:

	VERB	DIRECT OBJECT			
			SUBJECT	VERB	
I	don't know	what	this	is.	
Do you	know	what	this	is?	
I	wonder	how	he	can speak	so fast.
	Tell me	who		laughed.	
I	don't know	{ whether / if	John	finished	the test.

Indirect question (noun clause) = subject:

SUBJECT				
	SUBJECT	VERB		
What	this	is		is a mystery to me.
How	he	can speak	so fast	puzzles me.
Who		laughed		is not important.
Whether	John	finished	the test	will determine how well he did.

Indirect question (noun clause) = the object of a preposition:

	PREPOSITION	OBJECT
Pay attention	to	what I say.
John's grade will depend	on	whether he finished the test. whether or not he finished . . . whether he finished or not.

Indirect question (noun clause) = complement:

	ADJECTIVE	COMPLEMENT
I am not	sure	what this is.

Word Order: In indirect questions, the subject comes before the auxiliary and verb.

Word Choice: **Whether** introduces an indirect question formed from a *yes–no* question. **If** may also be used when the indirect question is the direct object, but not in other positions.

Punctuation: Commas are not used before or after an indirect question.

Exercise 1. Direct Questions (review)

Ellen Hoffman is the principal of a public elementary school. Recently a number of refugee children from Southeast Asia have enrolled in the school, and she needs to hire an ESL* teacher who can help them learn English.

Ms. Hoffman plans to interview several applicants for the job. She has made this checklist of the information she would like to obtain from each applicant:

ESL: English as a second language.

INTERVIEW CHECKLIST

Previous teaching experience:

1. years ______
2. grades ______
3. public ______ private ______
4. children:
   a. language background ________
   b. economic background ________
5. class size ______________________________
6. teaching methods ______________________________
7. discipline problems ______________________________
8. other problems/solutions ______________________________

Education:

9. Name of institution ______________ Degree ____ Major ______
   ______________ ____ ______
10. Education courses ______________________________
11. Certification: ESL ________
    Other ________
12. Languages ________ Years of study ____ Level of proficiency ____
    ________ ____ ____
    ________ ____ ____
13. Travel to other countries ________ Length of stay ________
    ________ ________
    ____

Outside interests:

14. Musical instruments ______________________________
15. Sports ______________________________
16. Other ______________________________

Personality:

cooperative	______	neat in appearance	______	sense of humor	______
courteous	______	patient	______	initiative	______
creative	______	relaxed	______		
direct	______				
friendly	______				

Form a question for each point on the checklist.

1. How many years *has the applicant been teaching* ?
2. What grades . . . he or she taught?
3. . . . public or private schools?

4. What kind of . . . ?
   a. . . .
   b. . . .
5. How . . . ?
6. . . .
7. How . . . handle . . . ?
8. What other problems . . . encounter and how . . . ?

9–16. (Continue to form questions orally or on your own paper. Are there any other questions Ms. Hoffman should ask?)

Exercise 2. Indirect Questions as Direct Objects (books open or closed)

A. Each applicant will send Ms. Hoffman a resume before his or her interview, so she will not have to ask all the questions on her checklist. What can she find out from the resume? Make sentences with these expressions:

She { can (probably) find out . . . / may be able to find out / probably won't need to ask }

The resume will (probably) { tell her / say / indicate }

Examples: **She can find out from the resume what university the applicant graduated from.**

The resume will probably tell her whether he or she is certified in ESL.

B. What won't the resume tell her?

Example: **It probably won't tell her how he or she handles discipline problems.**

C. What can she find out from observation during the interview?

Exercise 3. Indirect Questions as Objects of Prepositions

A. Ms. Hoffman will be interested in all the information that the applicants give her. Make sentences with the expressions in parentheses. Omit **will** in the noun clause.

1. The applicants will tell her something about themselves in the interview. (pay attention to)

   She will pay attention to what they tell her about themselves in the interview.

2. They will act in a certain way. (make a note of how)
3. They will speak in a certain way. (be concerned about)
4. They will say something about their teaching experience. (be interested in)
5. They will tell her something about their educational background. (think about)
6. They will give some names of people as references. (look at who)

B. What other information should Ms. Hoffman pay close attention to? Refer to the checklist.

Exercise 4. Indirect Questions as Subjects

Ms. Hoffman may ask some of the questions below, and she will probably not ask others. Why? Make statements with these expressions:

does not concern her	will be clear from the interview
doesn't matter	will (not) influence her decision
is relevant/irrelevant	is (not) related to (whether the applicant is a good teacher).
is none of her business*	
is (not) very important	

1. Are you courteous?

   Whether an applicant is courteous (or not) will be clear from the interview. She will not ask him/her directly.

2. Are you married?
3. Do you have a boyfriend/girlfriend?
4. Where were you born?
5. How old are you?
6. How big is your apartment?
7. What is your father's occupation?
8. What kinds of TV programs do you like?
9. Do you believe in physical punishment?
10. Do you like children?
11. Was it easy for you to learn a second language?
12. Can you describe your main strengths as a teacher?

*_None of (her) business:_ This expression can be rude. (See page 185, footnote.)

Exercise 5. Indirect Questions in Various Positions (books open or closed)

A. What factors will influence Ms. Hoffman's decision, in your opinion? Make statements with these expressions:

1. will (not) influence her decision

   How courteous an applicant is will influence her decision.

   or: **Whether an applicant is tall or short will probably not influence her decision.**
2. Her decision will be influenced by
3. is (not) related to

   Where he was born is not related to how well . . .
4. will indicate
5. depends on
6. is more important than

B. What are the most important qualifications for an elementary ESL teacher, in your opinion?

10.2 Indirect Statements

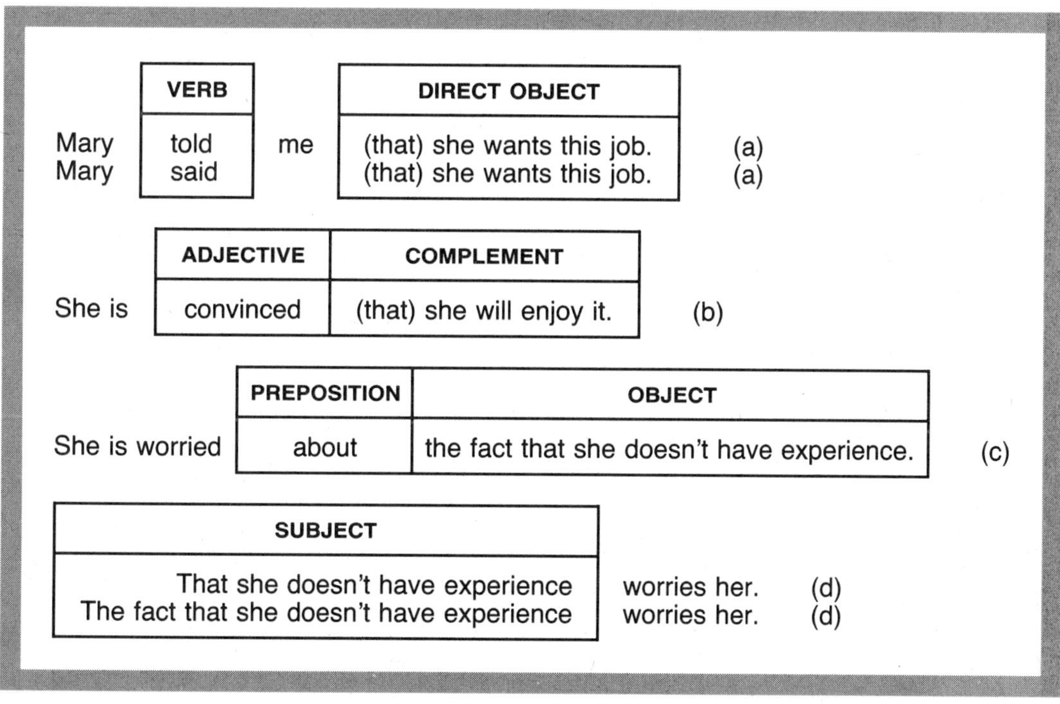

	VERB		DIRECT OBJECT	
Mary	told	me	(that) she wants this job.	(a)
Mary	said		(that) she wants this job.	(a)

	ADJECTIVE	COMPLEMENT	
She is	convinced	(that) she will enjoy it.	(b)

	PREPOSITION	OBJECT	
She is worried	about	the fact that she doesn't have experience.	(c)

SUBJECT		
That she doesn't have experience	worries her.	(d)
The fact that she doesn't have experience	worries her.	(d)

Word Choice: Use **that** or **the fact that** as follows:

a. Use **that** if the indirect statement is a direct object.

b. Use **that** if the indirect statement is a *complement.* Adjectives which may be followed by a noun clause generally express attitude or emotion. For example:

aware	happy	sure
certain	shocked	surprised
confident	sorry	worried

c. Use **the fact that** when the indirect statement is the *object of a preposition.*

d. When the indirect statement is the *subject* of the sentence, either **that** or **the fact that** may be used, but **that** is very formal and is used mainly in writing.

Punctuation: Commas are not used before or after an indirect statement.

Deletion: **That** may be deleted from a direct object or complement clause if the meaning is clear without it. Notice that in the following example, **that** is necessary to make the meaning clear:

unclear: **He told me on Friday he was going away.**
clear: **He told me that on Friday he was going away.**
clear: **He told me on Friday that he was going away.**

***Say** versus **tell**:* An indirect object always follows **tell** before a noun clause. We tell *somebody* something. We usually do not use an indirect object after **say.** (See example a.)

Backshifting

PAST TIME FRAME

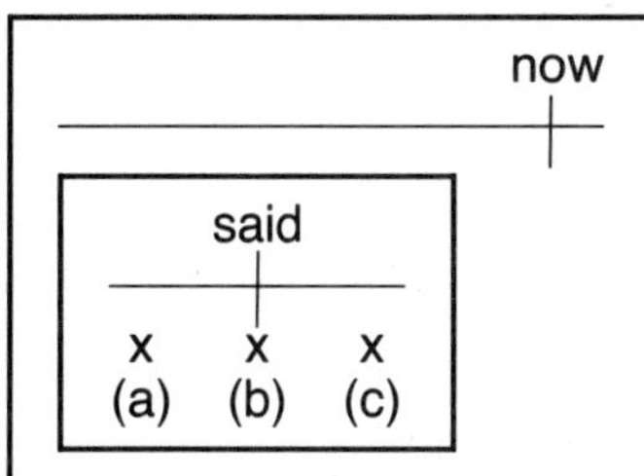

Lincoln said, "The world will not remember what we say here."

→ Lincoln said (that) the world *would not remember* (c) what they *said* (b) there.

He said, "It cannot forget the soldiers who fought here."

→ He said (that) it *could not forget* (c) the soldiers who *had fought* (a) there.

PRESENT TIME FRAME

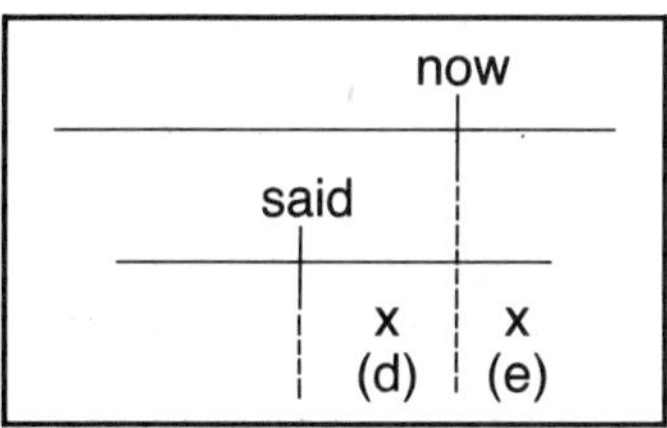

"I will correct your homework tonight."
→ The teacher said yesterday that she *would correct* our homework last night. (d)

"I will fly to Paris on Tuesday."
→ The President announced (that) he *will fly* to Paris on Tuesday. (e)
or: The President announced (that) he *would fly* to Paris on Tuesday. (e)

Tense Choice: When the main verb is past, we usually "backshift" the verb(s) in the noun clause as follows:

Present becomes *past:* **is eating → was eating**

Past / *Present perfect* } become *past perfect:* **ate** / **has eaten** → **had eaten.**

will → would
can → could
may → might
should / **must** } (no change)

d. We *must* backshift when the future time referred to in the original statement is now in the past.

e. Backshifting is optional when the future time is still in the future.

Word Choice: Here are some other words which often shift in indirect speech:

yesterday	→	the day before
tomorrow	→	the next day
today	→	that day, yesterday, etc.
now	→	at that time
here	→	there
this/these	→	that/those/the
that/those	→	the (or no change)

Indirect Statements from Short Answers and Exclamations

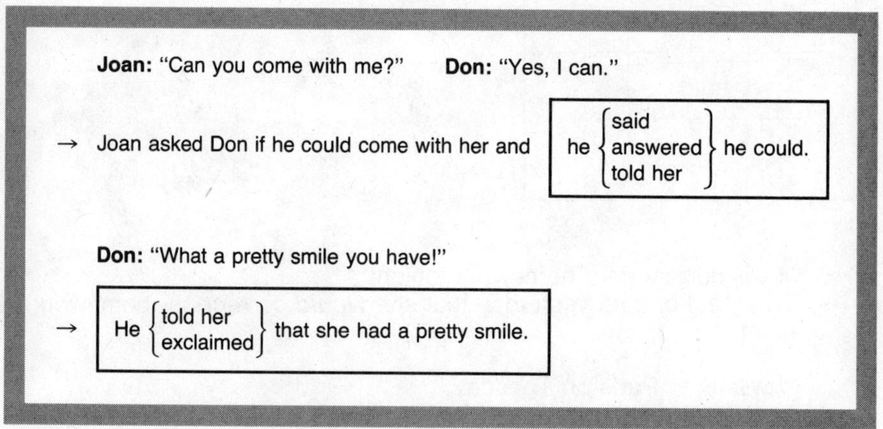

Joan: "Can you come with me?" **Don:** "Yes, I can."
→ Joan asked Don if he could come with her and he {said / answered / told her} he could.
Don: "What a pretty smile you have!"
→ He {told her / exclaimed} that she had a pretty smile.

Notes: 1. Indirect requests and commands use the infinitive. See Lesson 12.

"Sit down." **Ms. H. asked Mary *to sit down.***

2. Some brief everyday expressions are often reported in different words:

"Thank you."	→ **He thanked me.**
"You're right."	→ **He agreed with me.**
"No kidding!"	→ **He was surprised.**
"Maybe, but I doubt it."	→ **He wasn't convinced.**

Exercise 6. Indirect Statements and Questions as Direct Objects

Ms. Hoffman has just interviewed a young woman for the ESL teaching position. Here is part of the interview.

Report the information in indirect speech (indirect questions and statements), using these verbs. Use each verb once. Backshift the verbs in the noun clauses.

add	exclaim	say	want to know
answer	√notice	suppose	
√ask	reply	tell (her)	

Ms. H: Hello, Mary. It's nice to meet you. Please sit down over here. According to your resume, you majored in French. (1) Have you ever been to France? (2)

Mary: Yes, I spent my junior year there. (3)

Ms. H: What a wonderful experience that must have been! (4) Did you take any education courses in college? (5)

Mary: Yes, education was my minor. (6) I am certified in elementary education. In the fall, I'm going to take some courses in ESL (8). In fact, I'm planning to get an M.A. in language teaching (9). It'll probably take several years if I'm teaching at the same time (10).

1. **Ms. Hoffman noticed that Mary had majored in French.**
2. **She asked if . . .**

Exercise 7. Direct and Indirect Speech (oral)

Another applicant who has applied for the job is a young man named Edgar McCrea. Ms. Hoffman can see from his resume

that he has a B.A. from the University of Michigan, is certified in ESL, and has taught for two years. He seems like a good candidate for the job, and she is eager to interview him.

A. Role-play the interview between Ms. Hoffman and Edgar. Choose a student to play the part of Edgar. The others in the class can all take the part of Ms. Hoffman. If possible, tape-record the interview. If that is not possible, ask one student to take blackboard notes. You may also want to use the checklist in Exercise 1 for notes. Keep your interview brief.

B. Replay your tape recording of the interview or work from the notes on the blackboard and report the interview in indirect speech.

Exercise 8. Indirect Statements as Complements

Report some of the information from your interview in Exercise 7, using noun clauses after these expressions:

Ms. Hoffman is pleased
disappointed
aware
(not) convinced
(not) sure
She was surprised . . .

Example: **Ms. Hoffman is disappointed that Mary has not taught before.** (*Your* sentences will be about Edgar.)

Exercise 9. Indirect Statements with *the fact that*

Report some of the information from your interview in Exercise 7, using noun clauses with **the fact that** and these expressions:

1. Ms. Hoffman is (not) concerned about . . .

   Example: **Ms. Hoffman is not concerned about the fact that Edgar does not know the language of the refugee children.**

2. She is interested in . . .
3. . . . indicates that (he probably likes children).
4. . . . is a point in his favor.
5. . . . is a drawback.
6. . . . is more important than . . .
7. Except for . . . , he is a strong candidate for the job.

10.3 Direct Quotations

John said, "Smith called me yesterday."
"Smith called me yesterday," he said.
"Smith called me yesterday," said John.
"Smith," said John, "called me yesterday."
"Smith called yesterday. He wanted some information," John said.

"When did he call?" I asked.
I asked, "When did he call?"

Punctuation: Notice that

1. There is a comma after **he said, I asked,** etc., except at the end of the sentence.
2. The closing quotation marks are preceded by a comma, question mark, or period.

Word Order: A noun subject may precede or follow **said, asked,** etc., but a pronoun subject usually precedes the verb.

Exercise 10. Punctuating Direct Quotations

A friend of mine once told me this story about the time when, as a young man, he applied for a job as a lobster cook at a seafood restaurant.

Add the necessary punctuation and capitalization to the story. Notice that there is a new paragraph each time the identity of the speaker shifts. (Ignore the numbers in parentheses—they are for Exercise 11.)

have you cooked lobsters before the manager asked (1)
sure lied my friend (2)
you're hired said the manager you can start tomorrow (3) I'll pay you the minimum wage to start and you'll get a raise if you do well (4)

my friend reported for work the next day

the manager said the lobsters are in that refrigerator (5) if you will get half a dozen we'll make lobster salad (6)

my friend opened the door of the walk-in refrigerator and saw dozens of live, crawling lobsters. he completely panicked and ran out shouting there are lobsters in there! (7)

oh my God groaned the manager, and that was the end of my friend's career as a lobster cook.

Exercise 11. Indirect Speech

Change the numbered sentences in Exercise 10 from direct to indirect speech. You will need to use **and that** in 3, in 4, and in joining 5 and 6.

Transfer Exercises

1. Polite Questions (books closed)

Below are some questions that we might need to ask a stranger. When we ask a stranger for information, it is helpful to say a few words first so that the person has time to focus his or her attention on the question. Therefore we often begin with

Could you tell me . . . ?

or: **Do you know . . . ?**

When we stop someone on the street, we usually begin with **excuse me** or **pardon me** and then ask the question. Change the following direct questions to polite indirect questions.

1. Where is the bank? the escalator? the shoe department? the registrar's office? the bus stop?

   Excuse me. Could you tell me where the bank is?

2. Where can I get a ticket? a newspaper? a cup of coffee?
3. What time is it?
4. When will this class end?
5. How can I get to the cafeteria?
6. How much does this steak cost?
7. Whose coat is this?
8. Is this Professor Duffy's office?
9. Who is the foreign student advisor?
10. When does this bus leave?
11. Does this train stop at 42nd Street?

12. Is this Fifth Avenue?
13. What street is this?
14. Which way is East 43rd Street?
15. (Ask a question of your own.)

2. Curiosity

Mention something that you wonder about another student in the class. The other student can answer or can say, "No comment."

Examples: 1. **—I wonder why Mehrad was late this morning. She has never been late before.**

—I was late because our car broke down.

2. **—I wonder whether Julio has a serious girlfriend.**

—Whether I have a serious girlfriend or not is
{ my affair.
{ none of your business!*

or: **—I'm glad to say I have a wonderful girlfriend back home.**

3. A Fish Story

A. Punctuate the following story about the famous writer Mark Twain and add capital letters where you need them.

Once Mark Twain was fishing. A stranger came along and asked are you catching any fish

I caught fifteen trout in this stream yesterday Mark Twain said

is that so said the stranger do you know who I am

no said Mark Twain

I am the game warden* of this county** answered the stranger and trout are out of season

Mark Twain thought for a while and then asked do you know who I am

no replied the game warden

I am the biggest liar in this county said Mark Twain

B. Report the story in indirect speech.

**None of your business:* Except when we are joking with a good friend, *none of your business* is impolite and is used in anger.
**Game warden:* the man whose job is to enforce hunting and fishing laws.
***County:* a political area smaller than a state. There are many counties in every state.

Discussion Topics

A. Are the qualifications for a high school or university teacher the same as, or different from, the qualifications for an elementary school teacher, in your opinion? Which qualifications are the most important at each level? In your country, are certain qualifications considered particularly important at the elementary, secondary, or university level? If so, why?

B. What are the most important qualifications for someone in your present or future profession? Is talent important? training? knowledge? strength? honesty? Explain.

C. If you are not married yet, what are some of the most important qualities you will look for in a husband or wife?

If you are married, what are some of the qualities that you appreciate most in your spouse? (If you want to, you can also mention some qualities that you *don't* appreciate.)

D. What are some qualities that you appreciate in your best friend?

Composition Topics

1. Can you remember a conversation you had that was very important to you at some time in the past? Write about it. You might organize your composition into three paragraphs, as follows:

Paragraph 1

Set the scene: Tell when and where the conversation took place and who you were talking to. You might say why the conversation was important to you, or you might save this part to the end.

Paragraph 2

Report the conversation: Use indirect statements and questions except when you have a special reason to quote a sentence directly, for example, for emphasis. You don't need to remember the exact words or all the details of the conversation.

Paragraph 3

Give one or two concluding remarks: If you have not already explained why the conversation was important to you, do so here.

2. Write about a time when you were hired for a job. Tell something about the job interview and give the reasons why you were hired (if you know or can guess). Were you well qualified? During your first days on the job, what helped you the most? What factors made the first days difficult?
3. Write about one of the Discussion Topics.
4. Interview two classmates about the qualities that they consider important in a husband or wife (Discussion Topic C), and report their opinions.

Lesson 11

Times of Trouble: 1865, 1968

11.1 *It* in Place of a Noun Clause Subject

SUBJECT	PREDICATE
That John is intelligent	became clear yesterday. is a fact. is a good thing for us. delights the teacher.
Why Mary left	is uncertain. is a secret.

	SUBJECT	PREDICATE	NOUN CLAUSE
→	It	became clear yesterday is a fact is a good thing for us delights the teacher	that John is intelligent.
	It	is uncertain is a secret	why Mary left.

Form: Subject noun clauses are frequently replaced by **it** and moved to the end of the sentence.

Exercise 1. Indirect Statements and Questions

Abraham Lincoln is one of the best-known presidents in the history of the United States. He was president during the Civil War between the northern states and the southern states (the Confederate States of America), and during that war, he signed the declaration which abolished slavery in the United States.

On April 14, 1865, Lincoln was shot and killed while he was attending the theater. Some historians believe that the public has never been told all the facts about the assassination. They claim there is evidence of a conspiracy.

Make statements with **it** and the words in parentheses. With some of the verbs, you will need to use the passive form.

1. (know) Was the assassin an actor named John Wilkes Booth?

   It is known that the assassin was an actor named John Wilkes Booth.

2. (appear) Was Booth a Confederate spy?

   It appears that Booth was a Confederate spy.

3. (believe) Was Booth part of a conspiracy?
4. (not, know) Were high government officials part of the conspiracy?

   It is not known whether . . .

5. (a fact) Were several men and one woman tried for helping Booth after the assassination?
6. (not, know) How many others were involved?
7. (seem) Was Booth secretly married?
8. (possible) Was his wife also a spy?
9. (claim) Did someone destroy part of Booth's diary?
10. (think) Did a soldier named Boston Corbett kill Booth?
11. (also, say) Did Booth escape? Was he never caught?

    However, . . . and . . .

The events surrounding Lincoln's attendance at the theater leave many questions unanswered.

12. (was, clear) Was Lincoln's life in danger?
13. (surprising) Why did his military guard consist of only one man? (Use **that.**)
14. (not, clear) Why did the President have so little protection?

15. (very, odd) Why didn't the guard stay at his post outside the President's box?*
16. (turn out**) Did he take a seat where he could watch the play?
17. (know) Did Mrs. Lincoln hire the guard?
18. (not, understand) What was her relationship to the guard?
19. (suspect) Did they have a romantic involvement?
20. (probable) Did the guard not appear in court because of this suspicion?
21. (possible) Might his appearance in court have uncovered a scandal?
22. (a matter of opinion) Why did the government keep the case a secret for sixty-three years?
23. (obvious) Do many questions about Lincoln's death remain unanswered?
24. (shock the nation) Lincoln had been killed.
25. (a tragedy) Was he able to help the nation recover from the war?

11.2 Noun Clauses after Nouns

The world is flat.
→ People believed that the world was flat.

	NOUN	NOUN CLAUSE	
→	The belief	that the world was flat	was once widespread.

There was a conspiracy.
→ It is possible that there was a conspiracy.

	NOUN	NOUN CLAUSE
→ Historians have investigated	the possibility	that there was a conspiracy.

**Box:* a separate section in a theater.
***Turned out:* became clear later.

Exercise 2. Sentence Combining

Combine each sentence with the phrase which follows it, using each noun from the list once. Make all necessary changes.

evidence	√knowledge	possibility
fact	news	reason

1. "Someone may try to assassinate me."
   . . . caused Lincoln to ask for a bodyguard.

   The knowledge that someone might try to assassinate him caused Lincoln to ask for a bodyguard.

2. "Lincoln is going to Ford's Theater tonight."
   . . . traveled fast.
3. Everybody knew Lincoln was going to the theater.
   . . . increased the danger.
4. The guard was an unreliable person.
   There was already . . .
5. Mrs. Lincoln might have been romantically involved with the guard.
   The courts never investigated him. (Combine the two sentences.)
   . . . may be . . .

11.3 Subjunctive Noun Clauses

"Write me every week."

	VERB	NOUN CLAUSE		
			BASE FORM	
Phil's mother	insisted insists will insist	(that) he	write	her every week.

"Don't go to the theater."

	VERB	NOUN CLAUSE		
			BASE FORM	
Some of Lincoln's friends It was	urged recommended	that he that a bodyguard	not go be	to the theater. assigned.

"You must be on time."

	ADJECTIVE	NOUN CLAUSE		
			BASE FORM	
It is	important	that you	be	on time.
It is	essential	that she	have	finished the work by the time the boss arrives.

	NOUN	NOUN CLAUSE	
Her	insistence	that he write her every week	annoyed him.

Form: Certain verbs, adjectives, and related nouns can be followed by a noun clause with the verb or first auxiliary in the *base form.* To form the negative, use **not** before the base form. (Modal auxiliaries and the auxiliary **do** do not occur in this type of clause.)

Notice that the main verb may be *past, present,* or *future.*

Meaning: The base form in a noun clause means that an action is *desirable.* We do not know whether or not it occurred or will occur. *Compare:*

It is important that he *goes* to school. (He goes, and this fact is important.)

It is important that he *go* to school. (He should go, but we don't know if he will or not.)

Vocabulary: The following verbs can be followed by subjunctive noun clauses.

advise	direct	propose
arrange	forbid	recommend
ask	insist	request
beg	intend	require
demand	order	suggest
desire	prefer	urge

Note: We can also use a verb phrase with **should** after some of these verbs (especially **recommend** and **suggest**) with approximately the same meaning as the base form.

They recommended that he should not go to the theater.

Exercise 3. Subjunctive Noun Clauses after Verbs

During the late 1960s and early 1970s, student protests were widespread in the United States. The issues which concerned

the students included local and national political issues as well as university policies. The following is an account of a protest which took place at Columbia University in 1968.

A. Early in the spring, a group of radical students sent a list of demands to the president of the university. What did the students demand? Tell the story, using subjunctive noun clauses. In some cases, either an active or a passive clause is possible.

1. "Do not participate in military research."

   The students demanded that the university not participate in military research.

2. "Stop buying land in the neighborhood."
3. "Give students more voice in university affairs."
   a. *active:*
   b. *passive:* **They demanded that students . . .**
4. (The president did not accept their demands, and so they marched to his office.)
   "The president must meet with us."

B. When the president refused, the students occupied a classroom building and kept everyone else out. Continue, using the words in parentheses.

5. (president/request) "Leave the building peacefully."
6. (students/insist) "Accept our demands first."
   a. *active:*
   b. *passive:*

Exercise 4. Subjunctive Noun Clauses after Verbs and Adjectives

The protest spread, and soon students had occupied five buildings, including the president's office. The faculty and trustees met to advise the president, but they did not all agree. Some of them were conservative and others were liberal in their opinions.

What did the liberals recommend? What did they say was important? What did the conservatives recommend? Use these verbs and adjectives:

recommend	essential
request	important
suggest	urgent
urge	

1. "Call the police immediately."

   The conservatives recommended that he call the police immediately.

   or: **The conservatives recommended that the police be called immediately.**

   or: **The conservatives said it was essential that . . .**

2. "Don't call the police."
3. "Try to negotiate with the students first."
4. "Don't negotiate until the students leave the buildings."
5. "Appoint some of us as mediators."
6. "Try to find a compromise."
7. "Get the students out of the buildings immediately."
8. "There should be no violence."
9. When the police were finally called in, they said to the president, "For your own safety, don't come on campus while we are clearing the buildings." What did the police request?
10. "Don't punish the students."

    After the police had cleared the buildings and arrested many students, the liberals . . .

Exercise 5. *It* + a Passive Main Verb

The liberal faculty sent a memorandum to the president with their recommendations. What was recommended in the memorandum? Use the information in Exercise 4.

1. **It was recommended that the president not call the police.**

   or: **It was recommended that the police not be called.**

Exercise 6. Subjunctive Noun Clauses after Nouns

How did the president respond to the demands of the students and the advice of the faculty? Put the information below into complete sentences.

A. Student demands

	Accepted	Rejected
1. Do not participate in military research.		x

He rejected the students' demand that the university not participate in military research.

	Accepted	Rejected
2. Stop buying land in the neighborhood.		x
3. Give students more voice in university affairs.	x	
4. Meet with us.		x

B. Faculty advice (suggestions, recommendations, proposals)

5. Don't call the police.	x	

He accepted the advice of the liberal faculty that . . .

6. Try to negotiate first.	x	
7. Appoint some of us as mediators.	x	
8. Get the students out of the buildings immediately.		x

Transfer Exercises

1. Advice from Classmates

A. Working in groups of three or four, talk about a problem that you have, real or imaginary. Another student in your group can give you advice, using one of these verbs or adjectives:

suggest	essential
recommend	important

Examples: a. **—My shoes don't fit.**
—I recommend that you get a new pair and throw those away. It's important that you have shoes that fit.

b. **—My husband never helps me with the housework.**
—I suggest . . .

c. **—My girlfriend likes rock and roll, but I like classical music.**
—I recommend . . .

B. Report to the class the advice that was given in your group.

Example: a. **Felicia said that her shoes don't fit.**
Cheng recommended that she get a new pair of shoes and throw the old ones away. He said it's important that she have shoes that fit.

2. Advice on Leaving Home

What advice or suggestions did your family, friends, or teachers give you before you left your country to come here? Use a noun clause in your sentences.

Example: **My parents recommended that I live in the college dormitory.**

3. Customs

If you are studying abroad, give your reactions to some customs you have observed in this country. For example, do people speak fast? Do they dress informally? Do they eat strange things at strange times or in strange places? Do they do unusual things in their free time? If you are studying in your native country, give your reactions to customs that you have observed in foreign movies or television programs. Use **it** and some of these verbs and adjectives:

Verbs	*Adjectives*
annoy (me)	annoying
delight (me)	delightful, wonderful, nice
surprise (me)	surprising
upset (me)	upsetting
puzzle (me)	clear
	disappointing
	interesting
	sad
	strange, funny, odd, curious

Examples: **It surprises me that people eat in the street in the United States.**

It's nice that there are no-smoking sections in restaurants.

4. Facts and Opinions

Fit the sentences on the right into the sentences on the left. (There are a number of ways to do it.) Then think of another example of your own for each numbered sentence.

1. The idea that . . . is ridiculous

    Example: **The idea that the moon is made of green cheese is ridiculous.**

2. The belief that . . . is
   old-fashioned.
   widespread.
3. The possibility that . . . is
   frightening.
   encouraging.
4. My conviction that . . . is the reason I (came here)
5. The news that . . .
   upset me
   cheered me up
   (last night).

a. The Red Sox won the baseball game.
b. The number 13 is unlucky.
c. I can learn a lot here.
d. The moon is made of green cheese.
e. Women shouldn't work outside the home.
f. Nuclear war might destroy the world.

5. Prepositions

Fill in the correct preposition according to the preceding word. These combinations occur in this lesson.

1. If you give Bobby a nickel, he'll ask ______ a quarter.
2. Do you always participate ______ class discussion?
3. The two defendants are being tried ______ attempting to rob a bank.
4. If our class takes a class trip, I want to have a voice ______ deciding where we go.
5. This exercise consists ______ five sentences.

Discussion Topics

A. Have you seen or heard about a campus protest? If so, describe it. Where did it take place? Did the students occupy buildings? Were the police called in? Were classes canceled? How long did the protest last, and how did it end? What were the students' demands? Were they accepted or rejected by the administration? Did the faculty act as mediators?

(*Optional:* What is your opinion about the protest that you have described? Do you feel that the students' demands were justified? Do you agree with their actions? Did the administration handle the situation well, in your opinion, or should they have responded differently?)

B. Are student protests common in your country? If so, what are the issues that come up most often? How are the protests usually handled?

C. Has there ever been an important political assassination in the history of your country? If so, what facts are known about it? Are there unexplained aspects (that is, is there anything that is not clear about how it happened)?

Composition Topics

Write a short composition about one of the following topics. Use noun clauses in some of your sentences.

1. Write about your reactions to some customs that you have observed in a foreign country you have visited or in foreign movies and television programs. (See Transfer Exercise 3.)
2. Write about the advice that you received when you left home to go to the university or to travel to another country. What did your parents, teachers, or friends suggest or recommend?
3. Write about a campus protest. (See Discussion Topic A.)
4. Write about an assassination. First, give the facts, as far as you know them. Then discuss any questions about what happened which haven't been answered yet. (See Discussion Topic C.)

UNIT VI

VERBALS

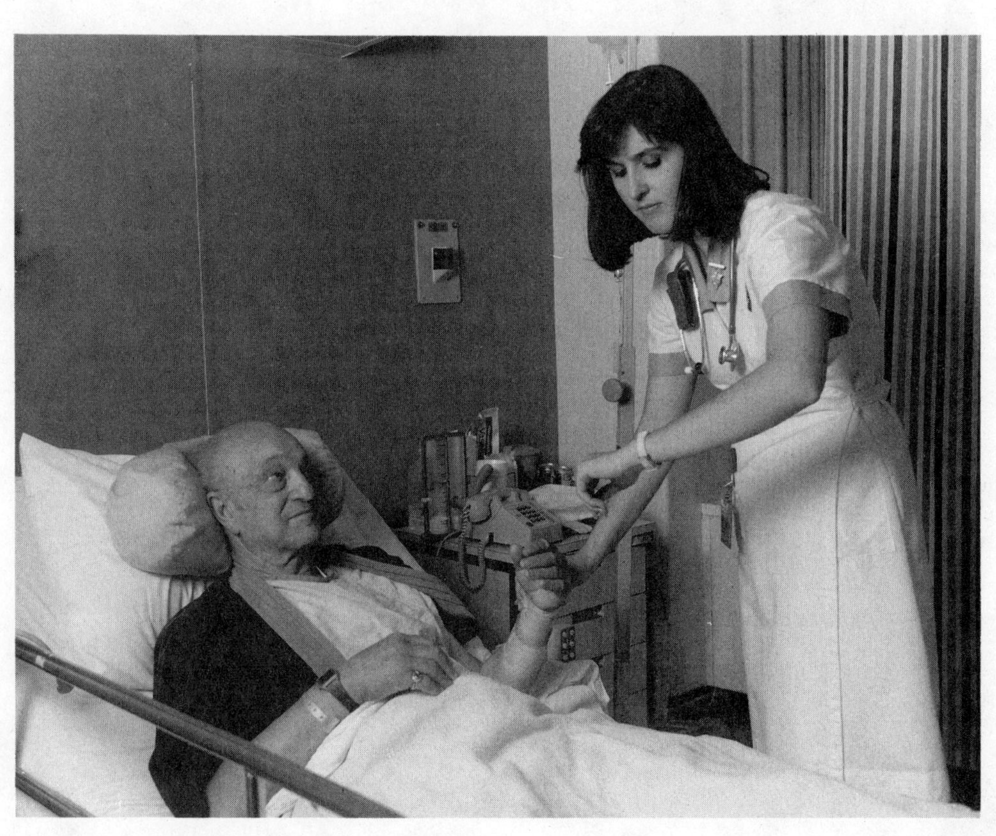

Lesson 12

Training and Working in the Health Professions

12.1 Infinitives and Gerunds as Verb Complements

Infinitives

SIMPLE INFINITIVE

Active

NEGATIVE	TO	BASE FORM
	to	eat
not	to	drive

Passive

NEGATIVE	TO	BE	PAST PARTICIPLE
	to	be	eaten
not	to	be	driven

	VERB	INFINITIVE PHRASE
Robert	decided	to speak English with his roommate.
He	decided	not to speak his native language at all.
Arthur	expected	to be elected president.

PROGRESSIVE INFINITIVE

NEGATIVE	TO	BE	VERB + ING
(not)	to	be	eating

(no passive)

Sarah	intended	to be waiting at the bus stop when the bus came.

Form: The infinitive consists of **to** plus the *base form*. In the passive, the base form **be** is followed by the past participle. In the progressive, the base form **be** is followed by the **-ing** form of the verb.

Function: An infinitive completes the meaning of the verb it follows. It may replace a direct object, an adjective complement, or a prepositional phrase.

Direct object:

The mayor demanded *an answer.*
The mayor demanded *to know the answer.*

Adjective complement:

The boy appeared *tired.*
The boy appeared *to have the flu.*

Prepositional phrase:

Susan hoped *for a miracle.*
Susan hoped *to go to Paris.*

Some verbs always have an infinitive phrase as complement:

Joe endeavored *to please his boss.*

Vocabulary: The following verbs can be followed by infinitives. See Appendix 5 for a longer list.

List A

(can) afford	choose	expect	plan
agree	decide	fail	pretend
appear	demand	hope	refuse
apply	deserve	long	resolve
attempt	endeavor	neglect	struggle

Gerunds

Active

NEGATIVE	VERB + ING
not	speaking eating

Passive

NEGATIVE	BEING	PAST PARTICIPLE
not	being being	spoken eaten

	VERB	GERUND PHRASE	
Robert	stopped	speaking French with his roommate.	
During vacation, I	enjoy	not having to get up early.	
The diver narrowly	escaped	being drowned	when his equipment failed.

Form: The gerund is the **-ing** form of the verb. The passive gerund is **being** + the *past participle.*

Function: The gerund generally functions as a noun, except in certain idioms. (*Note:* When it functions as an adjective or as part of a verb phrase, the **-ing** form of the verb is called a present participle.)

Vocabulary: The following verbs can be followed by the gerund. You will need to memorize this list. For a more complete list, see Appendix 6.

List B

appreciate	dislike	imagine	recommend
avoid	enjoy	include	resent
consider	finish	involve	risk
deny	give up	(don't) mind	suggest
discuss	(can't) help	recall	

Exercise 1. Infinitives (oral or written)

Complete each sentence with an infinitive phrase.

1. When I enrolled in this course, I resolved . . . **to do my best.**
2. Since the beginning of the term, I have attempted . . .

3. My roommate and I have agreed . . .
4. My roommate doesn't have a scholarship, so (he/she) can't afford . . .
5. In fact, (he/she) is struggling . . .
6. Sometimes I get really tired of studying and long* . . .
7. During the next break, I have decided . . .
8. When this course is over, I expect . . .
9. I plan . . .

Exercise 2. Gerunds (oral or written)

Last night, my best friend and I discussed our vacation plans.

Complete each sentence with a gerund phrase.

1. We are considering . . . **going to Florida.**
2. We'd like to go there because both of us enjoy . . .
3. However, Florida is a long way from here, and my friend doesn't like to fly. Whenever (he/she) can, (he/she) avoids . . .
4. There are other ways to get there besides flying. We discussed . . .
5. Another friend of ours recommended . . .
6. We finally decided to rent a car and drive nonstop. Each of us will sleep while the other drives. I don't mind . . .
7. My friend is glad that our trip will not involve . . .
8. It was late at night by the time we finished . . .

Exercise 3. Choosing the Infinitive or the Gerund (active)

Fill in the active form of the infinitive or the gerund. Use the progressive infinitive where indicated.

Hospitals in the United States have been experiencing a severe shortage of nurses in recent years. Why is this? For one thing, now that* more professions are open to women, fewer women are choosing

**Long:* want very much.
**Now that:* because now.

(1) to enter the nursing field. Moreover, because salaries are
(enter)
still relatively low, the profession fails (2) __________ many men.
(attract)
The number of high school graduates who apply (3) __________
(enter)
nursing school has dropped so sharply that some nursing schools have closed.

Another reason for the shortage is that more and more nurses are quitting hospital jobs and moving to jobs which offer better working conditions and which don't involve (4) working nights. The
(work)
result is even more difficult working conditions for those who remain.

Karen Doyle, for example, works in a large city hospital. She enjoys (5) __________ for the sick and does not even mind
(care)
(6) __________ on the night shift, but because her unit is so under-
(work)
staffed, she must constantly struggle (7) __________ up with the
(keep)
work. As soon as she finishes (8) __________ one patient his medi-
(give)
cation, she must rush to the next task. But if she neglects
(9) __________ a medication on time, she risks (10) __________ the
(give) (harm)
patient. For the same reason, she agrees (11) __________ overtime
(work)
several days a week: the patients must be cared for. A nurse's duties have always included (12) __________ patients sympathy and sup-
(give)
port, but Karen has had to give up (13) __________ down and
(sit)
(14) __________ to a patient for a few minutes because there just
(talk)
isn't time. "I don't see how I can avoid (15) __________ a mere tech-
(become)
nician** if I stay here," she said in a recent interview. "But talking to patients and caring about them is an important part of my job. I can't imagine (16) __________ on this job for very long." In fact,
(stay)
Karen has resolved (17) __________ as soon as possible and is con-
(quit)
sidering (18) __________ to medical school school next year. A career
(apply)
as a doctor has a number of advantages. "Five years from now

***A mere technician:* just a technician.

I hope (19) ______________ more money and
(*progressive:* make)
(20) ______________ more reasonable hours," she says.
(*progressive:* work)

To deal with the nursing shortage, some hospitals are planning (21) __________ salaries in order to attract more job applicants.
(raise)
Others, however, say they cannot afford (22) __________ their
(pay)
nurses more because federal regulations have limited their income. Money alone is not enough, according to the director of the National League of Nursing. She recommends (23) __________ nurses more
(give)
responsibility, status, and autonomy*** as well. In addition, many hospitals are endeavoring (24) __________ nurses from other coun-
(recruit)
tries.

Nevertheless, the nursing shortage appears (25) ______________ worse. The U.S. Department of Health
(*progressive:* get)
predicts that by the year 2000, the United States will have only about half the registered nurses that it needs.

Exercise 4. Active and Passive Infinitives and Gerunds

How does Karen feel about conditions in her hospital? Rewrite each sentence to include the verb in parentheses and a gerund or infinitive. In most cases, you will need the passive form of the gerund or infinitive, but in a few cases the active form is needed.

1. Karen's hospital gives nurses a lot of responsibility. (enjoy)

   Karen enjoys being given a lot of responsibility.*

2. However, they assign too many patients to each nurse. (dislike)

   However, she . . .

3. Moreover, they assign them jobs that are not really nurses' work (such as secretarial duties). (resent)
4. Karen has to work overtime a lot. (can't refuse)
5. She is tired a lot of the time. (can't help)

****Autonomy:* freedom to make decisions.

*In this sentence, the indirect object (*Karen* or *nurses*) is made the subject of the passive gerund. The direct object, *a lot of responsibility,* remains at the end.

6. She gets irritable when she is tired. (not, deny)
7. The head nurse occasionally criticizes her. (not, enjoy)
8. But more often the doctors and patients praise her for her outstanding work and conscientious attitude. (appreciate)

    She . . .

9. The hospital will promote her if she continues to do a good job. (hope)
10. She will receive more pay if she is promoted. (can expect)
11. Karen's work exposes her to infectious diseases. (not, mind)
12. She knows she won't be infected if she is careful. (can avoid)
13. Sometimes nurses are careless. (can't afford)
14. Carelessness might injure or even kill a patient. (risk)

    If Karen is careless, . . .

15. The patient's family might sue** a careless nurse. (risk)
16. The hospital might fire such a nurse. (deserve)

    In Karen's opinion, . . .

Exercise 5. Negative Infinitives and Gerunds

A. Complete each sentence with a negative infinitive phrase or a negative gerund phrase. There may be several ways to complete a sentence.

1. Karen attempts not to become irritable even when she is tired.
   or: not to make mistakes
2. She pretends ______________ when the head nurse criticizes her.
3. She doesn't mind ______________ time to sit down and relax on the job, but she resents ______________ to talk with patients.
4. On days off, she enjoys ______________ early.
5. Karen has decided ______________ in the field of nursing.
6. She is engaged, but her doctor friends recommend ______________ children until after she finishes medical school.

***Sue:* take someone to court.

7. In fact, she has resolved ________________ married until she has been accepted to a medical school and knows where she will be living.

B. Complete these sentences about yourself, using negative infinitives and gerunds.

8. On Sunday morning, I enjoy . . .
9. I considered . . . this morning, but then I changed my mind.
10. My classmates and I suggest . . .
11. When I do my homework, I always endeavor . . .
12. My teachers recommend . . . on the night before an exam.
13. I have decided . . .
14. I recall . . . when I first came to this country (or to this school). Now things are much better.
15. The other students from my country and I have discussed . . .
16. We have agreed . . .

12.2 Infinitive Subjects

Active Main Verb

		INFINITIVE PHRASE			
	MAIN VERB	FOR	INFINITIVE SUBJECT	INFINITIVE	
The teacher	permitted		John	to leave	the room.
The doctor	urged		his patient	not to overwork.	
You	can't force		yourself	to like	something.
That firm	requires		its employees	to be vaccinated	against rabies.
The teacher	arranged	for	John	to take	a makeup test.

Vocabulary: An *infinitive subject* must precede the infinitive after the following verbs. With these verbs, a reflexive pronoun (**myself, yourself, himself, herself, itself, ourselves, yourselves, themselves**) is used whenever the subject of the verb and the subject of the infinitive are the same. Appendix 5 gives more verbs of this type.

List C (must have an infinitive subject)

advise[G, *]	force	persuade
allow[G]	hire	recruit
assign	instruct	require
authorize	motivate	schedule
compel	oblige	tempt
enable	order	urge
encourage[G]	permit[G]	warn
forbid[G]		

After the following verbs, an infinitive subject is used when the subject of the verb and the subject of the infinitive are different.

I asked him to go. (*He* will go.)

When the two subjects are the same, no infinitive subject is used.

I asked to go. (*I* will go.)

List D (may have an infinitive subject)

ask	like[H]	get[J]
beg	prepare	need[J]
choose[F, *]	train	dare**
expect	want	help**

After the following verbs, we use **for** before the infinitive subject. When the subject of the verb and the subject of the infinitive are the same, no infinitive subject is used.

List E (**for** + infinitive subject)

arrange	mean (= intend)[J]
would hate	wait
intend[F, *]	

Passive Main Verb

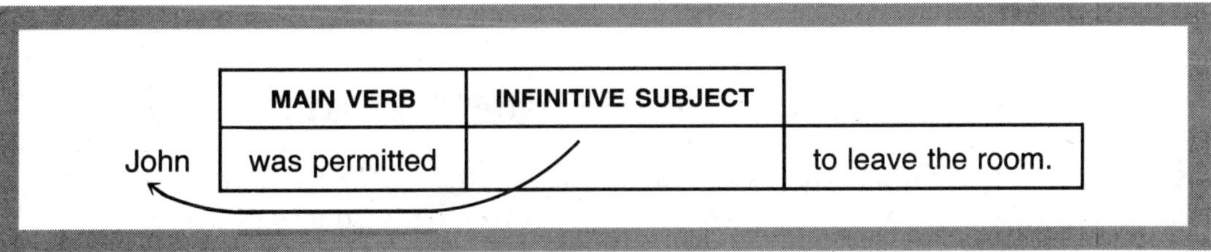

MAIN VERB
INFINITIVE SUBJECT
John
was permitted
to leave the room.

*A letter after a verb indicates that the verb also appears on that list.
**See also Lesson 15.

Form: An infinitive subject may become the subject of a passive main verb.

Exercise 6. Infinitive Subjects in Indirect Speech

Complete each sentence by including the relevant information from the preceding quotation.

1. "The hours here are long, the pay is low, and the working conditions are not good. I'd like to become a doctor." Karen's frustration with her job is motivating her to become a doctor.
2. "As a nurse, I can't make diagnoses, prescribe medicine, or decide on treatment plans." An M.D. degree will enable . . .
3. "As a nurse, I can't set up a private practice." The M.D. degree will also allow . . .
4. "It's a good idea to apply to medical school." Karen's friends are encouraging . . .
5. "You'd better apply to several schools because there's a lot of competition." Her friends who are doctors have advised . . .
6. "Going to medical school and bringing up a child at the same time was really hard for me. If possible, don't have kids* until after you graduate." One doctor, who is also a mother, warned . . .
7. "A baby-sitter came every morning." She said she had to arrange . . .
8. "Sometimes I was late to class because I couldn't leave until the baby-sitter came." Before she could leave, she had to wait . . .
9. "I hope you'll go to the medical school here in town." Karen's fiancé wants . . . the local medical school. He would hate . . . in a distant city.
10. "Please don't apply to schools that are too far away." He has begged . . .
11. "All right, I won't." He has persuaded . . .

Exercise 7. Infinitives after a Passive Main Verb

Becoming a doctor is not easy. Besides going to medical school, Karen will have to do a year of internship in a hospital.

Change the underlined main verb to the passive. Omit the **by** phrase.

Kids:* Use the word **children in your paraphrase. "Kids" is used in informal conversation only.

1. The American system of training doctors requires every new doctor to work in a hospital as an intern for one year after he or she graduates from medical school.

   Every new doctor is required to work in a hospital as an intern for one year after he or she graduates from medical school.

2. The hospital administration expects interns to work about 120 hours a week.
3. It schedules each intern to be "on call" every other night.
4. When an intern is on call, the administration obliges him or her to spend the night at the hospital.
5. The regulations permit interns to sleep a few hours at the hospital when and *if* they can find the time.
6. People expect them to be alert even after a sleepless night.
7. The courses in medical school have trained the new doctor to handle many different situations.
8. Furthermore, the administration encourages him or her to get help from more experienced doctors when necessary.
9. Nevertheless, situations which arise often force the intern to make life-and-death decisions before he or she feels ready.
10. Some interns feel the hospitals should not require them to make these important decisions when they are so tired and under such stress.
11. The hospital may assign medical students to help the interns.
12. The law does not authorize the medical students to make decisions on the treatment of patients.
13. Their rules instruct them to do what the interns and other doctors ask.
14. In some cases, however, an intern has asked a medical student to perform tasks which should only be done by a doctor.
15. Both medical students and interns are new and inexperienced. Their awareness of their own inexperience will tempt them to blame themselves if anything goes wrong.

Exercise 8. Infinitives after a Passive Main Verb (oral or written)

Below are some facts about another kind of problem that doctors face. Give an opinion or suggestion about each one. If you don't have a strong opinion, you can begin "Perhaps . . ."

You will need some of these verbs:

allow	forbid	permit
compel	instruct	require
encourage	order	urge

1. If a doctor makes a serious mistake, a patient can sue for millions of dollars.

   Examples: **Patients must be allowed to sue.**
   or: **Patients cannot be forbidden to sue.**
   or: **Perhaps patients shouldn't be allowed to sue for so much money.**

2. Doctors have to pay a lot, sometimes $50,000 a year, for malpractice insurance.*
3. (In some states, doctors' fees are controlled.) They cannot charge what they want for their services.
4. Sometimes doctors have gone on strike because of the insurance rates.
5. They have refused to see emergency patients (for fear of suits against them).
6. Because of the strikes, hospitals have sometimes closed their emergency wards.

12.3 Verbs Followed by Either the Infinitive or the Gerund

Same Meaning

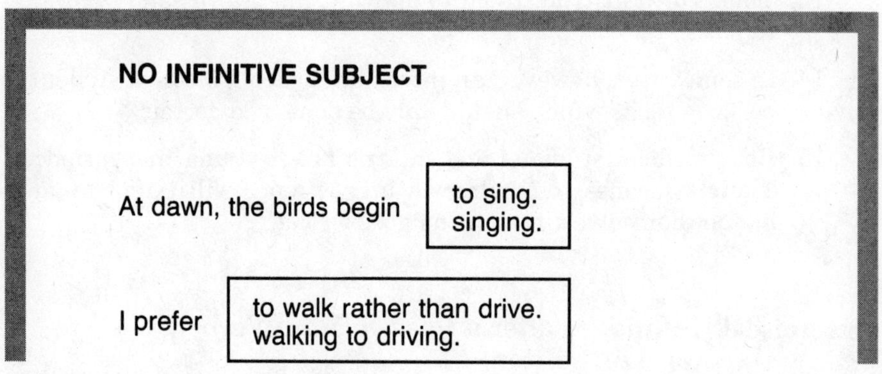

NO INFINITIVE SUBJECT
At dawn, the birds begin
to sing.
singing.
I prefer
to walk rather than drive.
walking to driving.

**Malpractice insurance:* insurance which protects a doctor when a patient sues.

INFINITIVE SUBJECT REQUIRED

I don't advise	you to walk walking	in the park after dark.

Vocabulary: The following verbs may take either an infinitive or a gerund with no change in meaning. Notice that **prefer** takes a different complement after the gerund and after the infinitive.

List F

	(The passive gerund is rare.)	*(The gerund is rare.)*
(can't) bear	begin	attempt
prefer	cease	choose*
(can't) stand	continue	intend
	start	

When a gerund is used with the following verbs, the subject of the main verb is not the subject of the gerund.
Compare:

I enjoy walking. (Meaning: *I walk.* List B)
I advise walking. (Meaning: *Someone else might walk.* List G)

List G

advise	forbid
allow	permit
encourage	

Choose* may or may not have an infinitive subject. **He chose (me) to go.

Different Meanings:

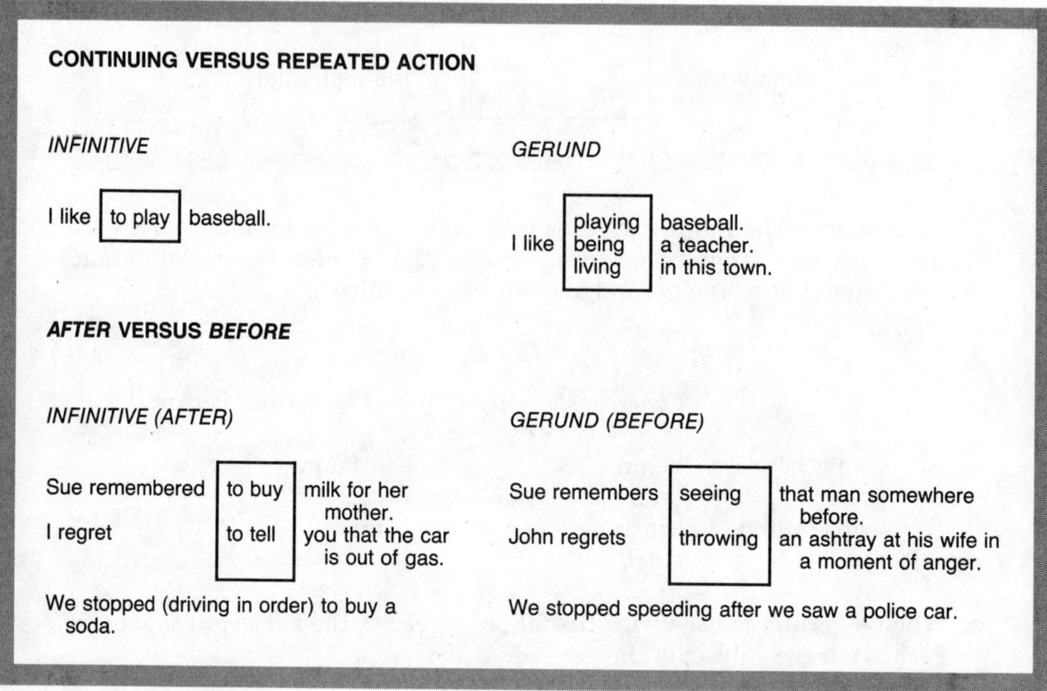

CONTINUING VERSUS REPEATED ACTION

INFINITIVE	*GERUND*
I like **to play** baseball.	I like **playing** baseball. / I like **being** a teacher. / I like **living** in this town.

AFTER* VERSUS *BEFORE

INFINITIVE (AFTER)	*GERUND (BEFORE)*
Sue remembered **to buy** milk for her mother.	Sue remembers **seeing** that man somewhere before.
I regret **to tell** you that the car is out of gas.	John regrets **throwing** an ashtray at his wife in a moment of anger.
We stopped (driving in order) to buy a soda.	We stopped speeding after we saw a police car.

Meaning: After **like, love,** and **hate,** the infinitive is used only for repeated action. The gerund is used for continuing situations or states (as well as for action).

List H

hate
like
love

After **forget, remember, regret,** and **stop,** an infinitive describes an event that happens *after* the action of the main verb. A gerund describes an event that happened *before*. Notice that with **stop,** there is always an earlier action that must be stopped, but sometimes it is not stated.

List I

forget	remember
regret	stop

Different Meanings: Miscellaneous

INFINITIVE	GERUND
I *meant to leave* a tip, but I forgot. (mean = *intend*)	100 years ago, going to school often *meant walking* ten miles or more. (mean = *involve, require*)
John *proposes to eat* that whole chicken. (propose = *plan*)	The chairman *proposed building* a new wing. (propose = *suggest*)
We *tried to open* the window, but we couldn't. It was stuck. (try = *make an effort*)	We *tried opening* a window, but the room was still very hot. (try = *experiment*)
We all *helped (to) move* the furniture. We all *helped Maria (to) learn* English.	Maria is a beginner, so she *can't help making* mistakes. (can't help = *can't prevent (herself) from*)
We *got to see* the President. (get = *succeed, with luck or permission*)	We *got going* at ten o'clock. (get going = *start*)
We *got Dad to take* us to Washington. (get = *persuade or cause*)	The mechanic *got the car going.* (get = *succeed in starting*)
John *went to look* for some chalk.	Sandra *went* {*swimming.* / *shopping.*} (a)
I *need to wash* the floor. I *need you to help* me. The floor *needs to be washed.* =	The floor *needs washing.* (b)

Meaning: a. An infinitive after **go** indicates purpose. Gerunds after **go** refer to active sports done outside the home. (We also go shopping and dancing.)

b. After **need,** the gerund is passive in meaning and usually refers to cleaning or fixing something.

List J

get
go
help
mean
need
propose
try

Exercise 9. Choosing the Infinitive or the Gerund

Fill in the infinitive or gerund form of an appropriate verb from the list.

add
√apply
argue
be
buy
camp
do
get
go
iron
mail
move
read
receive
sunbathe
work

1. When Tom spoke to his advisor, she encouraged him ___to apply___ to graduate school.
2. They don't allow __________ in that park.
3. Karen really likes __________ a nurse, but she doesn't like __________ overtime.
4. Sometimes she can't help __________ irritable.
5. Karen will probably go to medical school even if it means __________ to another city.
6. Could you boys please stop __________ and be nice to each other for a change?
7. When we drove to Chicago, we stopped three times __________ gas.
8. Olivia says she sent me a postcard from Paris, but I don't remember __________ it. Perhaps she forgot __________ it.
9. Tom meant __________ his homework last night, but when his girlfriend proposed __________ to a movie together, he couldn't say no.
10. What a lot of books you are carrying! Do you propose __________ them all?
11. —This stew doesn't taste very good, does it?
    —Try __________ a little salt. That should help.
12. I can't wear this jacket. It needs __________ .
13. —Where's Arthur?
    —He went __________ a cup of coffee.
14. —Where's Andrea?
    —She went __________ with some friends this weekend.

Exercise 10. Summary Exercise

Fill in the correct form (active or passive) of the verb in parentheses.

Hospitals are trying ___to cope___ (cope) with the shortage of registered nurses in several ways. In many hospitals, temporary nurses ___are being hired___ (hire) __________ (fill) the vacancies, but this means that staff nurses __________ (oblige)

__________ (spend) time orienting these temporaries to hospital procedures. Many hospitals have also considered (consider) __________ (recruit) nurses __________ (come) to the United States from other countries, and nurses aides can __________ (train) __________ (help) with the easier nursing tasks. In some cases, however, hospitals have __________ (force) __________ (close) beds because of the shortage of nurses.

For a long-term solution, we must somehow __________ (encourage) more young people __________ (become) nurses. Concerned congressmen have __________ (propose) __________ (increase) federal funds for nurses' training. Others advise __________ (give) more responsibility, status, and autonomy to nurses in order to attract more young people into the profession. And most observers expect salaries __________ (raise) in the next contract negotiations. Nevertheless, these observers predict that the shortage will continue __________ (worsen), and at some point the quality of hospital care will begin __________ (affect).

Transfer Exercises

1. Jobs

Ask a classmate about a job that he or she had in the past, a present job, or his or her future career.

First ask this question: What job do you want to talk about?

Answer: **I worked in a pizza shop once. I think I'll talk about that.**

or: **I'm going to be a civil engineer. I'd like to talk about that.**

Now continue:

1. enjoy

   What {did / do / will} you enjoy doing on your job?

   I enjoyed meeting a lot of people there.

   ***or:* I think I will enjoy designing bridges and highways.**

2. dislike
3. refuse
4. avoid
5. consider
6. never forget
7. encourage students (or trainees)
8. endeavor
9. hope
10. (not) mind
11. (never) regret
12. decide (when)
13. request
14. hire
15. oblige
16. (If time permits, ask questions with other verbs from the lists in this lesson.)

2. Giving Advice

Form groups of five to eight students; then follow steps A and B for one or more of the situations outlined below.

A. Role play the situation. One student (one or two in Situation 1) can play the role of the person who has a problem. Describe the problem, including some details. The other students give advice to the person with a problem. Each student in the group should try to give some advice or make a suggestion. You may have to ask some questions in order to give good advice.

Situation 1: A married couple have been quarreling a lot recently. They have come to you to try to save their marriage. Find out what the problems are. Then give the couple advice.

Examples: **You ought to help with the housework sometimes.**
You could buy an electric dishwasher.
Why don't you . . .

Situation 2: A friend tells you that he or she has fallen in love with someone that he or she has just met at a party. Your friend is shy and doesn't know how to approach the other person. Give your friend some suggestions or advice.

Situation 3: Does someone in your group have a problem that he or she would like to discuss? For example, do you have a problem with your roommate or with your studies? Do you wonder how to make friends with American students or how to act in a particular social situation? Describe your problem to the group and ask for advice.

B. Report to the class what happened in your counseling session. Use some of these verbs:

About the Counselors	*About the Person with a Problem*
advised	agreed
encouraged	will consider
tried to persuade	has decided
recommended	hopes
suggested	plans
urged	refuses
wanted	will stop
warned	

Examples: **Jun advised Robert to help with the housework.**
Robert agreed to help sometimes.

Discussion Topics

A. Are there enough hospitals in your country? Are the hospitals mainly in the big cities, or are there hospitals for people in the country also? Are the hospitals well equipped? Are there enough nurses and doctors?

B. In your country, are most nurses men or women? Are nurses well paid? Do they work under difficult conditions?

C. Are doctors' fees high in your country? Are they paid by the government? In your opinion, what are the advantages of a national health care system (a system in which the government pays for health care)? What are the disadvantages? Do the advantages outweigh the disadvantages, or are the disadvantages more important?

D. In your country, do patients sue doctors for malpractice (medical mistakes)? If so, does this create problems in your health care system? Do these suits help to protect the public, in your opinion, or do they hurt the public?

Composition Topics

Using infinitives and gerunds in some of your sentences, write a short composition on one of the following topics.

1. Write a description of your job. Use Exercises 3, 4, 5, and 7 for some ideas.
2. Write about the training required for your present or future job.
3. Write about some difficult or interesting experiences you have had on your job. For example, you could write about your first week on the job.
4. Write a report on the discussion that you had in Transfer Exercise 2. Choose only one problem to report on. You may wish to review Lessons 10 and 11 (indirect statements and questions) before writing your report.
5. In the United States, people sometimes write to a newspaper columnist for advice. The answers to their letters are printed in the column. One popular advice column is called "Dear Abby." Write a letter to Abby about a real or imaginary problem that you have. Then exchange letters with a classmate. Answer your classmate's letter with your best advice on his or her problem.

Letter form:

10 Juniper Street
Smithtown, Ohio
July 18, 1989

Dear Abby,

My roommate is a nice person and is usually very considerate, but ______________________________
____
____

Yours sincerely,

Troubled
Troubled

6. Write about the health care system in your country, or about one aspect of that system. Example topics: the training of doctors or nurses, working conditions in hospitals, problems in the health care system.

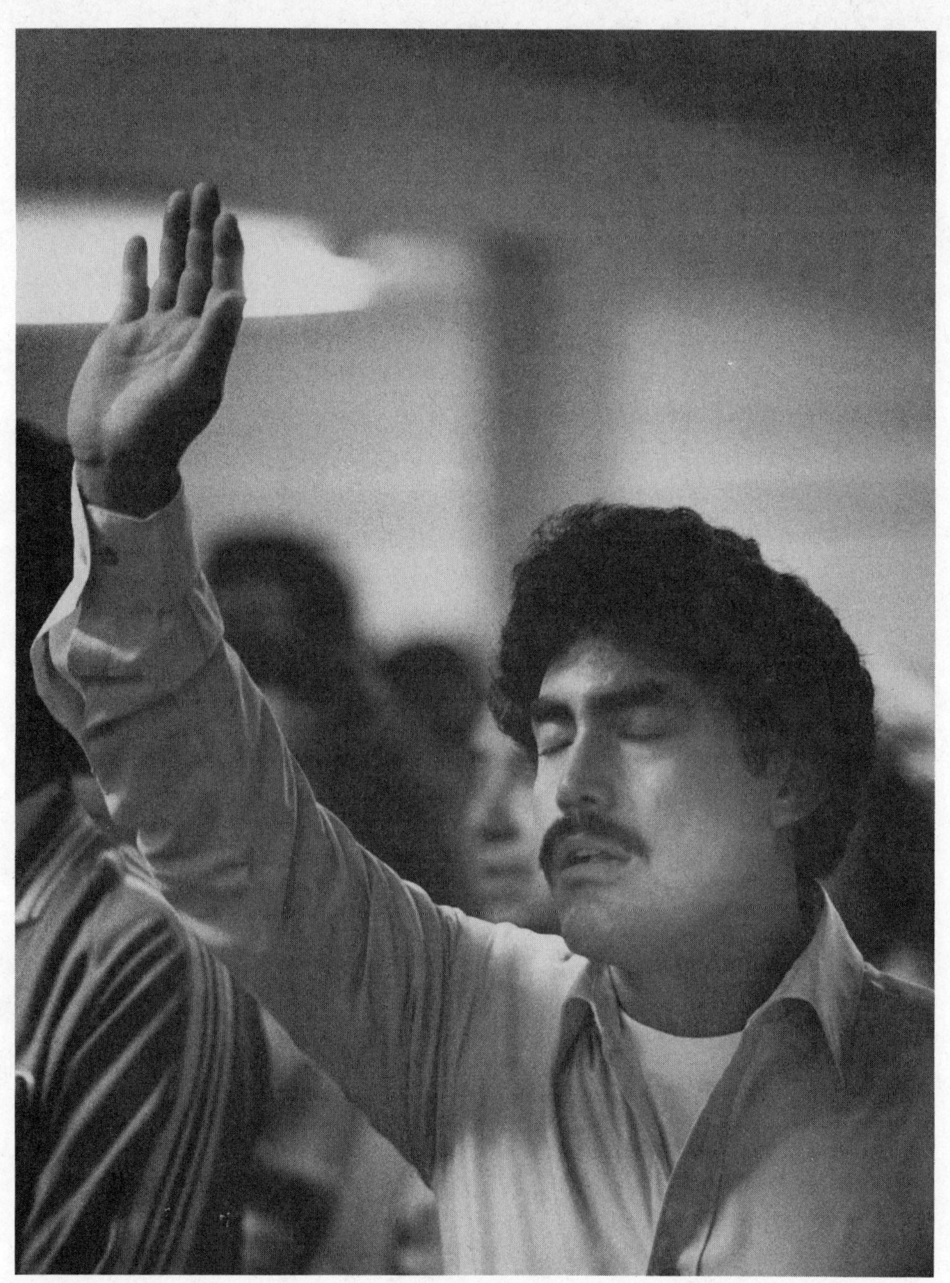

Lesson 13

Ancient Forms of Healing

13.1 Infinitives and Gerunds after *be*

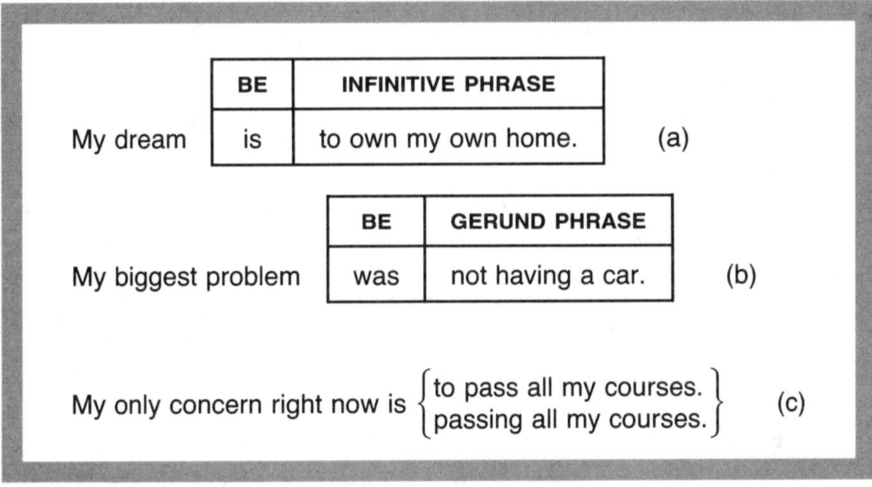

	BE	INFINITIVE PHRASE	
My dream	is	to own my own home.	(a)

	BE	GERUND PHRASE	
My biggest problem	was	not having a car.	(b)

My only concern right now is {to pass all my courses. / passing all my courses.} (c)

Meaning: An *infinitive* or *gerund* after **be** describes the subject.

a. To describe a purpose or future action, an infinitive is generally used.

b. To describe an ongoing situation, use a gerund.

c. In many cases, either an infinitive or a gerund may be used.

Note: In formal English, infinitives also occur after **be** to indicate a plan, regulation, or order which the subject will carry out. In this usage, **not** is not contracted.

Students are not to bring food into the library.
These reference books are to be used here.
They are not to be taken from this room.

Exercise 1. Infinitives after *be* (oral or written)

Complete each sentence with an infinitive phrase.

Example: **My ambition is to get a Ph.D. degree and become well known in my field.**

1. My ambition is . . .
2. Another dream of mine is . . .
3. Right now my main responsibility is . . .
4. The most important goal of a university education is . . .
5. The first duty of a teacher is . . .
6. A student's hope is usually . . .
7. After a student graduates from medical school, the next step is . . .
8. A doctor's first responsibility is . . .
9. A current problem in the field of medicine is . . .
10. The biggest challenge to my country's government in the next ten years will be . . .
11. The main job* of any government ought to be . . .
12. One way to achieve world peace would be . . .

Exercise 2. Gerunds after *be* (oral or written)

Complete each sentence with a gerund phrase.

Examples: When I moved to this town, my first problem was **not having any place to stay.** Therefore, my major concern was **finding a suitable apartment.**

1. When I first came to this (country/school),
   a. my biggest problem was . . .
   b. my major concern was . . .
   c. one big frustration was . . .
   d. the solution to that problem turned out to be . . .
   e. one mistake I made was . . .
2. As a child, one of my hobbies was . . .
3. My main job as a child was . . .
4. Right now, my favorite form of relaxation is . . .

**Job:* responsibility.

13.2 Infinitives Used as Modifiers

Modifies a Noun

	NOUN	INFINITIVE PHRASE
In our office, everybody has	a job	to do. (a)
We need	an expert	to do this job. (b)
We all need	something	to live for. (c)

Logical Relationships: An infinitive phrase may be connected to the noun which it modifies in several logical ways:

a. **Job** is the logical object of the infinitive. We *do a job.*

b. **Expert** is the logical subject of the infinitive. *The expert does* the job.

c. **Something** is the logical object of the preposition **for.** We live *for something.*

Modifies an Adjective

	ADJECTIVE	INFINITIVE PHRASE
Pierre is	eager	to learn English. (d)
This book is not	easy	to read. (e)
A house is	expensive	to take care of. (f)

Logical Relationships: An infinitive which modifies an adjective may have several logical connections to the noun which the adjective describes:

d. **Pierre** is the logical subject of the infinitive. *Pierre learns.*

e. **Book** is the logical object of the infinitive. We *read the book.*

f. **House** is the logical object of the preposition **of.** We take care *of the house.*

Modifies a Verb Phrase

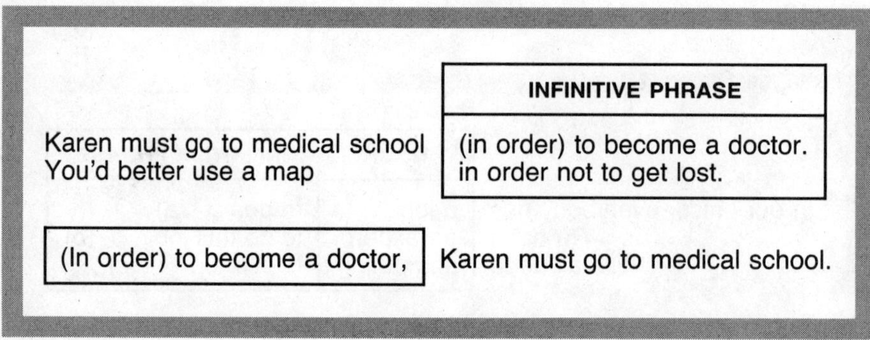

Meaning: Infinitives which modify the verb phrase express *purpose.* **In order to** is used before a negative infinitive. It may also be used for emphasis or to make the meaning clear.

Modifies a Sentence

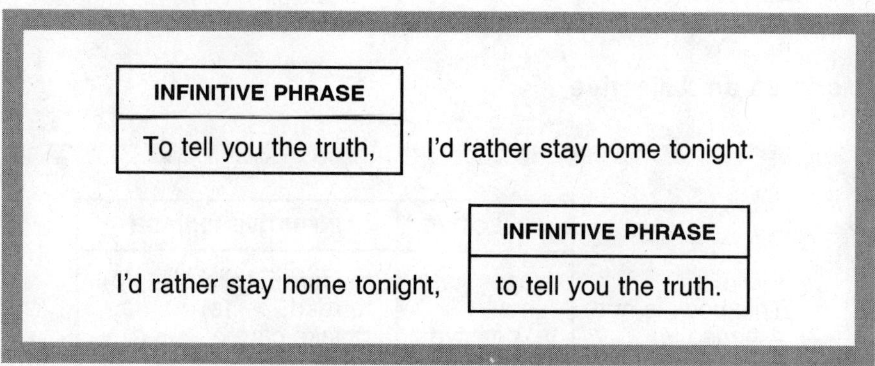

Function: **To tell you the truth** modifies the whole sentence which follows or precedes it. Logically, it means, "In order to tell you the truth, I am saying that I'd rather stay home."

Vocabulary: Other infinitive phrases used this way include

to put it in a nutshell (briefly)
to make a long story short
to put it politely
to be frank
to be honest

Exercise 3. Infinitives as Noun Modifiers

Combine each pair of sentences by reducing the second sentence to an infinitive phrase.

1. Modern medical research has given us some powerful medicines. We can take these medicines when we are sick.

   Modern medical research has given us some powerful medicines to take when we are sick.

2. We have antibiotics. These antibiotics cure infections.
3. There are tranquilizers. These reduce anxiety.
4. Vitamins can be obtained in any drugstore or supermarket. Vitamins give us energy and protect us against disease. (Place the infinitive phrase directly after the noun it modifies.)
5. We also have potent* anesthetics. They eliminate pain during operations.
6. However, people have not always had these "wonder drugs." They couldn't always turn to wonder drugs when they were sick.
7. Early cultures developed other ways. These ways could heal the sick.
8. Priest-doctors were the first people. These people treated the sick.
9. These shamans, medicine men and women, or witch doctors had several roles. They had to fulfill these roles.
10. The shaman had charms** and rituals. These protected people against black magic.
11. He or she had the power. With this power, he or she conducted dead souls to the next world. (Omit **with.**)
12. The shaman was also the person. He or she was consulted when someone was sick.
13. As an apprentice, the shaman learned the rituals. She or he used the rituals for each type of problem.
14. Shamans gathered herbs. They prescribed the herbs for various kinds of illness.
15. Some shamans even had a love potion, that is, a drink. The drink made someone fall in love.

**Potent:* powerful.
***Charm:* an object with magical power.

Exercise 4. Infinitives as Verb Phrase Modifiers

Change each sentence to include an infinitive phrase.

1. Ancient healers used herbs and spices when they treated illness.

   Ancient healers used herbs and spices (in order) to treat illness.

2. Shamans also used elaborate* rituals when they tried to cure the sick.
3. During the rituals, musicians played drums and other instruments because these called the spirits which helped the shaman.
4. The shaman danced to the music so that he or she could go into a trance.
5. The dance was performed around a fire at night, and an elaborate costume with mirrors was worn. This created a mysterious atmosphere.
6. Sometimes a headdress like the head of an animal was worn. This invoked the power** of that animal.
7. The shaman went into a trance and took possession of the soul or demon which had entered the sick person's body.

Another ancient form of medicine, which does not use magic or rituals, is the technique known as acupuncture. Acupuncture was developed in China more than 4,000 years ago.

8. An acupuncturist treats patients by inserting very fine needles into the body. This technique can relieve pain, restore hearing, induce sleep, and cure many kinds of illness.
9. The acupuncturist inserts the needles at various precise points on the body because this removes blocks in the flow of energy in the body.
10. In China today, acupuncturists also use a very weak electrical current because this increases the effect of the needles.
11. Doctors from western countries have gone to China because they were interested in studying acupuncture.

**Elaborate:* complicated.
***Invoke power:* obtain power through magic.

12. Nowadays there are many licensed practitioners in the west to whom you can go if you want to be treated with acupuncture.

Exercise 5. Infinitives as Adjective Modifiers and Sentence Modifiers

Complete each sentence with an infinitive phrase. Use these verbs, or others of your own, and any other words you need.

consult	learn	see
cure	perform	tell
hear	read (about)	treat

A. Shamanism

1. The subject of shamanism is fascinating to read about.
2. The rituals are complicated. They must be difficult . . .
3. Many people might be surprised ________ that voodoo and other forms of shamanism are practiced in New York City today.
4. Would people in your country be hesitant . . . ?
5. Would you yourself be willing . . . or would you be reluctant . . . ?
6. Sometimes herbs and spices are sufficient . . . , but many illnesses are more difficult . . .
7. . . . , I am interested in herbal medicine, but when I'm really sick, I go to a western doctor.

B. Acupuncture

8. Most people are relieved ________ that the slender acupuncture needles do not hurt much.
9. When western doctors first visited China, they were astonished . . .
10. Whatever the method of treatment, most patients are delighted . . .

13.3 Infinitive Phrases with *too* and *enough*

Too

The child shouldn't go out alone.

	TOO	QUANTIFIER	ADJECTIVE	NOUN	INFINITIVE PHRASE	
					INFINITIVE SUBJECT	
It is	too		dark		for the child	to go out alone. (a)
The child is	too		young			to go out alone. (a)
She is	too		young	a child		to go out alone. (b)
I have	too	many		packages		to carry. (b)

I can't wear this dress.

This dress is	too		small		for me	to wear.
This dress is	too		small		for me.	
I am	too		fat			to wear this dress.

Word order: a. **Too** occurs *before* an adjective or quantifier.
b. Both **too** and the adjective come before **a/an** + *noun*.

Deletion: The subject and object of an infinitive are not repeated if they occur earlier in the clause.

Meaning: An infinitive phrase after **too** gives an impossible or inadvisable action.

Compare:

The dress is *too* small. Therefore I can't wear it.
The dress is *very* small. It will fit my baby perfectly.

Enough

	NOUN	ADJECTIVE	ENOUGH	NOUN	INFINITIVE PHRASE	
					INFINITIVE SUBJECT	
The child is The book is		old simple	enough enough		 for a child	to understand that book. (a) to read. (a)
I have {	money		enough enough	money	}	to buy that book. (b)
Ted has {	a car	a big big	enough enough	car	}	to hold six people. (c)
That man knows			enough			to fill a dictionary.

Word Order: a. **Enough** occurs *after* an adjective.
b. It occurs either *before or after* a noun.
c. The order *adjective* + **enough** + *noun* is informal. In formal speech and writing, use the order *noun* + *adjective* + **enough.**

Deletion: The subject or object of the infinitive is not repeated if it occurs earlier in the clause.

Meaning: An infinitive phrase after **enough** states a *possible* action.

Note: **Too** and **enough** also occur with adverbs:

John ran too slowly to win the race.
He ran quickly enough to finish third.

Exercise 6. *Too* and *enough*

Combine or restate the sentences, using **too** and **enough.**

1. Aspirin is inexpensive. Most people can afford it.

   Aspirin is inexpensive enough for most people to afford.

2. Heart surgery is expensive. Most people can't afford it if they don't have health insurance.

    Heart surgery is too expensive for most people (to afford) if they don't have health insurance.

3. Many people don't have much money. They can't get adequate health care.
4. An intern doesn't have much experience. He doesn't treat patients without supervision.
5. Most herbal medicines are not very powerful. They cannot cure serious infectious diseases.
6. Antibiotics are very powerful, but even they cannot cure viral disease.

    Even . . .

7. Viruses are very small. We cannot see them with the naked eye.*
8. Nowadays, most people consider shamans old-fashioned. Most people don't consult them.
9. However, in primitive societies the shaman was often a frightening figure. People did not disobey him or her.
10. He or she knew strong black magic which could kill a person. (At least people believed that.)
11. It takes a long time to become an acupuncturist because there are many acupuncture points. One can't learn them in a day or a week.

Exercise 7. *Too* versus *very*

Fill in **too** where there is the idea of impossibility. In the other blanks, fill in **very** or **extremely.** (**Very** and **extremely** have approximately the same meaning.)

Examples: a. Mount Everest is _very_ high.
b. Until it was first "conquered" in 1953, people thought Mount Everest was _too_ high to climb.

1. The stars are ______ far away.
2. Scientists say they are ______ far away to influence our lives.
3. But people who believe in astrology disagree. They say that astrologers' predictions are ______ accurate to be ignored.

**With the naked eye:* without a microscope.

4. Astrologers say that some days are _______ auspicious* and recommend that people get married on those days.

5. According to astrology, people who are born in April make _______ good leaders.

6. But sometimes they are _______ self-centered to make good followers.

7. Whether you believe it or not, astrology is (a/an) _______ interesting subject to read about.

Transfer Exercises

1. Some Possibilities and Impossibilities

Complete the questions where necessary and ask them of a classmate. Use **too** and **enough** in your answers.

Examples: a. Can you buy _a car_? (money)

No, I don't have enough money to buy a car.

or: **Yes, I have enough money to buy a car.**

b. Can you buy _a Cadillac_? (expensive)

No, a Cadillac is too expensive for me to buy.

or: **Yes, a Cadillac is not too expensive for me to buy.**

1. Can you buy . . . ? (money)
2. Can you buy . . . ? (expensive)
3. Can you understand this lesson? (hard)
4. Did you do your homework last night? (easy)
5. Do you want to . . . this afternoon? (hot/cold)
6. Can you . . . tonight? (time)
7. Could you write a novel in English? (knowledge of English)
8. Could you be a rock star? (musical talent)
9. Could you teach English as a second language? (patience)

2. Limitations

Complete the sentence in (a) and add a contrasting sentence in (b).

1a. (young) In my country, a fifteen-year-old is legally **too young to drive a car.**

**Auspicious:* favorable.

1b. (old) **However, a fifteen-year-old is legally old enough to quit school.**
2a. (young) Ten-year-old children . . .
2b. (old) However, they . . .
3a. (experience) Very small children don't have . . .
4a. (old) In my opinion, someone who is ninety years old . . .
4b. (old)
5a. (young) Someone my age . . .
5b. (not/young)
6a. (usually/busy) Working mothers . . .
6b. (time) However, they have to find . . .
7a. (tired) After I finish my homework at night, I'm generally . . .
7b. (tired) However, . . .

3. Wishes

Make some wishes beginning **I would like to have** and ending with an infinitive phrase. You may be able to think of several wishes for each item.

I would like to have

1. a machine

   I would like to have a machine to bring a cup of coffee to my bedside every morning.

2. a house by the sea
3. a good book
4. a new (dress)
5. a friend
6. some medicine
7. a love potion
8. a fairy godmother
9. the power
10. the ability

4. Feelings

Ask a classmate about some of his or her feelings, now and in the past.

A. When you first came to this (city/school)

1. surprised

   When you first came to (San Antonio), were you surprised to hear Spanish in the streets?

2. eager
3. hesitant
4. ready
5. willing
6. disappointed
7. sad
8. happy

B. How about now? Are you . . .

9. eager
10. able
11. ready
12. relieved

5. Giving Reasons

Ask questions with **why.** Use infinitives in your answers. Give more than one reason if you can.

1. People work.

    Why do people work?

    (In order) to support themselves and their families.

    People work (in order) to support themselves and their families.

2a. People learn English.
2b. You are learning English.
3. You are going to study (business management).
4a. People watch TV.
4b. You watch TV.
5. People go to parties.
6. Some people carry a radio wherever they go.
7. Some people drink too much.
8. Some people wear contact lenses instead of glasses.
9. Many Americans are on diets.
10. Many Americans jog every day.
11. Many Americans have burglar alarms on their houses.
12. A lot of people consult astrologers.

6. Prepositions

Fill in the correct preposition. (If no preposition is needed, write Ø.) These preposition combinations occur in Lesson 12 and in this lesson.

1. People who live in a large city are constantly exposed ______ noise, crowds, and other forms of stress.

2. Some people cannot cope ______ the stress of life in the city.
3. If they become depressed or anxious, they usually *turn* first ______ their doctor.
4. If the doctor cannot *help* them ______ their problems, they may consult a psychiatrist.
5. A psychiatrist is a doctor who cares ______ the mentally ill.
6. The psychiatrist tries to find a solution ______ the person's problems.
7. He may *prescribe* tranquilizers ______ some conditions, while in other cases psychotherapy is more helpful.
8. To become a psychiatrist, one must graduate ______ medical school and then specialize in psychiatry.
9. A good psychiatrist really cares ______ his patients' happiness. He wants them to feel better.
10. You need patience and sympathy in order to enter ______ this profession.

Discussion Topics

A. Is any form of shamanism still practiced in your country? If so, what is it called? Do the priests or curers use herbs? rituals? other forms of healing? What kinds of people consult them? Are the ceremonies secret? Do you feel that the practices are helpful? Are they dangerous in any way?

B. Are there other traditional forms of healing in your country (besides shamanism)? If so, how do they work? Do they make use of herbs, massage, or other techniques?

C. Are people in your country becoming interested in healing traditions from other parts of the world (for example, acupuncture or shiatsu massage)? Is western medicine combined with other forms of healing in your country?

D. What form of treatment for illness is safest and most effective, in your opinion? Do you think it depends on the kind of illness?

E. Do you think that the stars are too far away to influence life on earth? Is it common for people in your country to consult astrologers? Do you have any good stories to tell about astrologers' predictions that did or did not come true?

Composition Topics

Write a short composition about one of the following topics. Use infinitives in some of your sentences.

1. Write about a form of healing or magic that is traditional in your culture. Describe the people who practice it, and the techniques and materials which they use. If the tradition is still practiced, say something about its place in your society today. Give your own opinion about its effectiveness or value.
2. Give your opinion about astrology and tell what role it plays in the life of your country. Include examples. (See Exercise 7 and Discussion Topic E.)

Lesson 14

Volunteer Archeologist

14.1 Gerunds and Infinitives as Subjects; *it* + Infinitive

	SUBJECT	PREDICATE	
	Learning another language	requires perseverance. is difficult. is a big job.	(a)
=	*To learn* another language	requires perseverance. is difficult. is a big job.	(b)

	IT	PREDICATE	INFINITIVE	
→	It	requires perseverance is difficult is a big job	to learn another language.	(c)

Sentence Structure: Gerunds and infinitives may be the subject of a sentence:

a. The gerund is more common in subject position than the infinitive, especially in informal English.

b. The infinitive may be used as a subject in formal English.

c. **It** frequently replaces the infinitive in subject position. The infinitive then comes after the predicate.

Note: Sometimes **it** is used with the gerund, although this is not always possible.

It's fun learning another language.

For/of + Infinitive Subject

IT	PREDICATE	INFINITIVE SUBJECT	INFINITIVE
It	will be a big job	for me	to learn Japanese. (d)
It	was intelligent	of John	to ask that question. (e)

For** versus **of: After **it,** the infinitive subject is usually introduced by **for,** but sometimes **of** is used:

d. Use **for** when the predicate refers to the whole infinitive phrase.

e. Use **of** after an adjective which describes only the subject of the infinitive.
Compare:

It was *difficult for* the boy to give away his candy.
(The *action* was difficult. The boy was not difficult.)

It was *generous of* the boy to give away his candy.
(The *boy* was generous. He gave away his candy *because* he was generous.)

Exercise 1. Gerund Subjects; *it* + Infinitive

Archeologists study early cultures by examining objects made and used in those cultures. They use a variety of techniques to find sites,* to excavate them, to record the data, and finally to analyze and interpret their findings. Some of their methods are described in the following account of an excavation that took place in England.

**Site:* a place where there are remains of an early culture.

Restate the sentences in two ways:

a. Use a **gerund** as subject.
b. Use **it and** an infinitive phrase.

Use each expression on the list once.

Adjectives	*Verb Phrases*
easy	gave the diggers new energy
essential	required time and patience
important	saved time
√impossible	was hard work
necessary	
possible	

1. The site could not be located from the ground.

    a. **Locating the site from the ground was impossible.**

    b. **It was impossible to locate the site from the ground.** (Notice that your sentences use an active gerund and an active infinitive, although the original sentence is passive.)

2. However, when they looked at a photograph taken from the air, the archeologists easily saw a geometric shape like a bicycle chain. (Omit sentence a.) (The shape was visible because the grass which grew where an ancient structure had existed was a little different in color from the surrounding grass.)

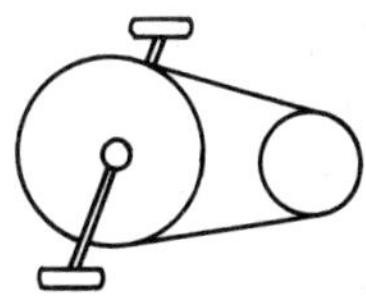

3. The archeologists next had to get permission to dig from the farmer who owned the field. (Omit sentence a.)

    Next . . .

4. A trench* was dug with a bulldozer in order to speed up the work.

5. When the trench had been dug, one could make out** the outline of an ancient ditch in the trench wall. (Omit sentence a.) (It was

**Trench:* a long narrow hole in the ground.
***Make out:* see.

visible because the dirt which filled the ditch was black and the dirt outside was a sandy color.)

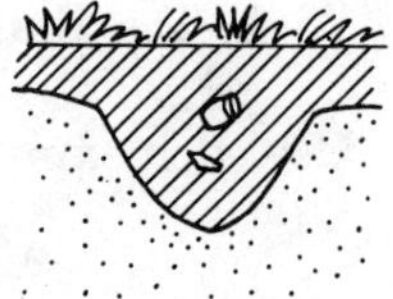

6. The archeological team began to dig out the dirt in the ditch with shovels and trowels.

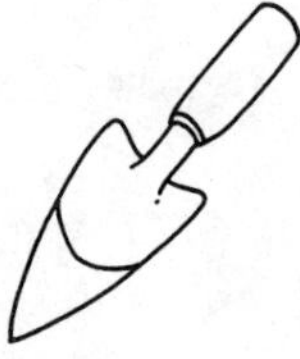

7. Several pots filled with charred*** bone were found. (These were prehistoric burial pots.)

However . . .

8. These had to be numbered, and their exact location had to be recorded on a map of the site.
9. (They were also photographed before they were moved.) They were marked with a number, a meter stick (to show size), and an arrow (to show direction) before the photograph was taken.

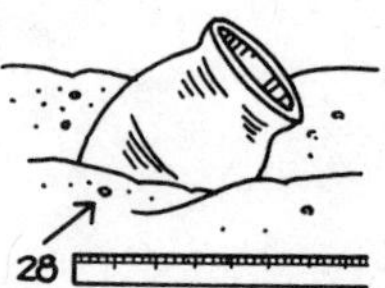

10. Finally, they were taken out with a small knife and cleaned with a brush.

Exercise 2. *For* + Infinitive

The archeological team consisted of two archeologists (the director and his assistant), several graduate students, and two volunteers from the United States. For the volunteers, it was a new, sometimes difficult, but thoroughly fascinating learning experience.

***Charred:* burned.

Form sentences with **It . . . for** . . . *infinitive.* Use each word or phrase on the list once.

√easy	impossible	an interesting and inexpensive way
difficult	necessary	require a lot of effort
hard	possible	take longer than expected

1. The director of the excavation could tell at a glance* which bits of stone were worked,** but the volunteers couldn't.

   It was easy for the director to tell which bits of stone were worked, but it ____________________ for the volunteers.

2. The volunteers couldn't guess the age of the artifacts that they found.
3. The director could estimate their age because he was familiar with artifacts of different periods. (He estimated that the burial pots were about 3,500 years old.)
4. The team couldn't finish their research the first summer, although they had hoped to.
5. They had to go back a second summer to complete it.
6. The volunteers weren't used to digging with shovels.
7. When their backs were aching, they couldn't easily keep working.
8. However, they spent a summer in England, made new British friends, and learned about archeology at the same time.

Exercise 3. *For* versus *of*

The archeologists and volunteers camped in the field next to the excavation site. The volunteers were inexperienced campers, and one of them, Nancy Wells, found it quite difficult at first.

Form sentences with **it . . . for/of** . . . *infinitive.* Use the pronouns **him, her,** or **them** in the infinitive subject. Use each expression on the list once.

more convenient	hard	be a new experience
foolish	kind	become a habit
friendly	nice	√take a long time
generous	uncomfortable	

**Tell at a glance:* know immediately, with only a quick look.
***Worked stone:* stone that has been cut by human beings.

1. Nancy put up her tent when she arrived at the "dig."

   It took a long time for her to put up her tent.

2. Some of the graduate students helped her.
3. She didn't enjoy sleeping in a tent.
4. She decided to get a room in the village.
5. One member of the team picked her up every morning when he drove to the village to buy a paper.
6. Nancy knew that England was a rainy country, but she didn't bring rubber boots.
7. Another volunteer lent her his extra pair.
8. They were too big, so she couldn't walk in them very well.

   In spite of the inconveniences, life at the dig was enjoyable. Nancy especially enjoyed the evenings.

9. The director invited the volunteers to go to the village pub* the first evening.
10. The Americans had never drunk beer that wasn't cold.
11. Everyone went there every evening to relax after the hard day's work.

14.2 Gerunds after Prepositions; the Possessive Subject of the Gerund

	PREPOSITION	GERUND PHRASE
Karen is interested She is thinking	in about	becoming a doctor. applying to medical school.

PREPOSITION	GERUND PHRASE	
Instead of After	remaining a nurse, obtaining her M.D.,	she plans to become a doctor. she will do her internship.

Form: Prepositions are followed by the gerund form of the verb.

**Pub:* Bar

To as a Preposition

	PREPOSITION	OBJECT
Karen is used	to	her schedule. working nights.
She objects	to	some of the regulations. being given too many patients.
She is looking forward	to	her vacation. being a doctor.

Form: In expressions where the preposition **to** is used with a noun, we also use **to** with a gerund. The infinitive is not used (with a few exceptions*).

Vocabulary: Some other expressions with the preposition **to:**

according to
(be) accustomed to
adjust to
in addition to
(be) open to
react to
resort to
respond to
return to

Note: Don't confuse the *adjective* **(be) used (to something)** with the *verb* **used (to do).**
Compare:

I *used to play* with dolls as a child. (*verb + infinitive*)
I *am used to* snow and ice. They don't bother me. (*adjective*)

One exception: They agreed *to our plan*. (**To** is a preposition.)
But: They agree *to go*. (**To go** is an infinitive.)

Idioms with the Preposition Omitted

	PREPOSITION	OBJECT
Sally is busy	with	her homework.
Sally is busy	Ø	doing her homework.
Did you have trouble	with	the last exercise?
Did you have trouble	Ø	understanding the last exercise?
I spent an hour	on	the dinner dishes.
I spent an hour	Ø	washing the dinner dishes.

Vocabulary: The gerund is used without a preposition after these expressions:

be busy
spend (time)

have {fun, difficulty, trouble}

have {a good time, a hard time, a difficult time}

Possessive Subjects of Gerunds (reduction of noun clauses with *the fact that*)

	NOUN CLAUSE
The teacher complained about	the fact that I came late.

	POSSESSIVE	GERUND PHRASE
→ The teacher complained about	my	coming late.
I can understand	Karen's	wanting to be a doctor.

POSSESSIVE	GERUND PHRASE	
My	coming late	upset the teacher.

Note: In informal conversation, some speakers use a noun or object pronoun before a gerund:

She complained about me coming late.

This usage is not correct in written English, except for certain verbs. (See Lesson 15, page 268.)

Exercise 4. Gerunds after Prepositions

Fill in the correct preposition and the gerund form of an appropriate verb. Write Ø in the first blank if there should be no preposition. The preposition combinations in this exercise are listed in Appendix 7.

1. The chief archeologist on the dig was responsible for training (train) the graduate students as well as ______ ______ (direct) the excavation.
2. One of the students was in charge ______ ______ (record) the location of each find on the map.
3. Another concentrated ______ ______ (photograph) the finds before they were removed from the site.
4. The director believed ______ ______ (include) his volunteers in as many aspects of the work as possible.
5. In addition ______ ______ with shovels and trowels, they participated ______ ______ (clean) and ______ (label) the artifacts that were found.
6. Their day consisted mainly ______ ______ (dig), however.
7. A cook took care ______ ______ the meals, but everyone helped ______ ______ the dishes.
8. The cook was busy ______ ______ most of the day.
9. Everyone had a voice ______ ______ (plan) the menus.
10. For a long time, Nancy had been interested ______ ______ England and ______ more about archeology.
11. She did not object ______ ______ (ask) to work hard.
12. At first, however, she was exhausted at night ______ ______ so hard.

13. She had trouble ______ __________ on the hard ground.

14. No one blamed her ______ __________ to sleep in the village.

15. Gradually she got used ______ __________ and didn't mind it.
(shovel)

16. By the end of the summer she was capable ______ __________
(recognize)
a "worked" stone.

17. She thanked the director ______ __________ her so much.

18. She was glad she had spent the summer ______ __________ on the dig.

19. In fact, she has become so interested in the field that she is thinking ______ __________ some courses in archeology this fall.

20. She is looking forward ______ __________ back to England to work on the dig again next summer.

Exercise 5. Combining Sentences with Preposition + Gerund

Combine each pair of sentences with one of the prepositions listed and a gerund. Omit the words in CAPITAL LETTERS and any other extra words.

{besides / in addition to}	by
	instead of
	without

1. Archeologists describe and classify the objects they find. They ALSO attempt to determine how old they are.

    In addition to describing and classifying the objects they find, archeologists attempt to determine how old they are.

    (Notice that the subject, **archeologists,** had to be used in the second part of the sentence because it was omitted from the first part.)

One important technique of dating is called dendrochronology, or tree-ring dating. This is how it works:

2. Tree trunks grow in diameter IN THE FOLLOWING WAY: They produce a thin layer of woody cells around the outside.

3. In temperate climates, they DON'T grow at a steady rate. They produce large cells in the wet spring and small cells in the drier fall. (This makes one visible ring in the wood each year.)

4. We can count the rings in the tree. We can find out how old the tree is THAT WAY.
5. Scientists count the rings. They ALSO measure the width of the rings. (This is because the tree forms a wider ring in years when there is more rain.)
6. They study the width of the rings. They can determine the exact dates of droughts,* fires, and other occurrences.

However, trees that can tell us about weather patterns are usually only a few hundred years old at most. Therefore, we have to match the sequence of rings in a living tree with the sequence in an older, dead tree from the same region. The center rings in a living tree match the outer rings in a tree that died when the first tree was young. In Arizona, a tree-ring chronology has been established that goes back 7,500 years.

7. We match the sequence of ring widths in a living tree with sequences in wood from older, dead trees. IF WE DON'T, we cannot go back more than a few hundred years.
8. Archeologists can date pieces of wood that they excavate. They can match the sequence of rings against the established tree-ring chronology.
9. Archeologists count tree rings. They ALSO count other kinds of annual layers, such as layers of guano,** layers of sediment,*** crusts formed on buried glass, and layers of ashes from volcanic eruptions.
10. They count layers. They ALSO date objects ANOTHER WAY. They measure the radioactivity in plant and animal remains.
11. They can determine when a plant or animal died. They measure the amount of radioactivity in bits of wood or bone.

In these and several other ways, archeologists attempt to determine the age of the events and cultures of prehistory.

**Drought:* a period with less rain than usual.
***Guano:* bird droppings.
****Layers of sediment:* clay brought by water.

Exercise 6. Possessive Subjects of Gerunds

Each sentence below includes a noun clause with **the fact that.** Reduce each noun clause to a gerund phrase.

> *Note:* To form the possessive of nouns, add **'s,** but after plural **-s,** add ' only.

Singular	*Plural*
the child's	the children's
the boy's	the boys'

1. Nancy appreciated the fact that another volunteer lent her his boots.

   Nancy appreciated another volunteer's lending her his boots.

2. She couldn't really complain about the fact that they were too big.
3. Everyone understood the fact that she wanted to sleep in a real bed.
4. The fact that she decided to go back the next summer didn't surprise me.
5. The cook didn't mind the fact that people asked, "What's for dinner?" every day.
6. But she resented the fact that they were constantly asking for snacks.
7. She couldn't bear the fact that the director tasted the food while she was cooking.
8. She disapproved of the fact that he was setting a bad example.
9. The fact that the dog stole food from the kitchen made her furious.
10. The fact that she shouted at the dog amused everyone.

14.3 Interrogative Infinitive Phrases (reduction of indirect questions)

	NOUN CLAUSE
The clerk didn't know	what he should say to the customer.

	INTERROGATIVE	INFINITIVE PHRASE
→ The clerk didn't know	what	to say to the customer.
Sally told Michiko	how much	to tip the taxi driver.
John and I tried to decide	where	to go on our vacation.
We talked about	whether	to take a trip or stay home.
Can you tell me	how	to get to the elevator?

Exercise 7. Interrogative Infinitive Phrases

Restate the sentences, reducing the indirect questions to infinitive phrases. Notice that the *active* infinitive is used.

Examples: a. Scientists have learned how tree rings can be counted without cutting down the tree.
Scientists have learned how to count tree rings without cutting down the tree.

b. Do you know whether we should count the annual rings inward from the outside of the trunk or vice versa?
Do you know whether to count the annual rings inward from the outside of the trunk or vice versa?

In organizing and carrying out an expedition, archeologists have to make many decisions.

1. Since they need money to conduct their research, they must worry about where they can get funding.
2. Since the expertise of botanists, chemists, and other specialists is often needed to help analyze archeological findings, the archeologist must consider whom he or she can ask for help.
3. Since these other scientists are very busy with their own research, the archeologist must figure out how he or she can interest them in his or her research.
4. When there is not enough money or time to excavate all the sites in an area, the archeologist must decide which sites should be excavated.
5. Then he or she has to determine where he or she should start digging.
6. An archeologist needs to know how samples are prepared for dating or for other forms of analysis.
7. He or she has to think about what method of dating he or she should use in each case.

8. Occasionally, an archeologist must decide whether an important object should be used for dating or (whether it should be) saved and placed in a museum. (Don't forget **it.**)

Transfer Exercises

1. American Customs

American life is changing rapidly. Some things we do today would have seemed strange to our grandparents. How do the following customs seem to people from your country? Which of them are also customary in your country? Which of them are not common? Which seem strange to you? Are any of these actions unacceptable, unthinkable,* or shocking in your country? Which of these customs do you enjoy? If possible, make two statements about each custom, as in the example.

1. Students sometimes wear shorts to classes.

   Wearing shorts to classes is customary in (Guatemala).
   It's common for both men and women to wear shorts to classes in (Guatemala).

2. People wear jeans to the theater, concerts, etc.
3. Some people get married in jeans.
4. Sometimes people eat while walking down the street.
5. People kiss in public.
6. A lot of people play radios while walking down the street.
7. People often live alone in apartments before they get married.
8. Many people change jobs every few years.
9. People hitchhike in the United States.
10. (What other customs have you noticed?)

2. Strategies

Complete and ask the questions below.

A. Use **by** in your first answer and **instead of** in your second.

1a. How can I lose weight?

You can lose weight by {not eating sweets. / giving up sweets.}

1b. How can I lose weight without **giving up sweets?**

Well, instead of giving up sweets, you could just eat less.

**Unthinkable:* completely unreasonable or never occurring.

2a. How can I keep in good physical shape?
2b. How can I keep in shape without . . . ?
3a. How can I save money?
3b. How can I save money without . . . ?
4a. How can I learn more English vocabulary?
4b. How can I do it without . . . ?
5. How did you learn your native language?
6a. How can I please my boss (teacher)?
6b. How can I please him/her without . . . ?

B. Use **besides** in your answer.

7. How do you study for an exam?

   Well, besides studying the book, I look over all my homework.

8. What do we do in this class?
9. What do you do in your spare time?
10. How do you keep up with the news?
11. How do you keep in touch with your family back home?

3. Understanding Across Cultures

Ask a classmate these questions. Begin the answers with **it.**

1. Can an adult learn a foreign language perfectly?

   I think it's impossible for an adult to learn a foreign language perfectly.

2. Can a child learn a foreign language perfectly?
3. Do you think someone from one culture can completely understand someone from another culture?
4. Can a husband and wife from different cultures be happy together?
5. Can classmates from different countries get along with each other?
6. Will capitalist countries and communist countries ever become friends?
7. Will we ever be able to achieve peace in the world?

4. A Class Party

A. Plan a class party. Each student in the class (or in your group) should volunteer to help, using these expressions:

I'll be responsible for
I'll be in charge of

I'll concentrate on
I'll take care of
I'll participate in
I'll help with

Here are some things you need to do. Can you think of others?

1. invite any special guests

   ***Example:* I'll take care of inviting our grammar teacher.**

2. bring a sound system
3. bring some records or tapes
4. buy snacks or other food
5. prepare food of various types
6. buy drinks
7. buy paper plates, paper napkins, etc.
8. decorate the room
9. plan games
10. . . .

B. There are some decisions to make. Complete the sentence as many ways as you can.
We need to decide

11. where **to have the party.**
12. when
13. who
14. how many
15. how much
16. what kind of
17. whether

C. What do you look forward to doing at the party?

5. Preparing a Meal (written)

Complete the following sentences about preparing a meal. Use gerunds and infinitives. Your story does not have to be true.

1. (cook) Once (name of person) asked me *to cook* dinner for *(25)* people.
2. (make) I decided . . .
3. I enjoyed . . .
4. However, I had trouble . . .

5. It was necessary . . .
6. It took quite a long time . . .
7. In fact, I spent . . .
8. In addition to . . .
9. . . . was hard work.
10. The guests had a good time . . .
11. Afterwards . . . thanked me . . .
12. (He/she/they) said it was nice . . .

Discussion Topics

A. Have you ever been camping? If so, were you comfortable? What was the weather like? Did you have a tent and other equipment? Was it easy to put up the tent, cook, find water, and so forth? What was most enjoyable about the trip? What was least enjoyable?

B. Are there many archeological sites in your country? How old are the most important sites? What culture or cultures built them? Where are they? Are they in or near modern cities? Are they in the jungle, in the desert, or underwater? How were they found? Is it difficult to reach them? Have many of these sites been excavated? If so, by whom? Do many tourists visit these sites? Are any of them closed to tourists, and if so, why?

C. Can volunteers participate in excavating archeological sites in your country? Do you know anyone who has worked on an excavation? If so, what did he or she tell you about it? Were important finds made? How did the excavators live at the site? Did they enjoy the work?

D. Have you visited any archeological sites (for example, an ancient temple, pyramid, fortification, or city)? Among the ancient places that you have seen, which one interested you the most? Where is it? How old is it? Who built it? Has it been excavated or restored? What interested you about it especially? Do many tourists go there?

E. Is it important to find out about ancient cultures, in your opinion? Is it important to preserve archeological sites? Why or why not? In your country, who is responsible for protecting and restoring sites? How are they protected?

Composition Topics

Write a short composition about one of the following topics. Use gerunds and infinitives in some of the patterns that you have studied in this lesson.

1. Write about a camping trip. Talk about deciding where to go, what to take, and so forth, and answer some of the questions in Discussion Topic A.
2. Write about planning and carrying out a project. (See Transfer Exercises 4 and 5 for some ideas.)
3. Write about cross-cultural understanding. What are some of the obstacles to understanding, and how can we overcome them? To what extent can we succeed in achieving understanding across cultures? You may want to write about a specific situation such as an inter-cultural marriage, studying in a foreign country, or emigrating to another country.
4. Write about some customs that surprised you when you came to this country (or when you visited another country or saw films from another country). How did you react when you saw these customs? Why? (See Transfer Exercise 1 for some ideas.)
5. Write about archeology in your country. Choose one of the topics in Discussion Topics B through E, or a similar topic of your own.

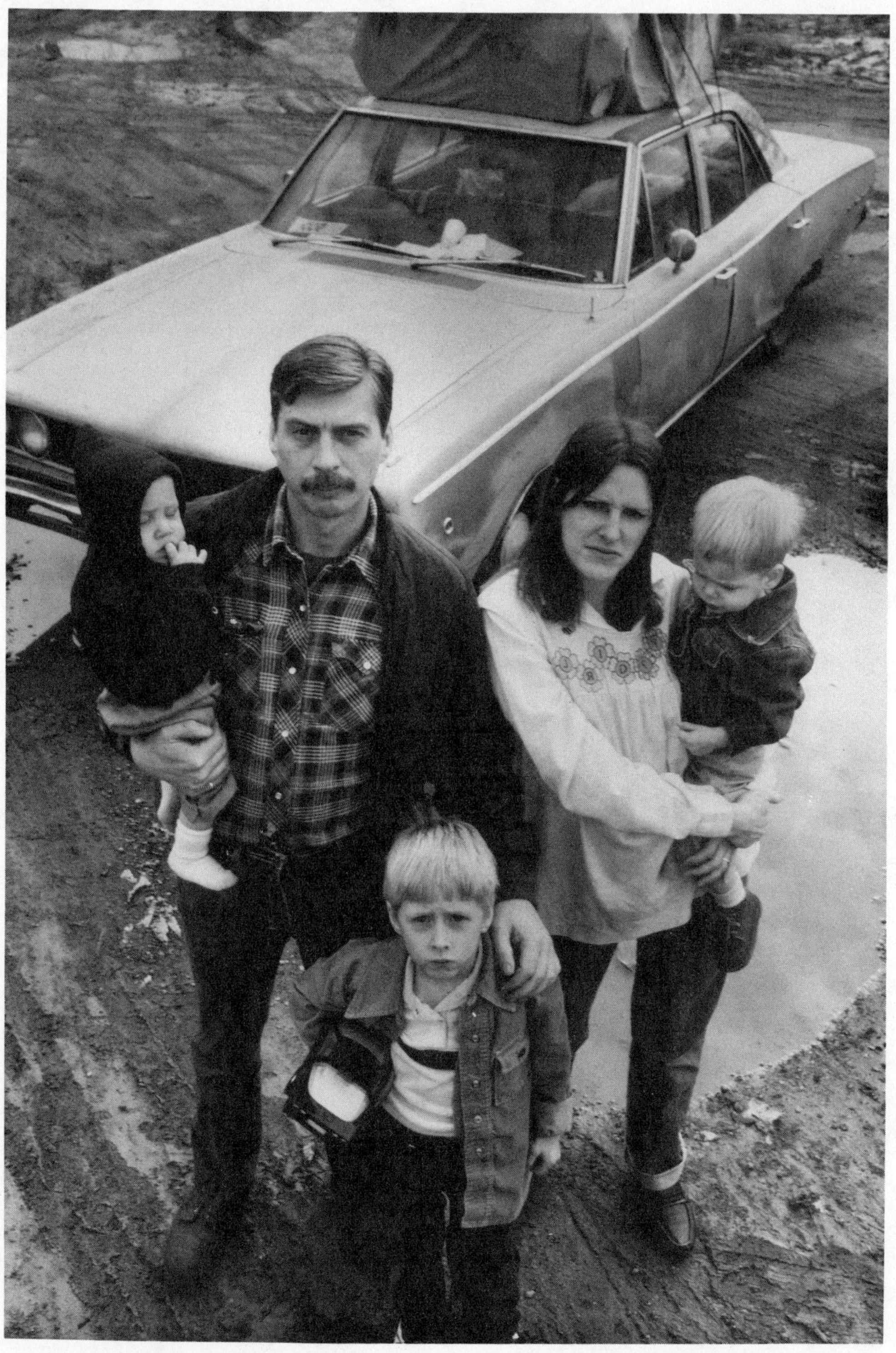

Lesson 15

A Home and Homelessness in New York City

15.1 Causatives: *make, let, have, help, get*

Active Main Verb + Base Form; *help, get* + Infinitive

Situation: Johnny likes to stay up late watching TV.

	CAUSATIVE VERB	INFINITIVE SUBJECT	BASE FORM	
The baby-sitter	lets	Johnny	stay	up until 10:00. (a)
His parents	don't let	him	stay	up late. (a)
They	make	him	go	to bed at 8:00. (b)
The baby-sitter	doesn't make	him	go	to bed early. (b)
The cold wind	makes	me	shiver. (b)	
The doctor	had	me	lie	down on his table. (c)
We	had	the postman	forward	our mail to our new address. (c)
Please	help	Johnny	tie	his shoes. (d)

			INFINITIVE	
Please	help	Johnny	to tie	his shoes. (d)
We	got	the teacher	to postpone	the test one day. (e)

Form: Active forms of **make, let,** and **have** + *infinitive subject* are followed by the *base form.* After **help,** either the infinitive or the base form is used. After **get,** we use the infinitive.

Meaning: a. **Let** means *permit* or *allow:* not to stop an action. Usually we *let* or *don't let* someone do what they *want* to do.

b. **Make** means *force*. Usually we *make* someone do what they *don't want* to do.

The subject of **make** and **let** is someone or something that has authority or control over the infinitive subject.

c. **Have** means to cause someone to do something by asking. We use **have** in situations where it is normal to ask. For example, a teacher may have students do something, but not the other way round. (The students *ask, persuade,* or *get* the teacher to do something.)

d. **Help** means to assist.

e. **Get** means to *persuade* some*one* to do something or *cause* some*thing* to do something.

Active Main Verb + *be* + Past Participle (passive base form)

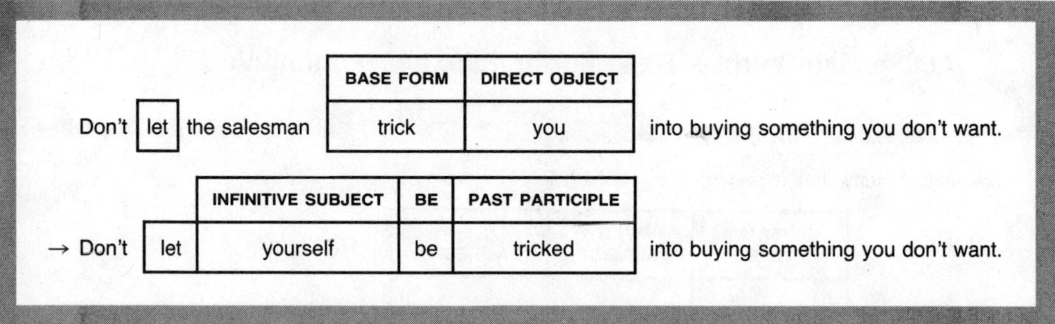

			BASE FORM	DIRECT OBJECT	
Don't	let	the salesman	trick	you	into buying something you don't want.

		INFINITIVE SUBJECT	BE	PAST PARTICIPLE	
→ Don't	let	yourself	be	tricked	into buying something you don't want.

Active Main Verb + Past Participle

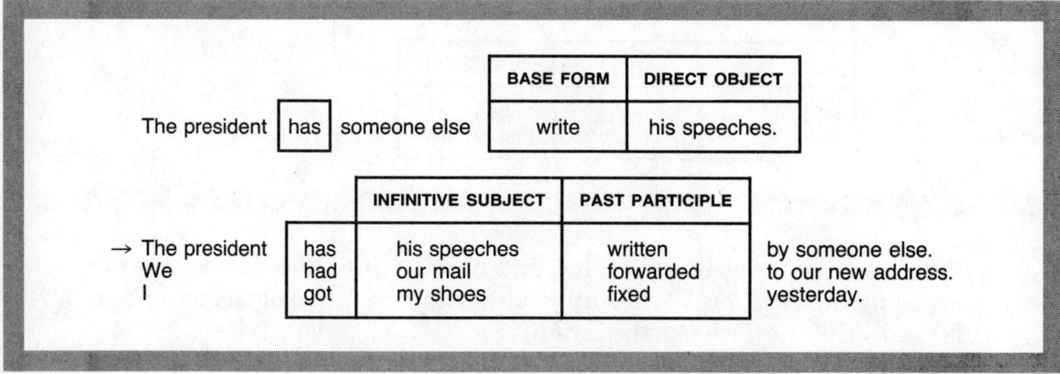

			BASE FORM	DIRECT OBJECT
The president	has	someone else	write	his speeches.

		INFINITIVE SUBJECT	PAST PARTICIPLE	
→ The president	has	his speeches	written	by someone else.
We	had	our mail	forwarded	to our new address.
I	got	my shoes	fixed	yesterday.

Form: After causatives **have** and **get,** the passive is shortened to the past participle.

Note: Two other verbs, **want** and **would like,** may be followed by either the past participle or the passive infinitive.

I {want / would like} this job done by 2:00 P.M.

I {want / would like} this job to be done by 2:00 P.M.

Passive Main Verb

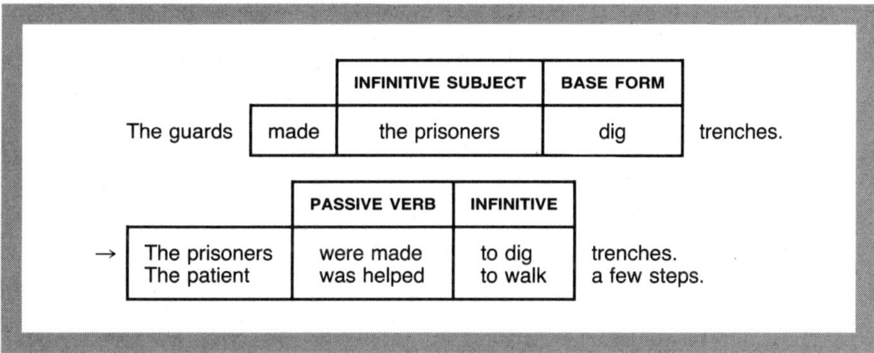

		INFINITIVE SUBJECT	BASE FORM	
The guards	made	the prisoners	dig	trenches.

		PASSIVE VERB	INFINITIVE	
→	The prisoners The patient	were made was helped	to dig to walk	trenches. a few steps.

Form: When **make** and **help** are in the passive, the infinitive with **to** is used.

Have and **get,** when causative in meaning, do not occur in the passive. **Let** rarely occurs in the passive except in the expression **let go.**

Because business was slow, several employees were let go.

Exercise 1. Choosing the Infinitive or the Base Form

Fill in the present tense (active or passive), the infinitive, or the base form.

Homelessness is a growing problem in many U.S. cities. Not only single men and women, but even families with children, have nowhere to live. Some low-income families (1) are forced (force) to leave (leave) their apartments when the rent is raised. Others are forced out by fire. Still others (2) ________ (make) ________ (leave) so that an old building can be torn down and replaced by a new one. If a family cannot find affordable housing, it may (3) ________ (force) ________ (live) in the family car or on the street.

City governments house many homeless families in special hotels while they try (4) __________ (help) them __________ (find) permanent housing. In addition, churches and synagogues, the Red Cross, and other organizations run shelters where homeless people (5) __________ (allow) __________ (stay) overnight. In very cold weather there are often more applicants than beds. Overcrowding is illegal, so the staff cannot (6) __________ (let) the extra people __________ (stay), but sometimes volunteers (7) __________ (permit) them __________ (sleep) on the floor or on chairs. Sometimes these centers also have extra winter clothing which they can (8) __________ (let) people __________ (have).

In New York City, you can see homeless people sleeping in the subways. It is illegal to sleep in the subway, so some police officers (9) __________ (make) the sleepers __________ (sit) up or __________ (leave) the train. But many officers (10) __________ (let) them __________ (sleep) because they know they have nowhere to go. In cold weather, homeless people may also go into a library or a MacDonald's to keep warm. However, they say that the librarians (11) __________ (not, let) them __________ (stay) there if they realize they are homeless. In parks, MacDonald's, museums, etc., they (12) __________ (ask) __________ (leave) as soon as it is known that they are homeless.

Exercise 2. *Make* and *let* (oral—books closed or pair work)

In some public parks there are many regulations, while in others there are very few. Ask a classmate questions with **make** and **let** about one or more of the following:

a. a park near your school
b. your school campus
c. parks in your classmate's home city

1. walk on the grass/stay on the paths

    Do they let people walk on the grass in (Washington Square Park), or do they make you stay on the paths?
    They let you walk on the grass.
    How about in (Buenos Aires)?

2. pay to enter
3. leave your bicycles outside the park/ride bicycles on the paths
4. walk dogs
5. keep dogs on a leash/run free
6. wade* in the fountains
7. play baseball, soccer, etc.
8. build fires and cook
9. put your trash in the trash can
10. listen to radios
11. sleep on the benches
12. stay overnight

Exercise 3. *Have* (oral or written)

A few years ago, Ken and Beth Ryan bought an old brownstone* on West 87th Street in New York City. The house had been a slum, but because it was in an "urban renewal" area, the Ryans were able to get financial aid from the city to fix it up. (The city had also helped the former tenants find new housing, so they were not homeless.) The Ryans planned to live in the house for many years, so they had it completely renovated.

When they bought the house, it contained four apartments, each with a kitchen and a bathroom. The Ryans wanted to rent the apartment on the top floor and to use the other three floors for their own home. Therefore, they had to have a lot of changes made.

A. What did the Ryans have each of these people do? Make sentences in the active using the words on the list as infinitive subjects. Then change each sentence to the passive.

carpenter	interior decorator	plumber
electrician	mason	√workmen
heating expert	painter	

1. Someone took out all the old appliances.

   Active: **They had workmen take out all the old appliances.**

   Passive: **They had all the old appliances taken out.**

2. Someone put in new bathrooms.

Wade: walk in shallow water.
Brownstone: A name given to the old four-story houses in New York City. Many of them have a front made of brown stone.

3. Someone rewired the house.
4. Someone installed a new central heating system.
5. Someone repaired the stone steps and balustrades.

6. Someone built closets, cabinets, and bookshelves.
7. Someone made suggestions about lighting, colors, and furnishings.
8. Someone painted the rooms.

B. What else did the Ryans have done? Make passive sentences with these verbs:

build	make	refinish
carpet	put in	tear out
√install	recover	

9. (a new kitchen/in the top-floor apartment)

   They had a new kitchen installed in the top-floor apartment.
10. They liked the old hardwood floors, so . . .
11. However, (the bedroom floor) . . .
12. They wanted a large living room, so (a wall) . . .
13. (a deck* on the back of the house)
14. (a dishwasher and garbage disposal unit/in their new kitchen)
15. (drapes/for the living room)
16. (their sofa/to fit the new color scheme)

Exercise 4. Active and Passive Forms after Causatives

Fill in the infinitive, base form, or past participle of any appropriate verb. In addition to verbs from earlier exercises, you can use these:

inspect   issue   pick out   replace

**Deck:* a porch without a roof.

Supply a pronoun where one is needed.

1. The four flights of steps were in bad condition, so the Ryans had the broken stairs replaced. While the carpenter was there, they also had him build some new closets in the bedrooms.
2. They asked an interior decorator ____________ the wallpaper for the living room and also had ____________ fabrics for the drapes and sofa.
3. They didn't have wallpaper ____________ (hang) in the bedrooms or the top floor apartment. Instead, they had those rooms ____________.
4. They had all the broken windows ____________ and also got a skylight ____________ on the top floor.
5. Instead of having the deck ____________, they asked the painter ____________ (stain) it.
6. After all the work was finished, they got the building inspector ____________ the building and ____________ them a certificate of occupancy.
7. Before they moved in, they had a locksmith ____________ strong locks on all the doors and also got a burglar alarm ____________.
8. Soon after they moved in, they had a housewarming party. The Ryans supplied the drinks, but they got each guest ____________ something to eat.

Shortly after the Ryans bought their house, the houseowners and the apartment dwellers on the block got together and formed a block association. They decided to plant trees and flower beds along the street, and they arranged block parties and barbecues.

A controversy arose over the welfare hotel on the block, which housed poor people who could not afford to pay rent.

9. Some of the homeowners wanted to have ____________ (evict) and have the building ____________ (convert) to middle-income housing, but another group got everyone ____________ (agree) to befriend and help the hotel tenants.
10. They organized social activities for them and even had a counselor ____________ (come) once a week to help them with alcoholism and other problems they might have.

15.2 Verbs of Observation and Depiction

Active Main Verb + Base Form

	VERB	INFINITIVE SUBJECT	BASE FORM		
We	saw	him	throw	a rock through the window.	(a)
We	heard	the glass	break. (a)		

			-ING FORM		
I	can hear	workmen	drilling	in the street.	(b)

Meaning: After verbs of observation:

a. The *base form* means that someone observes the *entire action.*

b. The ***-ing*** *form* means that someone observes the action *in progress,* but not necessarily from the beginning.

Note: A noun clause after the verb **hear** means that the subject learned about an event indirectly and did not observe it directly. *Compare:*

I heard Ann fall. (direct observation)

I heard that Ann fell. (Somebody told me about it afterwards.)

Vocabulary: These verbs of observation may be followed by an infinitive subject and either the *base form* or the ***-ing*** *form* of the verb:

List A

feel	look at	notice
hear	observe	see
listen to	overhear	watch

The following verbs may be followed by an infinitive subject and the ***-ing*** *form* of the verb. Notice that these verbs refer either to observation or to a picture or description.

List B

catch	depict	picture
discover	describe	portray
find	draw	remember
glimpse	imagine	show
spy	paint	visualize
smell	photograph	

Active Main Verb + *being* + Past Participle (passive *-ing* form)

The boy *was being arrested* when the reporter took the picture.

			BEING	PAST PARTICIPLE
The picture	showed	the boy	being	arrested.

Form: After verbs on Lists A and B, the passive **-ing** form (**being** + *past participle*) may be used.

See and *hear* + Past Participle

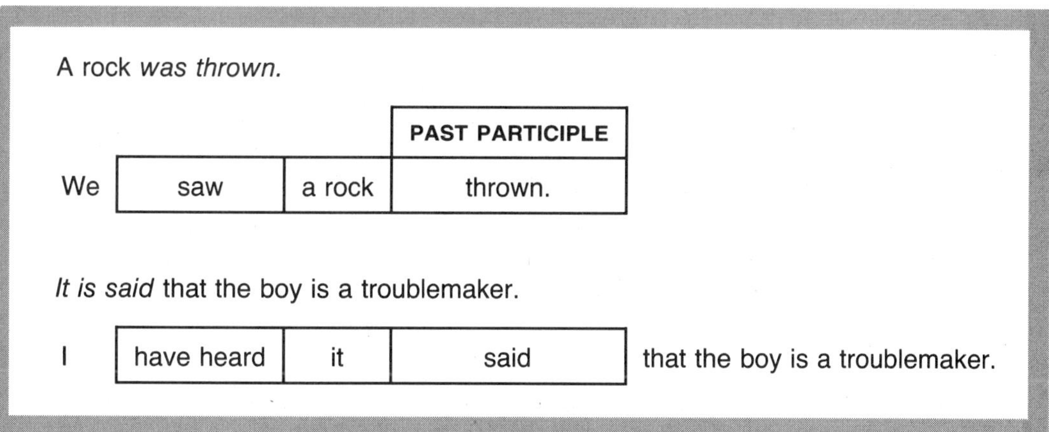

A rock *was thrown.*

			PAST PARTICIPLE
We	saw	a rock	thrown.

It is said that the boy is a troublemaker.

I	have heard	it	said	that the boy is a troublemaker.

Form: After **see** and **hear,** the passive of the base form is shortened to the *past participle.* **Hear** + *past participle* is limited to **hear it said.** Other verbs of observation do not usually occur in this pattern.

Passive Main Verb + Infinitive

	PASSIVE VERB	INFINITIVE	
A boy	was seen	to throw	a rock.
A bystander	was heard	to say	that the boy was a troublemaker.

Vocabulary: The passive of the following verbs of observation may be followed by an infinitive:

From List A: hear, observe, overhear, see.

Passive Main Verb + *-ing* Form

	PASSIVE VERB	-ING FORM	
The boy	was observed	running	away.
Later, he	was caught	stealing	fruit from a fruitstand.

Vocabulary: The passive of the following verbs of observation may be followed by the **-ing** form:

From List A: hear, observe, overhear, notice, see.
All the verbs on *List B*.

Exercise 5. Verbs of Observation

The Ryans reside in a mixed neighborhood where people of different races, nationalities, and income levels live side by side. When they moved to their new house from the suburbs, there were many new sights, sounds, and smells to get used to.

A. Using the verbs listed below, make sentences to describe the Ryan's new experiences. Use a verb from the list followed by a *base form, past participle,* or ***-ing*** *form*. Sometimes more than one form is possible, but with different meaning.

catch	hear	overhear	smell
discover	listen to	observe	watch
feel	notice	see	

There were the homeless.

1. Occasionally homeless people slept in doorways.

   Occasionally the Ryans saw homeless people sleeping in doorways.

2. People looked through the garbage cans for food.

There was the traffic.

3. Trucks went up Amsterdam Avenue all night long.
4. The garbage was picked up at 5:00 A.M.
5. The house shook every time the subway went by, even though it was a block away.

There were the neighbors.

6. In the summer, children played on the playground until midnight.
7. Food cooked on the neighbors' barbecue grills.
8. The neighbors quarreled in the house next to theirs.
9. On Tuesday evenings, the block was closed to traffic and everybody played volleyball together.

   On Tuesday evenings, they could play volleyball, or they could sit on the step and . . .

There were accidents.

10. Once something was burning. Once Ken . . .
11. Flames and smoke were coming out of an old car parked in front of the house.
12. The fire was put out by the fire department.

There was crime.

13. An old woman's purse was snatched. Beth . . .
14. The woman screamed.
15. The thief ran past the bus stop and turned the corner.
16. Nobody tried to stop him. Beth didn't . . .
17. Later he broke into an apartment. Later he . . .

And there were some other surprises.

18. Some pigeons were raising a family on their windowsill.
19. The baby birds were fed by the parents.
20. Eventually, the young birds took off and flew away.

B. Which of your responses in section A can be made passive? Follow these guidelines:

a. If a sentence already contains one passive, do not add another. Two passives are not used together in this construction.

b. Do not use the passive of **listen to, notice, smell,** or **watch.** Substitute another verb if possible.

c. You can make some of your sentences more general by using **can.**

Sentence 1: **Occasionally, homeless people can be seen sleeping in doorways.**

15.3 The *have* Passive and the *see* Passive

Have

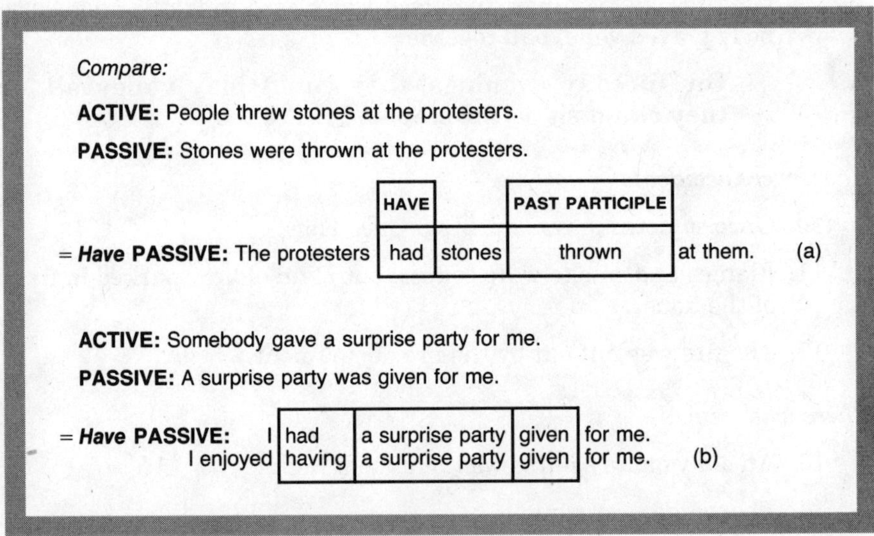

Compare:

ACTIVE: People threw stones at the protesters.

PASSIVE: Stones were thrown at the protesters.

	HAVE		PAST PARTICIPLE		
= ***Have* PASSIVE:** The protesters	had	stones	thrown	at them.	(a)

ACTIVE: Somebody gave a surprise party for me.

PASSIVE: A surprise party was given for me.

= ***Have* PASSIVE:** I	had	a surprise party	given	for me.	
I enjoyed	having	a surprise party	given	for me.	(b)

Meaning: The passive sentences above are formed in the same way as the passive with causative **have.** The meaning, however, is not causative, but is the same as the regular passive.

Usage: The **have** passive is useful because it allows us to have a subject which is different from the direct object of the active sentence. In the examples above, we make the object of a preposition into the subject to achieve focus and smoothness.

In (a), we want to focus on the *protesters*.
In (b), we want the subject of the gerund to be the same as the subject of **enjoy.**

See

Compare:

We would all like *something to be done* about the problem of homelessness.

	SEE		PAST PARTICIPLE	
= We would all like to	see	something	done	about the problem of homelessness.
We would like to	see	homes	found	for people.

Meaning: The **see** passive means the same as the regular passive but includes the idea of someone observing the event.

Usage: The **see** passive is often used with future expressions such as **would like, would rather, will, hope,** etc.

Exercise 6. The *have* Passive, the *see* Passive, and the Regular Passive

Combine the pairs of sentences, using the regular passive, the **have** passive, and the **see** passive as appropriate. In some cases, there is more than one possibility.

A. New York is a city of contrasts. It is a difficult city to live in in many ways, and both Ken and Beth have had some unpleasant experiences there.

1. Somebody robbed Ken on the subway. He didn't enjoy it.

   Ken didn't enjoy being robbed.

2. Somebody picked his pocket. He didn't enjoy that.

   He didn't enjoy having his pocket picked.

3. People stare at Beth on the subway. She hates it.
4. People step on her feet. She hates it.
5. The city should improve the subways. Both Ken and Beth would like that.
6. Somebody took Beth's purse while she was shopping. She was upset about it.
7. Moreover, salespeople have overcharged her. She complained to the manager about it each time it happened.
8. Somebody should do something about crime. New Yorkers would like that.
9. We should eliminate crime. However, it won't happen in our lifetime.

B. New York also offers many luxuries to tourists and to people with money.

10. At the luxury hotels, they treat you like royalty (kings and queens). Tourists enjoy that.
11. Everyone calls you "sir" or "madam." It makes people feel important.
12. A bellboy carries your bags for you. It's a relief after a long trip.
13. They serve you breakfast in bed. On vacation, people look forward to that.
14. At expensive restaurants, they park your car for you and bring it to the front door when you leave. That's a real convenience in a crowded city.
15. Developers will probably build more luxury hotels in New York in the future. Would New Yorkers like that?
16. They may tear down low-income housing to make way for hotels. Tenants' organizations don't want that.

Transfer Exercises

1. Childhood Experiences

Complete the sentences. If you work in groups, each member should supply his or her own answer to each item.

1. When I was a child, I always wanted (ice cream and candy), but my mother wouldn't let **me have it very often.**

2. I hated to (go to the dentist), but my parents made . . .
3. My mother (father) didn't let me . . . , but my grandfather (grandmother) . . .
4. My parents always made me . . . but my grandmother . . .
5. In elementary school, I hated to . . . , but my teacher . . .
6. The last letter I got from home made me . . .

2. Miscellaneous

Complete the sentences.

1a. When you enter the United States or Canada, the customs officials make you . . .

1b. They don't let you . . .

2a. When a policeman arrives at the scene of an accident, he has each driver . . .

2b. The driver who is at fault is made . . .

3. Hot, humid weather makes me . . .

4. Some professors are very easygoing. They let students . . . during a test.

5. Some students aren't very good typists, so they have their papers . . .

6. I am not a very good . . . , so I always have . . .

3. The Sights and Sounds of Your Neighborhood

A. Is your neighborhood (here or in your home town) similar to the one the Ryans live in? Talk about it using the verbs listed.

1. see, watch

   In my neighborhood, you can see (people jogging).
   You never see (homeless people sleeping in doorways).
   I have seen . . .
   Once I saw . . .

2. hear, listen to, overhear
3. observe
4. smell

B. What are some things that you can see or hear in the United States or Canada that you don't see in your country? For example, in your country, do you ever see people eating as they walk along the street? (If you have not been in the United States or Canada, talk about what you have seen in American movies or in another country that you have visited.)

4. Suggestions for Improving Your School

A. Imagine that your school administration has asked students for suggestions about improving the school. What would you like to see done? Consider the following:

1. the buildings and grounds

   Example: **I would like to see this old classroom building torn down and a new one put up in its place.**

   or: **I would like to see this building completely renovated.**

2. the facilities (library, sports facilities, cafeteria, club rooms, etc.)
3. the curriculum (course offerings and requirements)
4. the schedule of classes and vacations
5. the exam schedule
6. social activities

B. What improvements would you like to see in your neighborhood or in your city?

5. Redecorating Your Classroom*

A. Imagine that your school has hired your class as interior decorators to remodel and redecorate your classroom. They have given you the funds to hire people to do the work. Discuss the project with your classmates. What should you or could you have done?

Example: **We should have panels put on the ceiling to absorb sound.**

B. Are there other places at your school that you would like to redecorate? Give details, as in A.

6. Experiences

Talk about some experiences that you have had since you came to this city or school. Did you enjoy them or not? Use the active, passive, or *have* passive as appropriate.

*This exercise differs from Exercise 7B in Lesson 7 because in this case you will not be doing the work yourselves.

Examples:

1. An American family invited me to their home.
   I enjoyed being invited to their home.
2. Someone took my umbrella last week.
   I didn't enjoy having my umbrella taken.
3. I got lost in the subway.
   I didn't enjoy . . .

Discussion Topics

A. Have you or your family ever remodeled or renovated your home? If so, what changes did you make? What parts of the work did you do yourself, and what things did you have done by other people? Did the workmen do the work well and promptly? Were you pleased with the outcome?

B. Do you plan to make any changes in your present home? If so, what do you plan to do or have done? What improvements would you like to make sometime in the future? If you rent your apartment, what improvements would you like to see your landlord make?

C. Is there homelessness in your country? If so, what are the causes? Are the homeless mainly children? single adults? families? What do they do in the daytime? How do they get food and clothing? Where do they sleep at night? What do they do in very bad weather? Are they allowed to sleep in train or bus stations, subways, etc.? Are any agencies trying to help them? Are there special shelters for the homeless? What would you like to see done to solve the problem?

D. Are there block associations or neighborhood associations in your country? If so, are they important to the life of the neighborhood? Do they plan parties and other activities? Do they plant trees and flowers? Do they improve the neighborhood in other ways? Are they part of the city government? Do they have other functions?

E. Are there many luxury hotels in your country? What kinds of service do they offer? How does the presence of large hotels affect the area where they are built?

Composition Topics

Write a short composition about one of the following topics. Use causatives and verbs of observation in some of your sentences.

1. Write about ways in which you would like to improve your school. (See Transfer Exercise 4.)

2. Write about a time when you or your family made changes in your home. (See Exercises 3 and 4 and Discussion Topic A.)
3. Describe how you would like to remodel or redecorate your home, your classroom, or another room or building. (See Exercises 3 and 4, Transfer Exercise 5, and Discussion Topics A and B.)
4. Write about a neighborhood that you have lived in. Describe the sights and sounds of the neighborhood, its social or political organization, and improvements that have been made or that you would like to see made. (See Exercise 5, Transfer Exercise 3A, and Discussion Topic D.)
5. Compare some of the sights and sounds in the United States or Canada with the sights and sounds of your country. (See Transfer Exercise 3B.)
6. Write about the problem of homelessness in your country.

Lesson 16

England's Greatest Poet-Playwright

16.1 Perfect Infinitives and Gerunds

Infinitive

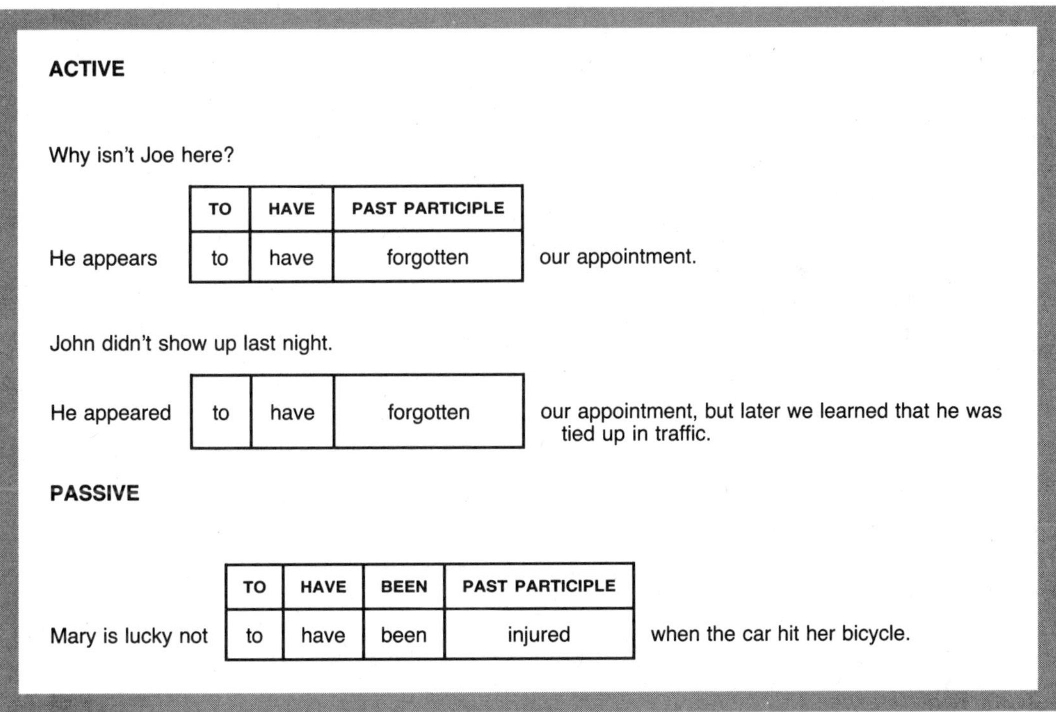

ACTIVE

Why isn't Joe here?

	TO	HAVE	PAST PARTICIPLE	
He appears	to	have	forgotten	our appointment.

John didn't show up last night.

He appeared	to	have	forgotten	our appointment, but later we learned that he was tied up in traffic.

PASSIVE

	TO	HAVE	BEEN	PAST PARTICIPLE	
Mary is lucky not	to	have	been	injured	when the car hit her bicycle.

Gerund

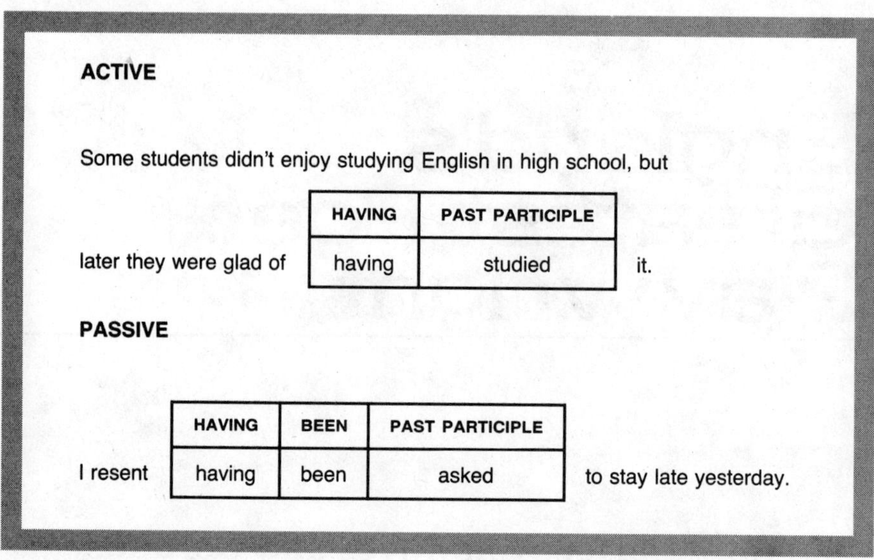

ACTIVE

Some students didn't enjoy studying English in high school, but

	HAVING	PAST PARTICIPLE	
later they were glad of	having	studied	it.

PASSIVE

	HAVING	BEEN	PAST PARTICIPLE	
I resent	having	been	asked	to stay late yesterday.

Meaning: The perfect infinitive and the perfect gerund indicate that an event occurred before the time of the main verb. Unlike the *present perfect* tense, perfect infinitives and gerunds can refer to definite or indefinite time.

Notes: 1. With a verb that points to the future, the perfect infinitive or gerund may mean that the action will occur before another future action.

I expect to have finished my homework by the time my husband finishes washing the dishes.
I won't be sure of having understood this until I take the exam.

2. When the context makes the time relationship clear, the simple gerund can often be used with the same meaning as the perfect gerund.

We remember Admiral Peary for having been the first to reach the North Pole.
= We remember Admiral Peary for being the first to reach the North Pole.

Exercise 1. Perfect Infinitives and Gerunds

Fill in the correct perfect form wherever possible. In two items, you will need the simple form.

The whole world admires the English poet and playwright William Shakespeare for (1) having written (write) *Hamlet, Macbeth, Othello,* and more than thirty other plays. We also remember him for (2) ______________ (compose) 154 sonnets* of great beauty.

Very little is known about Shakespeare's personal life, however. We know that he was born in Stratford-on-Avon in April 1564. He is almost certain (3) to have attended (attend) the local grammar school and (4) ______________ (learn) Latin there. However, his father seems (5) ______________ (have) financial problems at certain times, and this may be the reason that William did not continue his education at Oxford University. There is an official record of (6) ______________ (he, marry) Anne Hathaway when he was eighteen, and we also have records of the births of his children in 1583 and 1585. After this, we don't know where Shakespeare was until 1592. It is said that he was arrested for (7) ______________ (steal) a deer and was forced (8) ______________ (leave) Stratford. There are also accounts of (9) ______________ (he, be) a country schoolteacher and a soldier, but these are not documented.

We know that by 1592, Shakespeare was in London and was already a successful playwright. In addition to (10) ______________ (write) at least three plays, he was also an actor in the most successful theater company in London. He continued (11) ______________ (write) plays until about 1613, three years before his death. His sonnets were first published in 1609, but they appear (12) ______________ (write) over many years.

Perhaps because so little is known about Shakespeare's life, there has been controversy about who really wrote the plays and sonnets. Some scholars have said that it is impossible for the half-educated son of a merchant (13) ______________ (write) such profound and beautiful drama and poetry. They say that he could not have used the language of the court so well without

Sonnet: a form of poem with fourteen lines.

(14) ______________________ at the court. They believe that some-
(live)
one else wrote the plays but signed Shakespeare's name to them.

16.2 Reduction of Indirect Statements to Infinitive Phrases

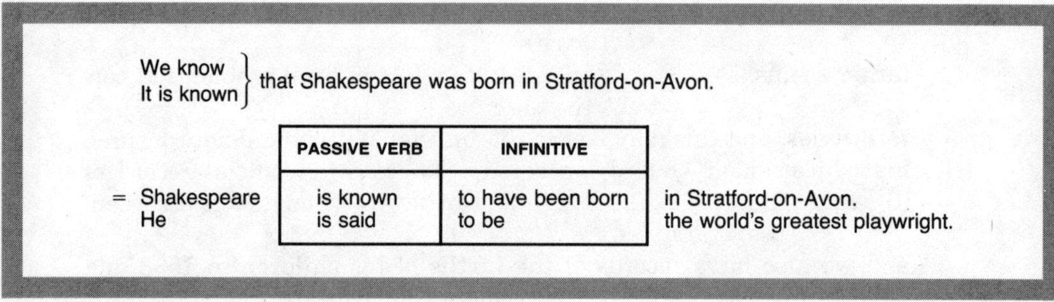

We know / It is known } that Shakespeare was born in Stratford-on-Avon.

	PASSIVE VERB	INFINITIVE	
= Shakespeare	is known	to have been born	in Stratford-on-Avon.
He	is said	to be	the world's greatest playwright.

Reduction: After verbs of *knowing, believing,* and *saying,* an indirect statement may be shortened to an infinitive phrase. The subject of the clause becomes the subject of the main verb.

Note: The active form also occurs with **believe, consider, judge,** and **know.**

Many believe him to be the world's greatest playwright.

I { know / judge / consider } John to be a responsible person.

Exercise 2. Reducing Noun Clauses to Infinitive Phrases

Restate the sentences to include a passive verb and an infinitive phrase.

1. Some historians believe that Shakespeare was born on April 23, 1564.

   Shakespeare is believed to have been born on April 23, 1564.

2. However, others say that he died on April 23 (1616). (also)
3. We know that he was baptized at Stratford-on-Avon on April 26, 1564.

4. It is assumed that he attended grammar school at Stratford.
5. We can suppose that he learned Latin and read Latin literature.
6. It is known that his father got into financial trouble during Shakespeare's youth.
7. It is thought that this is why he was not sent to the university at Oxford or Cambridge. (Use the simple infinitive.)

   This . . .

8. We know that Shakespeare married Anne Hathaway in 1582.
9. It is reported that she was eight years older than he was.
10. We believe Shakespeare left Stratford in 1585.
11. Some reports say he was caught stealing deer.

Exercise 3. Forming Statements with Infinitive Phrases (reduced noun clauses)

There is a great deal of conjecture* about Shakespeare's life and work after he left Stratford. No manuscript in his handwriting has come down to us, and there are few other documents. We don't even know when he began his career in the theater.

Answer the questions with the passive form of the verb in parentheses and an infinitive phrase.

1. When did Shakespeare arrive in London? (know/before 1592)

   Shakespeare is known to have arrived in London before 1592.

2. Had he written and acted in plays by that date? (know)
3. Was he a good actor? (report)
4. Did he join a company of actors? (believe/by some)

   He is believed by some . . .

5. Did he form his own company? (think/by others)
6. Did he bring his family to London? (not/think)
7. Did he visit Stratford? (know/after 1596)

**Conjecture:* guessing from incomplete evidence.

8. Where were his plays performed? (know/at the Globe and other theaters)

9. Were they performed at court? (The great tragedy *Othello*/for King James/1604/know)
10. Who played the women's roles? (boy actors/know)
11. Who were the earliest published versions printed by? (judge/pirates**)
12. Where were they obtained? (from actors who wrote them down from memory/think)
13. Have any plays been lost? (when the Globe Theater burned down in 1613/believe)
14. When did Shakespeare retire to Stratford? (believe/around 1610)
15. Was he living there when he died? (assume)
16. When was his last play (*Henry VIII*) performed? (know/1613)
17. Was it co-authored by someone else? (formerly/think/John Fletcher)
18. Was it created by Shakespeare alone? (now/believe)
19. Were all of Shakespeare's plays and poems written by someone else who was more highly educated than he was? (believe/by some)
20. Or were they the work of William Shakespeare? (but/think/by most serious scholars)

Exercise 4. Cumulative Exercise: Gerunds and Infinitives (oral—books closed)

Complete each sentence with **writing it, to write (it),** or **write it.**

1. We agreed . . . **to write it.**
2. I am considering . . .
3. I had trouble . . .
4. I meant . . .
5. She had us . . .
6. I have decided . . .

***Pirate:* someone who reproduces a literary work without permission.

7. They were seen . . .
8. He is busy . . .
9. I'm interested in . . .
10. How can I avoid . . .
11. I noticed her . . .
12. She advised me . . .
13. She allowed him . . .
14. It is necessary . . .
15. It was foolish of you . . .
16. She arranged for us . . .
17. I spent an hour . . .
18. She got us . . .
19. I wasn't used to . . .
20. Please attempt . . .
21. I observed him . . .
22. We were forbidden . . .
23. Have you finished . . .
24. Let them . . .
25. I recommend . . .
26. Does this involve . . .
27. I can't stand . . .
28. She wants us . . .
29. This will enable you . . .
30. Don't make him . . .
31. I urge you not . . .
32. I am endeavoring . . .
33. We discussed . . .
34. He is eager . . .
35. She instructed us . . .
36. I can't imagine . . .
37. I wasn't sure what . . .
38. I don't know whether . . .
39. I hope . . .
40. Are you looking forward to . . .
41. Can you recall . . .
42. We were made . . .
43. I don't mind . . .
44. I refuse . . .
45. Can you persuade her . . .
46. We were encouraged . . .
47. We stopped . . .
48. I advise not . . .
49. We watched them . . .
50. Don't fail . . .

Exercise 5. Cumulative Exercise: Gerunds and Infinitives

Fill in the correct form of the infinitive or gerund.

A Deserter of the 1960s

The Vietnam War, which ended in 1975, is known ____________ (be) the most unpopular war in U.S. history. Many young people in particular believed that the United States should not be fighting in Vietnam. Nevertheless, until 1973, every male citizen was required ____________ (register) for the military draft when he reached his eighteenth birthday.

When George Walker registered, he did not expect ____________ (draft) because he was a college student, and the government's policy was to let students ____________ (finish) their studies before ____________ (draft) them. However, he seems ____________ (forget) to mail in a form that was required.

The Draft Board claimed ______________ (not, receive) it and they drafted him. George was active in the anti-war movement at the time, but in spite of ______________ (say) previously that he would refuse ______________ (draft), when the time came, he did not refuse. He didn't look forward to ______________ (send) to Vietnam, but he knew that if he refused, he could expect ______________ (send) to jail.

Basic training in the army is known ______________ (be) tough and unpleasant. Besides ______________ (make) ______________ (cut) his hair, ______________ (wear) a uniform, ______________ (salute) officers, and ______________ (obey) commands, George was trained ______________ (use) a gun, ______________ (live) outside in all weathers, and ______________ (march) long distances. He got used to ______________ (order) to do things and didn't mind ______________ (get) up early and ______________ (work) hard. However, his conscience bothered him, and one day he deserted.

For several months, George avoided ______________ (catch). Instead of ______________ (try) to escape to Canada, he hitchhiked around the country. Everywhere he was helped by anti-war sympathizers. But of course he was always afraid of ______________ (question) by the police if they caught ______________ (he, hitchhike), since ______________ (hitchhike) is illegal

in many states. He longed ______________________ his family, but
(see)
it would have been dangerous ______________________ them. And
(he, visit)
it was impossible ______________________ a job because he didn't
(he, get)
dare ______________________ anyone his identity papers.
(show)

George enjoyed ______________________ around, but he always
(travel)
expected ______________________ some day, and eventually he was.
(catch)
Then everyone expected ______________________ to jail for several
(he, send)
years for ______________________, but he was discharged after only
(desert)
a few weeks. He was able ______________________ his family again
(see)
and ______________________ back to college. He is lucky
(go)
______________________ off so easily.* He will never forget the
(get)
people he met and will always be thankful to them for
______________________ him during that difficult time.
(help)

Transfer Exercises

1. Plans

Imagine the following situations and answer the questions.

Situation 1: You are going to have your final exam in (subject) on (date).
What do you intend to have done by that date? Use these verbs and/or others of your own:

ask	memorize	review
finish	reread	study
look over		

Example: **By that day, I intend to have memorized all the irregular verbs.**

Situation 2: You are going to start undergraduate or graduate studies in (month, year).

**Get off easily:* escape severe punishment.

What do you hope or intend to have accomplished before that?

By the time I start graduate school, I hope . . .

Situation 3: Ralph is in medical school and is a very bright student. Some day he hopes to win the Nobel Prize in Medicine.

What does he expect to have achieved by then? Use these and/or other verbs:

discover
figure out
invent

Situation 4: You are having a birthday party for your five-year-old child two weeks from now. You have invited about eight of his kindergarten friends to attend.

What do you expect to have done by the time the children arrive? Use these verbs and/or others of your own:

bake	choose	figure out	set
buy	decide	prepare	wrap

2. Famous People

Tell your classmates about writers, statesmen, and other well-known figures from your country's history. Use some of the expressions listed below.

A. Gerunds

1. (Name) {is known / is famous} for . . .
2. We {remember / admire} (name) for . . .
3. Some people criticize(d) him/her for . . .
4. There are stories about his/her . . .

Example: **Cervantes is famous for having written *Don Quixote.***

B. Infinitives

appear	know	seem
assume	report	suppose
believe	say	think
judge		

Examples: **Murasaki Shikibu is known to have lived at the Japanese court.**

Leif Eriksson appears to have come to America before Columbus.

3. Prepositions and Two-word Verbs

Fill in the correct prepositions and complete the two-word verbs. These preposition combinations and two-word verbs occur in Lesson 15 and in this lesson.

1. When I want to go to a movie, I look ______ the theater listings in the newspaper and pick ______ the movie I want to see.
2. **A:** Somebody just bought the old church in our neighborhood.

   B: Are they going to tear it ______ ?

   A: No, they want to convert it ______ a restaurant. They plan to put ______ a bar, a kitchen, and so forth. A lot of people are upset ______ it because the church is famous ______ its stained glass.

   B: If they are upset, what are they going to do ______ it?

   A: They want to buy the church, fix it ______ , and make it into a Shakespearean theater. But the new owner doesn't want to sell. There's a big controversy ______ it. In fact, there's an account ______ it in today's paper.
3. **A:** Anna is active ______ the anti-nuclear movement. Once she was arrested ______ trespassing on the land where a plant was being built.

   B: I would never do that. I'd be afraid ______ being hurt.

   A: Well, I admire her ______ doing what she believes in.

Discussion Topics

A. Have you seen any of Shakespeare's plays? If so, did you see a stage performance or a movie version? Was it performed in English? Did you feel that it was a great play? What made it great (or not), in your opinion?

B. Shakespeare wrote both tragedies and comedies. He wrote about love, ambition, and jealousy; politics and war; history and fantasy. His plays include humor as well as serious themes.

In your country, do people enjoy attending the theater? If so, what kinds of plays are the most popular? Who are your favorite playwrights and why? What themes do or did they write about?

C. Are there traditional forms of theater in your country? If so, how are they different from the modern theater? Is the style of acting different? Are the parts of women played by men? What are the plays usually about? Are they serious or comic?

D. Who is your country's greatest writer, in your opinion? What do you know about his or her life? Are there things that are not known about this writer? Did he or she write novels? plays? poetry? What themes did he or she write about? Was humor an important part of this person's writing? What makes the writing great, in your opinion?

E. Do you think that George Walker was justified in deserting from the army? Why or why not? Is it always wrong to desert from military service, in your opinion?

Composition Topics

Write a short composition about one of the following topics. If you can, include a few (not too many) perfect gerunds and infinitives.

1. Write about the theater in your country, or about one form of theater. Tell something about how and when it originated, and describe any special forms that it developed. How is the theater important in the life of your country? What kinds of plays and what themes are the most popular? (See Discussion Topics B and C.)
2. Write about an important historical figure from your country. (See Transfer Exercise 2 and Discussion Topic D.)

UNIT VII

ADVERB CLAUSES

Lesson 17

Sled Dogs of the Arctic

17.1 Introduction to Adverb Clauses; Time Clauses

Introduction

ADVERB	INDEPENDENT CLAUSE	ADVERB
	We went outside	yesterday.
Yesterday	we went outside.	

ADVERB CLAUSE		INDEPENDENT CLAUSE	ADVERB CLAUSE	
CONJUNCTION			CONJUNCTION	
		We went outside	when	the fire alarm rang.
When	the fire alarm rang,	we went outside.		
		I work after school	because	I need money.
Because	I need money,	I work after school.		
		I will take an umbrella	if	it rains.
If	it rains,	I will take an umbrella.		

Sentence Structure: An adverb clause is *dependent*—it is not a complete sentence but is used with an independent clause. (As you know from Lesson 10, an *in*dependent clause can stand alone as a complete sentence.)

Punctuation: An adverb clause is frequently followed by a comma when it precedes the independent clause. A comma is not used *before* an adverb clause except in special cases.

Time Clauses

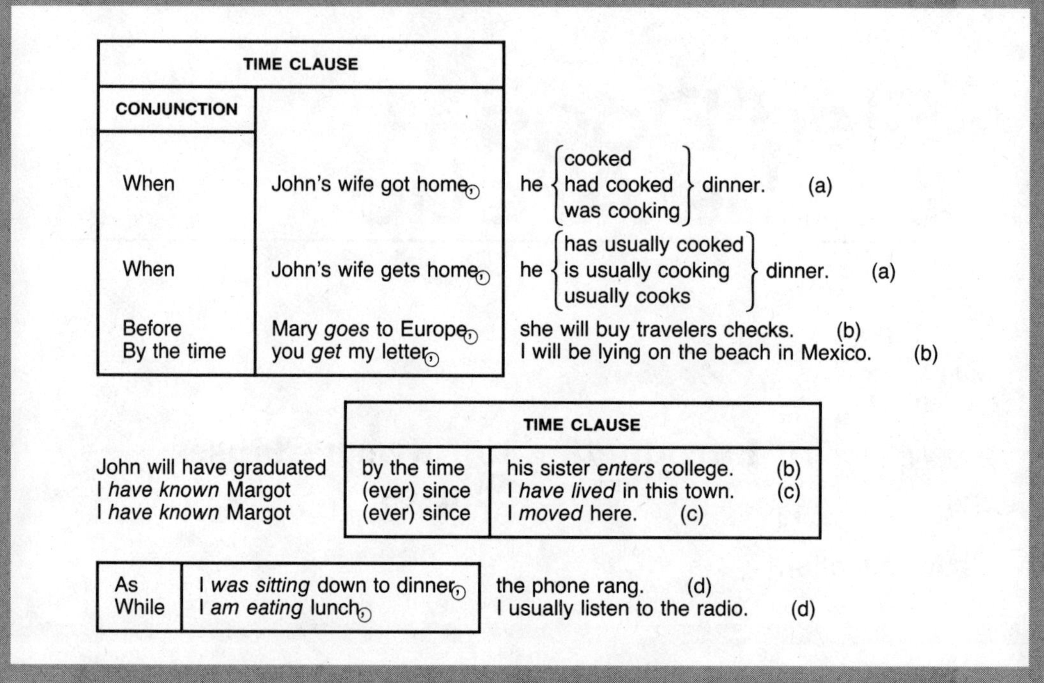

TIME CLAUSE		
CONJUNCTION		
When	John's wife got home,	he {cooked / had cooked / was cooking} dinner. (a)
When	John's wife gets home,	he {has usually cooked / is usually cooking / usually cooks} dinner. (a)
Before	Mary *goes* to Europe,	she will buy travelers checks. (b)
By the time	you *get* my letter,	I will be lying on the beach in Mexico. (b)

	TIME CLAUSE	
John will have graduated	by the time	his sister *enters* college. (b)
I *have known* Margot	(ever) since	I *have lived* in this town. (c)
I *have known* Margot	(ever) since	I *moved* here. (c)

As	I *was sitting* down to dinner,	the phone rang. (d)
While	I *am eating* lunch,	I usually listen to the radio. (d)

Choice of Tenses: a. The tenses in the two clauses show the time relationship between two actions.

b. In time clauses, the *present* tenses are used to refer to future time. The *future* tenses are not used in time clauses.

c. Clauses with **since** require a *perfect* tense in the independent clause. The verb in the **since** clause is *past* for past action and *present perfect* for action continuing to the present. (The *past perfect* may be used if the moment of focus is in the past.)

d. Time clauses with **as** and **while** often have a *progressive* tense.

Subordinating Conjunctions of Time:

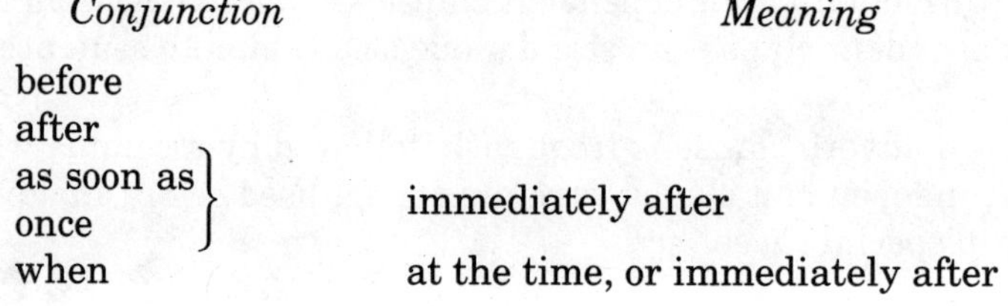

Conjunction	*Meaning*
before	
after	
as soon as } once }	immediately after
when	at the time, or immediately after

as	during the time, at the exact time
while	during the time
as long as	during the whole time
whenever	every time
every time	
until	up to the time, but not after
since	from that time up to now (moment of focus)
by the time (that)	before or at the time

Exercise 1. Identifying Adverb Clauses and Choosing the Correct Tense

The arctic, or extreme northern, regions of our earth have long, cold winters when the land is covered with ice and snow. In former times, the people who lived there used dogs to pull sleds across the snow. In that way they could cover long distances to find fish and game.* When Europeans began to settle these regions, they soon learned the value of the sled dog.

Underline the adverb clauses in the sentences below, and fill in the correct tense (active or passive) of the verbs in parentheses. In some cases, more than one tense is possible.

1. Before there ___were___ (be) planes and snowmobiles, the mail in Alaska was delivered by dogsled.
2. When diphtheria broke out in Nome, Alaska, in the winter of 1925, these dogsleds ______________ (travel) 600 miles through blizzards and 50-below-zero temperatures (F.) to deliver antitoxin** to the town.
3. The antitoxin was shipped partway by rail. By the time it reached the end of the railroad line in the interior of Alaska, the team drivers ______________ (notify) by telephone and the first team ______________ (wait) at the station.
4. The others were stationed along the route. As soon as a driver reached the next station, a fresh driver and a fresh team of dogs ______________ (take) over.

**Game:* wild animals that are hunted for food.
***Antitoxin:* medicine to prevent the spread of the disease.

5. During the last 77 miles, when blizzards ______________ (make) it impossible for a human being to find the trail, the lead dog, Balto, ______________ (sniff) out*** the way and ______________ (get) the serum to Nome.

To commemorate this race to save lives, a dogsled race of 1,150 miles was organized in 1973. It is called the Iditarod** Trail Race.**

6. There ______________ (be) a race every year since the first Iditarod Race was held in 1973.
7. The teams often encounter other difficulties besides bad weather. In 1985, almost half the sleds turned over as they ______________ (go) around curves in the steep, winding trail in the Alaska Range.*****
8. In the same year, one team ran into a moose while the team ______________ (run) at night.

9. Two dogs were killed when the moose ______________ (attack) the team.
10. The regulations to protect the dogs are very strict. Whenever a dog ______________ (injure), it must be carried on the sled to the next checkpoint.
11. When the first Iditarod Race ______________ (take) place in 1973, thirty-four teams entered.

****Sniff out:* find by smelling.
****Pronounced "I did a rod."
*****Alaska Range: The highest peak in this mountain range is Mount McKinley. It is 20,320 feet (6,250 meters) high.

12. When the race ____________________ place again next
(take)
March, more than twice that number will enter.

13. By the time the race starts next March, the racers ____________________ many months training their teams.
(spend)

14. Once the snowmobile ____________________ popular, sled
(become)
dogs began to disappear from Alaskan villages.

15. But since the race was established in 1973, dogs ____________________ popular again.
(become)

Exercise 2. Using Subordinating Conjunctions of Time

Read the following interview with a "musher" (sled-dog driver) and combine the pairs of sentences in the musher's responses to the questions. Make the underlined sentence into an adverb clause. Omit the words in capital letters and any other unnecessary words. Change the tense when necessary.

A. Use **as soon as** or **until.**

Interviewer: I notice that your dogs do a lot of barking.

Musher: 1. Yes, the dogs bark and pull against the sled brake. THEN we release the brake.

Yes, the dogs bark and pull against the sled brake until we release it.

2. THEN they begin to run. AT THAT POINT they are silent.

As soon as they begin to run, they are silent.

Interviewer: When did you start training the team?

Musher: 3. We started training them in mid-October. The ground was covered with snow BY THEN.

4. The dogs will be in condition* SOON. We are running them only a few miles a day FOR NOW.

5. They will be in condition AFTER A FEW MORE DAYS. THEN we'll run them fifty or sixty miles a day.

**In condition:* in good physical condition for racing.

Interviewer: How many dogs will you have on your team for the race?

Musher: 6. I'll use about eighteen dogs to climb the Alaska Range. AT SOME POINT, I'll get over the mountains.

7. THEN we'll drop a few dogs at a checkpoint. We'll be on flatter land.

B. Use **(just) before, (just) after, as long as, while,** or **whenever.**

Interviewer: When will you take the team to Anchorage (the starting point)?

Musher: 8. We'll truck the dogs to Anchorage ON MARCH 1. The race will start on March 5. (Use **a few days before.**)

Interviewer: Is it important for a racer to have a personal relationship with his or her dogs?

Musher: 9. Of course. For example, we'll start to race at 11:30. I'll pet and encourage each dog FOR A FEW MINUTES BEFORE THAT.

Interviewer: How often will you stop along the way?

Musher: 10. We won't stop FOR SEVERAL HOURS. The dogs will be running well DURING THAT TIME.

11. The dogs GENERALLY get tired AFTER SEVERAL HOURS. We'll pull off the trail and rest THEN.

12. We'll stop for rest. I'll feed and water the dogs FIRST. THEN I'll try to get a little rest myself.

13. EVERY FIFTY MILES, we'll come to a checkpoint. We must stop THEN.

14. A vet will examine each of the dogs for lameness, bruised feet, and so forth. We will be resting at the checkpoint DURING THAT TIME.

Interviewer: How fast do you think your dogs can go?

Musher: 15. We'll go up to 15 miles an hour (24 kilometers per hour) AT FIRST. They'll be feeling eager.

16. LATER, they'll get into a steady pace. We'll average about 10 to 12 miles per hour AFTER THAT.

Exercise 3. Combining Sentences

In 1985, the Iditarod Race was won by Libby Riddles, a twenty-eight-year-old woman from Teller, Alaska. Weather conditions were bad that year, and it took her eighteen days and twenty minutes to cover the 1,159 miles of trail.

Combine each pair of sentences. Make tense changes where necessary and omit unnecessary time expressions.

A. Use **as, by the time,** and **when.**

1. The mushers left Anchorage on March 2. The trails were clogged with heavy snow at that time.

   When the mushers left Anchorage on March 2, the trails were clogged with heavy snow.

2. They climbed the twisting trail into the mountains. Many sleds tipped over.
3. Riddles joined the top teams. She reached the Yukon River soon after that.

B. Use **when** and **while.**

4. She got only three or four hours of sleep a day. She was racing to pass the other teams.
5. She was dozing* on the sled one night. She was hit by the branch of a tree.
6. The branch knocked her headlamp onto her nose. It gave her a bloody nose, but it woke her up.

C. Use **by the time.**

7. She was among the top five contestants. She crossed Old Woman's Pass.
8. She arrived at Unalakleet in the middle of the night. She took the lead before that.
9. She came into the next checkpoint at dusk.** Strong winds and blowing snow were making it impossible to see the trail markers.

D. Use **once, whenever,** and **while.**

10. Riddles drove into the storm and the darkness. The other mushers were waiting for the storm to pass.
11. She got out onto the ice of Norton Sound. She began to wonder if she was crazy.
12. She didn't want to turn back, however. She had started.

**Dozing:* half asleep.
***Dusk:* nightfall.

13. Every few minutes, the dogs' eyes and ears became crusted with snow. She stopped to wipe it off.

E. Use **by the time, until,** and **when.**

14. They drove ten miles onto the ice. It became impossible to follow the trail.

    By the time . . .

15. Riddles stopped and spent the night in her sled. She realized that the dogs could not sniff out the trail.
16. She woke at dawn. She ate some seal oil and chocolate and started again.
17. (The last day of the race, she was clearly the winner, but she still didn't admit it. She said the following to reporters at the checkpoint.) "I won't brag now. I'll get to Nome first."
18. She arrived in Nome (the finish) on March 20. She left the second-place musher nearly three hours behind her.
19. Riddles won the race in 1985. No woman had ever won the Iditarod before that.

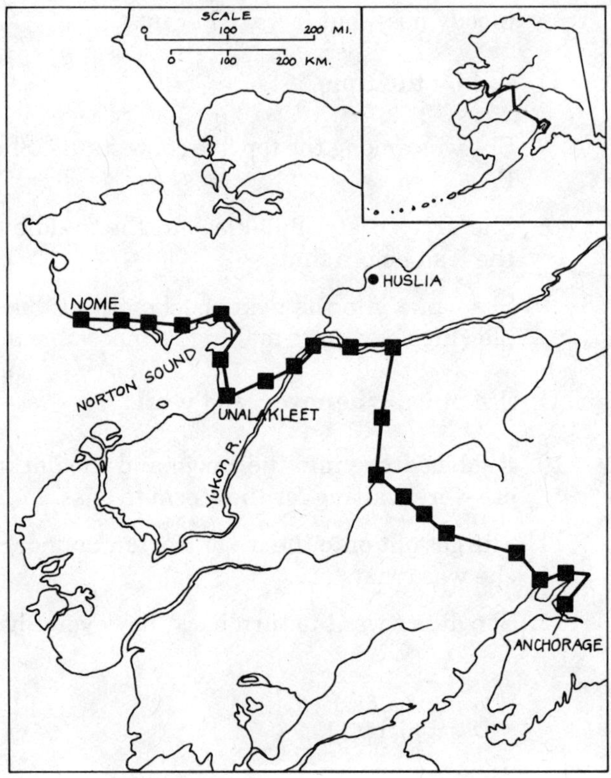

IDITAROD TRAIL RACE ROUTE

17.2 Reduction of Time Clauses

Active

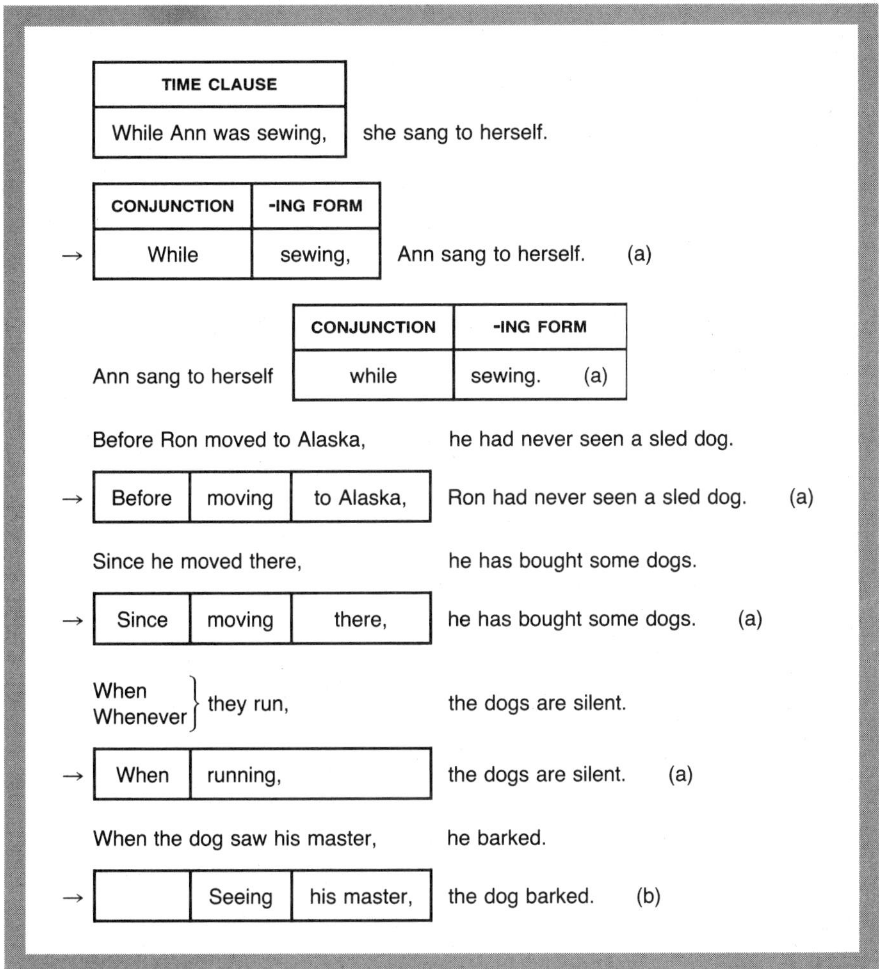

TIME CLAUSE	
While Ann was sewing,	she sang to herself.

	CONJUNCTION	-ING FORM	
→	While	sewing,	Ann sang to herself. (a)

	CONJUNCTION	-ING FORM
Ann sang to herself	while	sewing. (a)

	Before Ron moved to Alaska,			he had never seen a sled dog.
→	Before	moving	to Alaska,	Ron had never seen a sled dog. (a)
	Since he moved there,			he has bought some dogs.
→	Since	moving	there,	he has bought some dogs. (a)
	When / Whenever they run,			the dogs are silent.
→	When	running,		the dogs are silent. (a)
	When the dog saw his master,			he barked.
→		Seeing	his master,	the dog barked. (b)

Form: When a time clause and an independent clause have the same subject, the time clause may often be reduced to a phrase. In the active:

a. Omit the subject in the time clause and use the ***-ing** form* of the verb (present participle). Be sure that the subject of the sentence is still clear (substitute a noun for a pronoun if you need to). This type of reduction is common with the following conjunctions:

after	until
before	while
since	when (*meaning:* whenever)

b. The conjunction **when** is dropped except when it means *whenever.*

Passive

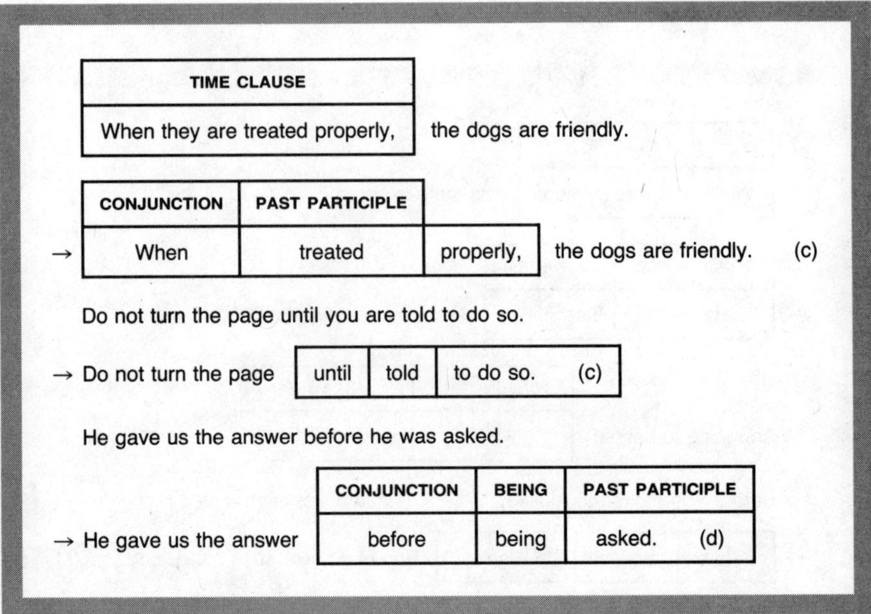

Form: For passive verbs:

c. After **until** and **when,** omit the subject and **be** and use the past participle.

d. After **after, before, since,** and **while,** use ***being*** before the past participle.

The Verb *be*

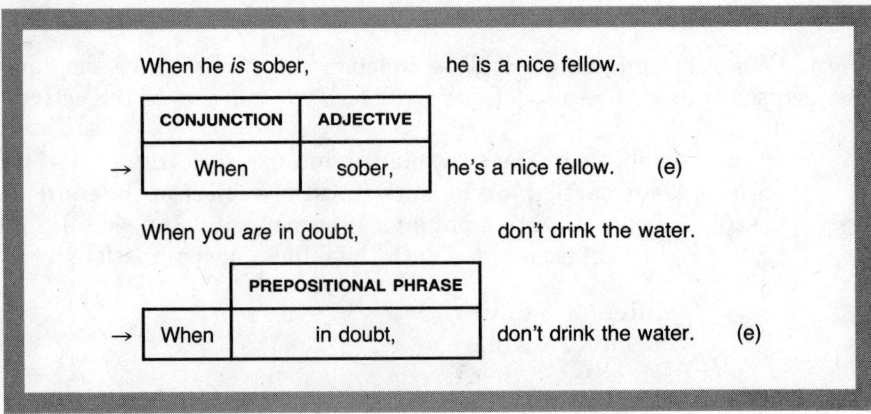

Form: e. The verb **be** is often omitted entirely before prepositional phrases and adjectives.

Note: When the subjects of the two clauses are different, no reduction is possible.

Compare:

While Ann was sewing, she sang to herself.
→ **While sewing, Ann sang to herself.**
While Ann was sewing, Maria prepared dinner.
→ **(No reduction possible.)**

There are a few common phrases which break this rule. In these, the subject **it** is understood.

Use a comma *when necessary.*
***If possible,* you should reserve a place beforehand.**

Exercise 4. Reductions

Underline the adverb clause in each sentence. Then, whenever possible, reduce the time clause to a phrase. Be sure that the subject of your sentence is clear.

1. Riddles has been raising sled dogs since she moved to Alaska at the age of sixteen.

   Riddles has been raising sled dogs *since moving* to Alaska at the age of sixteen.

2. When dogs are raised with a lot of friendly human contact, they will work hard for their drivers.

   When raised with a lot of friendly human contact, dogs will work hard for their drivers.

3. When their drivers treat them well, sled dogs will work hard. (No change.*)
4. They will sometimes run until they are exhausted.
5. When they are healthy, sled dogs love to run.
6. The dogs bark eagerly while they are waiting to be harnessed.
7. They jump and strain at the harness until they are permitted to run.

*This sentence can be made passive and then reduced: *When treated well, . . .*

8. They jump and strain at the harness until the sled brake is released.
9. A good lead dog must be intelligent. Some dogs seem to know the musher's wish even before they are given a command.
10. When a driver pulls off the trail to rest, he or she thinks about the dogs first.
11. After the dogs are fed and watered, the musher can sleep a few hours.
12. After the musher takes care of the needs of the dogs, he or she can rest.

17.3 Place Clauses; Factual Manner Clauses

As Complement

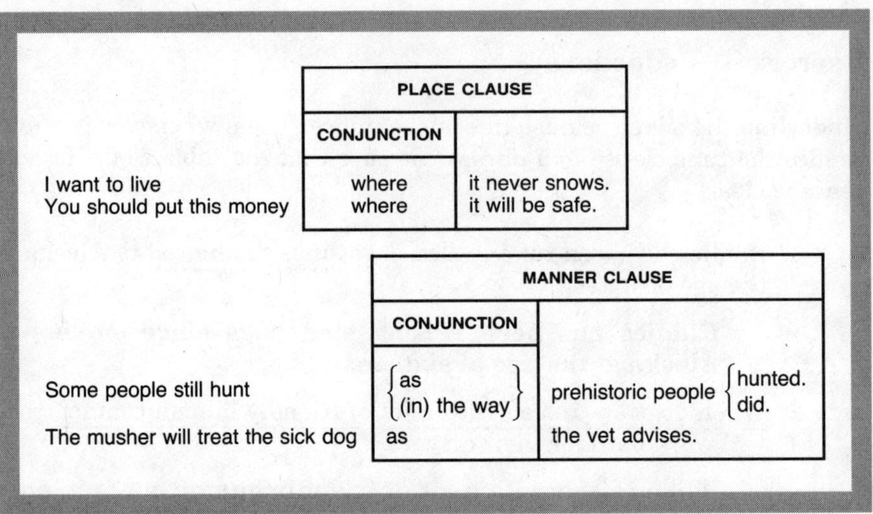

	PLACE CLAUSE	
	CONJUNCTION	
I want to live	where	it never snows.
You should put this money	where	it will be safe.

	MANNER CLAUSE	
	CONJUNCTION	
Some people still hunt	{as / (in) the way}	prehistoric people {hunted. / did.}
The musher will treat the sick dog	as	the vet advises.

Word Order: When a place or manner clause is a complement,* it comes after the independent clause. In this position, **the way** may be used to mean **as.**

Note: In informal conversation, **like** is often used instead of **as:**

Some Indians still live like their ancestors did.

This usage is not considered correct in written English.

*A complement is a phrase or clause which is necessary to complete the verb phrase. For example, *You should put this money* is not a complete sentence. We need to know *where.*

As Sentence Modifier

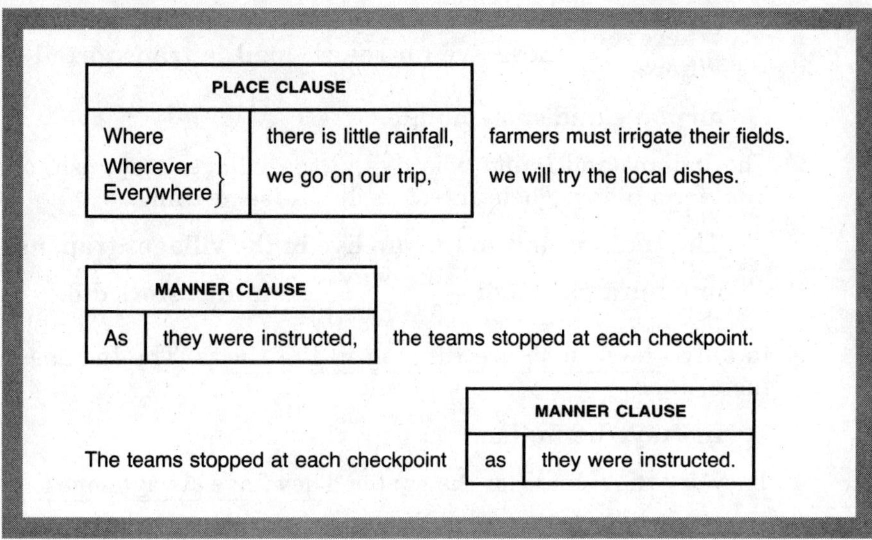

Word Order: Some place and manner clauses are not complements. They can either precede or follow the independent clause.

> *Note:* Place and manner clauses in the *passive* may be reduced to phrases:
>
> **Use a comma *where it is needed.***
> → **Use a comma *where needed.***
> ***As they were instructed,* the teams stopped . . .**
> → ***As instructed,* the teams stopped . . .**

Exercise 5. Combining with Place and Manner Clauses

Combine the pairs of sentences as follows:

a. Use **where, wherever, (just) as,** or **the way** to make the underlined sentence into an adverb clause.

b. Combine the clause with the other sentence, changing the order of the clauses if necessary. Omit unnecessary words and use **do, did,** etc., where you need them.

A. In large areas of the interior of Alaska, there are no roads or railroads. Life there is quite different from life in other parts of the United States.

1. There are no roads. Mail is transported by airplane and snowmobile.

   Wherever / Where } **there are no roads, mail is transported by airplane and snowmobile.**

2. The Indians and Inuit* who live in the villages trap, fish, and hunt for a living. Their ancestors did the same thing.

   The Indians and Inuit who live in the villages trap, fish, and hunt for a living the way / as } **their ancestors did.**

3. In July, the salmon are running in the rivers. The Indians go there.

   In July, the Indians . . .

4. They dry the salmon for the winter. They have always done that.
5. As soon as the ice is solid in the fall, they set fishing lines through the ice. The fishing is best in certain places.
6. In December and January, the scarce caribou can be found only in a few places. The men hunt there.

7. The women tan the skins of the animals and make boots and parkas.** Their mothers taught them how.

B. Life in the village of Huslia is an example of the Indian way of life. Huslia is located 60 air miles (100 kilometers) from the nearest village and 260 miles from the nearest road. The village is famous for its fine sled dogs.

8. The inhabitants go places. They must use plane, dogsled, or snowmobile.
9. (Yet they are not isolated from modern life.) In the summer, many men go away. They can find employment in other places.

**Inuit:* Eskimos. "Inuit" is the word that the Eskimos use for themselves.
***Parkas:* jackets with hoods.

10. There are high schools and colleges in other places. In the winter, the teenage children go there.
11. The children speak the Athabaskan language. Their grandparents do, too.
12. Their grandparents live in a certain way. But since the young people spend nine months of the year away at school, they no longer live that way.

Exercise 6. Cumulative Exercise

Combine the pairs of sentences using the conjunctions that you have studied in this lesson. Omit the words in capital letters and any other unnecessary words. Try to use most of the conjunctions. (There are some that you will not need.)

Conjunctions of Time		*Conjunctions of Place*
after	once	where
as	since	wherever
as long as	until	
as soon as	when	*Conjunctions of Manner*
before	whenever	as
by the time	while	the way

1. It is believed that dogsledding began AT A CERTAIN TIME. Siberian tribes around Lake Baikal first used dogs to transport game about 4,000 years ago.

   It is believed that dogsledding began when Siberian tribes first used dogs to transport game about 4,000 years ago.

2. The custom spread. EVENTUALLY, dogsleds were used IN MANY PLACES. The ground is covered with snow IN THOSE PLACES.
3. Arab tribes traveled through Siberia in the tenth century. They reported seeing dogsleds.
4. Marco Polo wrote about them. He returned to Italy from China in the thirteenth century.
5. European explorers in arctic regions had a very difficult time. THEN they learned to use sled dogs. The native peoples used sled dogs.
6. They learned the value of the sled dog. THEN they used dogs to

explore the arctic, to bring out furs, and to deliver mail and supplies. (Use **once.**)

7. Gold was discovered in Canada and Alaska at the end of the nineteenth century. RIGHT AWAY, dogs were put to use transporting gold.

8. Many dogs were stolen from the streets of Seattle, San Francisco, and Los Angeles. The gold rush was creating a demand for dogs.

9. Thousands of prospectors* moved into Alaska and Northwest Canada. Police patrols were needed to maintain law and order.

10. The last long dogsled patrol was made by the Royal Canadian Mounted Police in 1969. The "Mounties" had patrolled by dogsled for almost 100 years.

11. Peter Benjamin (a Loucheux Indian) made that last patrol. The Mounties have used snowmobiles and airplanes for long patrols FROM THAT YEAR UP TO NOW.

12. The mail was delivered by dogsled FOR ABOUT 100 YEARS. FOR ALL THAT TIME, the mail team was the most important team on the road.

13. The mail driver went to many places. IN ALL THOSE PLACES, he was given the right of way on the trail.

14. He came into an overnight roadhouse, bringing his lead dog with him. He was ALWAYS given the best seat at the table and the best bed.

15. Mail was delivered by dogsled in both Canada and Alaska. EVENTUALLY, planes and snowmobiles took over.

16. Airplanes replaced the last dog team in 1963. Even THEN the team was kept on a standby basis because in bad weather a dog team can go. A plane cannot fly AT SUCH TIMES.

Transfer Exercises

1. On Reading about the Iditarod

Complete each sentence with a clause.

Example: Until I read about sled dogs in this lesson . . .
I had never heard of them.
or: **I didn't know much about them.**
or: **I thought that they were no longer used.**

*_Prospectors:_ people who were looking for gold.

1. Until I read about sled dogs in this lesson . . .
2. I became more interested in them as . . .
3. By the time I finished doing the exercises . . .
4. I had never heard of Libby Riddles until . . .
5. Riddles will never forget the '85 Iditarod Race as long as . . .
6. I have never lived where . . .
7. I would(n't) enjoy driving dogs through a blinding blizzard the way . . .
8. I (don't) think I could live the way . . .
9. Whenever I learn something new about . . . , I . . .

2. Personal Questions

Complete each question with a *clause* (or *reduced clause*) and ask the question of a classmate.

Examples: Do you usually do your English homework as soon as **you get home?**
Do you usually finish your homework before **watching TV?**

1. Do you usually do your English homework as soon as . . .
2. Do you usually finish your homework before . . .
3. Do you usually listen to the radio while . . .
4. What did you see this morning as . . .
5. In the classroom, do you always sit where . . .
6. Would you like to speak English the way . . .
7. Are you going to study English until . . .
8. Are you going to quit studying once . . .
9. What do you hope to do after . . .
10. Have you been living in this city since . . .
11. Do you plan to stay in this country (or city) as long as . . .
12. *(For unmarried students)* Do you plan to get married as soon as . . .
13. *(For married students)* Do you plan to change your lifestyle as soon as your children . . .
14. By the time you retire, how long . . .

Discussion Topics

A. In your country, are dogs trained to work? Do they do any of the following jobs, and if so, *how?* What special abilities do they use?

Do they herd sheep, cows, or other animals? When and how?
Do they help the police? When and how?
Do they lead blind people? How?
Do they protect houses, factories, stores, etc.? When and how?
Do they help hunt or fish? How?
Do they transport goods? How?

B. In the United States, there are special beds and special food for dogs. Dogs sometimes wear raincoats, get their hair cut, and go to obedience school. There are even dog psychiatrists for dogs with behavior problems. Do these customs seem strange to you?

How are dogs raised in your country? Do they usually live in the house with the family, or are they kept outside? Do they run free, or are they tied up? Are they trained to be friendly and obedient? What are they fed? Are most dogs just pets, with no special work to do? Do you like dogs? Why or why not?

C. Is dog racing popular in your country? Is there sled-dog racing? Are there dog shows in which dogs compete for good looks or obedience? Have you ever entered a dog in a race or a show? If so, when? How did you train it?

D. Are there other animals that are important in the life of your country? If so, what animals, and what do they do? Are they trained to work? Have you ever trained an animal? If so, when? What did you train it to do, and how did you train it?

E. What animals are popular as pets in your country besides cats and dogs?

F. Are there isolated areas of your country where transportation by car or bus is impossible or difficult? If so, what forms of transportation are used to reach these areas? How did the local people travel traditionally? Do they still use the traditional ways? If not, when did they stop using them? How is mail delivered there? How do the police travel? Does weather sometimes interfere with transportation? When? What do people do when that happens?

G. Do you live, speak, and think the way your grandparents did? What are some differences?

Composition Topics

Write a short composition about one of the following topics. Include clauses of time, place, and manner in some of your sentences.

1. Write about the place of dogs in the life of your country. You can include a discussion of dogs as pets, dogs as useful animals, and dog racing, or you can limit your discussion to one of these topics. (See Discussion Topics A, B, and C.)
2. Write about another animal that is important or popular in your country. (See Discussion Topics D and E.)
3. Write about a pet or other animal that has been important in your life personally.
4. Write about a traditional means of transportation in your country. (See Discussion Question F.)
5. Write about a form of racing, for example, running, swimming, or dog racing, or racing with automobiles, boats, horses, or bicycles. Include some information about preparation for the race, the regulations, and the dangers and skills involved.
6. Write about how you are different from your grandparents. (See Discussion Question G.)

Lesson 18

The Inuit

18.1 Reason Clauses; Reduction of Reason Clauses

Full Clause

REASON CLAUSE		
CONJUNCTION		
Since } / As }	it was raining,	Sue took her umbrella. (a)
Inasmuch as	John is an excellent student,	he will probably get a scholarship. (b)
In view of the fact that	John is an excellent student,	he received a scholarship. (c)
Now that	Roberta has finished college,	she plans to look for a job. (d)

	REASON CLAUSE	
Sue took her umbrella	because	it was raining. (e)

Meaning: The conjunctions in this group introduce the *cause* of the event in the independent clause.

a. **Since** and **as** are used when the emphasis is on the result in the independent clause.

b. **Inasmuch as** is used mainly in formal speech and writing. It also emphasizes the result.

c. **In view of the fact that** is used when the cause leads to a decision (not a natural result).

Right: **In view of the fact that it is raining, we should take an umbrella.**

Wrong: **In ~~view of the fact~~ that it is raining, the streets are wet.**

d. **Now that** means *now because*. It indicates a change from the past situation.

e. To emphasize the *cause,* we use **because** and place the adverb clause after the independent clause. (When a clause with **because** comes first, it emphasizes the result.) **Because** is the only conjunction in this group used in answering questions with **why.**

—Why is the child crying?

—Because he has a stomachache.

He is crying because he has a stomachache.

Reduction

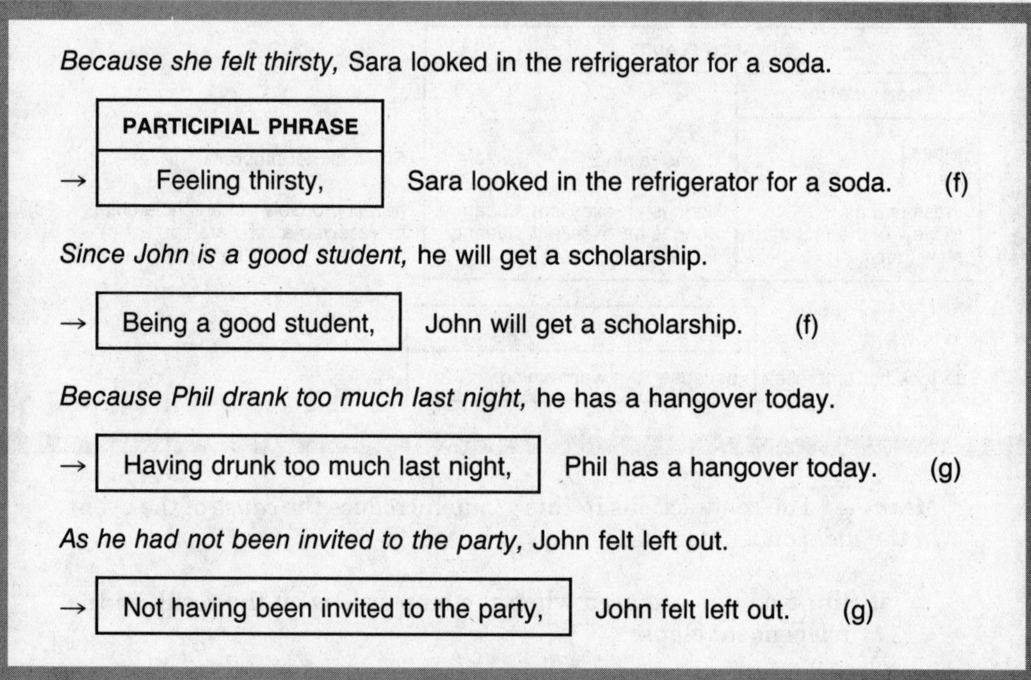

Because she felt thirsty, Sara looked in the refrigerator for a soda.

PARTICIPIAL PHRASE

→ Feeling thirsty, Sara looked in the refrigerator for a soda. (f)

Since John is a good student, he will get a scholarship.

→ Being a good student, John will get a scholarship. (f)

Because Phil drank too much last night, he has a hangover today.

→ Having drunk too much last night, Phil has a hangover today. (g)

As he had not been invited to the party, John felt left out.

→ Not having been invited to the party, John felt left out. (g)

Form: When the reason clause and the independent clause have the same subject, the reason clause may be reduced by omitting the conjunction and the subject and using a participle:

f. Use the *present participle* (**-ing** form) of the verb if the two actions or states refer to the same time. If the verb is **be,** use **being.**

g. Use **having** + *past participle* for an action that occurs before the action in the independent clause. In the passive, use *having been + past participle.*

Exercise 1. Using Subordinating Conjunctions of Reason

When Europeans began to explore the arctic regions of North America, they found a people already living there. We call these people Eskimos, but they call themselves Inuit, which means "human beings." The friendly Inuit helped the explorers and were in turn affected by their arrival in the Arctic.

Combine the sentences, using **because, since, as, inasmuch as,** and **in view of the fact that.**

A. Explorers learned from the Inuit how to survive in the severe arctic climate.

1. The early explorers were able to survive in the Arctic. The Inuit helped them.

   The early explorers were able to survive in the Arctic because the Inuit helped them.

2. The weather conditions were very severe. The explorers had to adopt Inuit ways of dressing, traveling, and finding food.

   Since . . .

3. The Arctic is covered with snow for more than six months of the year. Game was scarce and hunters had to travel long distances to find it.

4. Dogs could run long distances in snow and survive in extremely cold weather. The dogsled was perfectly suited to the Inuit's needs.

B. The early contact with Europeans created health problems for the Inuit, however.

5. Influenza, tuberculosis, and many other diseases were unknown among the Inuit. They had had no contact with other people.

6. Many of them died when they came into contact with Europeans. Their bodies had not developed resistance to these diseases.

C. Other people's politics have also interfered with the life of the Inuit. The cold war* between the United States and the Soviet Union is one example.

7. Many Alaskan Inuit used to visit Siberia. They have brothers, sisters, and cousins there.
8. Siberia and Alaska are only fifty miles apart. It was an easy trip by boat.
9. However, Siberia belongs to the Soviet Union and there is a "cold war" between that country and the United States. The Inuit have not been permitted to go back and forth since 1948.

However, . . .

10. Relatives who lived only two and a half miles apart on Big Diomede Island and Little Diomede Island cannot walk across the ice to celebrate Christmas together as they used to do. One island belongs to the Soviet Union and the other belongs to the United States.
11. The inhabitants of Little Diomede wanted to see their relatives again. They asked the Soviet government for permission to visit Siberia. (The inhabitants of Big Diomede had been moved to the mainland.)
12. The government in the Soviet Union is more liberal now. In 1988, they authorized the first "friendship flight" between Alaska and Siberia. (The visit took place in June 1988.)

Exercise 2. Distinguishing the Two Meanings of *since*

A. Which of the following clauses with **since** give a *reason?* Which indicate a period of *time?*

1. Alaska has had a governor since it became a state in 1959. time
2. Alaska has a governor since it is a state. reason
3. Since Alaska is a part of the United States, English is the official language there. ______
4. Since Alaska was sold to the United States by Russia, English has been the official language there. ______
5. The Inuit have been using dogsleds ever since they came to America from Siberia. ______

**Cold war:* political tension.

6. Nowadays, they have started using snowmobiles since they can go faster in deep snow. ______

B. Complete each sentence so that the **since** clause refers to *reason* or *time* as indicated. Make a guess if you don't know the facts.

7. (reason) Since farming is impossible in the Arctic, the Inuit . . .
8. (time) Since the Inuit learned how to use guns from the Europeans, . . .
9. (reason) In the interior of Alaska and the Northwest Territories, people have to travel by dogsled, snowmobile, and airplane since . . .
10. (time) Dogsleds have been less popular in the Arctic since . . .

Exercise 3. *Now that*

The transition to twentieth-century life has brought many changes for the Inuit.

Combine the sentences, using **now that.**

1. The residents of Big Diomede Island have been moved to Siberia. Friends and relatives from Little Diomede cannot walk across the ice to visit them.

   Now that the residents of Big Diomede Island have been moved to Siberia, friends and relatives from Little Diomede cannot walk across the ice to visit them.

2. However, they will be able to see each other again occasionally. The Soviet Union is permitting friendship flights to Siberia.
3. The Inuit use snowmobiles and guns. They need money to buy gas and ammunition.
4. They have to find paying jobs. They need money.
5. We have communications satellites. About 90 percent of Canadian Inuit have access to television.
6. The children are not learning the traditional Inuit ways. They spend their time watching American television programs like "Miami Vice" and "Dallas."
7. However, the Canadian government has started the Inuit Broadcasting Corporation. Programs are being broadcast in the Inuit language.
8. Inuit can watch programs about themselves in their own language. Perhaps the old ways will not be forgotten.

Exercise 4. Combining Sentences with Reduced Reason Clauses

Combine the sentences with reduced reason clauses. Decide which sentence gives a reason, change it to a participial phrase (reduced clause), and place the phrase *before* the other sentence. Be sure that the subject of your sentence is clear.

1. The town of Nome, Alaska, is not a big city, but it is the main center for an area the size of California. The town has a population of only 3,700.

    Having a population of only 3,700, the town of Nome, Alaska, is not a big city, but it is the main center for an area the size of California.

2. Many Inuit and Indians in the area depend on battery-operated radios. They have no other contact with the outside world.
3. Nome's radio station, KNOM, realizes this. It broadcasts personal messages.
4. For example, people depend on "bush" flights* for transportation. They listen to KNOM for announcements about these flights.
5. Fishermen listen to KNOM for important messages from their families. They don't have telephones or two-way radios.
6. Some people live fifty miles or more from the nearest post office. They depend on KNOM to tell them when something has been mailed to them.
7. The station was founded in 1971. It is now about twenty years old.
8. KNOM has served its community for almost twenty years. It has won several broadcasting awards.

18.2 Result Clauses *(so/such . . . that)*

So

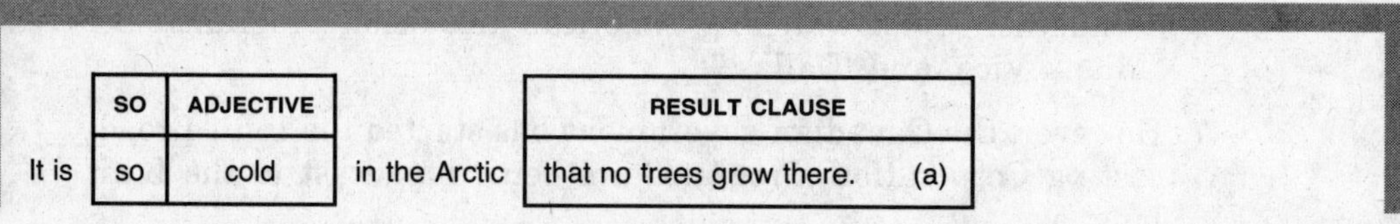

	SO	ADJECTIVE		RESULT CLAUSE
It is	so	cold	in the Arctic	that no trees grow there. (a)

**Bush flights:* flights in small planes, not regularly scheduled.

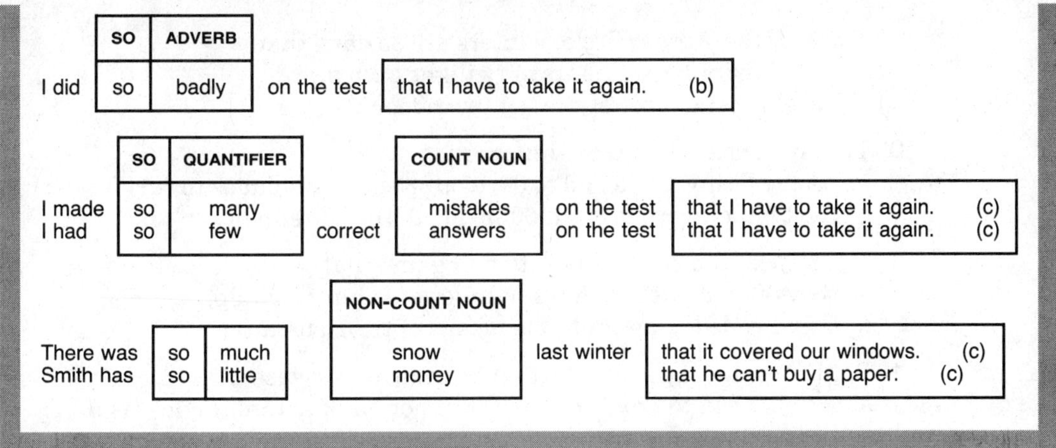

SO | ADVERB
I did so badly on the test that I have to take it again. (b)
SO | QUANTIFIER | COUNT NOUN
I made so many mistakes on the test that I have to take it again. (c)
I had so few correct answers on the test that I have to take it again. (c)
NON-COUNT NOUN
There was so much snow last winter that it covered our windows. (c)
Smith has so little money that he can't buy a paper. (c)

Such

	SUCH	A/AN	ADJECTIVE	NOUN		
I had	such	a	good	time	in Alaska	that I want to go there again. (d)
I met	such		interesting	people		that I want to go back. (d)

Word Choice: Use **so**

a. before an adjective that does not modify a noun
b. before an adverb
c. before quantifiers **many, few, much,** and **little**

Use **such**

d. before an adjective that precedes and modifies a noun. The article **(a/an)** comes after **such.**

Meaning: The result clause gives a *result* of the condition in the independent clause.

> *Note:* In informal speech, **that** may be omitted.
>
> **There was so much snow last winter it covered our windows.**

Exercise 5. Recognizing Result Clauses

Circle the letter of the clause which gives a *result* of the condition in the independent clause.

1. North of the Arctic Circle, winters are so dark that
   a. there are only two hours of twilight each day.
   (b) people spend most of the winter indoors.

2. The Arctic has such cold winters that
   a. people living there had to develop special techniques to survive.
   b. the temperature is often 60° below zero Fahrenheit.

3. Hunters had to travel so far to find game that
   a. they often went hundreds of miles on a hunting trip.
   b. they needed a fast, reliable means of transportation.

4. Big Diomede Island and Little Diomede are so close that
   a. people used to cross in small boats or walk across the ice regularly.
   b. they are only two and a half miles apart.

5. Nowadays, Inuit children watch so much American television that
   a. they are in danger of losing their own language and culture.
   b. they see "Dallas," "Miami Vice," and many other shows.

6. In the Arctic, there are so few roads that
   a. there are only three short roads leading out of Nome, Alaska.
   b. people depend on planes, dogs, boats, and snowmobiles.

7. There are so few telephones in northwest Alaska that
   a. most people don't have them.
   b. people depend on radio.

Exercise 6. Forming Sentences with Result Clauses

Restate the sentences so that each includes a result clause with **so/such . . . that.** Change the order of the clauses when necessary.

A. The traditional way of life of the Inuit.

1. There isn't much vegetation in the Arctic. The Inuit live almost entirely on meat and fish.

   There is so little vegetation in the Arctic that the Inuit live almost entirely on meat and fish.

2. Inuit hunters may be gone from their villages for days, weeks, or months at a time* when they travel long distances on hunting trips.

For (days) at a time: for several days without interruption.

Inuit hunters travel such long distances on hunting trips that they may be gone from their villages for days, weeks, or months at a time.

3. The hunters have to travel long distances to find food for their families because fish and game are scarce.

   Fish and game . . .

4. Traditionally, the Inuit built their houses of skins in the summer and snow in the winter because there isn't much wood in the Arctic.
5. Besides animals, birds, and fish, there are few resources. The Inuit used every part of these animals to make tools, clothing, boats, lamps, tents, etc.

B. Putting Inuit skills to work in the military.

6. The arctic region presents great difficulties for ordinary military forces. Both the Canadian government and the U.S. government use Inuit to conduct military patrols there.
7. The Inuit need little training and can help train other troops in winter warfare because they are already skillful at surviving in the Arctic.
8. They don't need a map or a compass to find their way even during a blizzard. They know the area within 300 miles of their village thoroughly.
9. They have an amazing ability to navigate** even during a blizzard. They have led other troops to safety who would have died otherwise.
10. They are already good marksmen. They don't have to be trained in shooting.
11. Hunting and fishing during the short summer months is important for the Inuit's survival. The Eskimo Scouts' military training must take place in midwinter.
12. The Eskimo Scouts and the Canadian Rangers enjoy their work, and the pay they receive helps their communities, which are poor. Almost every family is receiving government assistance.

***Navigate:* find one's way.

18.3 Purpose Clauses; Reduction of Purpose Clauses to Infinitive Phrases

Full Clause

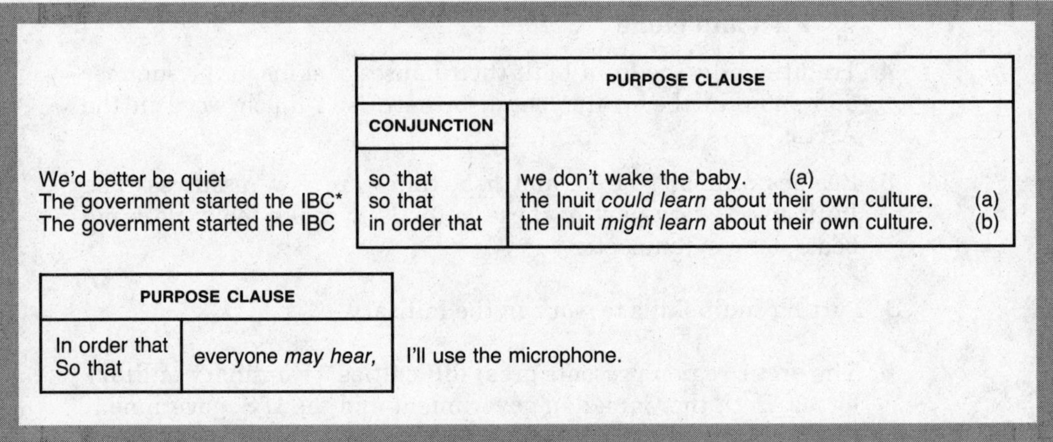

	PURPOSE CLAUSE		
	CONJUNCTION		
We'd better be quiet	so that	we don't wake the baby.	(a)
The government started the IBC*	so that	the Inuit *could learn* about their own culture.	(a)
The government started the IBC	in order that	the Inuit *might learn* about their own culture.	(b)

PURPOSE CLAUSE		
In order that So that	everyone *may hear,*	I'll use the microphone.

Meaning: Purpose clauses with **so that** and **in order that** give the *purpose* of the action in the independent clause.

Choice of Auxiliary:

a. **So that** is very often followed by auxiliaries **will, would, may, might, can,** or **could** to indicate that the event in the purpose clause happens after the event in the independent clause.

b. **In order that** is usually followed by **may** or **might.**

Formal and Informal Usage: **In order that** is used mainly in formal speech and writing.

Note: In informal speech, **that** is sometimes omitted after **so.**

Be quiet so you don't wake the baby.

Reduction

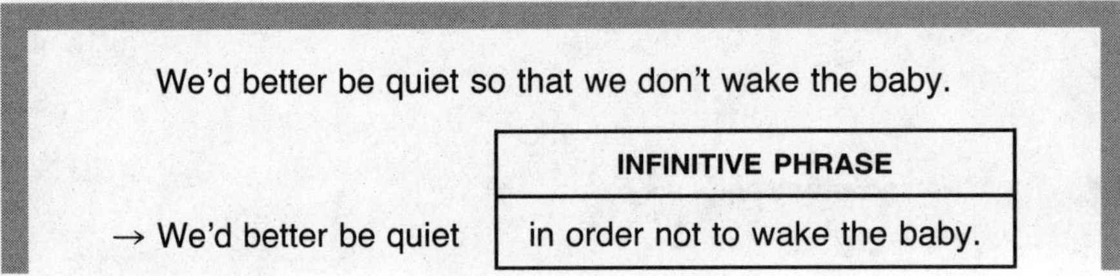

We'd better be quiet so that we don't wake the baby.

	INFINITIVE PHRASE
→ We'd better be quiet	in order not to wake the baby.

**IBC:* Inuit Broadcasting Corporation.

I studied hard so that I would pass the test.

→ I studied hard | (in order) to pass the test.

Form: When the independent clause and the purpose clause have the same subject, the purpose clause may be reduced to an infinitive phrase with **to** or **in order to. In order** may be deleted if the infinitive is affirmative. (See also Lesson 13, page 228.)

Exercise 7. Purpose Clauses and Phrases

Robert J. Flaherty's famous film, *Nanook of the North,* gives us a picture of Inuit life seventy-five years ago, before it had been changed greatly by contact with modern civilization. Flaherty wrote a vivid account of how he made the film.

a. Change each sentence to include a purpose clause with **so that** or **in order that.** Be careful that the *auxiliary* in the purpose clause shows the correct time relationship to the action in the independent clause.

b. If possible, reduce the purpose clause to a phrase with **in order to.**

1. In 1913, when Flaherty went to the far north to look for iron ore, he took a movie camera and film because he wanted to film the life of the Inuit.

   a. **In 1913, when Flaherty went to the far north to look for iron ore, he took a movie camera and film so that he *could film* the life of the Inuit.**
   b. **He took a camera and film in order to film the life of the Inuit.**

2. (Later Flaherty returned to the north solely to make a film.) On this trip, he took a movie projector because he wanted the Inuit to be able to see themselves on film.

3. He set up his camp near a stream because he needed a lot of water to develop the film.

4. Flaherty wanted to set up his camera inside an igloo* and film the Inuit's indoor activities.

5. The Inuit had to build an igloo 25 feet (8 meters) across because his camera would not fit inside an ordinary 12-foot igloo.
6. They were able to build it, but then it was necessary to remove the top of the dome because there wasn't enough light inside for filming.
7. Because Flaherty wanted to film them while they were sleeping, Nanook and his wife had to go to bed in the open air!
8. Once, Flaherty mounted his camera on a dogsled and filmed a caribou hunt.
9. Another time, he traveled eight weeks by dogsled in the hope of filming a bear hunt.
10. While they were traveling, Flaherty asked Nanook to carry the film and camera inside his jacket because the film cracked in the cold air. (The other Inuit teased Nanook about his new "babies.")

Exercise 8. Cumulative Exercise: Reason, Result, Purpose, Place, and Time

Alaska and the Northwest Territories are North America's "last frontier," where there are still large areas without roads and with few people. Two hundred years ago, however, the frontier began just west of the Appalachian Mountains, in the territory which is now Ohio, Indiana, and Illinois. Through this largely unsettled land, a strange figure wandered, carrying a bag of apple seeds. Today, few people recognize his real name, but every American school child has heard his nickname, Johnny Appleseed.

Combine the sentences with clauses and reduced clauses, omitting any unnecessary words. Use the following combining forms:

**Igloo:* a house made of snow.

	Clauses	*Phrases*
time:	after, before, until, when	*conjunction + participial phrase*
reason:	because, since, as	*participial phrase*
purpose:	so that	in order to
result:	so/such . . . that	
place:	wherever	

John Chapman was born in Massachusetts around the year 1775.

1. He was about twenty-five years old. He tied two canoes together.

   When he was about twenty-five years old, he tied two canoes together.

2. He filled them with rotten apples. Then he began to paddle west down the Ohio River.

   After { filling . . . / he had filled . . .

3. He knew that settlers would be coming to the new territories. He planted seeds everywhere. He went from place to place.
4. He planted the seeds. He wanted the settlers to have apples when they settled in their new homes.
5. In the first years, there were few settlers. Johnny scarcely met anyone except Indians.
6. Johnny was skilled in the use of medicinal herbs. He could sometimes cure the Indians' illnesses.
7. They saw him cure their sick. They considered him a great medicine man.
8. Each year, Johnny returned to where he had planted seeds and took care of the young trees. He wanted them to grow.
9. People came into Ohio and found the apple trees. They built their houses near them. They wanted to enjoy their fruit.
10. The settlers who moved into the territory were far from friends and relatives. They were always eager to see Johnny and hear the news that he brought.
11. Johnny wore an old coffee sack for a shirt and a metal pot for a hat. He looked strange. Some people thought he was crazy.
12. However, the Indians considered him their friend. He didn't carry a gun.

13. Johnny planted seeds throughout Ohio. Then he moved west into Indiana and Illinois.
14. Then he was about seventy years old. He started back to Ohio. He wanted to plant new trees there.
15. But he became sick. He didn't reach Ohio.
16. A family of settlers cared for him. He died.

He was buried under one of his own apple trees.

Transfer Exercises

1. Climate and Geography (oral)

There are many places in the world that have extreme climates. Expand the following sentences, using result clauses with **so/such . . . that.** Use the place names in parentheses or others that you think of. When you don't know the facts, guess.

1. There isn't much rain in the (Sahara Desert).

   There is so little rain in the Sahara Desert that nothing grows there.
2. The rain forests of (the Amazon Valley) are very wet.
3. (India) has a great deal of rain in the rainy season.
4. (Siberia) has very cold winters.
5. (Florida) has a pleasant climate in the winter. However, it's extremely hot in the summer.
6. (California) doesn't have much rain in the summer.
7. The Great Salt Lake in Utah is very salty.
8. It's only a short distance from (England) to (France).

2. Cause and Effect in Your Life (oral)

Change each sentence into a reduced reason clause (participial phrase), and add an independent clause which gives the result. Include the words in parentheses if they are true for you.

1. I wasn't taught to speak English when I was a child.

   Not having been taught to speak English when I was a child, I have to study it now.

2. I've studied English for (   ) years.
3. I've attended classes and done my homework regularly.
4. I (don't) have a car.
5. I have (never) been to Alaska.
6. I felt (tired/lonely/pretty good) last night.
7. I saw a friend of mine (at the cafeteria) last night.
8. I have (not) received a letter from (   ) recently.
9. I (don't) have a girlfriend/boyfriend here in (name of city).

3. Personal Goals (books closed or pair work)

Answer the questions, giving a purpose with **so that.**

1. Why are you studying English?

   I'm studying English
   { so that I can write business letters in English.
   { so that I can study at an American university.

2. Why did you enroll at this school?
3. What subject are you { majoring / going to major } in, and why?
4. When you finish your studies, where do you plan to live, and why?
5. When you retire, where do you plan to live, and why?
6. Where are you planning to go during your next vacation, and why?
7. Are you saving your money, and if so, why?

4. International Relations

Answer the questions. If the answer is *yes,* add a clause with **so that.**

1. Do you think that your country needs a strong military force? If so, why?
2. Is your government negotiating with other countries?
3. Do you think the superpowers should increase or decrease their supply of weapons?
4. What kind of aid should the big powers give to developing countries, and why?
5. Do you think the United Nations should have stronger powers?
6. Are there new laws or regulations that we need to establish in this country or in the world? If so, why do we need them?

Discussion Topics

A. Are there any areas in your country where the climate is severe? If so, what is the climate like? How does it affect the landscape and the lives of the people? Have people developed special ways of dressing, traveling, or obtaining food in order to survive? If so, give some examples.

B. Is there a group of people in your country who follow a traditional way of life? If so, what is their name, and what language do they speak? How do they live? For example, what are their houses made of? their clothes? Are they farmers, hunters, or fishermen? Do they have special arts, skills, or customs? Do they have much contact with other people in your country, or are they isolated? Do they have schools? television? Do they have any special problems? Is their way of life changing because of contact with other cultures?

C. The Canadian and U.S. governments are trying to help the Inuit preserve their culture. Is your government doing anything similar? Is it possible for a group of people to maintain their traditional culture in our modern world? Is it desirable? Why or why not? What is lost when a culture adopts modern ways, and what is gained? (If possible, give examples from your country.)

D. In your country, what languages are used for television and radio broadcasts? Are there special programs for special groups of people? Do most of the programs help to preserve the traditional culture or cultures of your country, or is television contributing to change? In general, do you think that television and radio have a good influence in your country? Do stations ever broadcast special messages for people (like KNOM)?

Composition Topics

Write a short composition about one of the following topics. Use reason, result, and purpose clauses (and their reduced forms) in some of your sentences.

1. Write about how the climate in your country (or one area of your country) affects the way people live. If the climate is a hard one, what techniques have people developed for survival? (See Exercise 6 and Discussion Topic A.)

2. Write about a group of people in your country who have a traditional culture. Answer some of the questions in Discussion Topic B.

3. All around the world, pre-industrial societies are experiencing rapid change as they come into contact with the modern industrialized world. How can we best help people in these societies? Can we, or should we, try to preserve traditional cultures? Give your opinion. (See also Discussion Topic C.)
4. Write about the effects of television on the culture of your country. (See Discussion Topic D.)

Lesson 19

The "I Have a Dream" Foundation

19.1 The Future Real Conditional

Statements

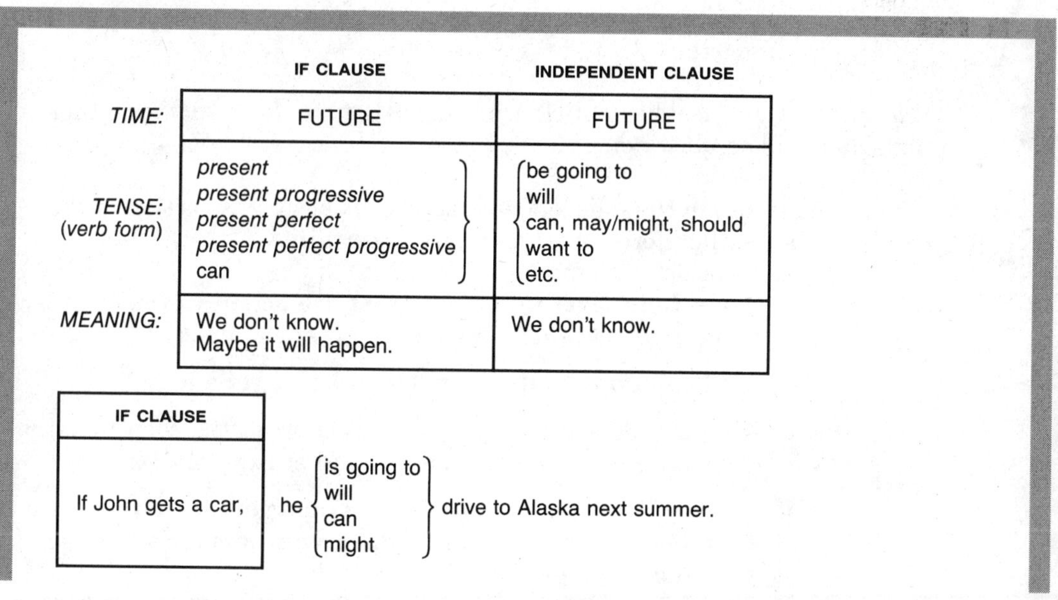

	IF CLAUSE	INDEPENDENT CLAUSE
TIME:	FUTURE	FUTURE
TENSE: (verb form)	*present* *present progressive* *present perfect* *present perfect progressive* can	be going to will can, may/might, should want to etc.
MEANING:	We don't know. Maybe it will happen.	We don't know.

IF CLAUSE		
If John gets a car,	he is going to / will / can / might	drive to Alaska next summer.

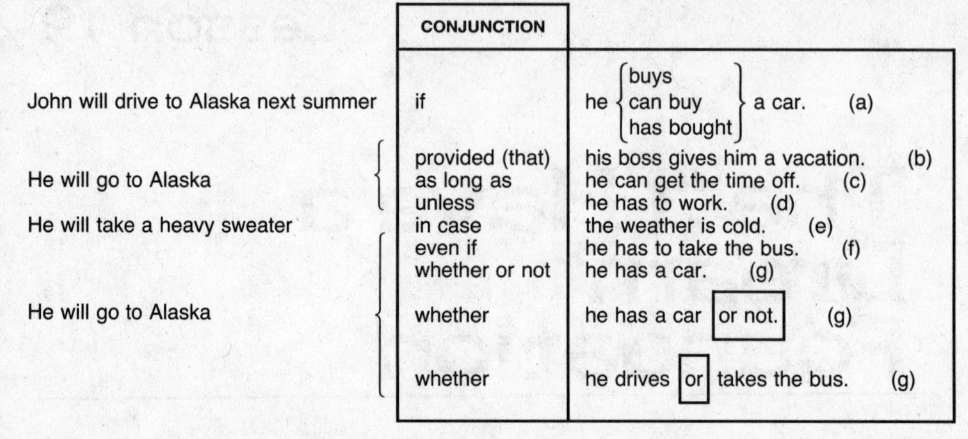

	CONJUNCTION		
John will drive to Alaska next summer	if	he {buys / can buy / has bought} a car.	(a)
He will go to Alaska	provided (that)	his boss gives him a vacation.	(b)
	as long as	he can get the time off.	(c)
	unless	he has to work.	(d)
He will take a heavy sweater	in case	the weather is cold.	(e)
He will go to Alaska	even if	he has to take the bus.	(f)
	whether or not	he has a car.	(g)
	whether	he has a car or not.	(g)
	whether	he drives or takes the bus.	(g)

Tense Choice: In real conditional clauses, the present tenses are used to express future time.

> *Note:* **Will** may be used in the **if** clause to express *willingness* (not refusing). We could say:
>
> **John will go to Alaska provided that his boss will give him a vacation.** (*Meaning:* if his boss doesn't refuse to give him one.)

Meaning: A real conditional clause means that we *don't know* whether an action will occur or not.

1. The action in the independent clause *depends on* the action in the **if** clause; therefore both actions are uncertain:
   a. **If** (no special emphasis).
   b. **Provided (that)** emphasizes that the action in the conditional clause is a *requirement.* Another example:

      I can go to college *provided* I can get a loan.

   c. **As long as** emphasizes that the action in the conditional clause is the *only* requirement. Another example:

      A U.S. citizen doesn't need a passport to go to Canada. *As long as* he/she has a valid driver's license he/she can get in.

   d. **Unless** means *if . . . not.*

      I cannot go to college if I cannot get a loan.
      = I cannot go to college *unless* I can get a loan.

2. The action in the independent clause *will* occur, even though we don't know about the action in the conditional clause:

e. **In case** means that we take an action *in order to be prepared* for another action, which might or might not occur.

I am going to take my umbrella *in case* it rains. (I don't know whether it will rain, but I want to be prepared.)

f. **Even if** means that the action in the conditional clause *will not prevent* the action in the independent clause.

Some people stay home when it snows, but I do not. I will go to school tomorrow *even if* it is snowing.

g. **Whether . . . or (not)** emphasizes that the action will occur *under any condition.*

I will come to school *whether* the weather is good *or not.*

Notes: 1. **Should** is sometimes used in conditional clauses with **if, unless, even if,** and **in case.** It emphasizes the uncertainty of the event.

If it *should* rain tomorrow, we won't be able to go to the beach.

Sometimes **if** is omitted and **should** is placed before the subject. The meaning is the same as in a clause with **if.**

Should it rain tomorrow, we won't be able to go to the beach.

2. In addition to future real conditionals, there are present and past real conditionals. These have two possible meanings:

i. **If** = *whenever.*

Present: **The children always complain if I don't give them a cookie after school.**

Past: **In the old days, the doctor came to your house if you were sick.**

ii. We don't know the facts.

Present: **I don't know why John isn't here today. If he is sick we should take him some soup.**

Past: **I don't know what the weather was like in (distant city) yesterday. If it rained, the baseball game was probably called off.**

3. In questions, **What will happen if** is often shortened to **What if** or **Suppose.**

   Suppose John doesn't get a vacation?
   What if John doesn't get a vacation?

Exercise 1. *If*

Eugene Lang graduated from elementary school in a poor neighborhood in New York City more than fifty years ago. He went on to high school, and as he was a bright student, he graduated when he was only fourteen years old. His parents were poor, and he didn't think about going to college. He worked as a dishwasher in a restaurant.

One day, however, he was asked to fill in for* a waiter who was sick. One of the customers he served took an interest in the bright young man. Shocked that someone so intelligent was not in college, he sent Lang a college catalog and encouraged him to apply. Lang received a full scholarship, finished college, and went into business, eventually becoming very wealthy.

Several years ago, the principal of P.S. (Public School) 121 heard of this successful man who had been a pupil at the school so long ago. He invited Lang to give the commencement address to the graduating sixth graders, and Lang accepted.**

Use **if** to restate the sentences in quotation marks ("...").

1. Lang prepared a typical commencement address. He decided to encourage the children by telling them of his own success in rising from poverty. "You can work hard, and you can succeed as I did."

   If you work hard, you can succeed as I did.

2. As he was sitting on the stage at P.S. 121 on graduation day, he felt uncomfortable. He thought, "I can give this address, but the children will be bored, and they won't believe me."

3. He knew that most of the children came from poor black and Hispanic families. "They can't go to college. Their families can't pay the tuition."

4. Lang knew that the dropout rate at that school was about 50 percent. "About half of the children will not finish high school. They don't have hope."

**Fill in for:* replace temporarily.
***Commencement address:* graduation speech.

5. "They will drop out, and then many will get involved in illegal drugs and crime."
6. "But they might be motivated to study hard and be able to graduate from high school."
7. "I don't want to give this speech. I can't offer the children anything but empty words."
8. Suddenly Lang thought of the black leader Doctor Martin Luther King, Jr., and his famous speech "I Have a Dream." Lang thought, "The children need to have a dream. Then they can do anything."
9. When Lang stood up to speak, he threw away the speech he had written and stunned*** the children, teachers, and parents with this announcement: "Graduate from high school, and I will pay your college tuition."

Exercise 2. *In case* and *provided that*

Here are some facts about the "I Have a Dream" project which Lang set up after making his promise to the sixth graders at P.S. 121. Combine the sentences using **provided that** or **in case.**

A. *News release (first year):*

1. Industrialist Eugene Lang will pay full college tuition for every sixth grader at P.S. 121. The child only has to graduate from high school and get accepted at a college.

   Industrialist Eugene Lang will pay full college tuition for every sixth grader at P.S. 121 provided that the child graduates from high school and gets accepted at a college.

2. (For each of the sixty-one children, Lang has put $2,000 into a special bank account.) He will add to the $2,000 every year. The child must stay in school another year.
3. Some of the sixty-one children may need help with a particular subject. Lang has promised to pay for tutoring.

   In case some of the children need . . .

4. A social worker has been employed by Lang to help the children. Some may have personal problems.

****Stunned:* surprised, amazed.

5. The social worker will visit their families. There may be family problems.
6. (Lang says that it's not the money but the "dream" that is really important.) The children can succeed. But they have to believe in their dream and work for it.

B. *News release (fourth year):* The students are now juniors in high school.

7. Lang keeps his door open in his downtown business office. Some of the children may want to talk to him about school or personal problems, exams, or applying to college.
8. (Lang believes his personal interest in each child is important.) Somebody must believe in him or her. Then a child can accomplish a lot.
9. These children can have the opportunity for a good life, Lang says. But they need to stay in school and graduate.

Exercise 3. *As long as* versus *even if*

Children of poor neighborhoods face a lot of problems. For example, girls in this neighborhood often become pregnant. Lang plans to deal with the problems as they come up. He will continue to encourage each child to finish high school no matter what obstacles arise.

Restate the sentences to include clauses with **as long as** and **even if.**

1. Some of the girls may get pregnant, but they can still remain in school.

   Even if some of the girls get pregnant, they can still remain in school.

2. They can remain in school and graduate with the others in the class.

   As long as they remain in school, they can graduate with the others in the class.

3. Some students may drop out, but Lang will encourage them to return to school.
4. They will graduate a little later than the others, but their college tuition will still be waiting for them.

5. They will graduate eventually, and their college tuition will be waiting for them.
6. A few students may have to leave school in order to work, but they can study at night for the high school equivalency exam.*
7. They can receive a high school diploma. They just have to pass the exam.

Although Lang is encouraging every child to aim for college, he doesn't consider college admission to be the main point of his efforts.

8. Lang doesn't really care if every child goes to college. The young people he has adopted now have the motivation to become useful citizens.

Exercise 4. *Unless*

A. Underline the clauses with **unless,** and restate them using **if** and a negative.

1. Lang's children cannot succeed unless they can resist pressure from other young people to get involved with drugs and gangs.

   Lang's children cannot succeed if they cannot resist pressure from other young people to get involved with drugs and gangs.

2. Crime is also a temptation. One of Lang's adoptees studied for the high school equivalency exam while in prison and has earned his diploma. But unless he is released from prison early, he will not be able to graduate with his class.
3. Lang has been negotiating for his release. He says that unless the prison authorities release him, he will ask the governor for a pardon.

B. Underline the clauses with **if** and restate them using **unless.**

4. Money is not enough. If there isn't personal involvement in the effort to help these children, they will remain isolated from mainstream society.
5. Furthermore, some students are behind in their studies and cannot catch up if they cannot get tutoring.

**High school equivalency exam (GED):* Students who pass this exam receive a high school diploma.

6. If they don't have counseling when family problems arise, these will interfere with their ability to study.
7. They will remain cut off from the larger world around them if field trips are not organized to take them out of the ghetto.*
8. In short, if support services and personal encouragement are not part of the program, it is not likely to succeed.

C. Punctuate and complete these sentences.

9. It is almost impossible to succeed today unless . . .
10. In poor neighborhoods, only one or two children out of a class will go on to college unless . . .
11. Unless children know that college is a possibility . . .
12. Lang believes that unless the children have a dream and believe in it and work hard for it . . .
13. Lang will not pay a child anything unless . . .
14. However, once a child in his adopted class is accepted to a college, Lang will pay full tuition unless ______________________ a scholarship from the college.

19.2 The Present–Future Unreal Conditional

	IF CLAUSE	INDEPENDENT CLAUSE
TIME:	PRESENT or FUTURE	PRESENT or FUTURE
TENSE: (verb form)	*simple past* *past progressive* could	would could might
MEANING:	The opposite is true.	The opposite is true.

True:
John *does not* have a car.
He *is taking* algebra this term.
I *will* probably *not win* the lottery tomorrow.

**Ghetto:* a very poor neighborhood in which a minority group lives.

IF CLAUSE	INDEPENDENT CLAUSE
If John *had* a car,	he {would / could / might} drive it to school tomorrow.
If he *were not taking* algebra,	he would not be studying for the test right now.
If I *won* the lottery tomorrow,	I would buy a house.

Agreement: In unreal conditionals, **were** is the preferred form for all subjects. In informal speech, however, **was** is often used for the first and third person singular.

Informal: **If that was my car, I would get it painted.**

Note: **Would** in the **if** clause means *willingness* (not refusing).

If John would speak louder, we could hear him better.

Exercise 5. Forming the Unreal Conditional (oral)

A. Form **if** clauses.

1. John studies (so he gets good grades.)

   If John didn't study, (he might not get good grades.)
2. He attends class regularly.

   If he . . .
3. He listens carefully in class.
4. He does all his homework.
5. He is a serious student.
6. He is taking interesting courses.
7. His professors are good lecturers.
8. He doesn't skip classes.

   If he skipped classes . . .
9. He doesn't come to class late.
10. He doesn't waste time.
11. He isn't working full time.
12. He isn't lazy.
13. He isn't taking advanced courses.

B. Form clauses with **would, could, might.**

14. (John studies a lot, so) he gets good grades.
(If he didn't study a lot,) **he might not get good grades.**
15. . . . he understands the material.
16. . . . he does well on all his tests.
17. . . . he asks intelligent questions in class.
18. . . . he is near the top of his class.
19. . . . he is getting A in math.
20. . . . he never fails tests.
21. . . . he doesn't want a full-time job.
22. . . . he doesn't have much free time. (Use **more.**)
23. . . . he is not failing math.
24. . . . the tests aren't difficult for him.

Note to the Teacher: If the students need more practice, read the sentences again, using a random order within A and within B.

Exercise 6. Present–Future Unreal Conditionals

Combine or restate the sentences, using **if.** Be careful in using the negative.

1. Most of the children at P.S. 121 come from poor families. They don't think about going to college.

   If the children at P.S. 121 didn't come from poor families, they {would probably / might} think about going to college.

2. They don't think of college as a possibility. They aren't motivated to succeed in school.

   If they thought . . .

3. Many students drop out before graduating because they don't see any reason to stay in school.

   Not so many students . . .

4. About half the students don't graduate. "Dropping out is considered normal,"[1] (one of the students told reporters).

   More students . . .

5. "Dropping out makes you big and important, so there is a big temptation."[1] (Use **such a big temptation.**)
6. But this student gets a lot of encouragement from Mr. Lang, so he is staying in school.
7. He is applying to several engineering schools because he wants to be an engineer.
8. The door of Lang's office is always open to these students, and they visit him to talk about everything from family problems to college applications.
9. (In addition,) the social worker keeps in touch with each of them, visits their homes from time to time, and arranges for tutoring and counseling when they need it. They are able to overcome many difficulties. (Use **might.**)
10. Other students tease the adoptees and say, "You've got an old man miser looking after you."[2] They envy the adoptees.
11. (However,) the other students are developing ambition (too,) because they are inspired by the success of Lang's adoptees.

19.3 *Were to*

	IF CLAUSE	**INDEPENDENT CLAUSE**
TIME:	FUTURE	FUTURE
TENSE: (verb form)	were to	would could might
MEANING:	I don't know. *or:* The opposite is true.	I don't know. *or:* The opposite is true.

[1]William E. Geist, "One Man's Gift: College for 52 in Harlem," *New York Times,* Oct. 19, 1985, p. 1 (paraphrased).
[2]William Raspberry, "Special People From P.S. 121," *The Washington Post,* Oct. 28, 1985, A–20.

True:
You might ask the teacher about it.
Water does not flow uphill.

IF CLAUSE	INDEPENDENT CLAUSE
If you were to ask the teacher,	he {would / might / could} give you some good advice.
If water were to flow uphill,	that would be breaking the law of gravity.

Agreement: **Were** is used for all subjects in conditionals with **were to.**

Note: Negatives are not used with **were to.**

Exercise 7. *Were to* (oral or written)

Answer the question and add a sentence with **were to.**

1. Do you think you'll win a million dollars in the lottery tomorrow?

   Probably not, but if I were to win a million dollars,

   I {would / could} . . .

   ***or:* I might. If I were . . .**

2. Will you ever become as wealthy as Lang?
3. Do you think you'll ever make a commencement address to a class of sixth graders?
4. Will you ever adopt a class of school children?
5. One of Lang's students says, "I want to do well so I can adopt a class of my own some day. Imagine if all fifty-two kids adopted classes, and those kids adopted classes . . ."[1] How do you think he finished that sentence?

   If all fifty-two kids . . .

6. Is a wealthy stranger going to pay for your education?
7. Do you think your children will drop out of high school?

[1]Michael deCourcy Hinds, "A Dream Come True," *New York Times Magazine,* April 26, 1987, p. 35.

8. Has the teacher ever asked you for advice about teaching this class?
9. Does the head of this school ever ask you for your advice?

19.4 Conditionals without an *if* Clause

OTHERWISE

	CONJUNCTIVE ADVERB	
Real: The students will have to study hard.	Otherwise,	they won't graduate.

*Implied **if** clause:* If the students don't study hard, . . .

Unreal: Mr. Lang is helping them. | Otherwise, | they probably couldn't go to college.

*Implied **if** clause:* If Mr. Lang weren't helping them, . . .

WITHOUT

	PREPOSITIONAL PHRASE
Real: An Englishman cannot enter the United States	without a visa.

*Implied **if** clause:* If an Englishman does not have a visa, . . .

You can't learn to drive | without practicing.

*Implied **if** clause:* If you don't practice, . . .

Unreal: | Without headlights, | we couldn't drive at night.

*Implied **if** clause:* If cars didn't have headlights, . . .

REASON CLAUSE

	REASON CLAUSE
Unreal: I don't want to drop out of school	because my father would be upset.

Implied: My father would be upset if I dropped out of school.

BUT

Unreal: I would go with you, | but I have to study. |

*Implied **if** clause:* If I didn't have to study, . . .

GERUND

	GERUND PHRASE	
Real:	Spending time with that gang	will get you in trouble.

Implied: If you spend time with that gang, it (that action) will get you in trouble.

Unreal: | Jumping out of a second-story window | would be dangerous.

Implied: If you jumped out of a second-story window, it would be dangerous.

INFINITIVE

	INFINITIVE PHRASE
Unreal: I would never dare	to jump out of a second-story window.

Implied: If you asked me to jump, I wouldn't dare.

COMPARISONS

	COMPARISON		COMPARISON
Unreal: I would be	happier	in	a bigger apartment.

*Implied **if** clause:* If I were living in a bigger apartment (than I am), . . .

TOO* AND *ENOUGH

Unreal: An apartment {wouldn't be / would be} | big enough / too small | } for my family.

Affirmative and Negative: **Otherwise** is used after an affirmative sentence. It means *if . . . not.* Notice that **otherwise** begins a new sentence and is followed by a comma.

Without after a negative verb phrase means *if . . . not.* After an affirmative verb phrase, it means *even if . . . not.*

U.S. citizens can enter Canada without a visa. (*Meaning:* . . . even if they don't have a visa.)

Note: There are other types of sentences with implied **if** clauses:

You could add those numbers faster *on a calculator.* (if you had a calculator)

John wouldn't make that mistake. (if he were doing that)

***With patience,* you can accomplish a lot.** (if you have patience)

Exercise 8. *Without* and *otherwise*

Complete the sentences.

1. In New York City, one hundred patrons have adopted sixth-grade classes.

   Without . . . **these patrons, the children wouldn't be able to go to college.**

2. Each patron is ready to pay college tuition for all the children in his or her class. Otherwise, these children . . .
3. However, the children have to be accepted to college. Otherwise, they won't . . .
4. Following Lang's example, about twenty U.S. cities now have "I Have a Dream" programs. Without . . .
5. Lang travels around the country helping people set up the programs. Otherwise, . . .

Exercise 9. Gerunds, Infinitives, and *because* (oral or written)

A. Make sentences with (a) a gerund phrase and (b) **it** + an infinitive.

1. adopt a class

   a. **Adopting a class would be a big responsibility.**

   b. **It would take a lot of money to adopt a class.**

2. have as much money as Eugene Lang
3. be the president of the United States
4. be an astronaut
5. walk from New York to San Francisco
6. eliminate poverty in the world
7. (Give an example of your own.)

B. Restate a few of your sentences in A, using **because.**

I'll probably never be able to adopt a class because it would take too much money.

Exercise 10. Unreal Conditions with *but* (oral or written)

Begin each sentence below with a clause that states the opposite of the true situation.

Example: **My little sister would visit me at Christmas, but she doesn't have the money for air fare.**

1. ____________________, but ______ (don't/doesn't) have the money.
2. ____________________, but ______ (don't/doesn't) have a car.
3. ____________________, but ______ (is/am/are) too busy.
4. ____________________, but I don't know how.
5. ____________________, but my English isn't good enough yet.
6. ____________________, but my parents don't want me to.
7. (Give one or two examples of your own.)

Transfer Exercises

1. Requirements (real conditional)

What is required in the following situations? Complete the sentences using **without, unless,** or **if.**

1. You can't learn to speak English without practicing.
   unless you practice.
   if you don't practice.
2. A foreign student can't get into an an American college . . .

3. You can't pass the TOEFL* . . .
4. You can't get an A in this course . . .
5. A child cannot grow up to be a responsible adult . . .
6. We can't eliminate poverty in the world . . .
7. We can't have peace in the world . . .

2. Improbabilities *(were to)*

Make statements with **If I were to** or **I would never . . . because.**

Example: marry an American
If I were to marry an American, we might not understand each other.
or: **I would never marry an American because my parents wouldn't like it.**

1. marry an American
2. rob a bank
3. teach an English class at this school
4. lose my (passport)
5. become a famous (rock star)
6. try out for the Olympic team in (soccer)
7. forget to hand in my homework tomorrow
8. write a letter to the president of this country
9. become (president/prime minister) of my country

3. Opinions and Principles (real and unreal)

Complete and punctuate the sentences.

1. As long as a person is content with what he has . . .
2. Even if I never become wealthy . . .
3. If I didn't have (   ) . . .
4. I would be happier (than I am) if . . .
5. My life wouldn't be worth living if . . .
6. I can achieve my goal in life provided that . . .
7. Everyone ought to have some kind of health insurance in case . . .
8. Provided that (   ) helps me . . .
9. I would never steal unless . . .

**TOEFL:* Test of English as a Foreign Language.

10. Unless my life were in danger . . .
11. A person can get into trouble unless . . .
12. I would never lie to (   ) even if . . .
13. My friends can borrow my (   ) anytime as long as . . .
14. If my wife/husband were to (   ) . . . (*Note:* You can speak of your present or future spouse.)
15. If I were(n't) a United States citizen . . .
16. If the whole world spoke one language . . .
17. If every child could go to college . . .

Discussion Topics

A. Is education very important for success in your country? Do most children graduate from high school? If not, at what age do they most often quit school? What are some important reasons why they quit school? Is motivation a problem among school children in your country? If so, how could their motivation be improved? Do you think it would be desirable for all children in your country to finish high school? Why or why not?

B. Is college expensive in your country? Can poor children go to college?

C. Do you think it would be a good idea for wealthy individuals to adopt classes in your country? Could it ever happen? Would it help to reduce poverty or crime?

D. How could poverty be reduced, in your opinion? Is more education the answer? Are there steps that the government could take? How about private individuals or groups?

E. If you won $100,000 in the lottery, what would you do with it? Would you give some of it away? If so, how much and to whom? Would you save some of it? Why? Would you spend some for yourself? How? Would you try to help other people? If so, whom would you help, and how?

F. Do you think people need a lot of money to be happy? What are the most important requirements for happiness, in your opinion?

Composition Topics

Write a short composition about one of the following topics. Use conditionals in some of your sentences.

1. Write about educational opportunity and attitudes toward education in your country. Discuss some of the questions in Discussion Topics A, B, and C.
2. Write about *one* of the other Discussion Topics (D through F).
3. Use one of the sentences in Transfer Exercise 3 as the opening sentence (topic sentence) of a paragraph.

Lesson 20

Singing Refugees

20.1 Past Unreal Conditionals

	IF CLAUSE	INDEPENDENT CLAUSE
TIME:	PAST	PAST
TENSE: *(verb form)*	*past perfect* *past perfect progressive*	would have could have might have
MEANING:	The opposite was true.	The opposite was true.

True:
It *did not rain,* so we *did not stay* home.
John *called* me, so I *knew* about the meeting.
Mary *was studying,* so she *couldn't go* with us.
The passenger's seat belt *was fastened.* He *was not injured* in the accident.

IF CLAUSE	INDEPENDENT CLAUSE
If it *had rained,* If John *hadn't called* me, If Mary *hadn't been studying,* If the passenger's seat belt *had not been fastened,*	we *would have stayed* home. I *would not have known* about the meeting. she *could have gone* with us. he *might have been injured* in the accident.

Note: Sometimes **if** is omitted and **had** is placed before the subject:

Had the passenger's seat belt not been fastened, he might have been injured in the accident.

Exercise 1. Using the Past Unreal Conditional

The movie *The Sound of Music* tells the story of a family's escape from political oppression. It is about young Maria von Trapp, her husband "the Baron," and the Baron's children by an earlier marriage.

Restate the sentences, using **if.**

1. The Trapp family left their home in Austria because their lives were in danger.

   The Trapp family would not have left their home in Austria if their lives had not been in danger.

They went first to a convent* where Maria had lived for a time.

2. The sisters offered to hide them, so they were not caught immediately.

   If the sisters had not offered to hide them, they {would / might} have been caught immediately.

3. When the soldiers came to look for them, they did not find them because they were hiding behind some gravestones in the courtyard.

   The soldiers ______________________ them if they ______________________ behind some gravestones in the courtyard.

As the soldiers were looking around the courtyard, the youngest child sneezed.

4. But they didn't hear the sneeze because one soldier happened to say something in a loud voice just at that moment.
5. The sisters led the family out to their car by the back gate and the family got away without being caught.
6. The soldiers rushed after them when they heard the car driving away.
7. But one of the sisters had disconnected some wires in the engine of the soldiers' vehicle, so they couldn't go after the fleeing family.

**Convent:* a home for women whose lives are dedicated to the religious life. These women are called nuns, or sisters.

8. The family were not followed as they drove up into the mountains. They were able to park the car among the trees and hike up over the mountains.
9. They hiked across the mountains into Italy and were safe.

Exercise 2. Using Past Unreal Conditionals

***The Sound of Music* is based on a true story but is partly fictional. The following account is taken from Maria von Trapp's books. You will see that it differs in some respects from the story in the musical.**

Restate the sentences, using **if.** Omit the words in parentheses.

1. After Baron von Trapp's first wife died, he needed a governess to teach one of his children.

   If Baron von Trapp's first wife . . .
2. The little girl was too sick to go to school.
3. Maria met the Baron when the convent sent her to teach the child.
4. The Baron fell in love with Maria, and (eventually) they were married.
5. As she loved to sing, Maria taught all the children to sing together.
6. (One day) the great opera singer Lotte Lehman overheard them singing in the garden as she was passing by.
7. She asked them to sing in the Salzburg Music Festival. (As a result,) they became known all over Europe.

In March, 1938, Adolf Hitler, the Nazi dictator, sent his army to occupy Austria. The Trapps were opposed to the occupation and to Nazism.

8. The Trapp family were invited to represent Austria at Hitler's birthday celebration because they had become famous in Europe.
9. (Moreover,) Hitler asked the Baron to join his navy because the Baron had been a submarine captain in World War I.
10. The Trapps did not want to accept these two invitations, so they could not safely remain in Austria.

11. Since they went hiking together often, they decided to walk to the railroad station wearing mountain boots.
12. People didn't notice anything unusual because they were wearing mountain boots and carrying backpacks.
13. They didn't take more luggage so that people wouldn't suspect anything.

They took the train into the mountains near the Italian border.

14. They walked across the Alps into Italy just one day before Hitler closed the border between the two countries. (Use *one day earlier.*)

20.2 Mixed-Time Unreal Conditionals

PAST CAUSE—PRESENT RESULT

True:
George *dropped* out of school two years ago. He *is not* a senior in high school now.

If George *had not dropped* out of school two years ago,	he *would be* a senior in high school now.

GENERAL CAUSE—PAST RESULT

True:
Sofia *doesn't understand* English well. She *didn't understand* the professor's instructions this morning.

If Sofia *understood* English better,	she {*would* / *might*} *have understood* his instructions.

Exercise 3. Combining Sentences

Combine the sentences using **if.** Be careful to keep the same time relationships.

1. The Trapp family did not stay in Austria. The Trapp Family Ski Lodge exists in Vermont today.

If the Trapp family had stayed in Austria, the Trapp Family Ski Lodge would not exist in Vermont today.

2. In 1949, Maria von Trapp published a book about her life. A firm in Europe offered her a contract for the movie rights.
3. The agent lied to her when she asked for royalties.* She sold the rights for $10,000.
4. (Later) the story of the Trapp family was made into a movie. People all over the world know and love "Maria."
5. The music in the film is beautiful. The movie was a great success.
6. Maria von Trapp did not receive any royalties. The Trapp family is not wealthy today.
7. *The Sound of Music* was shown all over the world. Children everywhere sing a song called "Do Re Mi."
8. "Do Re Mi" is an easy song to learn. It is loved by children everywhere.
9. A certain English teacher loved the movie. She decided to read the book.
10. She read the book and wrote some exercises about it. You are writing this exercise about the Trapp family right now.

Have you seen *The Sound of Music?*

Exercise 4. Transforming and Completing Sentences (oral—books closed)

A. Change each sentence to an **if** clause. Then complete the sentence with a *present* result.

1. Columbus discovered America in 1492.

   If Columbus had not discovered America in 1492, we might not be here today.

2. English-speaking people colonized the east coast of North America.
3. They did not colonize South America.
4. The English colonists won their war of independence.
5. Alaska was sold to the United States by Russia in 1867.

**Royalties:* a share in the profits.

6. You were not born in the United States.
7. You were born in (   ).
8. Your parents always encouraged you to (   ).

B. Answer the questions, including an **if** clause and a *past* result in your answers.

9. Do you need to learn English?

   Yes. If I didn't need to learn English, I wouldn't have enrolled in this class.

10. Are you a good student?
11. Do you like (name of person)?
12. Do you have a lot of free time these days?
13. Do your parents live near here?

Exercise 5. Cumulative Exercise: Understanding Real and Unreal Conditionals

Read each numbered statement. Then decide whether the information under it is *true, false,* or *not stated* in the sentence.

	True	*False*	*Not Stated*
1. If the Trapp family's recordings were available in this town, I would buy one.			
a. The recordings are available.	______	X	______
b. I am going to buy one.	______	X	______
2. If their songbook is available, I am going to buy a copy.			
a. The songbook is available.	______	______	X
b. I am going to buy a copy.	______	______	X
3. If I had seen the book in the bookstore, I would have bought a copy.			
a. I saw the book.	______	X	______
b. I bought a copy.	______	X	______
4. If I had known the family was giving a concert, I would have gone to hear them.			

a. The family was scheduled to give a concert. ______ ______ ______
b. I knew the situation. ______ ______ ______
c. I went to hear them. ______ ______ ______

5. If *The Sound of Music* is playing, we can go see it tonight.
   a. *The Sound of Music* is playing. ______ ______ ______
   b. We can see it. ______ ______ ______

6. If *The Sound of Music* were playing, we could go see it.
   a. *The Sound of Music* is playing. ______ ______ ______
   b. *The Sound of Music* was playing a while ago. ______ ______ ______
   c. We can see it. ______ ______ ______
   d. We were able to see it. ______ ______ ______

7. If the songs aren't sung in English, I won't understand them.
   a. The songs are sung in English. ______ ______ ______
   b. I will understand them. ______ ______ ______

8. If the songs weren't sung in English, I wouldn't understand them.
   a. The songs are sung in English. ______ ______ ______
   b. I understand them. ______ ______ ______

9. If the football game had not been more important to me, I would have watched *The Sound of Music* on TV last night.
   a. There was a football game last night. ______ ______ ______
   b. *The Sound of Music* was on TV last night. ______ ______ ______
   c. I watched *The Sound of Music* last night. ______ ______ ______
   d. I watched the football game. ______ ______ ______

10. If Ramon had gotten a high score on the TOEFL last spring, he wouldn't be studying English.
    a. Ramon got a high score on TOEFL. ______ ______ ______
    b. Ramon is studying English. ______ ______ ______
    c. Ramon was studying English last spring. ______ ______ ______

Exercise 6. Cumulative Exercise: Real and Unreal Conditionals (oral or written)

Change each sentence to an **if** clause and then complete the sentence.

1. English is not your native language.

   If English were my native language, I would not be in this class.

2. The teacher might give us a quiz on unreal conditionals.

   If the teacher gives us a quiz on unreal conditionals, I will probably . . .

3. You are not teaching this class.

   If I . . .

4. You did not write this textbook.
5. You might write a textbook some day.
6. You don't know English perfectly (yet).
7. Before you came here, you didn't know what you know now about this (country/school).

   If I ______________________ what I know now, I . . .

8. You might visit (Paris) some day.
9. You are not in (Paris) right now.
10. You probably will never go to the moon.
11. We (had/didn't have) a vacation last week.
12. You might have some free time this weekend.
13. Perhaps the weather will be good.
14. The weather was (not) very (hot/cold) yesterday.
15. You are (not) married.
16. You are not a bird, and you don't have wings, and you can't fly.

20.3 Noun Clauses after *wish* and *if only*

PAST

True:
My father *didn't send* me money last week.

NOUN CLAUSE: I wish	my father *had sent* me money.	
IF CLAUSE:	If only my father *had sent* me money,	(I could have gone to Chicago with you.)

PRESENT

True:
My father *never sends* me money.

NOUN CLAUSE: I wish	my father *sent* me money.	
IF CLAUSE:	If only my father *sent* me money,	(I wouldn't have to work.)

FUTURE

True:
My father *is not going to send* me money next week.

NOUN CLAUSE: I wish	my father *were going to send* me money.	
IF CLAUSE:	If only my father *were going to* send me money,	(I could go with you.)

COMPARE:

True:
I don't know.

	NOUN CLAUSE
I hope	my father will send me money.

Meaning: **Wish** and **if only** mean that the speaker is not happy with the true situation and would like reality to be the opposite of what it is.

Deletion: In informal speech, a clause with **if only** may be used alone, without an independent clause.

Choice of Tense: Noun clauses after **wish** are *unreal* and take the same tenses as unreal **if** clauses. **Were** (not **was**) is used for all subjects.

Past time: Use the past perfect tenses.
Present time: Use the simple past or past progressive.
Future time: Use **were going to. Would** is used for willingness.

I wish my father would send me money.

Note: **If only** occurs in real conditionals also.

If only he remembers to bring the money!

Exercise 7. Noun Clauses after *wish*

Imagine that you are one of the children in the Trapp family, a refugee from your native country. What are some of the things that you might wish?

A. *During the first months in the United States:*

1. We had to leave Austria.

   I wish we hadn't had to leave Austria.

2. I couldn't bring my clothes and books.
3. We don't have much money. (Use **more.**)
4. We had to borrow money to get here.
5. We have only visitors' visas.
6. Our application for an extension has not been granted.
7. We can't stay in this country.
8. We have to go back to Europe.
9. We are living in so much uncertainty.
10. I can't see my friends.
11. I wasn't able to say goodbye to them.

B. *Later:*

12. Mother signed a movie contract for only $10,000.
13. She didn't consult her lawyer.
14. We aren't receiving any royalties for *The Sound of Music.*

20.4 Manner Clauses with *as if* and *as though*

Present/Future

REAL (nearly certain)

True situation:
I believe Joe probably *knows* a lot about cars.
I believe he's *not going to have* any trouble.

	MANNER CLAUSE
Joe talks	{as if / as though} he *knows* a lot about cars.
Joe talks	{as if / as though} he *isn't going to have* any trouble.

UNREAL/UNCERTAIN

PRESENT TIME

True:
I don't know. I don't feel sure that he *knows* a lot.
His wife *isn't* five years old.
Sue *doesn't pay* her rent.

Joe talks	{as if / as though} he *knew* a lot about cars.	(a)
His wife acts	{as if / as though} she *were* five years old.	(a)
Sue talks	{as if / as though} she *paid* her rent (but she doesn't).	(a)

FUTURE TIME

True:

The Leaning Tower of Pisa { *is probably not going to* / probably *will not* } *fall* soon.

The Leaning Tower of Pisa looks { as if / as though } it { *were going to* / *would* } *fall.* (b)

Past

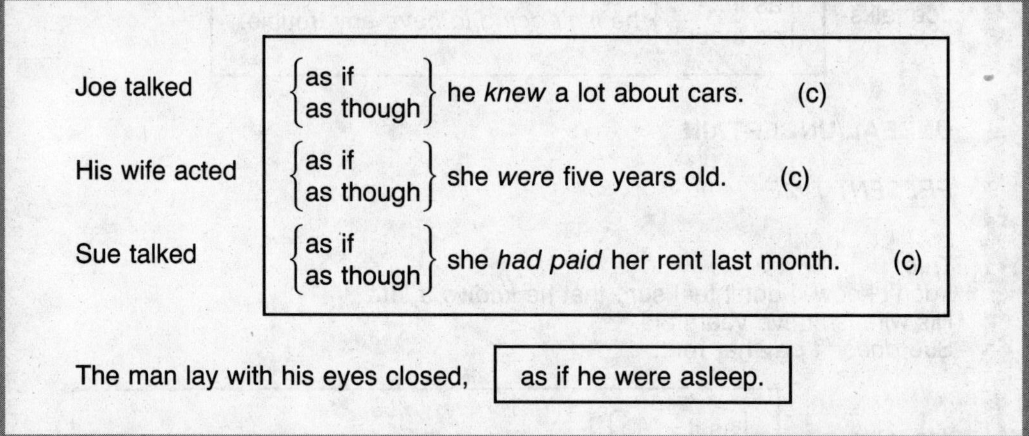

Joe talked { as if / as though } he *knew* a lot about cars. (c)

His wife acted { as if / as though } she *were* five years old. (c)

Sue talked { as if / as though } she *had paid* her rent last month. (c)

The man lay with his eyes closed, as if he were asleep.

Meaning: Clauses with **as if** and **as though** tell how something appears, not how it is.

Choice of Tense:

a. *Present time:* To say that an event is uncertain or untrue, use the *simple past* or *past progressive.* **Were** (not **was**) is used for all subjects.

b. *Future time:* To say that an event is uncertain or untrue, use **were going to, would,** or **could.**

c. *Past time:* The tense shows the time relationship between the action in the manner clause and the action in the independent clause.

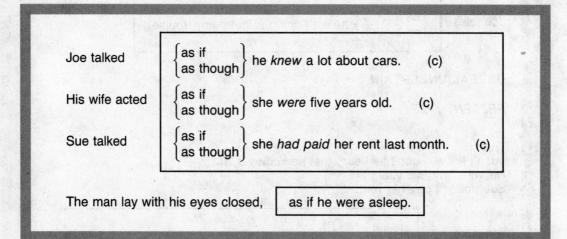

Punctuation: When the manner clause modifies the whole sentence, it is sometimes preceded by a comma. No comma is used when the clause is the complement of the verb.*

> *Note:* In informal conversation, **like** is often used to mean **as if/ as though:**
>
> **Joe talks like he knows a lot about cars.**
>
> This usage is not considered correct in written English.

Exercise 8. Completion

Complete the sentences, using **as if** or **as though** and the verbs in parentheses.

1. The Trapp family left home wearing mountain boots and carrying backpacks, {as if / as though} they were going to climb a mountain (climb).
2. **A:** I've been studying for five hours and I can't understand anything!
   B: It sounds {as if / as though} you need (need) a break. Let's go get a cup of coffee.
3. When I say "Roll over!" to my dog, he rolls over with his feet in the air ______________ (be) dead.
4. Listen to that noise in the engine! It sounds as if something ______________ (be) wrong with the car. We'd better take it to the garage.
5. I understand English pretty well, but when the customs official spoke to me I just stared at him ______________ (never, hear) English before. When he looked at my passport, he scratched his head ______________ (be) wrong with it.
6. My throat is sore and I ache all over. I feel ______________ (get).

**Complement of the verb:* See page 306, footnote.

7. **A:** Ted keeps nodding. He looks ______________ some
(need)
sleep.
B: You're right. And he has bags under his eyes. He looks ______________ for a week.
(not, sleep)

8. Alice is very shy. When Rob asked her to marry him, she looked upset, ______________, but really she adores him. She
(not, love)
opened her mouth ______________, but she couldn't say
(speak)
a word.

Exercise 9. Metaphors with *as if* and *as though* (oral)

Listen to the information and complete the sentences using **as if** and **as though.**

1. I can't eat a horse, (but I'm hungry).
   I feel . . . **as if I could eat a horse.**
2. A heavy load has been lifted from my shoulders. (I'm relieved.) I feel . . .
3. I wasn't going to die, but I was embarrassed. When I spilled my drink on the teacher's jacket . . .
4. I wasn't losing an old friend, (but I was sad). When I had to sell my car, . . .
5. John has a head on his shoulders, (but sometimes he acts stupid). He acts . . .
6. Ralph was not walking on air, (but he was happy). When Katie agreed to marry him, Ralph felt . . .
7. Money does not grow on trees. Some people spend money . . .
8. The rain will stop sometime, (but it's very heavy). It's raining . . .
9. My mother will see me again, (but she was sad). When I said good-bye, my mother cried . . .

Transfer Exercises

1. Complaints

Life is never perfect. For each of the items below, think of something that you would like to be different. If you want, you can add a reason.

Examples: your boyfriend/girlfriend

I wish my boyfriend didn't smoke so much.

I wish my girlfriend had called me last night. It would have cheered me up.

1. your apartment/dormitory room (Is it big enough? quiet enough? Does it have enough light?)
2. this school
3. the English language
4. the school cafeteria
5. your mother/father/parents
6. your best friend
7. your husband/wife/boyfriend/girlfriend
8. the weather
9. the president of this country
10. (other)

2. Good and Bad Luck

A. Remember an unlucky experience that you have had. On a piece of paper, list all the events that led to the unfortunate outcome. Then tell a classmate about it, using **if**.

Example: **I was robbed once while I was shopping at the supermarket.**

List:

1. **I put my bag in my shopping cart.**
2. **I left the cart and went to look for something.**
3. **I wasn't paying attention to what I was doing.**

If

1. **If I hadn't put my bag in the shopping cart, it wouldn't have been taken.**

2. **If I hadn't left the cart and gone to look for something, the thief couldn't have taken it.**
3. **If I had been paying attention to what I was doing, I wouldn't have left it alone in the cart.**

B. Repeat the exercise in A, but this time remember a piece of *good* luck. List the events that led up to the lucky event, and then tell a classmate about it, using **if.**

Discussion Topics

A. Have you ever had to escape from your home or country? (Or, do you know anyone who has?) If so, were you escaping from a fire, flood, earthquake, war, or political oppression? How did you do it? Was it a dangerous escape? How were you lucky or unlucky? Did you suffer hardships, going without water, food, or shelter? Did anyone help you? What would have happened if something had gone wrong?

Did you go to a different country? What happened when you got to your destination? Was life easy there? What are some of the difficulties of being a refugee?

B. Have you ever had trouble getting a visa to go to another country? If so, what did you have to do in order to get it? Did you finally get it? What would have happened if the outcome had been different? What could you have done?

C. Do you know anybody who is waiting for a visa? What will help him or her get it? What will the person be able to do as soon as he or she gets it? What if the person cannot get it?

D. What would happen if all the countries of the world opened their borders and passports were abolished? Who would move, and why? Where would they go? Would the world be a better place? What kinds of problems might occur?

Composition Topics

Write a short composition about one of the following topics, using **wish** and **if** in some of your sentences.

1. Write about a lucky or unlucky experience that you have had. What made it happen? What would have happened if you (or someone else) had acted differently? (See Transfer Exercise 2.)

2. Write about something that you cannot change in your life although you would like to change it. What do you wish, and why? (See Transfer Exercise 1.)
3. Write about an escape. (See Discussion Topic A.)
4. Write about someone who had trouble getting a visa. (See Discussion Topics B and C.)
5. Give your opinion about what would happen if passports were abolished. Answer the questions in Discussion Topic D.

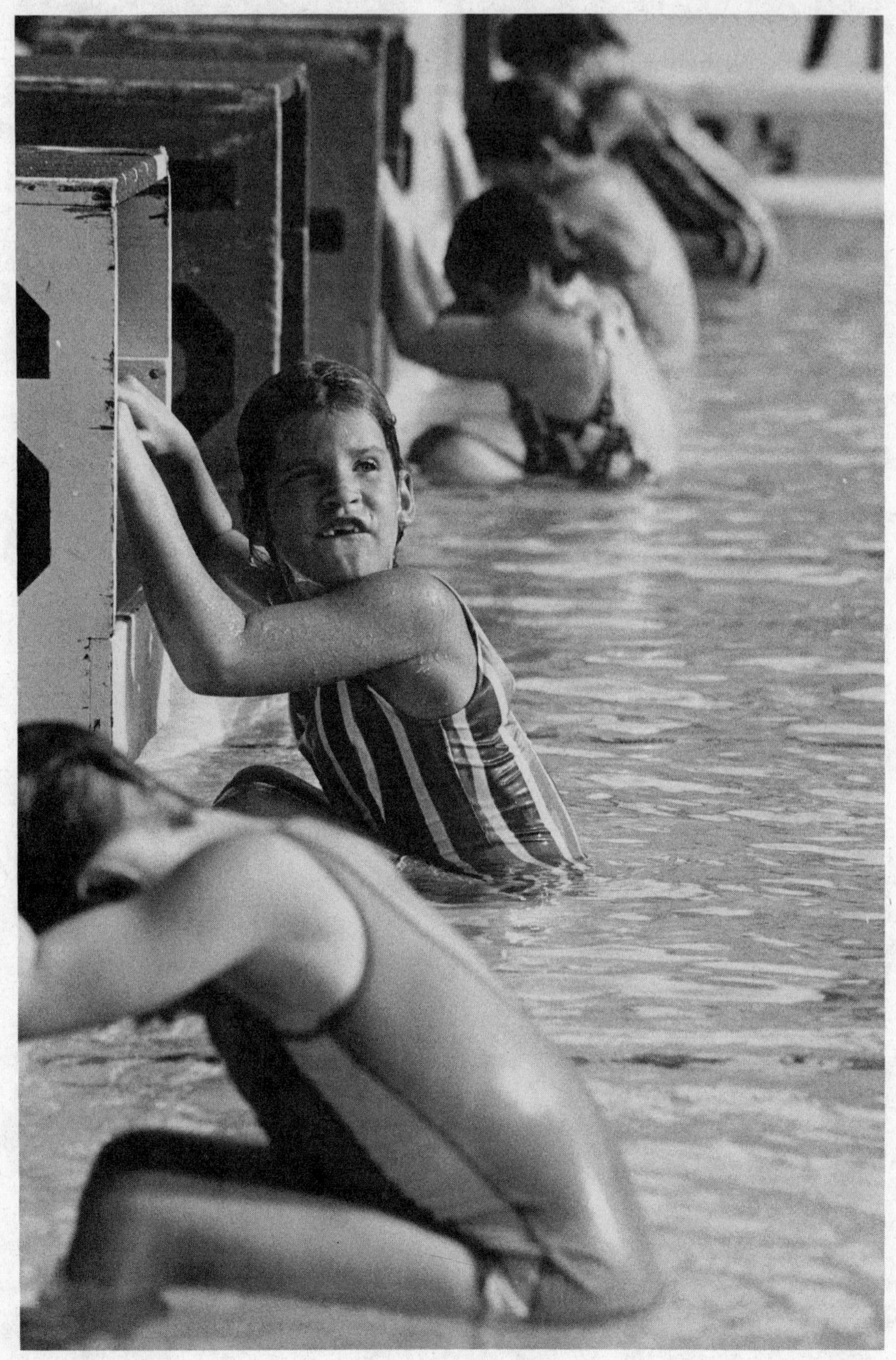

Lesson 21

Contrasting Ideas of Time

21.1 Incongruity/Concession: *although, though, even though, in spite of the fact that, while*

Incongruity

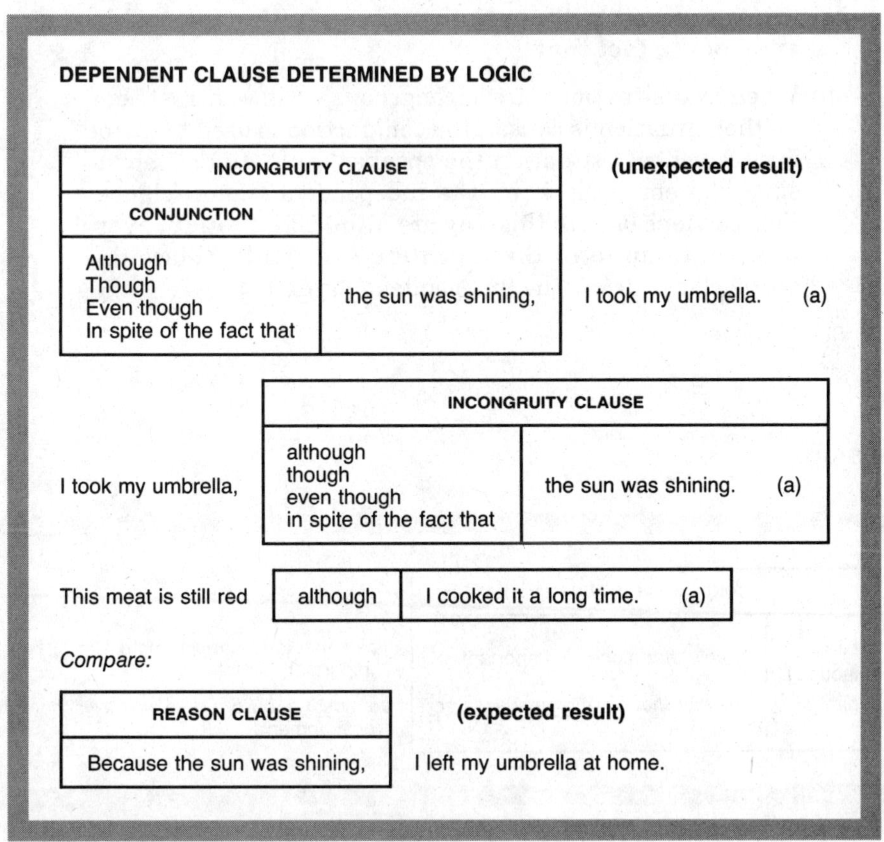

DEPENDENT CLAUSE DETERMINED BY LOGIC

INCONGRUITY CLAUSE		(unexpected result)	
CONJUNCTION			
Although Though Even though In spite of the fact that	the sun was shining,	I took my umbrella.	(a)

	INCONGRUITY CLAUSE		
I took my umbrella,	although though even though in spite of the fact that	the sun was shining.	(a)

This meat is still red	although	I cooked it a long time.	(a)

Compare:

REASON CLAUSE	(expected result)
Because the sun was shining,	I left my umbrella at home.

DEPENDENT CLAUSE DETERMINED BY EMPHASIS

INCONGRUITY CLAUSE		**(negative emphasis)**
While	I like this country as a whole,	I don't like the food here. (b)
Although Though	the sun was shining,	there were clouds on the horizon. (b)
		(positive emphasis)
While Although	I don't like the food here, there were clouds on the horizon,	I like this country as a whole. (b) the sun was shining. (b)

The sun was shining,	although though	there were clouds on the horizon.

Meaning: a. Clauses of incongruity introduce an "ineffective cause" which does not have its expected result. Usually sunny weather makes us leave our umbrellas at home. **I took my umbrella** is logically unexpected. Conjunctions used in this pattern are **although, though, even though,** and **in spite of the fact that.**

b. When two situations are incongruous or in contrast, but neither situation is causal, the conjunction is used to introduce whichever situation the speaker wants to *de*-emphasize. The emphasis is on the independent (main) clause. Conjunctions used in this way are **although, though, even though, in spite of the fact that,** and **while.** (Place the **while** clause *before* the independent clause.)

Concession

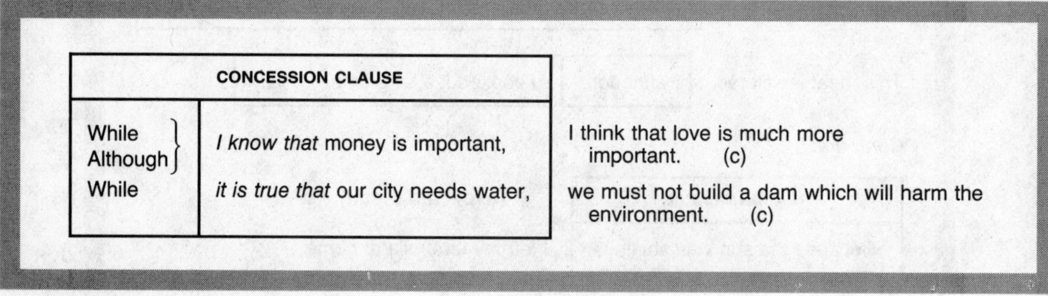

CONCESSION CLAUSE		
While Although	*I know that* money is important,	I think that love is much more important. (c)
While	*it is true that* our city needs water,	we must not build a dam which will harm the environment. (c)

Meaning: c. **While** is often used to concede (admit) a counterargument before stating an opinion. The **while** clause comes first, and the emphasis is on the independent clause. (**Although** and **though** are also used in this way.)

Punctuation: A comma is often used before the conjunctions in this group in order to emphasize the logical separation between the unexpected result and the clause of incongruity.

Exercise 1. Logical Placement of *although*

In American culture, competition, teamwork, and time are highly valued. One of the ways that American children learn these values is through their participation in competitive sports. Children's competitive swimming is an example.

Combine the sentences using **although, though, even though,** and **in spite of the fact that.** Be careful to place the conjunction so as to make a logical sentence.

1. Richard spends many hours a week swimming. He is only eight years old.

   Richard spends many hours a week swimming, although he is only eight years old. (*Logic:* We cannot place **although** before the first clause because swimming can not "cause" Richard's age.)

2. Richard participates in many children's meets* every year. This takes a lot of his parents' time.
3. The meet last week was held an hour's drive from his home. His father was willing to drive him there.
4. Richard went to the meet. He woke up with a slight cold that day.
5. He didn't feel very well. He couldn't let his teammates down.**
6. Each swimmer's time was recorded electronically during the different races at the meet. Every parent also held a stopwatch to make sure there was no mistake.
7. The children can remember exactly how fast each of the others has swum in past races. They are only five to eight years old.
8. Many children compete in each race. Richard is most interested in competing with his own previous best time.

**Meet:* an athletic competition. One meet may involve several races.
***Let down:* fail to help.

9. For example, Richard didn't win the first event last Saturday. Everyone congratulated him on having bettered his time.
10. However, Richard was disappointed in his time in the relay race.*** His team won the relay.

Exercise 2. Choosing the Intended Emphasis

Combine the following sentences to emphasize the *positive* aspects of children's swim meets in the United States. Use **although, though, even though,** and **in spite of the fact that.**

1. In each race, every child can hope to better his time. Only one child can receive first prize in that particular race.

   In each race, every child can hope to better his time, although only one child can receive first prize in that particular race. (*Logic:* This sentence emphasizes the encouragement that the system gives all the children. Placing **although** at the beginning would emphasize the negative idea that only one child can win. Give your sentences a *positive* emphasis.)

2. Richard was not fast enough to win any of the races last week. He was able to better his time in two of them.
3. Only the official winners receive the medals and ribbons. Every child who betters his or her time receives recognition* and feels like a winner.
4. Thus, Richard was pleased with his performance at the meet. He did not win any medals.
5. Only the faster swimmers can compete in the "A" group. There are also races for slower swimmers ("B" and "C" groups).
6. Therefore, Richard was able to enter several events that day and gain valuable experience. His time was not fast enough to place him in the "A" group for every race.
7. The American emphasis on time, competition, and achievement may have drawbacks**. These values probably help U.S. athletes succeed in international competitions such as the Olympics.

******Relay race:*** a team race in which each team member swims part of the total distance and then another continues the race.
**Recognition:* favorable attention.
***Drawbacks:* disadvantages.

Exercise 3. Expressing Opinions with *while* (oral or written)

Complete each sentence with a contrasting opinion. Include or omit the expressions in parentheses according to your own ideas.

Example: While I can('t) understand your interest in competitive swimming, . . .

While I can understand your interest in competitive swimming, I prefer to lie on the beach myself.

or: **While I *can't* understand your interest in competitive swimming, I enjoy swimming for relaxation.**

1. While I know that English is an important language in the world today, . . .
2. While I can('t) understand the importance that Americans place on time, . . .
3. While I like certain aspects of American culture, . . .
4. While I (don't) enjoy watching American TV (or American movies), . . .
5. While I believe it is important to learn about other cultures, . . .

21.2 Contrast: *whereas* and *while*

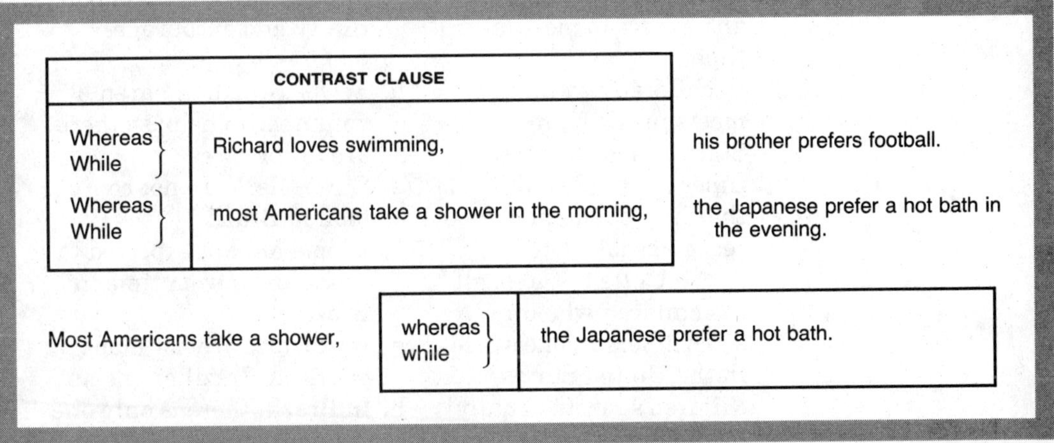

CONTRAST CLAUSE		
Whereas / While	Richard loves swimming,	his brother prefers football.
Whereas / While	most Americans take a shower in the morning,	the Japanese prefer a hot bath in the evening.

	CONTRAST CLAUSE	
Most Americans take a shower,	whereas / while	the Japanese prefer a hot bath.

Meaning: **Whereas** and **while** are used to contrast two situations where no causality or unexpected result is involved.

Punctuation: We use a comma before contrast clauses with **whereas** and **while.**

Exercise 4. Contrasts with *while* and *whereas*

An American anthropologist recently wrote an article contrasting American and Brazilian attitudes toward time. He described children's competitive swimming in those two countries as an example of the differences in attitude. Some of his observations are listed below.

For each sentence on the left, find a contrasting sentence on the right and write the appropriate letter to the left of the number. Then join the two sentences, using **while** or **whereas.**

Example: b 1. **While / Whereas Americans are obsessed with time, according to many Brazilians, people are more relaxed about time in Brazil.**

or: **Americans are obsessed with time, according to many Brazilians, while / whereas people are more relaxed about it in Brazil.**

b 1. Americans are obsessed with* time, according to many Brazilians.

___ 2. Americans often make appointments for exact times (like 4:15 or 2:50) and expect to meet on time.

___ 3. In children's swimming meets in the United States, each child's best times are made public so that improvement can be recognized.

___ 4. In the United States, all the children who improve are winners in one sense.

___ 5. In the United States, children's meets usually include relay races, which emphasize teamwork.

a. Relay races are not common at Brazilian meets.

b. In Brazil, people are more relaxed about time.

c. Young Brazilian swimmers are given less opportunity and encouragement.

d. Fewer Brazilian parents volunteer to help, so there are fewer races.

e. Car pools** are not common in Brazil.

f. People are not expected to arrive exactly on time in Brazil.

g. Best times are not made public at Brazilian meets.

h. In Brazil, there is only one winner for each race.

i. In Brazil, information about meets is often not

**Obsessed with:* preoccupied with, always thinking about.
***Car pool:* An arrangement in which one parent transports several children.

_____ 6. In the United States, meets are organized a year in advance.

_____ 7. American parents organize car pools to take children to distant meets.

_____ 8. American parents contribute a great deal of time in organizing races for their children.

_____ 9. American children often swim in many meets each year.

_____ 10. The anthropologist concludes that the American system of training encourages many young swimmers to aim for an Olympic medal.

available ahead of time, so children often miss them.

j. In Brazil, there are fewer meets, so children gain less experience.

21.3 Contrasting Conjunctions and Prepositions (reason and incongruity)

ADVERB CLAUSE			
CONJUNCTION	SUBJECT	VERB	
Because	it	was raining,	I took my umbrella.
Although	it	was raining,	John left his umbrella at home.
In spite of the fact that	he	had	a cold, John went out without his umbrella.

PREPOSITIONAL PHRASE		
PREPOSITION	NOUN	
Because of	the rain,	I took my umbrella.
In spite of / Despite	the rain,	John left his umbrella at home.

	GERUND PHRASE	
In spite of	having a cold,	John went out without his umbrella.

Structure: **Because, although,** and **in spite of the fact that** are examples of subordinating conjunctions. Subordinating conjunctions are followed by a *clause,* which contains a *subject* and *verb.* **Because of, in spite of,** and **despite** are prepositions and are followed by a noun or gerund.

> *Note:* A gerund is not often used after **because of.** It is simpler and better to use **because** + *clause.*

Vocabulary: Other expressions which mean *because of* include

on account of
as a result of
in view of

Exercise 5. Choosing a Conjunction or a Preposition

Fill in the blanks. Use

because	although
because of	in spite of, despite

1. Because the earth is tilted at an angle in relationship to the sun, the days are longer in summer and shorter in winter.
2. ____________ its shorter days, winter is colder than summer.
3. ____________ the long hours of daylight, the Arctic is not hot in summer, however.
4. ____________ the days are longer in summer, our hours are always sixty minutes long.
5. This was not always true. In the ancient method of measuring time, the hours were longer in summer ____________ the days were longer.

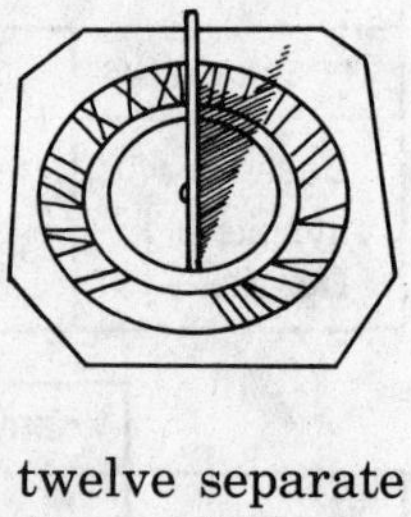

6. ____________ the changing length of the hours, twelve separate scales had to be marked on water clocks and sundials, one for every month of the year.

7. __________ it was complicated, this method of keeping time was used for several thousand years.

8. Apparently the idea of twenty-four equal hours was first adopted __________ its usefulness in astronomy.

Exercise 6. Cumulative Exercise: Conjunctions and Prepositions

Fill in a conjunction or preposition from the list. Use each expression at least once.

	Time	*Incongruity/Contrast*	*Cause/Purpose*	*Condition*	*Manner*
Conjunctions:	as by the time since until when whenever	√although though whereas while	as because since so that	as long as	as
Prepositions:		despite	because of on account of		

Although clocks have been in use for at least 5,000 years, the methods of measuring time and the accuracy with which it is measured have changed a great deal __________ someone first measured the length of a shadow to determine the hour. The first clocks were nothing more than vertical posts which cast a shadow. __________ the shadow was short __________ the sun was high in the sky at noon and became longer and longer __________ the sun sank toward the horizon in the evening, its length indicated roughly* the time of day. This was the first sundial.

More and more sophisticated sundials were developed by the Greeks, Romans, and Arabs. __________ they worked well __________ the sun was shining, they were useless at night and __________ it rained. __________ this limitation, the water clock was developed. The water clock was a bowl or jar with hours marked on the side and a small hole in the bottom. __________ the water dripped slowly out the bottom, the water level fell from one mark to the next. The Chinese developed large, complicated water clocks with bells to sound the hours.

__________ the ancients measured time quite accurately, they did not divide the day into twelve equal parts __________ we do. To

**Roughly:* not exactly.

them, every complete day had twelve daylight hours and twelve nighttime hours. __________ the sun rises earlier and sets later in the summer, each daylight hour was longer in the summer than in the winter, __________ each nighttime hour was shorter. __________ this variation, twelve separate scales had to be marked on the clock __________ the hours could be measured during each of the twelve months of the year.

The idea of having twenty-four equal hours was apparently unknown __________ it was introduced by an Arab named Abū al-Ḥasan about 800 years ago. This idea spread __________ its usefulness to astronomers. __________ the first mechanical clocks were made, the idea of equal hours had been known for about 100 years.

__________ the first mechanical clocks were very large, smaller models were gradually developed. Watches came into use around the year 1500. __________ these advances, however, people's concept of time must still have been quite different from ours __________ there were no minute hands on these timepieces for another 170 years!

Transfer Exercises

1. Surprises

Tell a classmate about something that surprised you in one (or more) of the situations listed. Use sentences of this type:

Although I	knew had been told was aware	that . . . , I	wasn't prepared	for . . . to (see) . . .
			was surprised	that . . . when . . . to (see) . . .

Examples: 1. **Although I knew that Americans were very exact about time, I was surprised when our first class began exactly on time.**

2. **Although I had been told that this class would be hard, I wasn't prepared to have a quiz every single day!**

What surprised you when

1. you took a trip?
2. you came to the United States?
3. you began to study at a new school?
4. you started a new job?
5. you signed up for this English course?

2. Contrasting Cultures

A. Below are some statements about American values and family life. Is life in your country different? Make statements of contrast using **while** or **whereas.** (Omit those sentences where there is no contrast. Or, if your country is similar to the United States, you can choose another country to contrast.)

Example: **In the United States, people eat sweet things such as pancakes for breakfast, whereas in (Japan), we like soup and salty food for breakfast.**

1. In the United States (and Canada), individual independence is considered very important.
2. In the United States, older people don't like to depend on their children to take care of them.
3. It is not common to find grandparents living in an American family.
4. Most American women have jobs outside the home.
5. In the United States, many high school students have after-school jobs.
6. Many American children are cared for in day-care centers while their mothers work.
7. Parents often hire baby-sitters one or more nights a week in the United States.
8. American children often spend part of the summer living away from home at a children's camp.
9. American homes typically have many appliances, but no servants.

B. Make sentences of your own about some other aspects of culture. For example:

marriage and divorce
family size and family planning
health care

the system of government
education
ways of celebrating holidays
attitudes toward women
etc.

3. Open-ended

Complete the following sentences:

1. Even though this course is . . .
2. In spite of the fact that the teacher . . .
3. English is . . . , while . . .
4. While I agree that . . . , I think . . .
5. I like . . . , even though . . .
6. Though I would like to . . .
7. I have had some failures in my life, though . . .
8. My life now is . . . , whereas (last year) it was . . .
9. Although I will never . . .

Discussion Topics

A. Are children's competitive sports highly organized in your country? If so, are the teams organized by schools, churches, clubs, or towns? Do parents help to organize events and transport the children? Are there regional and national competitions for children? Do most children participate in one or more sports? How old are the youngest competitors? What sports are the most popular?

B. Were sports important to you as a child? What were your favorite sports? How much time did you spend playing or practicing per week? Did you participate all year, or only in certain seasons? Was individual competition important to you? Team competition? How often were competitions held? Did your parents participate in organizing games or competitions? Did they encourage you to work hard to improve? Was time important in your sport? Was it more important than winning?

C. How do people feel about time in your country? Do they consider punctuality to be very important? For example, is it important to be exactly on time for business appointments, classes, dinner parties, concerts, etc.? Are you expected to be a little late when visiting someone's home? If so, how late can you be without being impolite? Is it all right to be early?

How do you feel about time? If you are now in an English-speaking country, do you find that you pay more attention to time than you did when you were in your country?

D. Are competition and teamwork important values in your culture? What do you consider to be your country's most important cultural values? Are they learned through sports or other organized activities for children? Can you give examples?

Composition Topics

Write a short composition about one of the following topics, using adverb clauses of incongruity, concession, and contrast in some of your sentences.

1. Write about something (or several things) that surprised you when you visited a foreign country, when you started a new job, or when you enrolled at a new school. (See Transfer Exercise 1.)
2. Contrast some important attitudes in your country with corresponding attitudes in the United States (or another country). (See Transfer Exercise 2 and Discussion Topic D.)
3. Write about how people in your country feel about time. (See Discussion Topic C.)
4. Write about children's competitive sports in your country. (See Exercises 1, 2, and 4, and Discussion Topic A.)
5. Write about your own participation in sports as a child. (See Discussion Topic B.)

UNIT VIII

ADJECTIVE CLAUSES

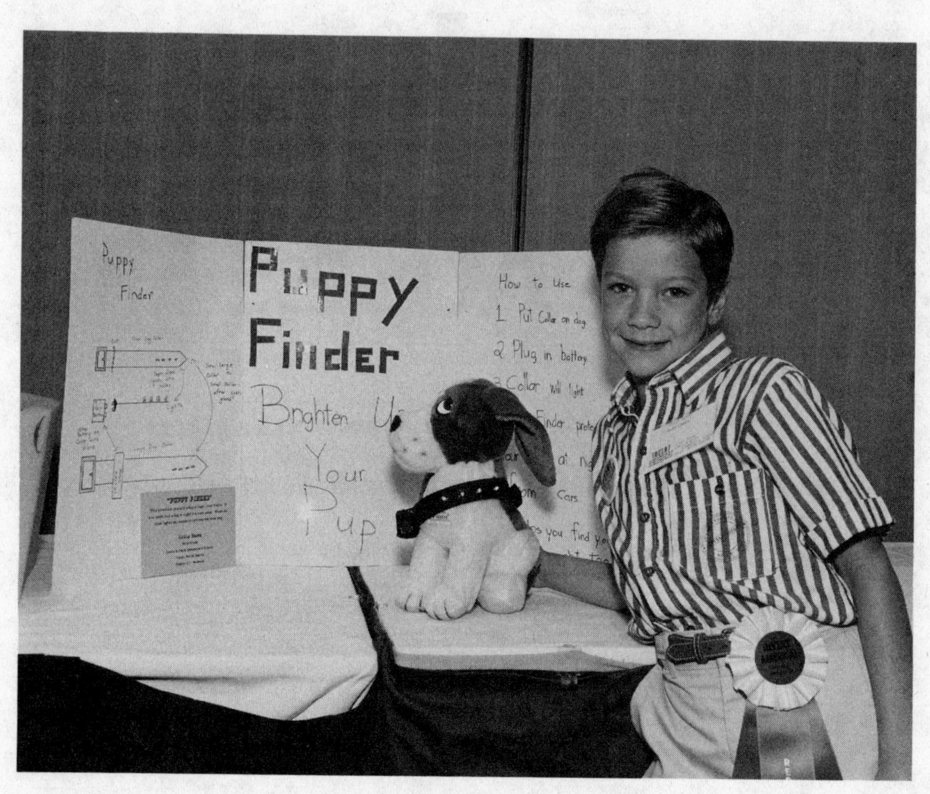
Puppy
Finder
PUPPY
Finder
Your
Pup
How to Use
1. Put Collar on dog
2 Plug in battery
3 Collar will light

Lesson 22

Young Inventors

22.1 Essential Adjective Clauses: Subject Focus

Statement			*Adjective Clause*	
SUBJECT			**SUBJECT**	
The teacher	taught the class yesterday.	→	who	taught the class yesterday
The book	explains the grammar.	→	which	explains the grammar

EMBEDDING THE ADJECTIVE CLAUSE IN THE INDEPENDENT CLAUSE

The teacher [who taught the class yesterday] didn't give any homework. (a)

We need *a* book [which / that } explains the grammar. (b)]

Definition: An adjective clause is a dependent clause which follows a noun or pronoun and gives more information about it.

Meaning: Essential adjective clauses identify the noun they follow:

a. A clause after **the, that,** or **those** tells *which one.*
b. After other words, the clause tells *what kind of.*

The first word in the adjective clause (the relative pronoun) means the same as the noun it follows.

Choice of Relative Pronoun:

People:

Who refers to a person or people.
Which is used for nouns which refer to a *group* of people:

> **The committee *which* decides those questions will meet tomorrow.**

Things:

Which is used to refer to animals, things, and all other nouns. (However, if an animal is referred to by name, use **that.**)

That:

That can be used in place of **who** or **which.** However, **who** is preferred as the subject in written English.

The subject pronoun is never omitted from an adjective clause.

Word Order: An adjective clause follows directly the noun which it describes.

Exception: If the noun is modified by both a prepositional phrase and a clause, the phrase comes first.

> **The aspect** *(phrase:)* **of the language** *(clause:)* **which is hardest for me is grammar.**
>
> **John told me something** *(phrase:)* **about you**
> *(clause:)* **which I had never heard before.**

Vocabulary: Adjective clauses can modify the following pronouns:

everyone	someone	anyone	no one
everybody	somebody	anybody	nobody
everything	something	anything	nothing
all	some	any	none
much	one(s)	that	
many	others	those	
most			

Examples: **Everyone who passes the final exam will graduate.**
No one who studies will fail.

Note: Generally adjective clauses are not used after personal pronouns (**he, she, him, them,** *etc.).*

Exceptions: **those of us** and **those of you.**

Those of us who passed the exam will be taking the advanced course next term.

Those of you who haven't registered yet should do so after this class.

Punctuation: We do not use commas before or after essential adjective clauses.

Exercise 1. Subject Relative Pronouns

Since the U.S. Patent Office issued its first patent* two hundred years ago, about five million inventions have been patented in the United States. In recent years, however, more and more of the patents have been issued to foreigners. Educators are worried that Americans are losing their inventiveness, so they have introduced invention as a subject in schools and colleges. There are now several annual contests for young inventors from kindergarten age up. The largest—called "Invent America!"—has several million entries each year from children around the country. The finalists bring their inventions to Washington, D.C., and the winners receive a savings bond*** and a handshake from the Vice President of the United States. Here are some facts about some of the winners in recent years.**

Combine the sentences with **who, which,** or **that.** Make the first sentence in each pair the independent clause.

1. One boy invented a bird cage. The cage is easy to clean.

   One boy invented a bird cage which is easy to clean.

2. The cage can be cleaned just by pulling on a roll of paper. The roll of paper passes through slots on the floor of the cage.

Patent: a statement issued by the government which gives an inventor the rights to his or her invention so that others may not copy and sell it.
***Finalists:* the top group from which the winners are chosen.
****Savings bond:* a certificate which can be exchanged for money after several years.

3. A girl invented a diaper. It can be folded into its own plastic pouch for easy disposal.

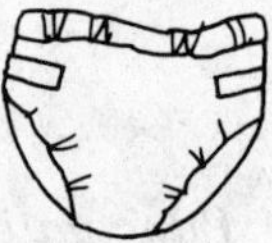

4. One fifth grader didn't want the person to fall asleep on his shoulder. The person was sitting next to him on a plane trip.
5. A headrest was his solution to the problem. It can be attached to an airplane seat.
6. The "School Bus Safety Control Board" was invented by a fourth grader. She rides the school bus every day.
7. The safety control board is an ingenious device. It signals the bus driver whenever a child's seat belt is unfastened.
8. A seventh grader invented a bathtub.
   The boy didn't like to clean the bathtub.
   This bathtub cleans itself.
9. An eighth grader was worried about the disappearance of the fish. He lives in Florida. The fish live in the coastal waters.
10. He invented an artificial reef. The reef provides shelter and a feeding ground for the fish.

22.2 Essential Adjective Clauses: Object Focus

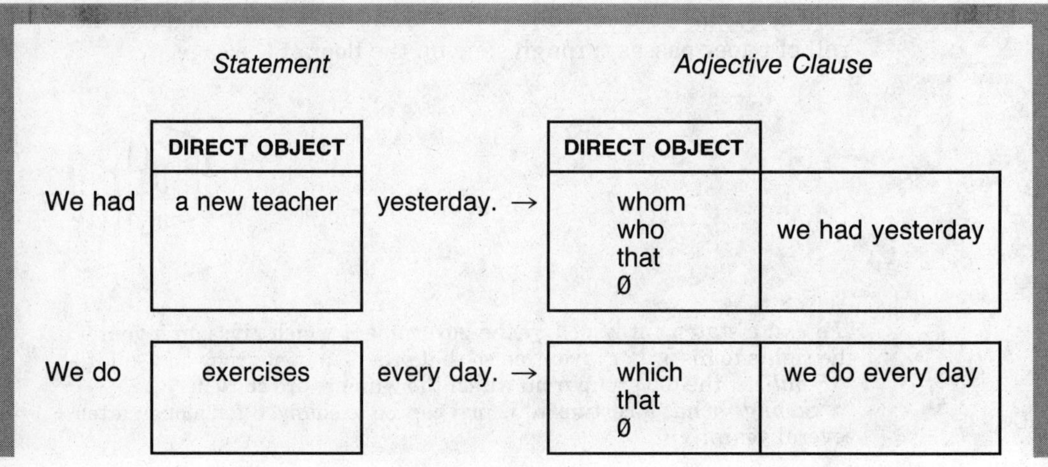

	Statement			*Adjective Clause*	
	DIRECT OBJECT			DIRECT OBJECT	
We had	a new teacher	yesterday.	→	whom who that ø	we had yesterday
We do	exercises	every day.	→	which that ø	we do every day

EMBEDDING THE CLAUSE

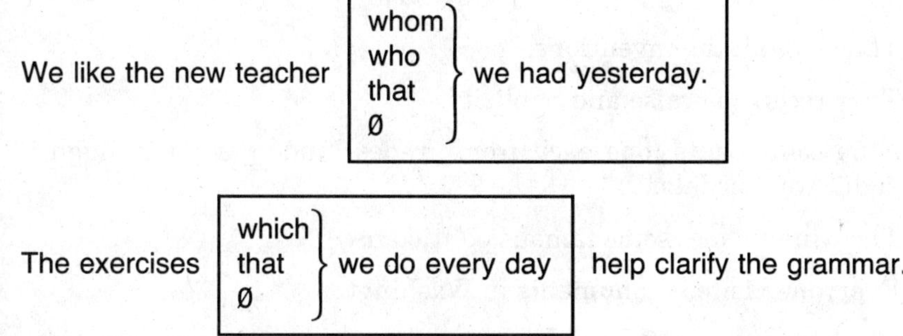

Choice of Relative Pronoun:

Whom refers to a person or people. (Informally, we use **who.**)
Which is used for nouns which refer to a group of people, and for animals, things, and all other nouns.
That can be used in place of **whom** or **which.**

Deletion: The direct object relative pronoun may be omitted.

Note: A relative pronoun may be the direct object of an infinitive, gerund, or noun clause:

The book which I tried *to read* last night was difficult.
One book which I enjoyed *reading* was *The Red Pony.*
The book which he said *he wanted* was *The Red Pony.*

Exercise 2. Object Relative Pronouns (oral—books closed)

Last year, the forty-five finalists in the Invent America! contest were invited to come to Washington, D.C., and exhibit their inventions there. Naturally, they enjoyed the trip and all the activities that took place.

A. Change each sentence below to an adjective clause and insert it in the sentence, "They liked . . ." Give the different variations which are possible.

1. The forty-five children saw a lot of people.

They liked the people { whom they say. / who they saw. / that they saw. / they saw. }

2. They saw all the inventions.
3. They received praise and publicity.
4. Nine contestants (one each from grades kindergarten through eight) won medals.
5. The winners met some famous politicians.
6. Everyone visited monuments in Washington.

B. Change the first sentence in each pair to an adjective clause. Then combine it with the second sentence. Give all the possible variations.

7. The children brought their inventions to Washington. The inventions were all clever.

   The inventions which . . .

8. They won money. The prize money was a savings bond.
9. They met politicians. One of the politicians was the Vice President.
10. They met lots of people at the exhibit. The people included all the other finalists and their families.

Exercise 3. Object Relative Pronouns (formal)

Combine or restate the sentences so that they include an adjective clause after the underlined word(s). Use **whom** or **which.** Be sure that your sentences make good sense.

1. A teacher in Oklahoma read about a contest. The magazine *The Weekly Reader* was sponsoring it.

   A teacher in Oklahoma read about a contest which the magazine *The Weekly Reader* was sponsoring.

2. She was teaching a class of six-year-olds. She asked the children to think of inventions.

   She asked the six-year-old children . . .

3. She suggested that they think about daily tasks. Perhaps they could make them easier.
4. Or they could think about people in their families if they wanted to help them.
5. One of the children, Suzy G., fed cat food to the family's cats. She hated the smell of the canned cat food.
6. She used a spoon to dish out the cat food, but afterwards she hated to clean the spoon.
7. So she thought of making a new kind of spoon. The cats could eat it.
8. She made a spoon-shaped cracker with some help from her mother and grandmother. The spoon-shaped cracker is strong enough to get the catfood out of the can but can be broken and fed to the cat.
9. She used a recipe. The recipe is a secret but includes lots of garlic, she says.
10. Another first-grade teacher was concerned about the safety of the children as she led them along a busy street to the town library.
11. One of her pupils has devised a rope with handles. The children hold the handles.
12. The teacher carries a box. Whenever a child lets go of his or her handle, the box buzzes a warning.

Exercise 4. Choosing Subject and Object Pronouns

Improve the style of the paragraph below by following these steps:

a. Underline the relative pronoun **that** wherever it occurs. (But do not underline **that** if it is not a relative pronoun.)

b. Write **who, whom** or **which** above **that.**

c. Put parentheses around the relative pronouns which can be deleted (the object relative pronouns).

d. Copy the paragraph, using a variety of relative pronouns and **Ø**.

Some guidelines:

Use **who** (not **that**) for the subject if it refers to a person.
Omit the object pronoun in short clauses.

The children that participate in the invention contests often think of inventions (that) can help people (that) they know. For example, one kindergarten child had an older brother that had to walk to the school-bus stop in the dark on winter mornings. The flashlight umbrella that she invented helped him get there without stepping in a mud puddle. Another kindergarten child had a little sister that was always throwing her plate and spoon (as well as the food!) on the floor at mealtime. This child devised a plate that could not be thrown and then attached a fork and spoon to it with elastic cords. One boy's mother complained that she couldn't get the food out of the bottom of glass jars. The jar that he created for her has a lid on each end. Another child likes to take hot meals to an old couple that she knows that find it hard to prepare good meals. The insulated casserole cover that she devised has two handles for easy carrying. Finally, one boy invented a bicycle rack that keeps his bicycle wheel straight when he parks the bike in the garage. That solved the problem of scratches on the family car and improved family relations.

22.3 Focus on the Object of a Preposition

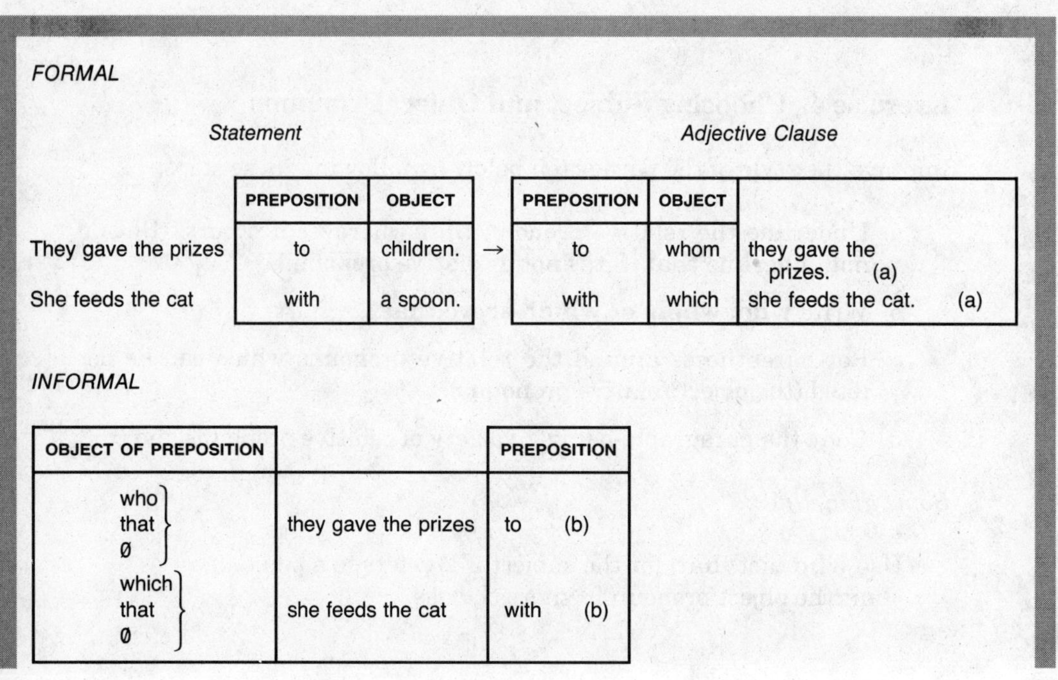

FORMAL

Statement	PREPOSITION	OBJECT		PREPOSITION	OBJECT	*Adjective Clause*	
They gave the prizes	to	children.	→	to	whom	they gave the prizes.	(a)
She feeds the cat	with	a spoon.		with	which	she feeds the cat.	(a)

INFORMAL

OBJECT OF PREPOSITION		PREPOSITION	
who / that / Ø	they gave the prizes	to	(b)
which / that / Ø	she feeds the cat	with	(b)

EMBEDDING THE CLAUSE

The children	to whom	they gave the prizes		came from all over the country.
	who / that / Ø	they gave the prizes	to	

The spoon	with which	she feeds the cat		can be eaten by the cat.
	which / that / Ø	she feeds the cat	with	

Choice of Relative Pronoun:

a. *After a preposition,* we use **whom** and **which.** They are never deleted.

b. When the clause begins with a relative pronoun and the *preposition remains at the end,* use **who** or **that** for people and **which** or **that** for other meanings. The relative pronoun may be deleted in this case.

Note: If the adjective clause is long, the preposition should be placed at the beginning.

Exercise 5. Informal Position for Prepositions (oral—books closed)

Answer each question *yes* and add a sentence with an adjective clause that ends in a preposition. *Optional:* Another student can give the possible variations on the first student's answer.

Example: Did you sit next to another student in class yesterday?

First Student: **Yes, the student I sat next to was Maria.**

Second Student: **The student {who / that} Mustafa sat next to was Maria.**

1. Did you sit next to another student in class yesterday?
2. Did you get a letter from somebody last week?
3. Did you write to somebody a few weeks ago?
4. Are you looking at something or somebody?
5. Did you eat at a restaurant last week?
6. Did you give a tip to the {waiter? / waitress?}
7. Has a friend told you about a good movie recently?
8. Have you gone to a good movie recently?

Exercise 6. Formal Position for Prepositions

Besides invention contests for children, there are also courses in inventing at a few colleges in the United States. One of them, called "How to Develop, Patent, and Market an Idea," is taught by Robert Krolick at San Francisco State College.

Make the underlined sentence into an adjective clause that begins with a preposition. Then combine the clause with the other sentence.

A. Professor Krolick's class is not for engineers, but for people from many walks of life.* Many of the problems the students tackle** are rather small ones. For example:

1. One student devised a large plastic bag. <u>You could wash your dog in the bag without getting splashed</u>.

*Walks of life: occupations.
**Tackle: try to solve.

Clause: **in which you could wash your dog without getting splashed**

Sentence: **One student devised a large plastic bag in which you could wash your dog without getting splashed.**

2. Another made a plastic disk. You could insert your socks into the disk so that they wouldn't get lost in the washing machine.

   Clause: **into which . . .**

B. Some ideas, however, have made money for their student inventors.

3. Patients' heads are held with clamps during some kinds of medical treatment. A medical technician in the class noticed that the clamps are uncomfortable.
4. She invented a vacuum clamp. The head can be held comfortably with this clamp.
5. One student invented a plastic handle. You can pick up two-liter soda bottles with it.
6. He sold the invention to a company. The company has sold 200,000 handles in five years.
7. Another student filled a big plastic bag with an oozy gelatin-like substance in order to make a chair. You could relax comfortably in the chair.
8. Later, when he changed the chair to a mattress, he decided that the gelatin was too thick. He had filled the chair with gelatin.
9. He became a millionaire for his invention. The invention is called a waterbed.

C. Professor Krolick is also a successful inventor, but some of his inventions have been failures because of marketing problems.

10. For example, a plastic rack didn't sell. You could measure out helpings of uncooked spaghetti with the rack.

11. He tried to sell it to a large food company. The company turned it down because they hoped spaghetti users would continue to cook too much spaghetti.

Exercise 7. Summary Exercise

Rewrite the following paragraphs, combining sentences with adjective clauses. (Not every sentence needs to be combined—some can remain as they are.)

Are Americans losing their inventiveness? This is a question. It is being asked by educators and industrial analysts. In 1986, the U.S. Patent Office was still as busy as ever, but about half the patents went to foreigners. The office issued the patents. This is a fact. It has some Americans worried.

Some experts believe that the Japanese are rapidly outstripping the United States in inventiveness, partly because they have had an invention education program in the schools since as early as 1941. They also point to the Americans' desire for immediate results. For example, Americans give their children building toys. The building toys work immediately, without any need for experimentation. Other experts hold that Americans have as many bright ideas as ever. Americans are weak in one area. The area, they say, is the area of process innovation—that is, in manufacturing and marketing new ideas. Contests will not remedy that weakness, in their view. The contests encourage "breakthrough thinking." One writer has written a book on inventing. He feels that the way children use crayons to color in pictures shows the difference between the American and the Japanese creative styles. Japanese children color the pictures. They stay within the lines of the pictures, whereas American children tend to go outside the lines. This shows, he feels, that "American kids are the ones. They make the breakthroughs, and Japanese kids are the ones. They perfect them."[1]

The people are not worried about which experts are correct. They sponsor the invention contests. In their opinion, the contests can only benefit the children. The children participate in them. They believe that any activity will help them throughout their lives. The activity encourages children to think creatively.

[1]Steven Caney, quoted in Barbara Bradley's article "From Fake Reefs to Diapers—Kids Turn Inventors," *Christian Science Monitor,* June 26, 1987, page 1. Your combined sentence will be the quotation.

Transfer Exercises

1. Some Firsts

Ask and answer questions about what happened when you first came to this country (or when you first enrolled in this school). Use the word **first,** and include the sentences below as adjective clauses in your questions.

1. You spoke to somebody first.

   Who was the first person you spoke to when you came to this (country/school)?
   The first person I spoke to was the (immigration official/ secretary).

2. You did something first.

   What was . . .

3. You ate your first meal here.

   How was . . .

4. You went to a restaurant near school.
5. You saw your first movie (in this country).
6. You bought your first book after coming here.
7. You had your first piece of good luck.
8. Somebody wrote you a letter.
9. Somebody called you up.
10. Something shocked or confused you.
11. Something made you feel at home.

2. Attitudes

Complete the sentences with an adjective clause.

1. I pay attention to everything . . . **that the teacher writes on the blackboard.**
2. I like everyone . . .
3. I don't know anyone . . .
4. I don't buy anything . . .
5. Nothing . . . will make me change my mind about (   ).
6. I am suspicious of anyone . . .
7. I like to study with professors . . .
8. Next year I want to take courses . . .

3. What Are These Inventions For?

The following inventions have been exhibited in classrooms or in the National Inventors Exposition in Washington, D.C. Can you guess what they do or what they are used for? Use an adjective clause in each sentence. (Use your imagination.)

A. Invented by children

1. a floating jigsaw puzzle

   A floating jigsaw puzzle is a puzzle that floats so that a child can play with it in the bathtub.

2. a bottomless jar
3. a lunch-box alarm
4. the "Lazy-Boy Light Switch"

B. Invented by adults

5. a see-through cereal box
6. an electric ice-cream scoop
7. flashlight slippers
8. a fold-up cello

4. What's Your Invention?

A. Think of something that you hate doing, something you need, or something that would help a friend. Tell the class what you would like to invent.

Example: **I hate to carry heavy books. I would like to invent a small balloon that would carry my books from the parking lot to school.**

B. *Optional:* Think about your invention at home, draw a picture of it, and be prepared to tell your classmates how you would construct it and how it would work.

Discussion Topics

A. Americans consider themselves a nation of inventors. Since they consider the first person to patent a machine at the U.S. Patent Office the inventor of that machine, American history books give the impression that almost every nineteenth-century invention was an American idea. Even dictionaries contain errors of this kind. For example, they state that Elias Howe invented the sewing machine in 1846. In fact, a Frenchman named Barthélemy Thimonnier had already built a sewing machine sixteen years earlier.

Do you know of inventions that come from your country? If so, what are they? Who invented them and when, approximately? You might want to look up one or more of these inventions in an American encyclopedia. Who is given as the inventor in the encyclopedia? Is the inventor from your country mentioned?

B. Have you ever wanted to invent something? If so, what was it? Did you want to make a toy more interesting or a job easier? Did you just dream about your idea, or did you actually construct the device? If you constructed it, how did you do it? Did it work well? Do you think other people you know could benefit from your idea? Would it sell well if you marketed it for the general public?

C. Which of the inventions that have been discussed in this lesson seem most useful or valuable to you? Which ones seem least useful? Are there some that are ingenious* even though they are not important or useful?

D. Have you heard of an invention contest for children in your country? If you have, what do you remember about it? If you haven't, do you think such a contest would be a good idea?

E. Inventing is only one form of creativity; there are many others. What forms of creativity are particularly valued in your country? How are children encouraged to develop their creativity?

Composition Topics

Write a short composition on one of the following topics, using adjective clauses in some of your sentences.

1. Write about one (or more) inventions from your country. What is the purpose or function of the invention? Who invented it, and when? How did it improve on previous methods or machines? Is

**Ingenious:* clever.

the invention used in your country or around the world today? Do most people know that it originated in your country?

2. Write about an invention of your own. (See Transfer Exercise 4 and Discussion Topic B.)

3. What is the most important invention in the history of humankind, in your opinion? Explain.

4. Write about a form of creativity that seems important to you. Why is it important? Can it be taught to everybody? Can it be taught to children? How can children (or adults) be encouraged to develop this form of creativity?

5. Write about some of your first experiences in the country (or at the school) where you are studying now. (See Transfer Exercise 1.)

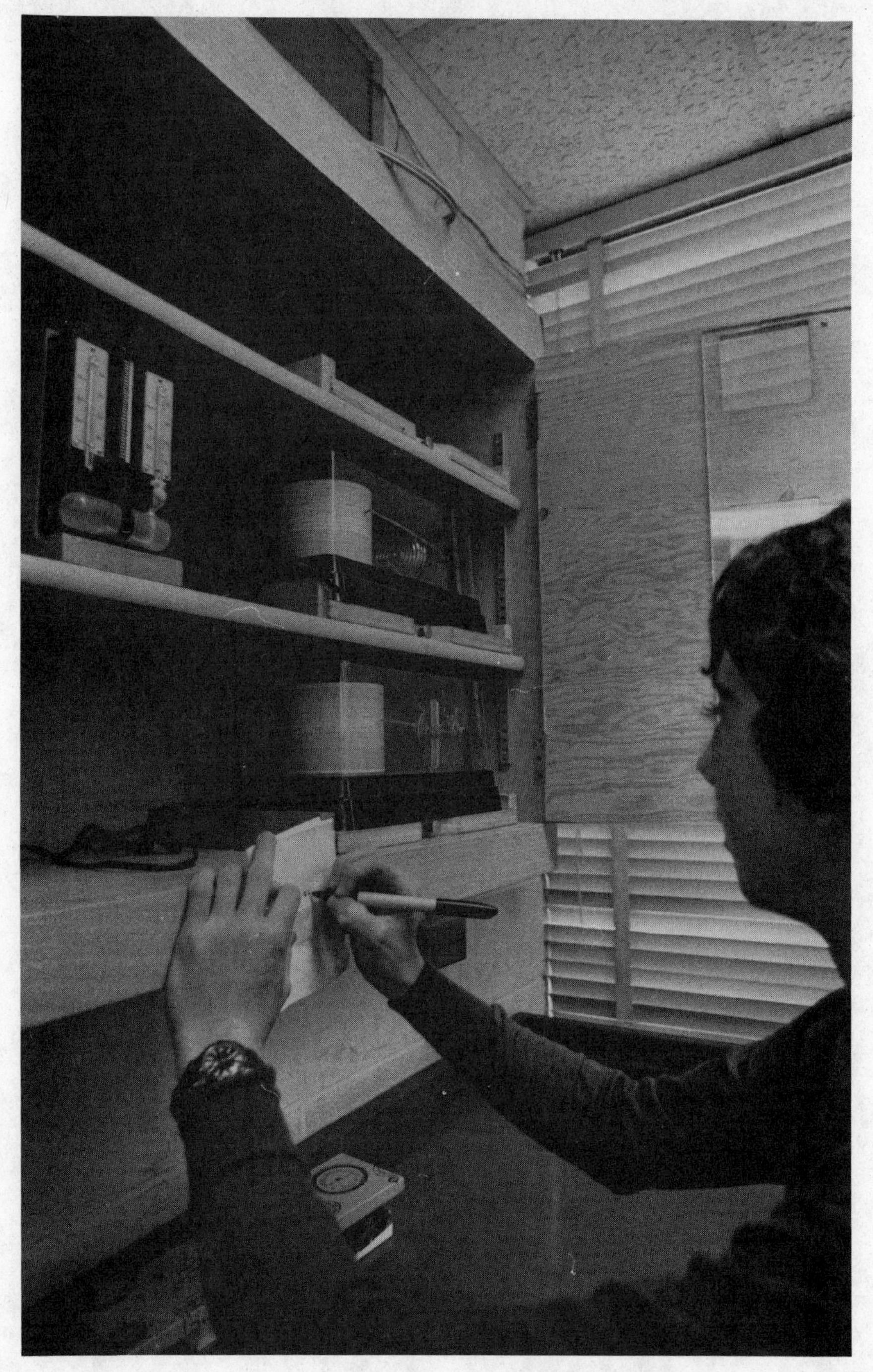

Lesson 23

Children in All Walks of Life

23.1 Essential Adjective Clauses with *whose*

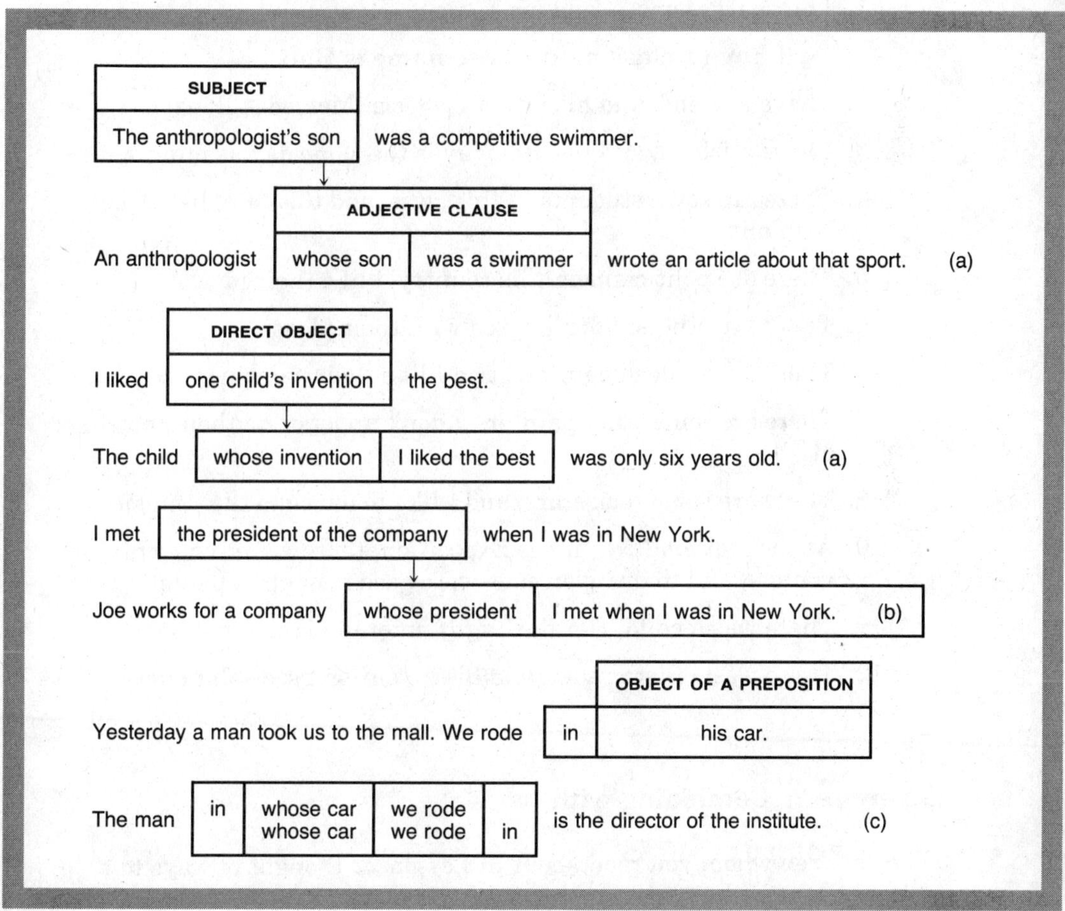

Choice of Relative Pronoun: **Whose** refers to a possessive form:

a. a noun + **'s** or **s'**
b. a phrase with **of**
c. a possessive adjective (**my, your, our, his, her, its, their**)

Whose may refer to people or things.

Word Order: In adjective clauses, **whose** is always followed by the noun it modifies. No deletion is possible.

Exercise 1. Combining with *whose* (oral—books closed)

Restate the sentences using **whose.** Your sentences will be much clearer than the ones given here.

1. I have a classmate, and his name is (Hao).

   I have a classmate whose name is Hao.
2. I have a friend, and his father drives a (Mercedes-Benz).
3. I have a friend, and his birthday is the same day as mine.
4. There are some students in this class, and their English is better than mine.
5. There are politicians in this country. I like their ideas.
6. There are others. I don't agree with their ideas.
7. There are modern painters, and I like their paintings.
8. There are some other painters. I don't understand their paintings at all.
9. There are some rock stars, and I like to dance to their music.
10. At the National Inventors Exposition, there were some child inventors, and their inventions were good enough to patent.
11. There was a child. Her flashlight umbrella received a prize.
12. There was a first grader, and his invention used solar energy.

Exercise 2. Combining with *whose*

The children whom you read about in Lesson 22 thought of ways to help someone who had a special problem.

Find the sentence on the right which best matches each sentence on the left, and combine the two sentences with **whose.**

Example: __c__ 1. **A girl whose older brother had to walk to the school-bus stop in the dark invented a flashlight umbrella.**

	Problem	*Solution*
__c__	1. A girl's older brother had to walk to the school-bus stop in the dark.	a. She invented the "Toddler* Plate."
____	2. A child's little sister liked to throw her plate and spoon on the floor.	b. A rider on a school bus invented the "School Bus Safety Control Board."
____	3. A boy's parents complained that his bicycle had scratched their car.	√c. She invented a flashlight umbrella ("Mud-Puddle Spotter").
____	4. A child's teacher was concerned about taking her pupils along a busy street.	d. The exhibitor was the six-year-old creator of the edible pet-food spoon.
____	5. A six-year-old's mother always made her clean up after feeding her cats.	e. He invented a new bicycle rack.
____	6. A boy's mother made him clean the bathtub when he wanted to go out to play.	f. He invented an artificial reef to increase the supply of fish in his area.
____	7. An eighth grader's father was a commercial fisherman.	g. The "Self-Cleaning Bathtub" was invented by him.
____	8. The driver of a school bus was concerned about the children's safety.	h. Do you think they will be more successful when they grow up?
____	9. Photographers at the National Inventors Exposition especially liked to take one exhibitor's picture.	i. The edible pet-food spoon was invented by her.
____	10. Some children's parents and teachers encourage them to be inventive.	j. The child devised a safety rope with handles and a warning system.

**Toddler:* a child who is just learning to walk.

23.2 Essential Adjective Clauses with *where, when,* and *why*

Where

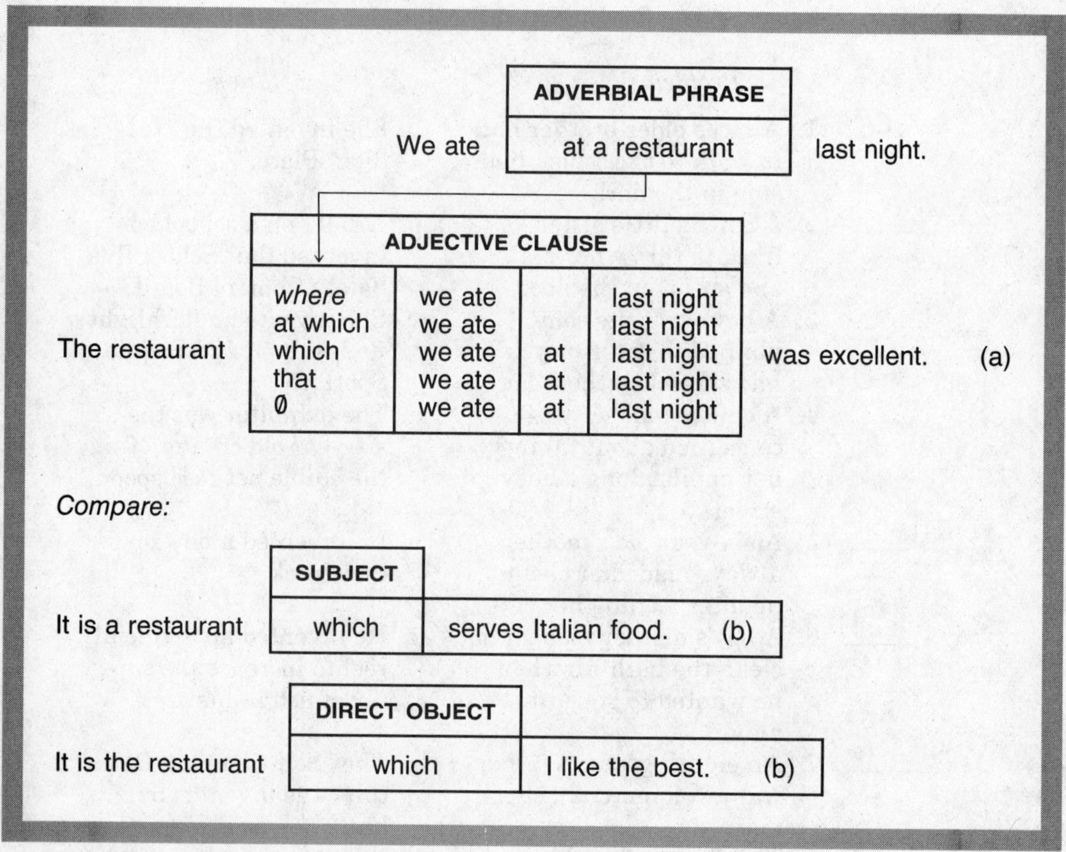

Choice of Relative Pronoun:

a. **Where** can begin an adjective clause which refers to a place. No preposition is used with **where.** (Notice that a preposition *is* used with **which, that,** and **Ø.**)

b. **Where** cannot be used as a subject or object relative pronoun.

When

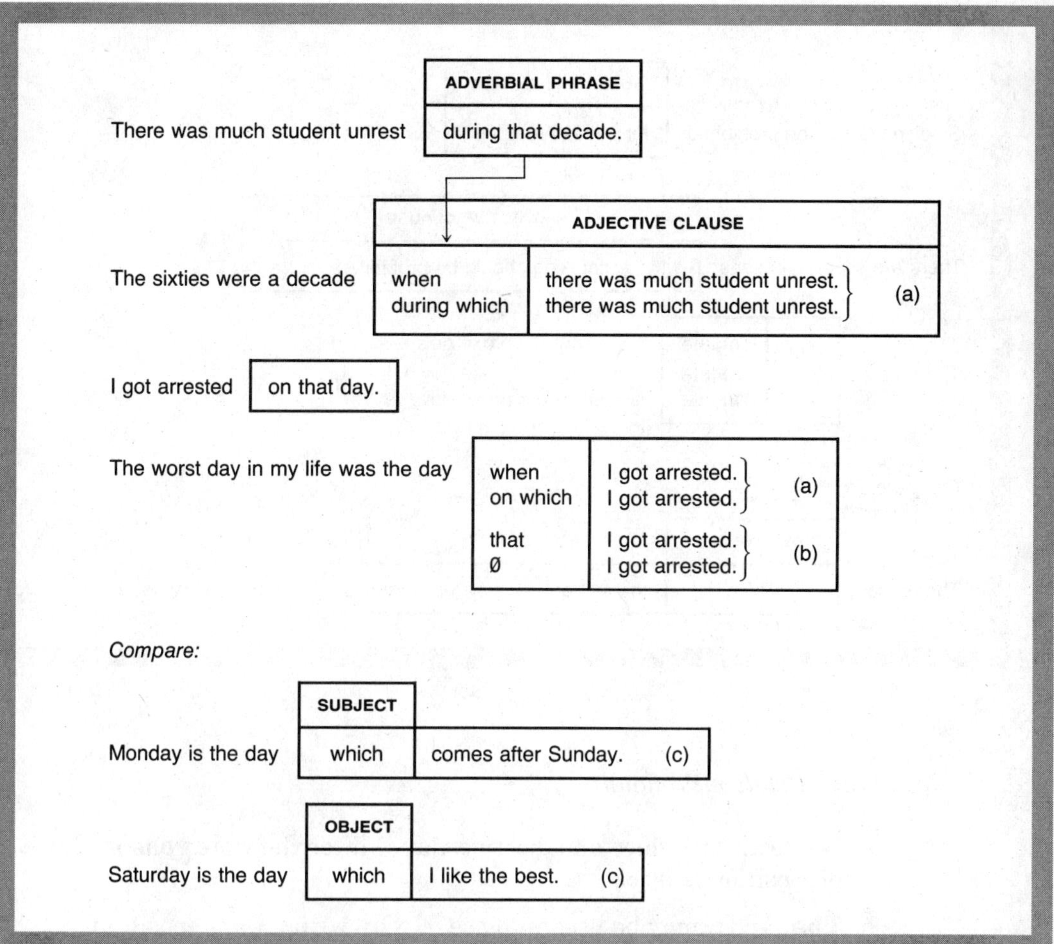

Choice of Relative Pronoun

a. **When** can begin an adjective clause which modifies a noun of time. No preposition is used with **when.** (Notice that a preposition *is* used with **which** and that it must *precede* **which.**

b. **That** and **Ø** are used only after common nouns of time such as **day, year,** or **time.** No preposition is used with **that** and **Ø** in clauses referring to time.

c. **When** is *not* used as a subject or object pronoun.

Why

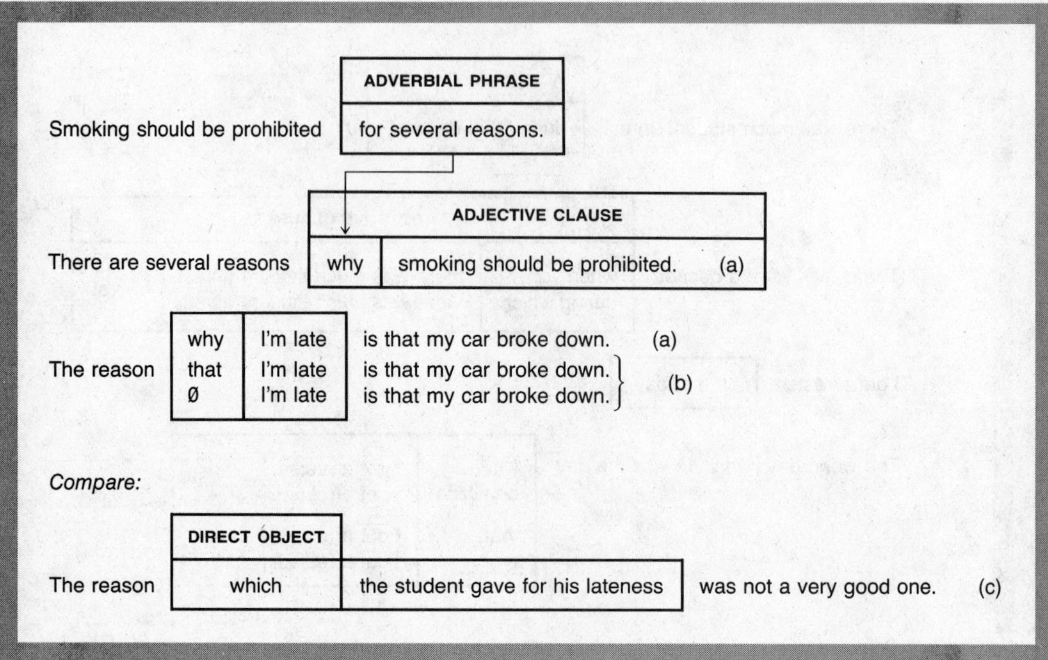

Choice of Relative Pronoun:

a. **Why** can introduce an adjective clause after the word **reason.** No preposition is used.

b. **That** and **Ø** may be used in place of **why** without a preposition.

c. **Why** is not used as a subject or object relative pronoun.

Exercise 3. Combining with *when, where, why,* and *which*

Programs to foster children's inventiveness were the subject of the previous lesson. Science education is another area in which the United States is thought to lag behind other countries, and science museums and zoos around the country are trying to do something about it. This exercise describes some of the innovative science programs they offer both teachers and children.

Join the sentences using adjective clauses with **when, where,** and **why** wherever possible. Use **which** only as the subject or object. In some cases, the first sentence should become the adjective clause, while in other cases it makes more sense to make the second sentence into an adjective clause.

Be sure that your sentences make good sense as a paragraph. Write them in paragraph form.

1. We live in a technological age. Science is considered very important in our age.

   We live in a technological age when science is considered very important.

2. The United States needs to improve the quality of its science education. According to educators, an important reason is that the country is behind in that area.
3. Most of us have been to museums. You can look at the exhibits in the museums, but you cannot touch them.
4. However, science museums exist in many cities around the country. At these museums, children are invited to touch the exhibits.
5. During after-school hours, the children can come to the museum by themselves. Many parents are at work during after-school hours.
6. Furthermore, these museums now plan weekends. Girl Scout and Boy Scout troops bring their sleeping bags, sleep among the museum exhibits, and spend the days working on science projects.
7. Weekends are popular. Teachers can sleep over and learn new teaching methods. (Use **also.**)
8. In addition, there are zoos. These zoos offer educational programs for children.
9. For example, at the Museum of Natural History in Washington, D.C., there is an insect zoo. Children act as caretakers at this zoo.
10. The Philadelphia Zoo has a special discovery center. In the center, children can ride a life-sized model of a dinosaur, get inside a huge bird's egg and hear the mother bird's heartbeat, look through a large model of a bee's eye, or climb inside a giant frog's mouth.
11. They can do all these things in the center. The center also contains a four-story tree (independent clause). The tree has a staircase inside for the children to climb.
12. The children love this center. The sounds and smells are one reason. The sounds and smells are part of the exhibits.

Exercise 4. Cumulative Exercise: Essential Adjective Clauses

Children are involved in many unusual activities, both as amateurs and as professionals. Some of their achievements are reported below.

Combine the sentences with adjective clauses. Use **who, whom, which, whose, when, where, why, that,** or **Ø.** You will need to shift nouns and pronouns in some cases in order to make meaningful sentences. In some sentences, three dots (. . .) indicate where to put the adjective clause.

1. A picture of Santa Claus was used on a U.S. postage stamp in December 1984. A boy of nine drew the picture (independent clause).

   A boy of nine drew the picture of Santa Claus {which / that} was used on a U.S. postage stamp in December 1984.

2. A ten-year-old girl . . . published a book about her grandfather. Her grandfather led a group of soldiers to safety when he was fourteen.
3. A class of children . . . made a field trip to dig up dinosaur fossils.* They live in an area of Colorado. . . . Dinosaurs were once prevalent** in that area.
4. A boy of fourteen started a successful company. It puts out inexpensive portable computers.
5. A Texas boy writes a syndicated newspaper column.*** His book about home video games was published when he was fourteen. In the column he rates**** video games and accessories.
6. The column . . . is called "The Vid Kid." He writes the column.
7. Two young brothers love to collect all kinds of old things, from automobile hubcaps to elegant horse-drawn carriages. The boys live in West Virginia.
8. They collect the things. They display the things in a large shed (independent clause). Their father built the shed for them.
9. During (certain) hours their museum is open to visitors. They are not in school during those hours. The visitors pay fifty cents to see the collection.
10. When the sports director of radio station WROR in Boston quit his job, the replacement was a twelve-year-old girl, Kelly Michelle. The station hired a replacement.

**Fossil:* a trace preserved in stone.
***Prevalent:* common.
****Syndicated newspaper column:* articles which are published frequently in newspapers around the country.
*****Rate:* evaluate, decide how good something is.

11. Kelly asked for something. The only thing was a Mickey Mouse telephone, which she uses to phone in reports to the station.
12. An eleven-year-old girl . . . has interviewed more than 200 people on the air during the four years. . . . Her radio show is heard on FM stations around the country. She has co-hosted***** the show for four years. (Use **Ø**.)
13. She enjoys doing the show. The reason is that it is "fun and exciting," and she likes (certain) activities. These activities keep her busy.
14. In Poughkeepsie, New York, elementary school children help resolve disputes between children. They are trained as mediators. The children get into fights.
15. A thirteen-year-old boy in South Carolina writes a weather column for his local newspaper. He says that the weather column . . . is 80 percent accurate in its predictions.

Exercise 5. Cumulative Exercise: Adjective Clauses, Adverb Clauses, and Noun Clauses

Combine the sentences and write them in paragraph form, omitting the expressions in parentheses. Use each of the following at least once:

In Adverb Clauses	*In Noun Clauses*	*In Adjective Clauses*
although	how much	where
even if	that	which
since		who
so that		whom
until		whose
when		
whereas		
while		

Paragraph 1:

1. Nearly 12,000 volunteer observers record temperatures and precipitation levels* for the U.S. National Weather Service. Nine-year-old Cindy Scott is one of them (independent clause).

   Nine-year-old Cindy Scott is one of nearly 12,000 volunteer observers who . . .

******Co-host:* be the host or hostess together with another person.
**Precipitation levels:* amount of rainfall and snowfall.

2. A woman was recording the weather in Roy, New Mexico. The woman . . . retired. (Then) the Weather Service needed someone (independent clause). That person could take over.

   When . . .

3. Cindy was only nine. She volunteered (anyway) and was accepted.

4. Cindy has an electronic thermometer. It records the maximum and minimum temperatures every day, as well as the 6:00 P.M. temperature.

5. Near her home there is a vacant lot. She keeps equipment in this lot. The equipment measures rainfall and snowfall.

6. A tape inside the machine records (this data). How much rain and snow fell in the past month?

7. Every month, Cindy sends the data to the National Weather Service. She has collected the data.

Paragraph 2:

8. The Cannonball River was threatening to flood in April 1982. Another young observer stayed on a dangerous bank. (On the bank) he could take water level readings every fifteen minutes.

9. He sent the readings to Weather Service officials. The Weather Service officials . . . issued reports to worried people. The people lived near the river.

Paragraph 3: Not all the volunteer observers are young, however.

10. In Gosper County, Nebraska, there was a farmer. He recorded the weather for seventy-five years. He died in 1980.

11. In rural Minnesota, there is one observer. He is one hundred years old.

12. And there is another Minnesota family. . . . Members of the family have been recording temperatures, precipitation, and wind velocities. An ancestor began monitoring weather in November 1888, over one hundred years ago.

Paragraph 4:

13. Cindy has modern electronic equipment. Some of the equipment . . . is as old as the oldest observer. The equipment is used by the observers.

14. Cindy can read the outside temperatures without leaving her house. Many observers have to go outside to read their instru-

ments. The weather may be forty or more degrees below zero (Fahrenheit).

Paragraph 5:

15. Many different kinds of people depend on the weather information. The volunteer observers collect the information.
16. The Weather Service receives inquiries. Almost one fourth of the inquiries . . . are from lawyers. The lawyers' clients have been involved in traffic accidents. The accidents involve weather.
17. Weather summaries are also important to contractors, farmers, insurance companies, and vacationers, among others. Contractors design heating and air conditioning systems. Farmers need to know when to plant their crops. Insurance companies need to estimate costs for crop insurance. Vacationers want to know when to travel.
18. The Weather Service employs professional meteorologists and uses satellites and other modern equipment. It nevertheless depends to a great extent on its 12,000 volunteers. It is interesting . . .

Transfer Exercises

1. Childhood (oral or written)

Complete the sentences with adjective clauses. (If this exercise is done in pairs, one student can keep his or her book closed while the other reads the incomplete sentences.)

A. Remember your school days.

1. In elementary school, I had a teacher . . .

   who taught us the names of all the seashells.

2. I didn't like classes . . .
3. I used to enjoy days . . .
4. There was a child at our school . . .
5. I had several friends . . .

B. Recall some experiences outside of school.

6. When I was a child, I didn't like movies in which . . .
7. I loved movies . . .
8. At the zoo, my favorite place was the building . . .
9. I liked (didn't like) museums . . .

10. Summer vacation was the time . . .
11. Sometimes we went to a place . . .
12. I'll never forget the time . . .

C. Think about other children in the world.

13. Every child needs at least one person . . .
14. It is a sad fact that there are children in the world . . .
15. Children whose . . .
16. Some children don't even have a place . . .
17. An unhappy childhood is one reason . . .
18. Childhood should be a time . . .

2. Error Correction

Each of the sentences below contains one or more errors. Find and correct the errors.

1. I have a sister who she lives in New York.
2. Some of the stories she tells me about New York they are hard to believe.
3. One experience she had it in the subway was frightening.
4. I'm glad I live in a place there isn't too much crime.
5. My sister goes to a university has a particularly good department of filmmaking.
6. She was accepted at all the universities which she applied to them last year.
7. She especially likes one professor who his main interest is Italian films.
8. The students are taking his courses they are all graduate students.
9. My sister showed me a book which it contains many pictures from old films.
10. One of the pictures shows a number of actors and actresses which putting on makeup.

Discussion Topics

A. When you were a child, did you enjoy going to the zoo? What exhibits at the zoo interested you the most? Were there any special programs or exhibits to teach science to children? What is the most interesting zoo that you have visited? Were all the animals kept in cages? If not, how were they separated from the people visiting the zoo?

B. Are there museums for children in your country? Are there special programs for children at other museums? Are there exhibits which children can touch and experiment with? What is the most interesting museum in your country, in your opinion, and why?

C. What are some other places in your country where children can learn and enjoy themselves at the same time? For example, do national parks have programs for children? Are there summer camps for children?

D. Do you know of children who have unusual abilities or accomplishments? If so, what are they? Would it be possible in your country for a child to run a company, a small museum, or a television show? Are there children who write for newspapers or who publish books? Are there children who perform in concerts, dances, or plays?

What are the most usual jobs for children in your country? Do many children work?

E. Do volunteers collect weather data for the government of your country? Would you like to be a volunteer weather observer?

Composition Topics

Write a short composition about one of the following topics. Use adjective clauses in some of your sentences.

1. Write about a zoo, museum, or other place which you especially enjoyed visiting as a child and where you learned something at the same time. (See Exercise 3 and Discussion Topics A, B, and C.)
2. Write about a child who had unusual ability or who accomplished something unusual. Or write about several children or a group. (See Exercise 4 and Discussion Topic D.)
3. Write about something unusual that you did as a child.
4. Write about the life of children in your country in general. What are the most common activities for children outside of school? You may want to discuss children of poor and rich families separately.

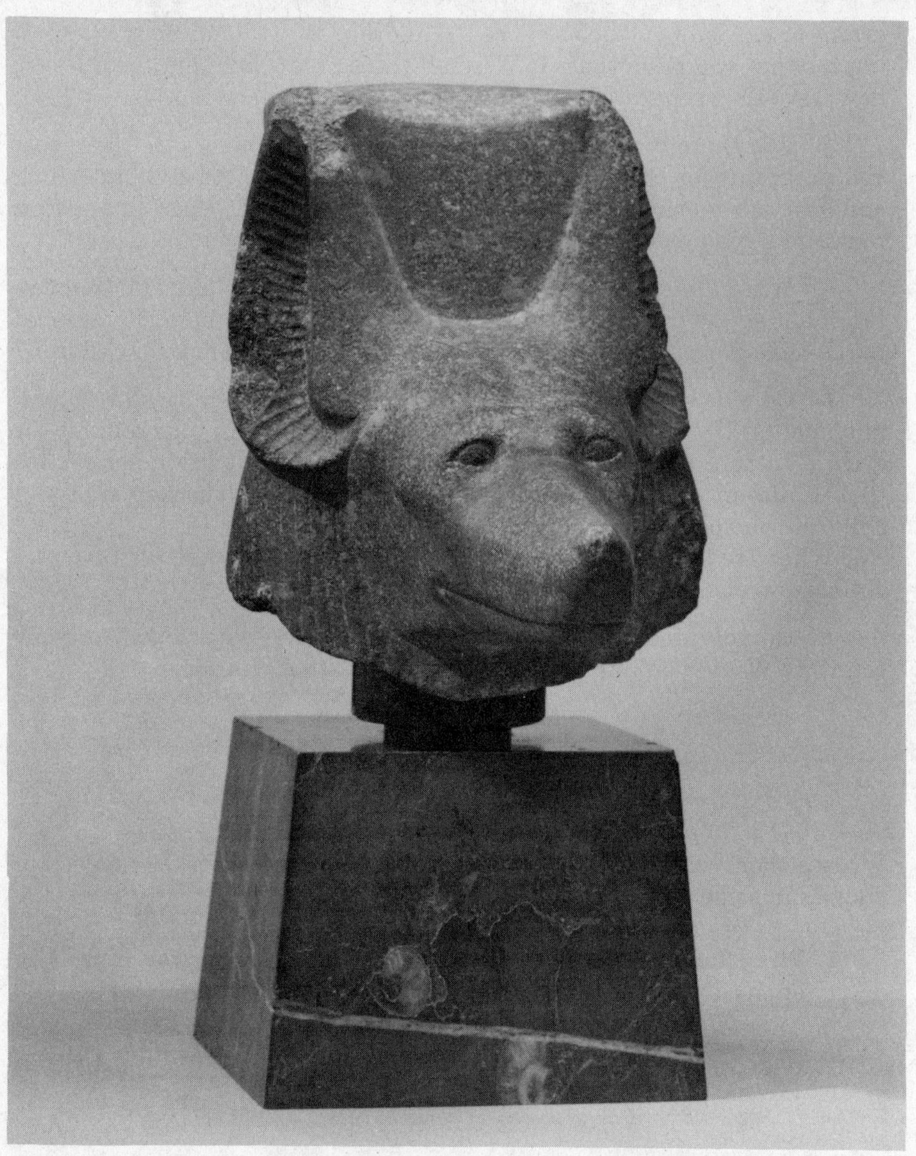

Head of Anubis. *16th to 8th century B.C. Diorite, 11¾ × 9½ in. (29.8 × 24.2 cm.) Smith College Museum of Art, Northampton, MA. Gift of Mr. and Mrs. Richard Lyman (Charlotte Cabot '32), 1970.*

Lesson 24

Art Smugglers

24.1 Nonessential Adjective Clauses

Modifying a Noun

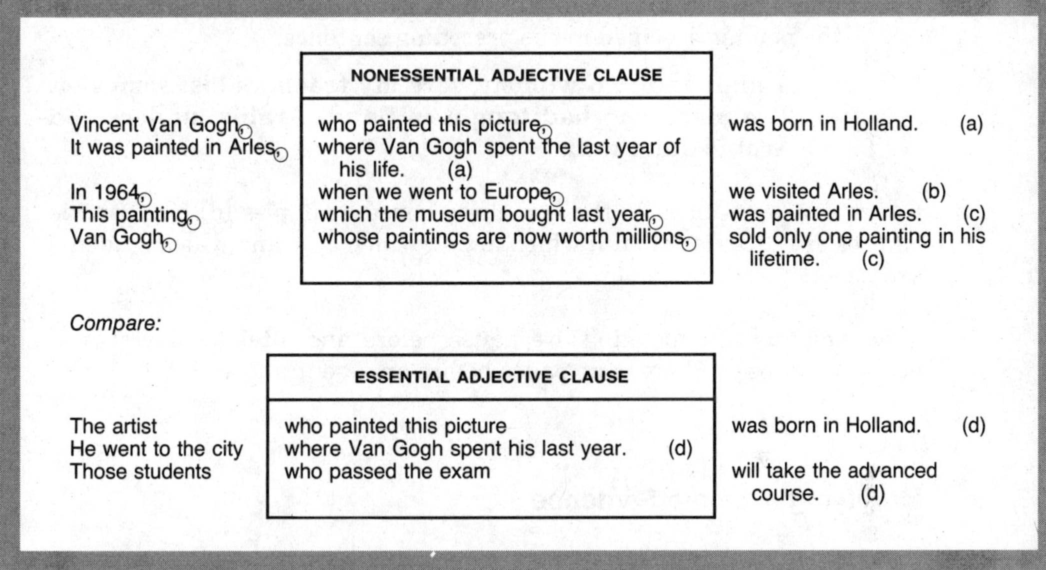

	NONESSENTIAL ADJECTIVE CLAUSE	
Vincent Van Gogh,	who painted this picture,	was born in Holland. (a)
It was painted in Arles,	where Van Gogh spent the last year of his life. (a)	
In 1964,	when we went to Europe,	we visited Arles. (b)
This painting,	which the museum bought last year,	was painted in Arles. (c)
Van Gogh,	whose paintings are now worth millions,	sold only one painting in his lifetime. (c)

Compare:

	ESSENTIAL ADJECTIVE CLAUSE	
The artist	who painted this picture	was born in Holland. (d)
He went to the city	where Van Gogh spent his last year. (d)	
Those students	who passed the exam	will take the advanced course. (d)

Meaning: A *nonessential* adjective clause adds information to a sentence but is not needed to identify the noun it modifies. The sentence is still meaningful without the adjective clause. In contrast, if an essential adjective clause is omitted, the sentence becomes meaningless or the meaning changes.

Choice of Relative Pronoun: **Who, whom, which, whose, when,** and **where** are used to introduce nonessential adjective clauses. The relative pronoun is never omitted, and **that** is not used.

Punctuation: A comma is used before and after a nonessential adjective clause.

Identifying Nonessential Adjective Clauses: It is not always easy to decide whether to use commas or not, but commas are clearly needed if

a. the clause modifies a *proper noun,* such as the name of

a person: **Vincent Van Gogh, Ronald Reagan, John**
a place: **Arles, Boston, the Pacific Ocean**
a book: ***Lust for Life, Romeo and Juliet***
a movie: ***Gone with the Wind, The Sound of Music***
etc.

b. the clause refers to a *specific time:*

at 11:15
July 10th
October 1988
etc.

c. the clause modifies a noun which is already specific. Sometimes the noun is specified in the preceding sentence:

A man and two women were my teachers last semester. *The man,* who had taught in Saudi Arabia, understood Arabic quite well.

Commas are not used in the last three boxed examples (d) because the clauses are necessary to tell which artist, which city, and which students are meant.

Pronunciation: In speaking, we pause before and after a nonessential adjective clause. (There is no pause before an essential clause.)

Modifying a Whole Sentence

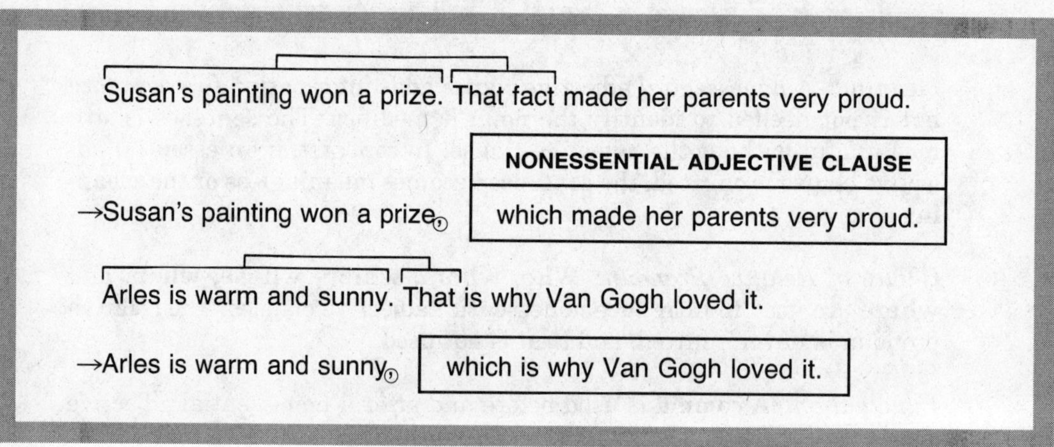

Choice of Relative Pronoun: Use **which** for adjective clauses which refer to a whole sentence.

Punctuation: Commas are always used with this type of adjective clause.

Exercise 1. Using Adjective Clauses to Modify a Sentence (oral or written)

Repeat each sentence, adding a clause that modifies the whole sentence. If you write the sentences, don't forget the commas.

A. Use **which means/meant that**

1. Arthur passed his driving test.

   Arthur passed his driving test, which means that he can get his license.

2. Sarah got all A's in high school.
3. Joelle wants to get married, but she is under sixteen.
4. A policeman arrested Harry for drunken driving and took away his license.
5. Sue's bicycle got a flat tire.
6. Van Gogh's paintings are very expensive today.

B. Use **which made (me).**

7. I got a letter from my girlfriend yesterday.

   I got a letter from my girlfriend yesterday, which made me homesick.

8. I got a bad grade on my last composition.
9. Sometimes people are rude on the bus.
10. The little boy climbed a tall tree. (His mother was nervous.)
11. Van Gogh had a rare illness. (He was depressed* and irrational during periods of his life.)

C. Use **which makes/made it** + *adjective* + *infinitive.*

12. Some people talk very loud in the library.

    Some people talk very loud in the library, which makes it *hard* to *study.*

**Depressed:* unhappy.

13. My roommate plays his stereo late at night.
14. The words in the dictionary are arranged alphabetically.
15. Many banks have automatic machines that operate 24 hours a day.
16. Most museums charge low entrance fees.

D. Use these verbs:

help	please	terrify
irritate	√surprise	upset

17. My lazy roommate decided to go mountain climbing.

    My lazy roommate decided to go mountain climbing, which really surprised me.

18. On the way up the mountain, he got bitten by mosquitoes.
19. He put on some insect repellent.
20. He saw a bear on the trail in front of him.
21. He forgot to tell his girlfriend that he was going away for the weekend.
22. However, he brought her a bunch of flowers.

Exercise 2. Nonessential Adjective Clauses

Combine the sentences, using adjective clauses and commas.

1. In February 1988, paintings and drawings worth six million dollars were stolen from a commercial gallery* in New York City. This constitutes the largest art theft ever reported in the city.

   In February 1988, paintings and drawings worth six million dollars were stolen from a commercial gallery in New York City, which constitutes the largest art theft ever reported in the city.

2. The gallery is one of the few places where it is still possible to purchase paintings by the old European masters. The gallery was founded in London in 1760.

   The gallery, which was founded in London in 1760, is one of the few places where it is still possible to purchase paintings by the old European masters.

**Commercial gallery:* a store which sells works of art.

3. The theft occurred sometime between 6:15 P.M. and 10:30 P.M. The gallery closed at 6:15 P.M. A burglar alarm was accidentally set off at 10:30 P.M.
4. The thieves lowered themselves through a skylight** and down a stairwell by means of a rope. This was a daring acrobatic act.
5. If one of them had slipped, he would have fallen four flights down the stairwell. The stairwell was located directly beneath the skylight.
6. Detective Thomas Moscardini was called in on the case. Detective Moscardini specializes in art theft.
7. Moscardini said the thieves did not take the most valuable works in the gallery. Moscardini's full-time job is working on art theft cases.
8. Two paintings by the Italian artist Fra Angelico were the best known of the works they took. The thieves will probably be unable to resell the two paintings.
9. The International Foundation for Art Research will publish photographs of the paintings. The Foundation has compiled a list of 278,000 stolen works.

Exercise 3. Generalizations about Whole Classes and Sub-classes

a. Decide whether the first sentence of each pair is true for *all* or only *some* of the group mentioned.

b. Then make the first sentence into an adjective clause and combine it with the second sentence. You will need commas if the clause is about the *whole* class. But if the clause tells which *sub-class* is meant, do not use commas.

(*Note to the Teacher:* This exercise may be done orally if the students are introduced to the intonation patterns which distinguish essential from nonessential clauses.)

1. Art is three-dimensional. *some*
   It is called sculpture.

   Art which is three-dimensional is called sculpture.

***Skylight:* a window in the roof.

2. Sculpture is three-dimensional. *all*
It often uses stone or metal as a medium.

Sculpture, which is three-dimensional, often uses stone or metal as a medium.

3. Sculptures are displayed in parks. ______
They are often quite large.

4. Paintings are generally made with a brush. ______
They are two-dimensional.

5. Paintings are not covered with glass. ______
They must be cleaned periodically.

6. Works of art have moving parts. ______
They are called mobiles.

7. The parts of mobiles move. (*Ask: all* mobiles or *some* mobiles?)
______
Mobiles are often hung from the ceiling.

8. Drawings are not produced with a brush. ______
They are often in one color only.

9. Photographs are taken with a camera. ______
They cost less than paintings.

10. The subject of a photograph is a person's face. ______
It is called a portrait.
A photograph ____________________ portrait.

Exercise 4. Recognizing Essential and Nonessential Adjective Clauses

Underline the adjective clauses and add commas where needed.

1. In 1986, an art collector bought a sculpture of a Roman goddess in Switzerland and had it shipped to his New York office, where he intended to put it on display.

2. A few months later he was looking at a magazine that publishes photographs of stolen art and saw a picture of the work he had bought.

3. The magazine is published by the International Foundation for Art Research which is devoted to recovering stolen art.

4. Constance Lowenthal who is the executive director of the Foundation says that every year one billion dollars' worth of art and cultural artifacts are stolen around the world.

5. Works that are true masterpieces are easier to recognize and therefore more difficult to resell than those that are a little less valuable.
6. The sculpture the collector bought was of the latter type.
7. The collector who specializes in ancient Greek and Roman art was told about the piece by an art dealer he had dealt with in Switzerland.
8. The thief who had taken it from the site where it was on display was never caught.
9. The sculpture was returned to Italy. The dealer who had sold it to the collector refunded his money in exchange for a promise that his name would not be disclosed.
10. According to Lowenthal, artifacts that are excavated from archeological sites are the most frequently stolen.
11. In Mexico, Peru, Egypt, and other countries where there are undiscovered and unguarded sites, it is easy for treasure hunters to take things out.
12. It is reported that in Egypt where the desert is full of unguarded sites some of the thieves are Americans who are working for the U.S. government.
13. Egypt's tourist police whose job is to guard museums and important archeological sites do the best they can.
14. But they cannot possibly guard all the sites which include many that have not yet been excavated and whose location may not even be known.

Exercise 5. Forming Essential and Nonessential Adjective Clauses

Nowadays almost every country has laws to protect its cultural heritage. These laws make it illegal to export important art objects without a permit. But many countries with rich cultural heritages are finding it difficult to enforce these laws.

Combine the sentences, using essential and nonessential adjective clauses. Leave out unnecessary words and add commas where you need them.

1. One country is having difficulty protecting its cultural treasures. This country is Peru.

   One country which is having difficulty protecting its cultural treasures is Peru.

2. In January 1981, a certain New York art dealer was met by custom's officials. He returned to the United States from Peru at that time.

3. Since they had heard that drugs were being smuggled on the flight, they searched every piece of baggage. The passengers had brought the baggage with them.

4. They searched the art dealer's four suitcases. They found nearly $300,000 worth of pre-Columbian artifacts in the suitcases, including a feather cape.

5. A specialist was asked to authenticate the artifacts. He said that some of the treasures were unique and unknown even in museum collections.

6. Authorities later searched the art dealer's apartment. They found over one million dollars' worth of additional pre-Columbian artifacts in the apartment.

7. The thief was not jailed and was fined only $1,000. This meant that he could continue to work as an art dealer.

24.2 Nonessential Adjective Clauses Beginning with Quantifiers

Most of the artifacts were from a newly discovered site.

The art dealer smuggled in valuable artifacts,

ADJECTIVE CLAUSE		
QUANTIFIER		
most	of which	were from a newly discovered site.

Many art smugglers are Americans.

Art smugglers, | many of whom | are Americans, | are rarely punished.

Many of China's treasures were destroyed during the Cultural Revolution.

The People's Republic of China,

many of whose treasures	were destroyed during the Cultural Revolution,

is now trying to protect its rich heritage.

Vocabulary: Below are some examples of quantifiers which may begin a nonessential adjective clause. **Which, whom,** and **whose** are the only relative pronouns used after a quantifier. Commas must be used.

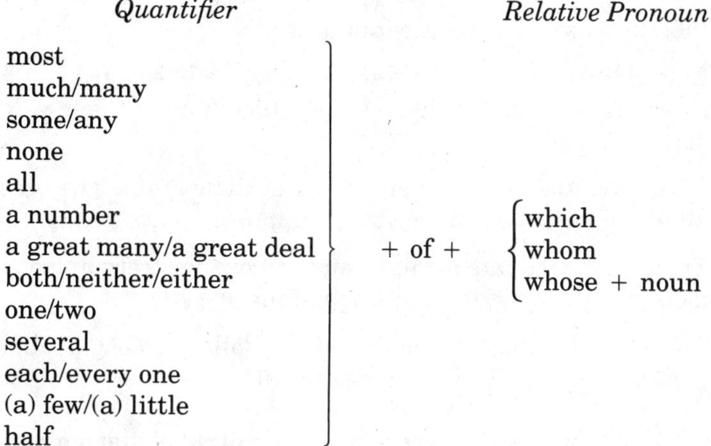

Quantifier		*Relative Pronoun*
most much/many some/any none all a number a great many/a great deal both/neither/either one/two several each/every one (a) few/(a) little half	+ of +	which whom whose + noun

Note: Nouns, superlatives, and prepositional phrases are sometimes used at the beginning of a nonessential adjective clause in formal speech and writing.

Shea's most recent book, *the title of which* I have forgotten, is about the drug trade.

James's books, *the most famous of which* is *Smoky,* were about cowboys.

We will have a final exam, *in preparation for which* we will review everything in the book.

Exercise 6. Adjective Clauses with Quantifiers

Below are some facts reported in a magazine article about art smuggling around the world. Combine the sentences, using quantifiers to introduce adjective clauses.

1. In Hong Kong, antique stores offer ceramics, bronze sculptures, and jade objects. Most of the objects have been smuggled in from the People's Republic of China.

   In Hong Kong, antique stores offer ceramics, bronze sculptures, and jade objects, most of which have been smuggled in from the People's Republic of China.

2. The smugglers prefer to get high prices from Westerners rather than turn in the art objects for rewards offered by the Chinese government. Many of the smugglers are Chinese.

3. In Thailand, antique stores are well stocked with eleventh-century pieces. Only a few of the pieces are originally from Thailand.

4. Europeans and Americans encourage smuggling by offering high prices for art objects. Some of these people are diplomats and therefore have diplomatic immunity.*

5. In El Salvador, two smugglers regularly robbed burial sites in territory that was controlled by guerrillas. Both of them were Salvadoran.

6. They gave the rebels a percentage of their profit. The rebels used all of the money to buy military supplies.

7. They excavated late at night and removed pottery and other artifacts. They also restored** some of the objects.

8. The buyers generally paid in U.S. dollars. Most of them were American journalists covering the war.

Guatemala, more than any other Central American country, polices its borders and protects its cultural property. Guards have been stationed at the important Mayan sites such as Río Azul.

9. Río Azul is now guarded by eight men. Most of Río Azul's tombs have already been robbed. Each of the men carries a submachine gun.

24.3 Reduction of Adjective Clauses to Phrases

Essential

PRESENT PARTICIPLE (active)

Clause:	All the students	who were taking Professor G.'s course	passed the exam.	
Phrase:	All the students	taking Professor G.'s course	passed the exam.	(a)

Diplomatic immunity: Their baggage is not inspected by customs officials.
***Restored:* repaired.

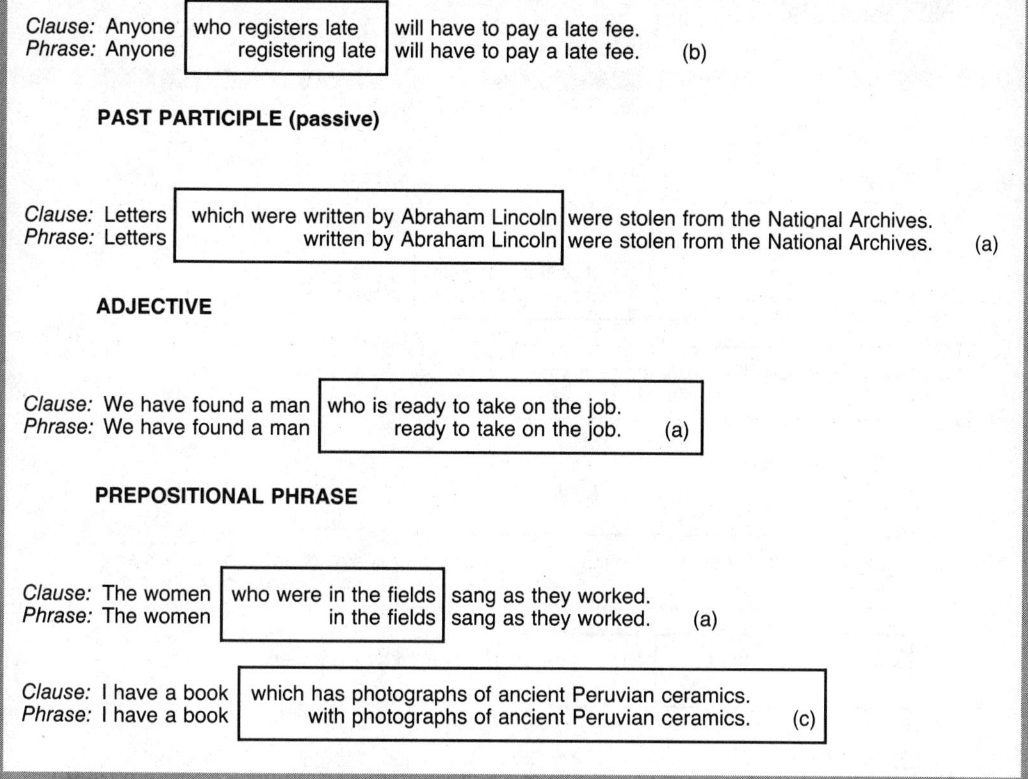

Clause: Anyone | who registers late | will have to pay a late fee.
Phrase: Anyone | registering late | will have to pay a late fee. (b)

PAST PARTICIPLE (passive)

Clause: Letters | which were written by Abraham Lincoln | were stolen from the National Archives.
Phrase: Letters | written by Abraham Lincoln | were stolen from the National Archives. (a)

ADJECTIVE

Clause: We have found a man | who is ready to take on the job.
Phrase: We have found a man | ready to take on the job. (a)

PREPOSITIONAL PHRASE

Clause: The women | who were in the fields | sang as they worked.
Phrase: The women | in the fields | sang as they worked. (a)

Clause: I have a book | which has photographs of ancient Peruvian ceramics.
Phrase: I have a book | with photographs of ancient Peruvian ceramics. (c)

Form: Adjective clauses beginning with a subject relative pronoun (**who, which,** or **that**) may often be reduced to phrases.

a. If the clause contains a form of **be,** omit the relative pronoun and **be.**

b. If there is no **be** in the adjective clause, the verb may often be changed to the **-ing** form.

c. A relative pronoun + **have** is often reduced to a phrase with **with.**

Nonessential

PRESENT PARTICIPLE

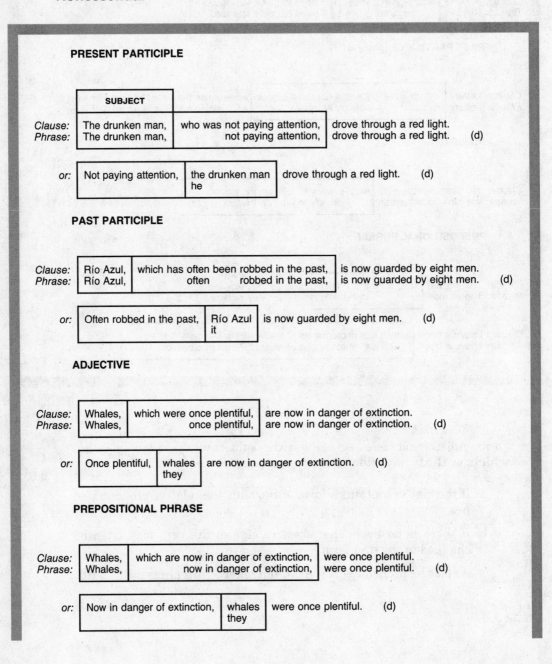

	SUBJECT			
Clause:	The drunken man,	who was not paying attention,	drove through a red light.	
Phrase:	The drunken man,	not paying attention,	drove through a red light.	(d)

or:	Not paying attention,	the drunken man he	drove through a red light.	(d)

PAST PARTICIPLE

Clause:	Río Azul,	which has often been robbed in the past,	is now guarded by eight men.	
Phrase:	Río Azul,	often robbed in the past,	is now guarded by eight men.	(d)

or:	Often robbed in the past,	Río Azul it	is now guarded by eight men.	(d)

ADJECTIVE

Clause:	Whales,	which were once plentiful,	are now in danger of extinction.	
Phrase:	Whales,	once plentiful,	are now in danger of extinction.	(d)

or:	Once plentiful,	whales they	are now in danger of extinction.	(d)

PREPOSITIONAL PHRASE

Clause:	Whales,	which are now in danger of extinction,	were once plentiful.	
Phrase:	Whales,	now in danger of extinction,	were once plentiful.	(d)

or:	Now in danger of extinction,	whales they	were once plentiful.	(d)

APPOSITIVE (noun phrase)

Clause:	Whales,	which are the largest animals on earth,	are mammals, not fish.	
Phrase:	Whales,	the largest animals on earth,	are mammals, not fish.	(e)

or:	The largest animals on earth,	whales they	are mammals, not fish.	(e)

		DIRECT OBJECT	
Phrase:	I want to study	whales,	the largest animals on earth. (e)

Form: Nonessential adjective phrases are formed in the same way as essential adjective phrases—by omission of **who** or **which** and **be.**

Punctuation: Commas are used before and after nonessential adjective phrases.

Restriction: d. Nonessential adjective phrases (reduced clauses) always modify the *subject* of the main clause, with the following exception:

e. Appositives may modify nouns in other positions.

Word Order: Nonessential phrases which modify the subject may be placed at the beginning of the sentence. When the subject is a personal pronoun (**he, she, we,** etc.), the phrase *must* precede the subject. Full clauses are not used with personal pronouns.

Note: Phrases placed before the subject may look and mean the same as the reductions of adverb clauses which you studied in Lessons 17 and 18.

Exercise 7. Reducing Adjective Clauses to Phrases

A. Restate the sentences, reducing all adjective clauses to phrases. Be careful to keep the commas.

1. Art theft, which is already the most extensive form of international crime next to* narcotics, is increasing at an alarming rate.

**Next to:* except for, second to.

Art theft, already the most extensive form of international crime next to narcotics, is increasing at an alarming rate.

2. In response to the problem, Italy has organized a police unit which specializes in combatting this form of crime.
3. It is rare, however, that the eighty-man squad, which was the first and is one of the most unusual detective units in the world, arrests criminals who deal in stolen art.
4. Instead, the detectives who are on the squad concentrate on recovering unharmed as many as possible of the thousands of works which are stolen every year from Italy's churches, museums, and archeological sites.
5. The squad publishes a bulletin which has photographs and descriptions of the stolen works.
6. This bulletin, which is distributed to art dealers and museums, makes it hard for anyone who holds a work which has been identified as stolen to say that he or she didn't know.
7. The art squad detectives, who are like narcotics police, often put on disguises to do their work.
8. Their operations, which are often secret and sometimes dangerous, were the subject of a 1986 Italian television series which was called "To Hunt a Thief of Genius."
9. In contrast to Italy, the United States has very few policemen who are assigned to work on art theft.
10. Washington, D.C.'s art squad, which was formed in 1973, now has only one part-time member.
11. Thomas Moscardini, who is the New York City Police Department's expert on art theft, is the only police detective in the United States who is working full time on the problem of stolen art.
12. The country needs many more such specialists, for the United States, which has long been an importer of art, is now being robbed of its own cultural heritage.
13. Antiquities which are plundered from archeological sites which are in the American Southwest are being sold abroad in ever-increasing numbers.

B. Which of the reduced clauses in A can be placed at the beginning of the sentence?

1. **Already the most extensive form of international crime next to narcotics, art theft is increasing at an alarming rate.**

Exercise 8. Cumulative Exercise: Adjective Clauses and Phrases

Combine the sentences with adjective clauses and phrases (reduced clauses).

Peru, Mexico, and other countries have rich cultural heritages. These countries have passed laws. These laws state that all ancient artifacts are national property. The artifacts were produced within their borders. Many objects were exported before the laws were passed. These two countries claim that the laws apply even to those objects. These two countries are the home of the Inca, Maya, and Aztec civilizations. Some objects are in the possession of private citizens. In these countries, private citizens are not permitted to sell the objects because their real owner is the government. Many Peruvian and Mexican objects are on display in American museums. Theoretically, these governments could request the return of every Peruvian or Mexican object.

The question "Who rightfully owns the objects of antiquity?" does not have a clear answer. Some journalists and diplomats smuggle art from countries. They work in these countries. They apparently feel that anyone clever enough to get through customs without being caught should have a right to the high profits. High profits are so easily obtainable in the art market. Some people will restore and preserve precious art works carefully. Some collectors feel that precious art works should be owned by those people. These collectors knowingly buy smuggled art. Other art historians ask whether the descendents of Europeans should be the rightful owners of art objects. Europeans colonized the New World. The objects were produced by the people. They conquered the people. According to André Emmerich, no country can rightfully claim ownership of works. The works were produced by ancient peoples within its territory. André Emmerich is a well-known art dealer. Emmerich says, "Ancient cultures flourished in a particular geographic spot. The art of mankind is part of mankind's cultural heritage and does not belong exclusively to that particular geographic spot."[1]

What do you think?

[1]Peter S. Greenberg, "Smuggled Treasures," *Art and Antiques,* Summer 1986, p. 83. Combining the sentences will result in the direct quotation.

Exercise 9. Cumulative Exercise: Adjective Clauses and Phrases

The picture on the opposite page was painted by the well-known American artist Mary Cassatt (1844–1926). Describe the picture by completing the sentences below with adjective clauses and phrases. Add commas where you need them.

Examples: The woman **in the picture has black hair.**

The woman, **who has black hair, is giving her daughter a bath.**

The woman **holding the little girl looks very gentle.**

1. The woman . . .
2. The woman whose . . .
3. The dress she . . .
4. The child she . . .
5. The child who . . .
6. The child whose . . .
7. The towel around . . .
8. The basin in . . .
9. The basin which . . .
10. The pitcher . . .
11. Squatting . . .
12. Holding . . .
13. Held . . .
14. Seated . . .
15. This picture which . . .
16. Mary Cassatt . . .
17. Cassatt lived in a period when . . .

Transfer Exercises

1. Geography (oral or written)

Fill in the words in parentheses. Then form a longer sentence which includes the first. Use both adjective clauses and phrases.

Example: **Paris** is the capital of **France.**

Clause: **Paris, which is the capital of France, is a romantic city.**

Phrase: **Paris, the capital of France, is a romantic city.**

1. (_______) is the capital of (_______).
2. (_______) is a country in (South America).

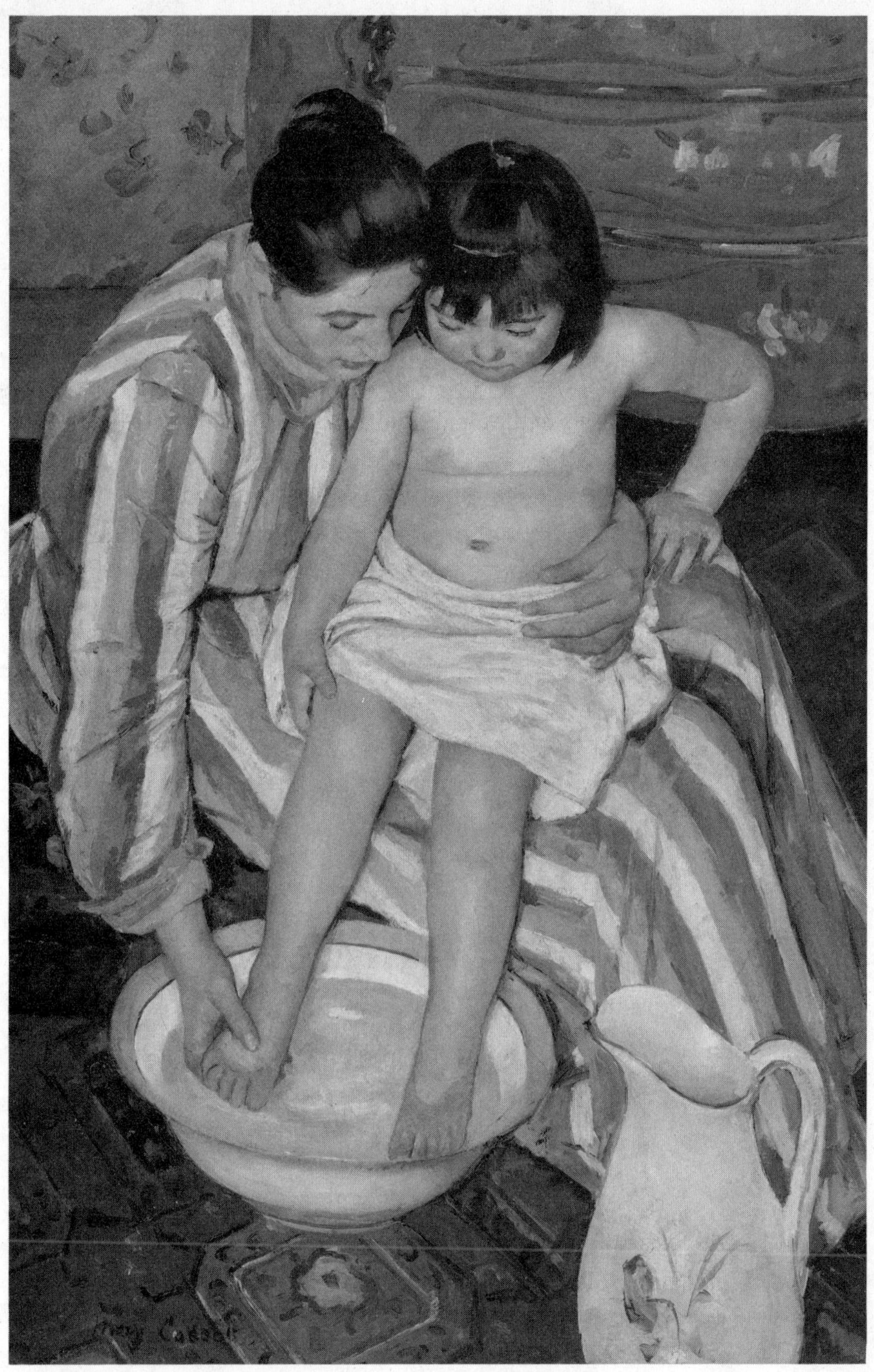

Mary Cassatt, The Bath, *1891/92, oil on canvas, 99.2 × 66.1 cm, Robert Waller Fund, 1910.2*

3. (______) is on the (Atlantic/Pacific) coast.
4. (______) is one of the most interesting cities I have ever visited.
5. (______) is the king/queen of (______).
6. (______) is the (president/prime minister) of (______).
7. (______) (is/was) a famous (______).
8. Continue with examples of your own.

2. Some People and Things in My Life

Complete the sentences with adjective clauses. Begin each clause with **most, all, both, none, two,** etc. (See the list on page 427.) If the total number is only one (for example, if you have only one teacher), omit that item.

Examples: I have (   ) classmates, . . .

I have twelve classmates, three of whom speak Arabic.

most of whom are from Latin America.

all of whom live in the dorm.

1. I have (   ) classmates, . . .
2. In the class, there are (   ) men, . . .
   (   ) women, . . .
   (   ) students from (   ), . . .
3. This term (I/we) have (   ) teachers, . . .
4. We are using (   ) textbooks, . . .
5. The chairs in this room, . . . , are made of (plastic).
6. On the walls of this/my room, there are (   ) pictures, . . .
7. I have (   ) brothers, . . .
   (   ) sisters, . . .
   (   ) roommates, . . .
   (   ) pens with me, . . .
8. Each month I receive a limited amount of money, . . .
9. I have (a lot of/only a few) clothes, . . .

3. About Your Country

Ask a classmate the questions below. In answering the second question, include the information from the first question and answer.

1. What food products are grown in (Colombia)?

   We grow coffee.

   Is the (coffee) high quality?

   Yes, the coffee grown in Colombia is the best!

2. What products are manufactured there? Are they (well-made/expensive/exported, etc.)?
3. Do you eat special food on your biggest holiday? Does it take a long time to prepare?
4. Do you ever wear traditional costumes and if so, when? What are they like?
5. Are traditional dances performed on certain days? Can you tell me about them?
6. Are different dialects spoken in different parts of your country? What are they like?
7. Are different kinds of food served in different parts of the country? Can you describe them?
8. What kinds of movies are shown on TV in your country? Are most of them in your native language?
9. What kind of music is performed in night clubs? Is it popular with everybody in your country or only certain groups?

Discussion Topics

A. What are some of the great masterpieces in the art of your country? What artists or periods of art in your country are the most famous around the world? (If you aren't sure, look in an encyclopedia or an art book in your library. You can ask the librarian for help.)

B. In your country, do you frequently hear about art thefts? Are objects stolen from museums or archeological sites? In general, are the thieves poor people? members of organized crime gangs? foreigners? Are there special police units to protect art?

C. Apparently, many people feel that taking objects from archeological sites is not wrong. Perhaps they feel that it does not harm anybody. Do you agree, or disagree?

D. Do you think that the art of antiquity belongs to all humankind? Who should own it? Should it be kept in museums? Should private collectors be permitted to buy rare works? Should countries nationalize their art treasures and try to reclaim art objects that were taken out by foreigners (many years ago or recently)?

E. Stolen works of art are often smuggled from one country to another. What other objects are frequently smuggled? What forms of smuggling, if any, are a problem in your country?

F. What other kinds of theft are common in your country? Who are the thieves? What is their motivation? How do people try to protect themselves against theft?

Oral Report (optional)

Bring to class pictures of some of the important art of your native country, and tell the class about it. You may wish to limit your presentation to one particular period or style of art, or to one artist. Include some of the following information:

who the artists were
who the works were created for
when they were created
the name given to the style of art
what factors influenced the particular style of art
where the works are now

Where to find pictures:

1. Check books out of your school library or the public library.
2. If you cannot take the books out, photocopy a few pages.
3. Buy postcards at a local bookstore, art store, or museum.
4. Pick up a brochure at a travel agency.

Composition Topics

Write a short composition on one of the topics listed below. Include adjective clauses and phrases (reduced adjective clauses) in some of your sentences, and be sure to check your punctuation after you have finished.

> *Note on Style:* Varying sentence structure and length helps make writing interesting. Therefore, try to include some long and some short sentences as well as a variety of structures in your composition.

1. Write about art theft or art smuggling in your country. (See Discussion Topic B.)
2. Write about another form of theft or smuggling.

3. Tell the story of an art theft (real or imaginary). Include information about how the work of art was taken, what happened to it, and how police tried to catch the thief and recover the work. (Did a detective disguise himself or herself as an art history professor? You can use your imagination.)
4. Should objects buried in the earth belong to whoever finds them? (See Discussion Topic C.)
5. How should governments regulate the exportation of ancient art objects and artifacts, in your opinion? Answer some of the questions in Discussion Topic D.
6. Write about an important period in the art of your country. (See the section titled Oral Report.)

UNIT

COORDINATION

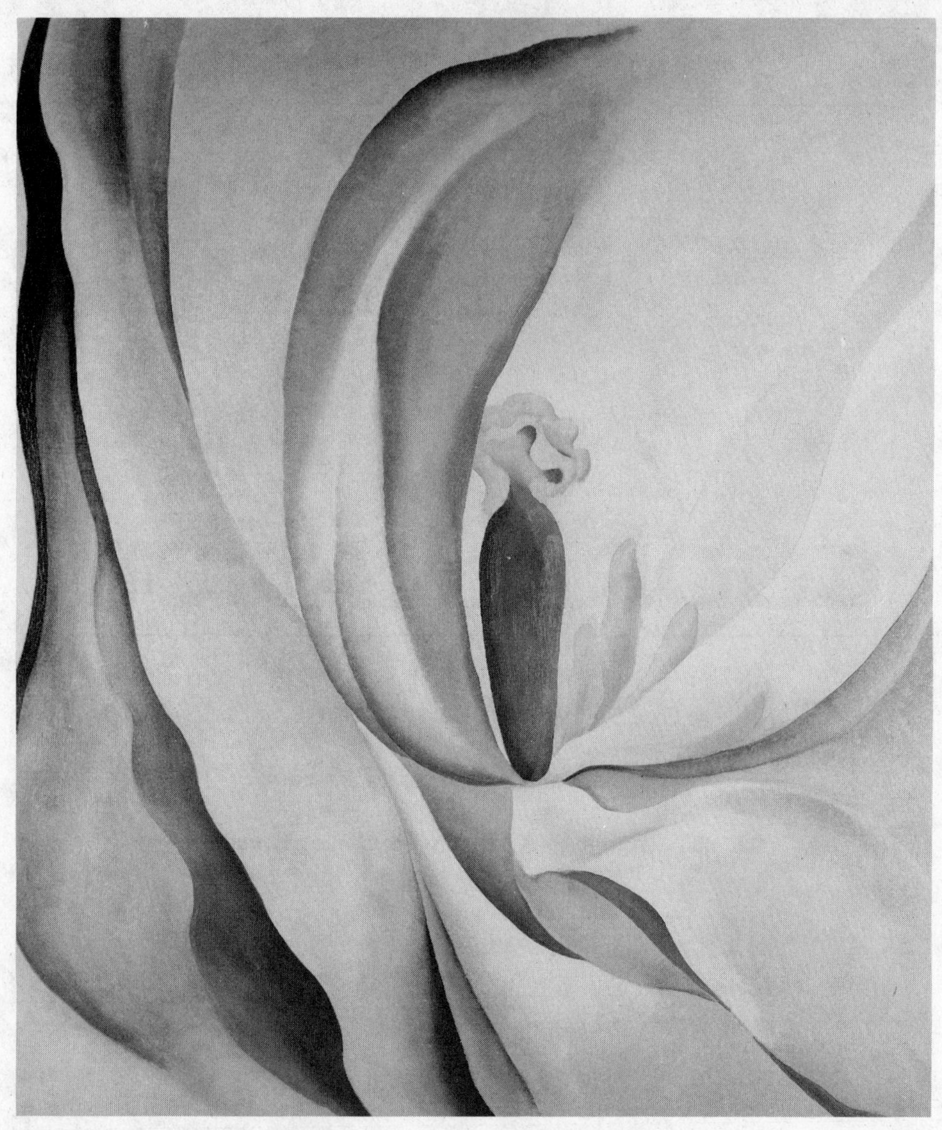

Georgia O'Keeffe (American, 1887–1986). Pink Tulip, *1926. Oil on canvas; 36 × 30″ (91.5 × 76.2 cm.) Bequest of Mabel Garrison Siemonn in Memory of her Husband George Siemonn. BMA 1964.11.13.*

Lesson 25

Two Modern Artists

25.1 Coordinating Conjunctions: Joining Independent Clauses

Affirmative

INDEPENDENT CLAUSE	COORDINATING CONJUNCTION	INDEPENDENT CLAUSE
We hand in our homework every day,	and	the teacher corrects it. (a)
I come from China,	but	my roommate is from India. (b)
I have been in the U.S. for two years,	{yet / but}	I still have problems with English. (c)
I can go home for summer vacation,	or (else)	I can take a trip to Europe. (d)
You had better decide soon,	or (else)	it will be too late to get a reservation. (e)
Europe needs tourists,	for	they help the economy. (f)
My classmates come from many countries,	so	we have to talk English. (g)

Negative

	COORDINATING CONJUNCTION	AUXILIARY	SUBJECT		
My classmates don't know my language,	nor	do	I	know theirs.	(h)

Word Order: After **nor,** we use *question word order;* that is, we use an auxiliary before the subject. (See page 471 for other cases of reverse word order after negatives.)

Meaning: a. **And:** The second clause *adds* to the first and continues the same idea in some way.

b. **But:** The second clause *contrasts* with the first.

c. **Yet, but:** The second clause shows *incongruity* or gives an unexpected result.

d. **Or (else):** The second clause gives *another possibility.*

e. **Or (else):** When the first clause contains **have to, must, should,** or **had better,** the meaning is often conditional. (*If* you *don't* decide soon, it will be too late to get a reservation.)

f. **For:** The second clause tells *why.* (Europe needs tourists *because* they help the economy.)

g. **So:** The second clause gives a *result.*

h. **Nor:** The first clause is negative, and the second continues the idea with another negative. (My classmates don't know my language, *and* I *don't* know theirs, *either.*)

Punctuation: A comma is often used before a coordinating conjunction which joins independent clauses, especially if the clauses are long.

Formal and Informal Usage: **For** and **yet** are used mainly in formal speech and writing.

Note: A coordinating conjunction may begin a new sentence (as well as joining sentences). This gives more emphasis to the second clause.

I have been in the United States for two years. Yet I still have problems with English.

Series

Mary got an A on the test, John got a B, **and** Sarah got a C.

You can stay here for vacation, you can come to my house, **or** you can fly home.

Punctuation: When three or more independent clauses are joined with **and** or **or,** use commas after each clause. The conjunction occurs only before the last clause.

Exercise 1. Understanding Coordinating Conjunctions

Circle the letter of the clause which logically and grammatically completes the sentence.

1. The American artist Georgia O'Keeffe (1887–1986) was born in Wisconsin, but . . .
   a. she became a well-known painter.
   (b.) she lived more than forty years in New Mexico.
2. Alfred Stieglitz, the famous photographer, became interested in her work in 1916, and . . .
   a. in 1924 they were married.
   b. they hadn't known each other before that.
3. O'Keeffe did not paint like other artists, nor . . .
   a. she wanted to.
   b. she didn't want to.
   c. did she want to.
4. She painted natural objects such as trees, flowers, and bones, yet . . .
   a. she didn't produce many abstract* paintings.
   b. her style has an abstract quality.
5. She loved the New Mexican desert, so . . .
   a. she often painted desert themes.
   b. she also lived in New York City.
6. She painted skyscrapers in the 1920s, for . . .
   a. she preferred desert themes.
   b. she lived in New York City then.
   c. she also painted many flowers.
7. You can find books about Georgia O'Keeffe in most bookstores, or . . .
   a. you can take one out of the library.
   b. can you take one out of the library.
   c. she is very popular nowadays.

**Abstract:* not representing real objects.

Exercise 2. Choosing the Correct Conjunction

In 1916, Georgia O'Keeffe sent several drawings to a close friend in New York, and that was a turning point in her life.

Fill in the coordinating conjunction which most logically joins the two clauses. Use each conjunction at least once.

and	yet	for	nor
but	or	so	

1. O'Keeffe asked her friend not to show the drawings to anyone, {but/yet} the friend showed them to Alfred Stieglitz, the photographer and gallery owner.
2. Stieglitz liked them very much, ______ he decided to exhibit them.
3. O'Keeffe was angry when she heard that he was exhibiting them, ______ he had not asked her permission.
4. She went to the gallery to demand that Stieglitz take the pictures down, ______ when she got there, he was away.
5. She went back a week later and repeated her demand. At first, Stieglitz did not know who she was, ______ he had never met her.
6. Stieglitz argued with her, questioned her, and took her to lunch, ______ in the end, the drawings stayed on the gallery walls.
7. O'Keeffe continued to send her work to Stieglitz, ______ a year later he put on a solo exhibition of her works.
8. O'Keeffe's drawings stimulated a great deal of discussion, ______ she did not like the critics' comments.
9. She rejected their psychoanalytic interpretation of her work, ______ did she like the later feminist interpretations.
10. The following winter, O'Keeffe became seriously ill. Stieglitz was worried about her since she was living alone in a place where she had few friends, ______ he offered her an apartment in New York City and took care of her.
11. He felt that he had better take care of her, ______ the world might lose a great artist.
12. Stieglitz was married to another woman, ______ he soon moved in with O'Keeffe, ______ he was in love with her ______ his marriage was not a happy one.

13. Stieglitz and O'Keeffe were married in 1924, ______ after the first ten years of marriage they lived apart a great deal.
14. After 1934, O'Keeffe insisted on spending at least half of each year in the desert country of New Mexico, ______ Stieglitz had to make a choice: He could go with her to New Mexico, ______ he could be content to spend only six months with her each year.
15. He chose the latter, ______ he continued to take photographs of O'Keeffe until he was an old man, altogether taking more than 500.

Exercise 3. Forming Sentences with Coordinating Conjunctions

Complete the sentences. When you see the word **never** in parentheses, keep it or omit it so that the sentence is true for you.

1. I had (never) seen O'Keeffe's work before I read this lesson, so . . .
2. I had (never) seen O'Keeffe's work before I read this lesson, but . . .
3. The painting by O'Keeffe which is reproduced in this lesson is not completely abstract, nor . . .
4. It is different from most paintings of flowers, for . . .
5. It is different from most paintings of flowers, yet . . .
6. Many of O'Keeffe's paintings of flowers are in private collections, so . . .
7. Although O'Keeffe spent part of every year in New Mexico, her husband never went there with her. Perhaps he did not like the desert, or perhaps . . .
8. I have (never) been to New Mexico, but . . .
9. If I were a painter, I would live in (place), and . . .
10. (   ) is a good place for an artist to live, for . . .
11. I don't really like (style of art*), nor . . .

*If you don't know the name of a style of art in English, give it in your own language.

25.2 Coordinating Conjunctions: Joining Parallel Structures

Affirmative

	NOUN	COORDINATING CONJUNCTION	NOUN	
	Peru	and	Mexico	have similar laws to protect their art.

	NOUN		NOUN	
Did O'Keeffe use	oil paint	or	water colors?	

	VERB		VERB	
The old artists	ground	and	mixed	their own paint.
Do you	own	or	rent	your house?

	PREDICATE		PREDICATE
John	framed his painting	and	hung it on the wall.
You can	frame your painting	or	protect it with plastic.

	ADJECTIVE		ADJECTIVE
O'Keeffe's paintings are	large	and	colorful.
Jane's fiancé is	attractive	but	penniless.

	PREPOSITIONAL PHRASE		PREPOSITIONAL PHRASE
Is the bread	in the refrigerator	or	on the shelf?

	INFINITIVE		INFINITIVE
She learned	to draw	and	(to) paint.

	GERUND		GERUND	
By 8:00, we had finished	washing	and	drying	the dishes.

ADVERB CLAUSE		ADVERB CLAUSE	
As soon as John arrived	and	before he could say hello,	the child threw her arms around him.

	ADJECTIVE CLAUSE		ADJECTIVE CLAUSE	
Someone	whom I met once	but	whom I don't know well	called and asked me for a loan.

	NOUN CLAUSE		NOUN CLAUSE
I don't know	who she is	or	what she wants.

Negative

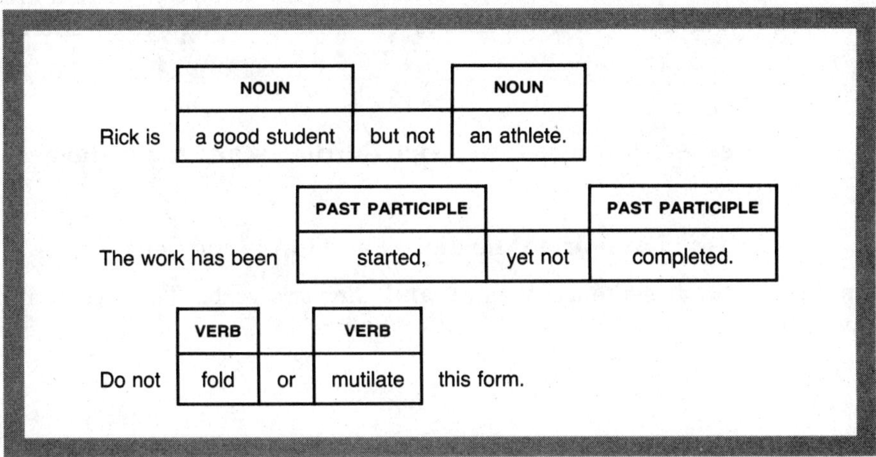

Series

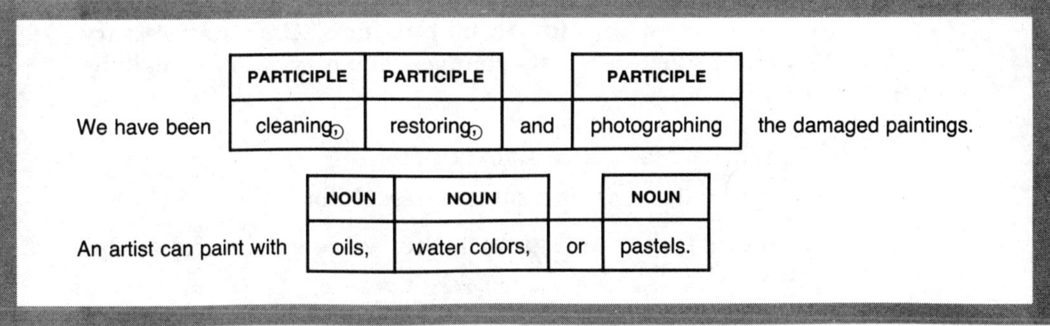

PARTICIPLE
PARTICIPLE
PARTICIPLE
We have been
cleaning,
restoring,
and
photographing
the damaged paintings.
NOUN
NOUN
NOUN
An artist can paint with
oils,
water colors,
or
pastels.

Form: **And, or, but, but not,** and **yet not** may be used to join two parallel structures. (Parallel structures are structures with the same grammatical form.) **And** and **or** may also join series of three or more parallel structures.

> *Note:* **But not** sometimes joins structures which are not parallel. This pattern results from the reduction of a longer form.

I drink coffee, but I don't drink it in the afternoon.
→ **I drink coffee, *but not in the afternoon.***

Punctuation: A comma is not used when two parallel structures are joined. (*Exception:* A comma is sometimes placed before **but not** and **yet not.**) With series of three or more parallel structures, commas are required.

Style: In good writing, we generally use **and** or **or** only once in a series of three or more parallel structures. However, the same conjunction may be used several times in a sentence to join parallel structures of different types.

Poor style:

Ron washed the dishes and dried the dishes and made the beds.

Good style:

Ron washed and dried the dishes and made the beds.

In the acceptable sentence, the first **and** joins two verbs. The second **and** joins two predicates.

Exercise 4. Joining Parallel Structures

Another American artist who lived at the same time as Georgia O'Keeffe was Alexander Calder (1898–1976). Calder created a new form of sculpture called a mobile.

Combine the sentences with **and, or,** or **but (not).** Omit unnecessary words and made any other necessary changes. You may want to begin by circling parallel structures.

1. Calder's father was a successful sculptor.
   Calder's grandfather was a successful sculptor.

   Calder's father and grandfather were successful sculptors.

2. As a boy, Calder loved to work with his hands.
   As a boy, Calder loved to construct toys for himself.
   As a boy, Calder loved to construct toys for his playmates.
3. He was good with his hands.
   He decided to become a mechanical engineer.
4. He obtained a degree in mechanical engineering in 1919.
   He was not successful as an engineer.

5. He tried a number of jobs.
   In every case, he soon quit. (Omit **he.**)
   He was soon fired.

6. Finally he realized that he wanted to be an artist.
   He began to take courses in drawing.
   He began to take courses in painting.

7. Calder tried to make a living as an artist.
   He didn't have much luck at first.

8. Moving to Paris in 1926, he began to meet other artists.
   Renting a small room in the artists' quarter, he began to meet other artists.
   He met American artists.
   He met European artists.

9. He first attracted attention with his miniature circus, which he operated by means of pulleys.
   He first attracted attention with his miniature circus, which he operated by means of strings.

10. People were delighted with the performances, in which tiny acrobats leapt through the air.
    In the performances, dogs jumped through hoops.
    In the performances, horses raced around the miniature ring.

11. Lions which roared ferociously (with Calder's voice) were also among the performers.
    Seals which tossed and caught balls were also among the performers.

12. (Calder was a genius at remote control through wires and strings.)
    When he brought his new bride to his Paris apartment in 1931, she found that he could open the front door while sitting in the bathtub.
    She found that he could turn on the gas stove from his bed.
    She found that he could bring a pot of coffee to his bed in a basket which hung from two wires.

13. Calder also made full-size sculptures of animals by twisting wire into three-dimensional forms.
    He also made full-size sculptures of people by twisting wire into three-dimensional forms.

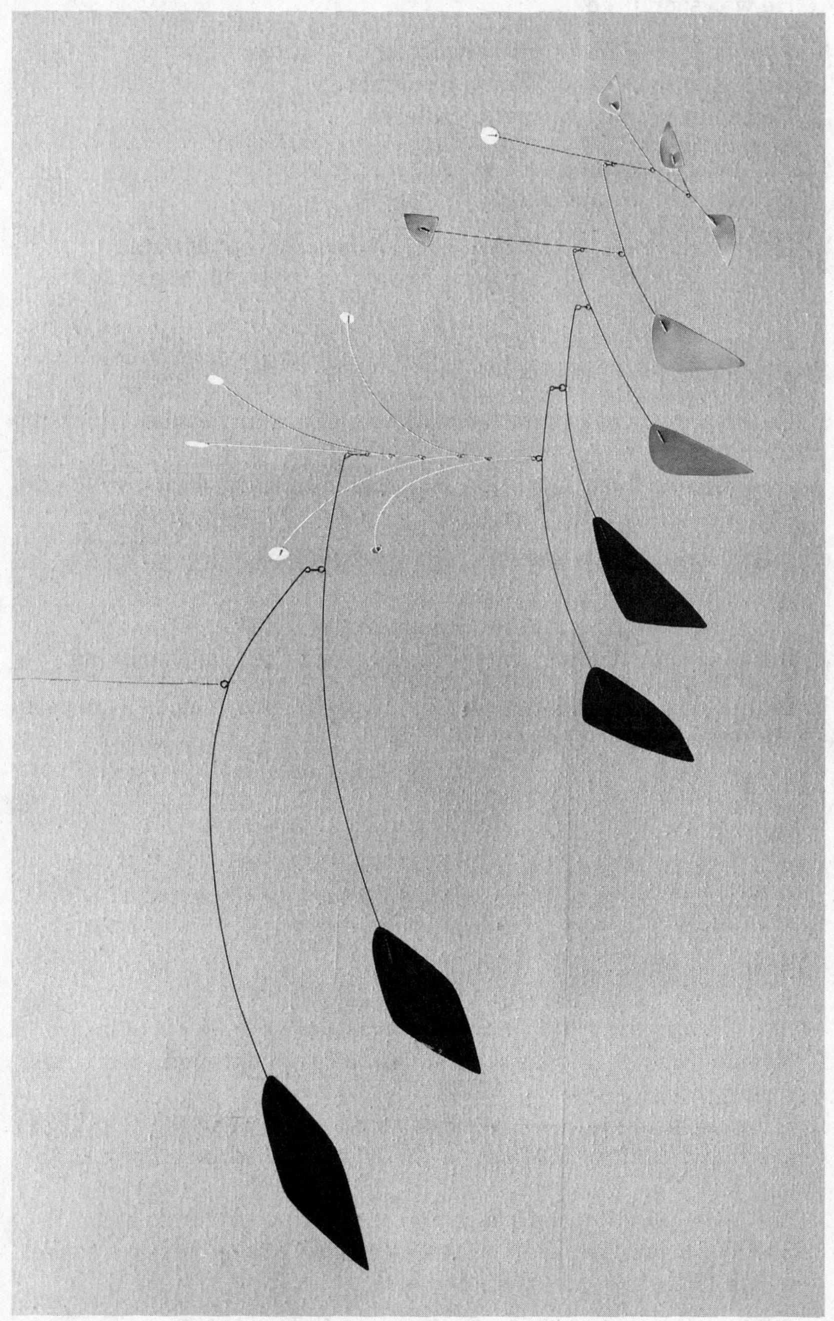

Alexander Calder. American, 1898–1976. White Spray. *1964. Painted metal, 34 × 73 × 40½ in. (86.5 × 185.4 × 102.8 cm.) Smith College Museum of Art, Northampton, MA. Purchased with funds given by the estate of Mrs. Chapin Riley (Mary Alexander '30), 1965.*

14. When he first exhibited these humorous pieces in New York, viewers could not decide whether they were real art.
    Viewers could not decide whether they were just something to amuse.
15. They enjoyed the pieces.
    They did not buy them.
16. In Paris, the wire sculptures were well received.
    In Paris, the wire sculptures were not taken seriously.
17. Up to this point, Calder's work had been highly original.
    Up to this point, Calder's work had not been abstract.
18. When Calder began to make abstract sculpture, he began to have more success.
    When he added motion to his sculpture, he began to have more success.
19. His first mobiles could be set in motion by switching on a motor.
    His first mobiles could be set in motion by pulling strings.
    His first mobiles could be set in motion by turning a crank.
20. Later, Calder hung his mobiles from the ceiling.
    He allowed natural currents of air to move the delicate wires.
    He allowed natural currents of air to move the delicate metal pieces.

Exercise 5. Making Structures Parallel

Correct the following sentences so that the coordinating conjunctions join parallel structures. Use your dictionary to find related words if you need to. Some sentences can be corrected in more than one way.

1. Calder made his first mobiles move with a motor or turning a crank.

   Calder made his first mobiles move by *switching on a motor* or *turning a crank.*

   or:* Calder made his first mobiles move with *a motor* or *a crank.

2. Calder made his first mobiles move by switching on a motor, cranking gears, or he pulled a string.

   Calder made his first mobiles move by *switching on a motor, cranking gears,* or *pulling a string.*

3. Because of his sense of humor and he was so friendly, everybody liked "Sandy" Calder.

4. People enjoyed meeting him and to see his circus performances.
5. His mobiles are admired for their grace, imaginative, and originality.
6. The later mobiles are lightweight, and a natural current of air is enough to move the parts and makes them rotate slowly.
7. Calder met his wife Louisa while crossing the Atlantic Ocean and falling in love with her.
8. They fell in love and get married in 1931.

Exercise 6. Combining Sentences with Coordinating Conjunctions

Use coordinating conjunctions **(and, but, yet, or, nor, for, so)** to combine independent clauses and parallel structures. Use each of the conjunctions at least once.

1. O'Keeffe and Calder were extremely different in their personalities.
   O'Keeffe and Calder were extremely different in their artistic styles.
   Both of them were highly original.
   Both of them have had a great influence on the art of our time.

   O'Keeffe and Calder were extremely different in their personalities and artistic styles, yet both of them were highly original and had a great influence on the art of our time.

2. Living in Paris had a strong influence on Calder.
   He turned to abstract art after seeing the work of European artists such as Piet Mondrian.
   He also saw the work of the European artist Joan Miró.
3. O'Keeffe, on the other hand, never went to Europe until she was in her sixties.
   O'Keeffe did not admit that other artists influenced her ideas.
   She did not admit that other artists influenced her work.
4. Her paintings of flowers do not resemble the work of other modern artists.
   Her paintings of bones do not resemble the work of other modern artists.
   Her paintings of clouds do not resemble the work of other modern artists.
   These paintings do reflect the same willingness to discard traditional ideas.

5. Some women have considered O'Keeffe a feminist because of her style of painting.
   They have considered her a feminist because of her outspokenness.
   They have considered her a feminist because of her fierce independence.
6. O'Keeffe always rejected such labels.
   O'Keeffe did not accept psychoanalytic interpretations of her work.
7. O'Keeffe preferred to spend much of her time in solitude.
   She had an unlisted phone.
   She often refused to grant interviews.
8. Calder, on the other hand, was friendly and sociable.
   As a young man in Paris, he liked to spend time in cafes.
   Later in his life, he had frequent visitors.

Exercise 7. Cumulative Exercise: Using Commas and Periods

Fill in the needed punctuation as follows:
Use a *comma*

a. after an adverb clause at the beginning of a sentence
b. before clauses with **while, whereas,** and **although**
c. before and after a nonessential adjective clause or phrase
d. before a coordinating conjunction (**and, or, nor,** etc.) which joins independent clauses
e. to separate three or more parallel structures

Use a *period* between two sentences. (Don't forget to capitalize the word after the period.)
Leave the other spaces blank (or write **Ø**).

1. Georgia O'Keeffe __Ø__ and Alexander Calder were both great artists __Ø__ who influenced the art of the twentieth century __,__ yet it would be hard to imagine two more different people.
2. While O'Keeffe was small ____ thin ____ and rather severe-looking ____ and wore her hair pulled straight back ____ Calder was large ____ and fun-loving with a pink face ____ and tousled* hair.

Tousled: not neatly combed.

3. Calder ____ whose father and grandfather were both well-known sculptors ____ felt equally at home in France ____ and in the eastern United States ____ whereas O'Keeffe ____ who grew up on a Wisconsin farm ____ preferred the open spaces of New Mexico.

4. Calder turned to art ____ only when he failed to find a career as an engineer ____ O'Keeffe knew ____ when she was twelve ____ that she would become an artist.

5. O'Keeffe wanted her art to reflect her own vision ____ she rejected the influence of other painters.

6. Calder ____ always open to suggestions from others ____ acknowledged his debt to important artists of his time.

7. Colorful ____ and dramatic ____ O'Keeffe's painting seems to convey passion ____ and intensity ____ but not humor.

8. In contrast, much of the work ____ that Calder produced ____ has a humorous quality.

9. Both of these artists made innovations ____ which have been important for the development of twentieth-century art ____ and Calder has even added a new word ____ "mobile ____ " to the dictionary.

Transfer Exercises

1. School Subjects

Ask a classmate these questions about subjects he or she is taking now in school (or subjects that he or she took in high school). In answering the questions, use the coordinating conjunctions given in parentheses. (*Note:* **for, nor,** and **yet** are included in the exercise for practice even though they are not used much in conversation.)

1. What are your two favorite subjects? (and)
   or: What were your two favorite subjects in high school?

   My two favorite subjects (are/were) (chemistry) and (math).

2. Is (chemistry) difficult? (but)
3. How do you spend the class time in (math class)? (and)

   We spend the class time . . .

4. What subjects don't you like very much? (or . . . so)
5. What subject do you especially dislike? (for)
6. What do you have to do in that class? (and)

7. Does the teacher try to explain things clearly? (yet)
8. What *doesn't* the teacher do? (nor)
9. In high school, what three subjects did you do best in? (and)
10. Did you get good grades in all your subjects? (but not)
11. What subjects can you take next term? (or)

2. Professions

Ask and answer questions about a job that you have had (or about your future job). Use the expressions in parentheses in your answers.

1. What kind of job did/do/will you have?

    I was a _______ .

    ***or:* I worked in a _______ .**

    ***or:* I'm going to be a _______ .**

2. What did you do on your job? (and)
3. Did you mind doing those things? (or . . . but)
4. What did you have to get used to? (for)
5. Was the work difficult? (yet)
6. Tell me three reasons why you liked or didn't like it. (and)
7. Did the job pay well? (so)

3. Television

Complete the sentences.

1. When I watch television, I like to watch . . . , for . . .
2. However, my (roommate/sister/brother) prefers . . . , so . . .
3. (He/she) doesn't like . . . , nor . . .
4. I always tell (him/her) . . . , yet . . .
5. Sometimes (he/she) . . . , but . . .
6. Since we don't agree about . . . , we have to . . . or . . .
7. I'm planning to . . . , and . . .

Discussion Topics

A. Give some of your impressions of the three works of art reproduced on pages 435, 442, and 452. You cannot see the color, but you can comment on the following points:

Do you like the subjects? the composition? the sense of balance or design?

Are these works realistic or abstract?
Do they have a sense of motion?
Do they communicate the artists feelings?
Are all of them good enough or important enough to be in a museum?
Are they beautiful?
Would you like to have them in your home?
Which one do you like best, and why?

B. In general, do you prefer realistic art or abstract art? Can you give a reason for your preference? Do you think it is important for an artist to be original? Can an artist be great if he or she stays within a tradition without contributing new ideas? What is the purpose of art?

C. Do present-day artists in your country generally work in traditional styles, or are there modern styles as well? Are there many abstract artists? Which contemporary artists from your country do you consider the greatest, and why? (You may wish to bring some postcards, books, or photocopies to show the class as illustrations of the points you make.)

Composition Topics

Write a short composition about one of the following topics, using coordinating conjunctions in some of your sentences.

1. Write about one, two, or all three of the works of art reproduced in this lesson and Lesson 24. (See Discussion Topic A for some questions.)
2. Write about a style of art that you especially admire. Describe the style and tell why you like it. (See Discussion Topics A and B.)
3. Write about twentieth-century art in your country. You may want to focus on a particular artist, group of artists, or period in the twentieth century. (See Discussion Topic C for ideas.)

Lesson 26

The Nobel Peace Prize

26.1 Correlative Conjunctions: Joining Phrases and Dependent Clauses

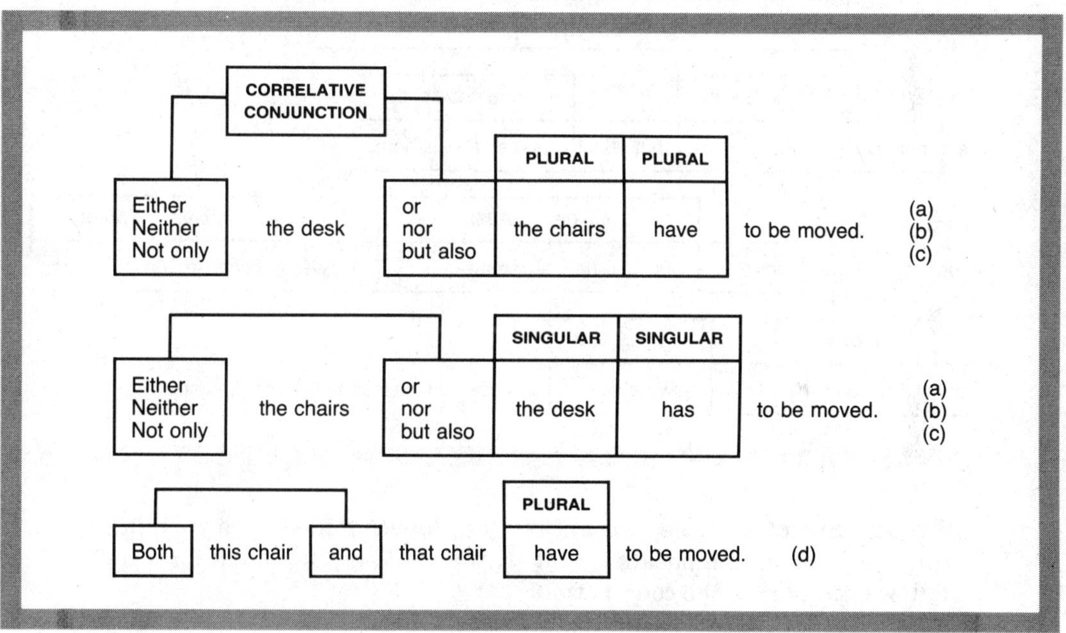

Meaning: Correlative conjunctions correspond in meaning to coordinating conjunctions, but they add emphasis by calling attention to the two phrases or clauses which they join.

a. **Either . . . or** emphasizes the meaning *or.*

b. **Neither . . . nor** emphasizes the meaning *and . . . not.*

c. **Not only . . . but also** means *and.* It adds emphasis to the second phrase.

d. **Both . . . and** emphasizes the meaning *and.*

Agreement: a,b,c. The verb agrees with the second part of the two-part subject for the first three expressions.

d. After **both . . . and,** the verb is always plural.

Punctuation: A comma is not used when joining two phrases or dependent clauses.

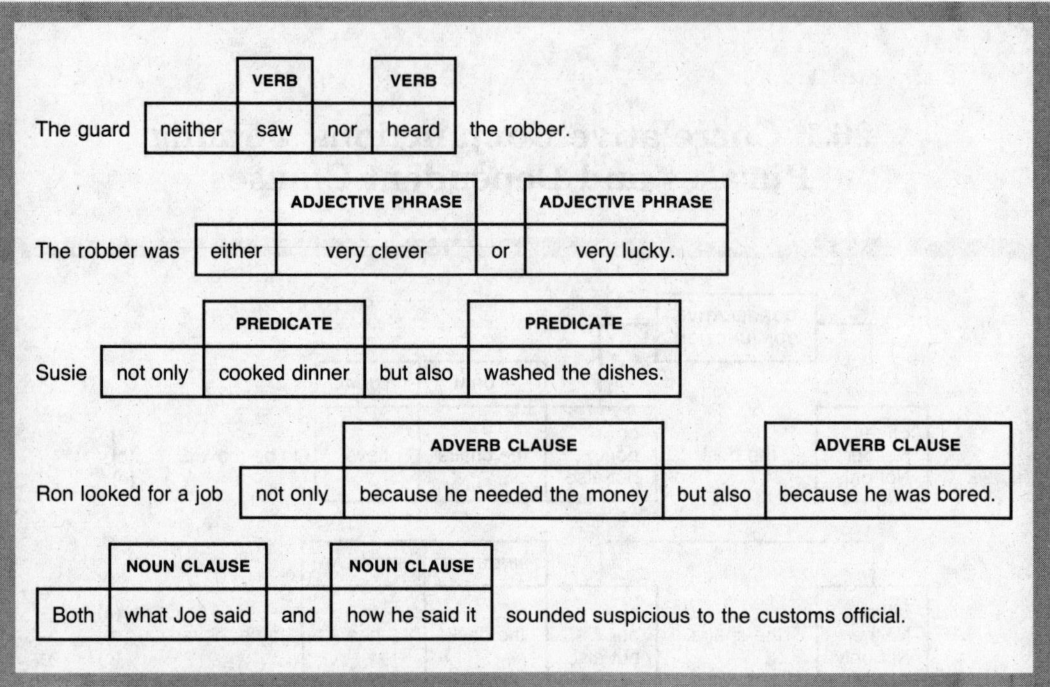

VERB
VERB
The guard
neither
saw
nor
heard
the robber.
ADJECTIVE PHRASE
ADJECTIVE PHRASE
The robber was
either
very clever
or
very lucky.
PREDICATE
PREDICATE
Susie
not only
cooked dinner
but also
washed the dishes.
ADVERB CLAUSE
ADVERB CLAUSE
Ron looked for a job
not only
because he needed the money
but also
because he was bored.
NOUN CLAUSE
NOUN CLAUSE
Both
what Joe said
and
how he said it
sounded suspicious to the customs official.

Parallel Structure: The two phrases or clauses joined by a correlative conjunction must be parallel; that is, the same grammatical form must follow each part of the conjunction.

Word Order: It is poor style to insert **not only . . . but also** between a preposition and its object. It is better to repeat the preposition.

Poor: **Shakespeare is famous for not only his plays but also his poems.**

Better: **Shakespeare is famous not only for his plays but also for his poems.**

When there are two auxiliaries before the verb, **either, neither,** and **not only** usually go between them.

The book may {either / neither} be used here {or / nor} (be) taken home overnight.

Note: **Either . . . or** and **neither . . . nor** can also be used with series:

You can *either* buy, rent, *or* borrow a bicycle.
He *neither* attended class, read the assigned books, *nor* turned in his homework.

Exercise 1. Subject–Verb Agreement

Fill in the singular or plural of the word in parentheses.

1. Not only the United States but also the U.S.S.R. wants (want) an arms reduction treaty.
2. Not only the citizens but also the President ______ (hope) a treaty can be signed.
3. Not only the President but also the citizens ______ (hope) a treaty can be signed.
4. Both the citizens and the President ______ (want) an arms reduction treaty.
5. Neither the President nor his aides ______ (have) spoken to reporters about the progress of the negotiations.
6. Either the President's aides or the President himself ______ (be) going to speak with reporters soon.
7. Neither the President's advisors nor the press secretary who will speak to reporters ______ (have) the ability to predict the outcome of the talks.

Exercise 2. *Not only . . . but also*

The Nobel Prizes, awarded every year for outstanding work in physics, chemistry, medicine (or physiology), literature, economics, and peace, are the highest of all international awards. Below are some facts about Alfred Nobel, the man who established the prizes.

Combine the sentences with **not only . . . but also.** You may want to circle the parallel structures first.

1. Alfred Nobel was descended from scientists on his father's side.
   Alfred Nobel was descended from scientists on his mother's side.

   Alfred Nobel was descended from scientists not only on his father's side but also on his mother's side.

2. He was a chemist. He was an industrialist.
3. Dynamite was among his inventions. Other explosives were among his inventions.
4. Dynamite has important uses in war. Dynamite has important uses in peacetime engineering.
5. Nobel invented explosives. He manufactured explosives, so he became extremely wealthy.
6. As a young man, science interested him. As a young man, poetry interested him.
7. He spoke Swedish, his native language. He was fluent in English, French, German, and Russian.
8. Nobel was involved in manufacturing weapons. He was deeply concerned about peace. (Use **but was also.**)
9. Today he is remembered for having invented dynamite. Today he is remembered for having established the Nobel Prizes.
10. A prize for literature is included among the six Nobel Prizes. A prize for peace is included among the six Nobel Prizes.

Exercise 3. *Both . . . and*

Nobel stated in his will that his Peace Prize should go to people who had promoted the peace movement, arms reduction, and harmony among nations. He also outlined procedures for selecting the recipients.

The sentences below are repetitious and lack proper emphasis. Restate them using **both . . . and** and eliminating all unnecessary repetition.

1. Nobel stated the purpose of the Peace Prize and he stated the procedures for selecting the recipients.

    Nobel stated both the purpose of the Peace Prize and the procedures for selecting the recipients.

2. The Nobel Foundation of Sweden owns the funds, and it administers the funds, but it does not choose the prizewinners.
3. A separate group, the Norwegian Nobel Committee, selects the winner each year, and the Committee also awards the prize each year.
4. The discussion during the selection process is secret, and the voting is also secret.
5. The Nobel Peace Prize has been awarded to individuals, and it has been awarded to organizations, too.
6. Men have received the prize, and women have received it also.
7. Besides money, each recipient receives a diploma, and every winner receives a gold medal.
8. At the award ceremony, a representative of the Norwegian Nobel Committee makes a speech, and the Nobel laureate* makes a speech at the ceremony, too.

Exercise 4. *Either . . . or; neither . . . nor*

Restate the sentences using **either . . . or** and **neither . . . nor.** Eliminate unnecessary repetition. (When you use **neither . . . nor,** omit **not.**)

1. The Nobel Foundation does not award the Nobel Prizes, and it doesn't select the recipients, either.

    The Nobel Foundation neither awards the Nobel Prizes nor selects the recipients.

2. An institution may be selected to win the Peace Prize. One or more individuals may be selected to win the Peace Prize.
3. Generally, the Committee selects one individual to win the prize, but sometimes it selects two individuals to win the prize.

    Generally, . . .

4. The Committee's discussion of the nominations is not made public, and the final vote isn't made public, either.

**Laureate:* winner.

5. Some years the Peace Prize has not been awarded because no worthy candidate could be found. Some years it has not been awarded because the world has been at war and the necessary information could not be gathered. (Repeat **because.**)
6. For four years during World War II, the Prize for Literature was not awarded, and the Peace Prize was not awarded during those years, either.

The last two items are more difficult: *(optional)*

7. If prize money is not awarded one year, it may be awarded the following year, but if it is not awarded the following year, it must be paid back into the fund. (*Hint:* Use **must.**)

   If prize money is not awarded one year, . . .
8. A prizewinner who declines the prize will not receive the money, and the money will be paid back into the fund. A prizewinner who fails to collect the money by a set date will not receive the money, either.

Exercise 5. Using Correlative Conjunctions

Restate the sentences using **both . . . and, not only . . . but also, either . . . or,** and **neither . . . nor.** Eliminate unnecessary repetition and make any other necessary changes.

1. According to the provisions of Nobel's will, individuals may receive more than one prize, and organizations may receive more than one prize.
2. For example, Marie Curie shared the Physics Prize with two others in 1903, and she received the entire Chemistry Prize in 1911.
3. The Office of the United Nations High Commissioner for Refugees won the Peace Prize in 1954, and it won the prize again in 1981.
4. Linus Pauling, the only individual to win two unshared prizes, won the Chemistry Prize in 1954, and then he won the Peace Prize in 1962.
5. Sometimes a recipient declines a Nobel Prize for political reasons, and sometimes he or she declines it for other reasons.

6. For example, Adolf Butenandt was not able to receive his prize in 1939 because his government would not permit him to, and Gerhard Domagk was not able to receive his prize that year for the same reason. (Use **neither . . . nor.**)
7. A prize may be awarded to a single individual. A prize may be shared by two or more individuals.
8. The 1973 Peace Prize, awarded to an American and a North Vietnamese, is an example of a shared prize. The 1978 Peace Prize, awarded to the heads of state of Egypt and Israel, is an example of a shared prize. (Use **both . . . and** to join the two sentences.)
9. It is interesting that Mahatma Gandhi, who taught the principles of nonviolent political protest, never received the Nobel Peace Prize. And John F. Kennedy, who founded the Peace Corps, didn't receive the prize. (Use **neither . . . nor.**)
10. However, the Nobel Prize can only be awarded to a living person, and Gandhi was assassinated in mid-career. Kennedy was also assassinated in mid-career.
11. The list of Peace Prize recipients includes the names of men and women who have dedicated their lives to establishing peace in the world, and it includes the names of others who have dedicated their lives to helping the victims of war.
12. Yet after almost a century of prizes, it is uncertain whether the recipients' efforts have brought the world closer to peace, and it is also uncertain whether their efforts have reduced suffering.

26.2 Correlative Conjunctions: Joining Independent Clauses

Statement Word Order

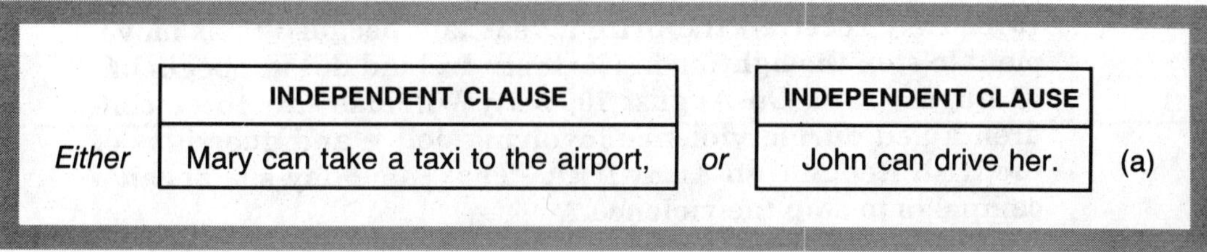
INDEPENDENT CLAUSE
INDEPENDENT CLAUSE
Either
Mary can take a taxi to the airport,
or
John can drive her.
(a)

Question Word Order

	AUXILIARY	SUBJECT		AUXILIARY	SUBJECT	
Neither	will	the workers	return to work, *nor*	can	the government	require them to do so. (b)

					SUBJECT	AUXILIARY		
Not only	do	they	want more pay, *but*	*also*	they	have		asked for health benefits. (c)
					they	have	*also*	

Word Order: Three of the correlative conjunctions are used to join independent clauses:

a. **Either . . . or:** Use statement word order.

b. **Neither . . . nor:** Question word order is used in both clauses.

c. **Not only . . . but also:** Question word order is used in the first clause. Statement word order is used in the second clause. Notice that there are two positions for **also:** after **but** or after the first auxiliary.

Formal and Informal Usage: The correlative conjunction **neither . . . nor** is used mainly in formal speech and writing. Its use to join independent clauses is infrequent and very formal.

Exercise 6. Combining Sentences

In 1977, two women from Northern Ireland, Mairead Corrigan and Betty Williams, were awarded the Nobel Peace Prize for 1976. They received the prize a year late because their movement to stop the fighting in Northern Ireland did not begin until August 1976. On August 10, Betty Williams saw three children killed during violence involving police and guerrillas of the Irish Republican Army (IRA). That same day she began a campaign to stop the violence.

Combine the sentences, using **either . . . or, neither . . . nor,** and **not only . . . but also.**

1. On February 1, 1976, the deadline for Nobel Prize nominations, the two women's names had not been nominated. Their peace movement had not even begun.

   On February 1, 1976, the deadline for Nobel Prize nominations, neither had the two women's names been nominated, nor had their peace movement begun.

2. In fact, until August 10th of that year, the two women did not know each other. They had not been active in any political movement.

Williams was appalled* by the children's deaths. That same day, she went from house to house, asking women to sign a petition for peace.

3. Williams thought, "The fighting must stop. Otherwise, more people will die."
4. Both Catholics and Protestants signed the petition. Four days later, 10,000 joined in a peace march.
5. Protestant extremists did not approve of the movement. The IRA did not stop its struggle against the British rule in Northern Ireland.
6. However, widespread support developed in Northern Ireland. The peace campaign attracted sympathy internationally.
7. According to the two women, living conditions would have to be improved in Northern Ireland. Otherwise the violence would continue.

They needed money for building projects. When the Nobel Committee could not award them the Peace Prize in 1976 because of their regulations, twenty-two Norwegian newspapers collected $340,000 for a "People's Peace Prize" and sent it to them.

8. They received the People's Peace Prize in 1976. The following year, the 1976 Nobel Peace Prize was awarded to them.

Exercise 7. Cumulative Exercise: Coordinating Conjunctions and Correlative Conjunctions

One of the best known recipients of the Nobel Peace Prize is Martin Luther King, Jr. (1964), whose efforts to obtain freedom

**Appalled:* shocked and very upset.

and equality for black Americans brought about great changes in the United States.

Combine the sentences with the following conjunctions. Use each conjunction at least once.

and	or	either . . . or
nor	for	neither . . . nor
but	yet	not only . . . but also
so		both . . . and

1. Martin Luther King, Jr., was born in 1929 in Atlanta, Georgia. He died in 1968 in Memphis, Tennessee.
2. His father was a pastor* in Atlanta. His grandfather was a pastor in Atlanta.
3. By 1955, when King was twenty-six, he had received two bachelor's degrees. By 1955, he had also earned a doctorate in philosophy.
4. At that time, blacks were not permitted to eat at store lunch counters in the South. They could not sit in buses if there were not enough seats for white passengers.
5. That year (1955), a black woman was arrested in Montgomery, Alabama, where King was working as a pastor. She refused to give up her seat in the bus to a white man.
6. The black community was not willing to accept such injustice. Organized by King, blacks boycotted the city buses in Montgomery.
7. They rode to work in car pools. They walked to work.
8. Many had to walk many miles to work. They continued the boycott for over a year.
9. King was arrested. His home was bombed.
10. His family was also threatened. He did not give up his philosophy of nonviolent resistance.
11. During the thirteen years that he led the movement for racial equality, King taught the principles of nonviolent struggle. He felt that it was "the only morally and practically sound method open to oppressed people in their struggle for freedom."[1]

**Pastor:* protestant minister.

[1]As quoted in *Champions of Peace* by Tony Gray (London: Paddington Press Ltd., 1976): p. 273.

12. During those years, the protesters carried no arms. They did not fight back when attacked.
13. For King said, "We do not want to instill fear in others. We do not want to instill fear in the society of which we are a part."[2] (or)
14. King was shot and killed on April 4, 1968. His efforts to achieve equality for black Americans are remembered every year on his birthday, January 15th.

26.3 Negative Adverbials at the Beginning of a Sentence

NEGATIVE ADVERBIAL	AUXILIARY	SUBJECT	
Never	have	I	seen a more unusual work of art.
Seldom / Rarely	have	I	enjoyed a movie that showed violence.
Nowhere	has	that question	been more hotly debated than in California.
Not once	did	the child	ask for his mother.
Not since 1922	have	we	had so much rain.
In no case	do	they	permit a customer to use the phone.
Under no circumstances	should	you	leave the phone off the hook.
Only once during the hours of waiting	did	a passenger	complain.
Only after they inspected all the bags	did	they	permit passengers to leave.

Word Order: After a negative adverbial, the auxiliary comes before the subject. **Seldom, rarely,** and **only** are adverbials of negative force and so require reverse word order.

Punctuation: No comma is used between the negative adverbial and the auxiliary.

Formal and Informal Usage: Negative adverbials come at the beginning of a sentence in formal speech and writing. This pattern is rare in conversation.

[2]Ibid. p. 274.

Exercise 8. Placing Negative Adverbials at the Beginning of a Sentence

Restate the sentences so that a negative adverbial comes before the subject.

1. The Norwegian Nobel Committee awards a Peace Prize only in years when a worthy recipient can be found.

   Only in years when a worthy recipient can be found does the Norwegian Nobel Committee award a Peace Prize.

2. A Peace Prize winner has seldom declined the award unless forbidden to accept it by his or her government.
3. An Englishman has not received the Prize since 1959.*
4. A nomination cannot be accepted after February 1 of a given year under any circumstances.
5. Two women have received the Peace Prize in the same year only once in the history of the prize.
6. In the history of the Peace Prize, such a young man had never won the prize (when Martin Luther King, Jr., received it at the age of thirty-five.)
7. Peace has been difficult to achieve in the Middle East. It hasn't been more difficult anywhere (else). (Use **nowhere** and combine the sentences.)
8. We can hope to have peace in the world only when we have peace in our hearts. (Do you agree or disagree?)

Exercise 9. Placing Negative Adverbials at the Beginning of a Sentence

Restate the sentences so that a negative adverbial comes before the subject. When you have done so, each sentence will be an exact quotation.[1] You may want to discuss these quotations as you do the exercise. (*Note:* Three dots (. . .) mean that some words have been omitted from the quotation, but the meaning has not been changed.)

1. "It was never possible before for one nation to make war on another without sending armies across the border." —Albert Einstein, 1946

*As of 1988.

[1]As quoted in *Champions of Peace* by Tony Gray (London: Paddington Press Ltd., 1976): (1) p. 269, (2) p. 224, (3) p. 232, (4) p. 241, (5) p. 273.

2. "So many peoples* have never in human history experienced freedom. Yet freedom itself . . . is widely endangered." —Ralph Bunche, Nobel Peace Prize acceptance speech, 1950 (Change the first sentence only.)
3. "The institutions set up to maintain this peace will fulfill the function expected of them only when an ideal of peace is born in the minds of peoples." —Albert Schweitzer, Nobel Peace Prize acceptance speech, 1952
4. "Today we can defend ourselves by force less than ever, for there is no effective defense against the all-destroying effect of nuclear missile weapons." —Lester Pearson, Nobel Peace Prize acceptance speech, 1957 (*Note:* **Less** is a word with negative force.)

   Today . . .

5. "[The Negroes] have only rarely acted against the principle given to them [by King] by requiting violence with violence, even though for many of us this would be the natural reaction." —Chairman of the Nobel Committee, 1964

Transfer Exercises

1. Some Types of People (oral—books closed)

Make statements about the following, using **neither . . . nor.** Use your dictionary if you need to.

1. an only child

   An only child has neither sisters nor brothers.

2. an orphan
3. a childless couple
4. an illiterate
5. a newborn baby
6. a foreign student without a resident's visa
7. a medical student

2. Some Differences and Similarities

Ask how the pairs are (a) different and (b) the same. Use **neither . . . nor** and **both . . . and** in your answers.

**Peoples:* races or nations of people.

1. a fish and a bird
   a. **How is a fish different from a bird?**

      A fish has neither wings nor legs. (A bird has both.)

      or: **A fish can neither fly nor walk.**

   b. **How are they the same?**

      Both a fish and a bird { **are good to eat.** / **have a skeleton.** }

2. a chicken and a duck
3. a lion and an elephant
4. a bicycle and a car
5. an ocean liner and an airplane
6. Continue with examples of your own.

3. Alternatives

Suggest two or more possible courses of action for each situation. Use **either . . . or.**

1. How can I get to (   ) from here?

   You can take either a bus or a train.

   or: **You can either walk, take a bus, or call a taxi.**

2. I need something to wake me up.
3. How can I get rid of my headache?
4. I'd like to look at a newspaper.
5. What should I do if I don't know how to spell a word?
6. How can I find a girlfriend/boyfriend?
7. I want to work in the field of health.
8. How can I win the Nobel Prize?

4. Interviewing a Classmate

Ask a classmate the following questions. In answering, give an affirmative answer (if you can) with **not only . . . but also.** Then give a negative answer with **either . . . or.**

> *Note:* In using **not only . . . but also,** place the *least* expected answer last. For example, for a Chinese student:
>
> *Wrong emphasis:* **I speak not only Arabic, but also Chinese.**
>
> *Right emphasis:* **I speak not only Chinese, but also Arabic.**

1. What cities have you lived in?

    a. **I have lived not only in (city where you are now), but also in (   ).**
    b. **I haven't lived either in (Berlin) or (Moscow).**

2. What countries have you traveled in?
3. What languages do you speak?
4. I imagine you have met people from many different countries, haven't you?
5. What sports are you good at?
6. What do you enjoy doing in your spare time?
7. What do you like to read about in the newspaper?
8. Who are some well-known people that you admire?

Discussion Topics

A. Do you know of any men or women from your country who have won a Nobel Prize? If so, who were they? Which prize did they win, and for what work?

B. Consider these two statements by Nobel Peace Prize laureates.[1] Do you agree or disagree with them? Explain your opinion.

1. "All nations must come to the decision to renounce force as a final resort of policy. If they are not prepared to do this, they will cease to exist." —Linus Pauling, 1962 laureate
2. "Nonviolence is a powerful and just weapon. Indeed, it is a weapon unique in history, which cuts without wounding and ennobles the man who wields it." —Martin Luther King, Jr., 1964 laureate

C. In your opinion, what could governments do to bring the world closer to peace? Do you think that disarmament reduces the danger of war or increases it? If you favor disarmament, how do you think it could be regulated?

D. What can individuals do to promote peace? Do you think that demonstrations and marches are effective? If you decided to work for peace, what kind of organization would you join? Are there ways to work for peace without joining an organization?

[1]Gray, *Champions of Peace:* (1) p. 267, (2) p. 274.

Composition Topics

Write a short composition on one of the following topics. Use correlative conjunctions in some of your sentences.

1. Write about a man or woman from your country who has won a Nobel Prize. Tell something about his or her life and answer the questions in Discussion Topic A.
2. Write about a man or woman who has made a contribution to peace, in your opinion.
3. Write about a peace movement or a nonviolent struggle which has taken place in your country. (See Exercises 6 and 7 for examples.)
4. Write about one of the quotations in this lesson (in Exercise 9 and Discussion Topic B). Do you agree or disagree with the quotation? Give reasons to support your opinion.
5. How can the world achieve peace, in your opinion? (See Discussion Topics B, C, and D.)

Lesson 27

Into the Twenty-first Century

27.1 Introduction to Conjunctive Adverbs; Conjunctive Adverbs of Addition, Result, and Time

Introduction

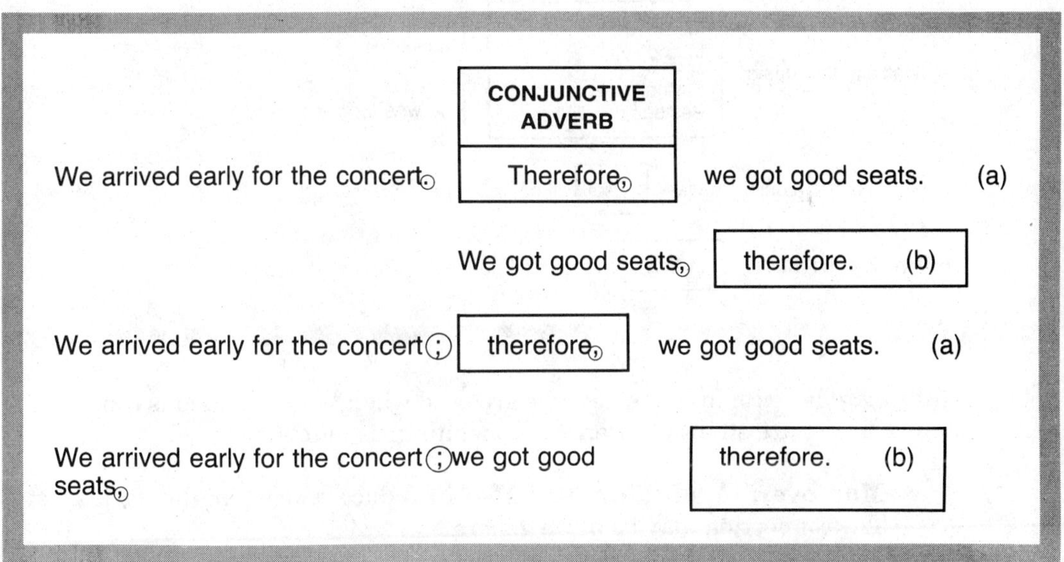

CONJUNCTIVE ADVERB
We arrived early for the concert. Therefore, we got good seats. (a)
We got good seats, therefore. (b)
We arrived early for the concert; therefore, we got good seats. (a)
We arrived early for the concert; we got good seats, therefore. (b)

Meaning: Conjunctive adverbs show the relationship between two sentences. **Therefore,** for example, means that the event in the second sentence is a result of the event in the first sentence.

Word Order: A conjunctive adverb can occur at the beginning or end of the sentence it modifies.

Punctuation: A conjunctive adverb does not join sentences grammatically. We use a *period* (.) or a *semicolon* (;) between the two sentences just as if the conjunctive adverb were not there.

A *comma* is generally used

a. after a conjunctive adverb at the beginning of a sentence, and
b. before a conjunctive adverb at the end of a sentence.

Note: Conjunctive adverbs also occur in the middle of a sentence. One common position is after the subject. Commas are used if the subject is different from the subject of the previous sentence.

There weren't many people at the concert. Those who wished, *therefore,* could sit in the front row.

Addition

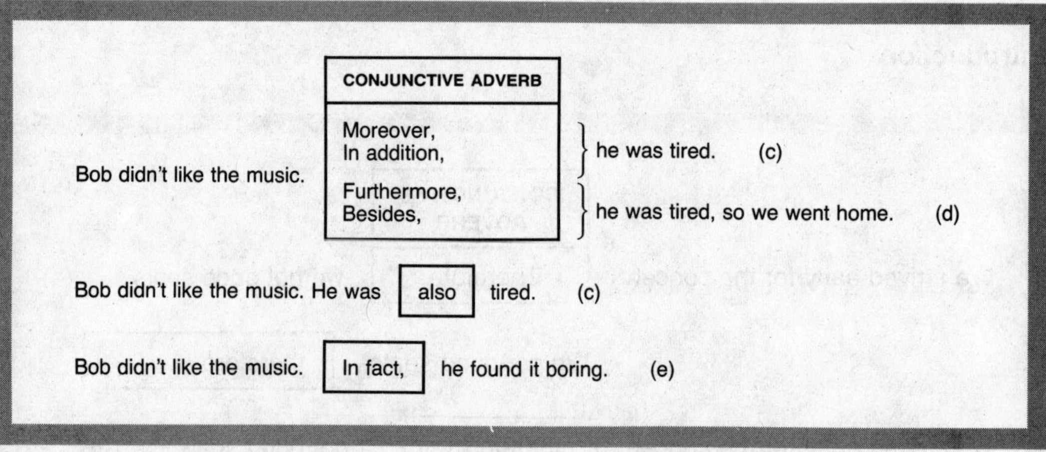

Meaning: These conjunctive adverbs are used when the same idea is continued. There are slight differences in meaning, as follows:

c. **Moreover, in addition,** and **also** introduce a new similar fact. The connection may be quite general.

Bob didn't like the music. *Moreover,* he doesn't like modern painting.

d. **Furthermore** and **besides** often add another reason for an action or a conclusion.

e. **In fact** introduces a restatement or more detailed explanation which emphasizes the first statement. Another example:

Bob was tired. *In fact,* he was falling asleep in his seat.

Word order: **Also** most often occurs between the auxiliary and the verb. Do not use commas with **also** in this position.

Result

Bob didn't like the music.	Therefore, Consequently, As a result,	we left early and went home.	(f)
We left the concert early.	Thus,	we missed the piece by Mozart.	(g)

Meaning: f,g. **Therefore, consequently, as a result,** and **thus** mean *because that (previous sentence) is true.*

g. **Thus** often introduces a logical conclusion.

The champion won the fight in ninety-one seconds. *Thus,* it was one of the shortest fights in history.

Time

We bought our tickets.	After that,	we went into the hall.	(h)
	Then	we went into the hall.	(h)

Meaning: h. **After that** and **then** indicate sequence in time.

Punctuation: No comma is used after **then.**

Note: There are many other conjunctive adverbs of time, each with its own meaning.

Exercise 1. Punctuating Sentences with Conjunctive Adverbs

Fill in commas, semicolons, and periods where they are needed.

1. The inventor and thinker R. Buckminster Fuller (1895–1983) believed that war can be avoided only if we develop a high standard of living for all human beings ____ Therefore ____ he spent his life developing inventions that would help all people live well.
2. In 1927, he designed a new type of house called a Dymaxion House ____ This lightweight, movable house cost about the same as an inexpensive car ____ moreover ____ it included automatic vacuum cleaners and a system for turning garbage into power.
3. Fuller patented the design for his Dymaxion House ____ Then ____ he went on to design a three-wheeled automobile that could go 100 miles an hour.
4. One of these cars was in an accident with another car ____ consequently ____ people lost interest in the Dymaxion Car.
5. The other car in the accident had driven away by the time reporters arrived ____ as a result ____ the reporters wrote that the Dymaxion Car had killed its driver.
6. A world map designed by Fuller in 1943 was the first map ever to receive a U.S. patent ____ It ____ also ____ attracted the attention of scientists because it did not distort either land or water areas.

Exercise 2. Choosing the Correct Adverb

Restate or combine the sentences to include a conjunctive adverb from the list. You can punctuate your responses either as one sentence (with a semicolon) or as two sentences (with a period). But do not use more than one semicolon in a sentence. Use each conjunctive adverb on the list at least once.

Addition	*Result*
also	as a result
√besides	therefore
furthermore	thus
in addition	
in fact	
moreover	

1. Fuller investigated the geometry of natural forms, for he believed this study would help solve problems, and he was fascinated with the subject.

Fuller investigated the geometry of natural forms, for he believed this study would help solve problems; besides, he was fascinated with the subject.

2. The geodesic dome, which grew out of this study, was the discovery that made Fuller famous. It made him a wealthy man.

Geodesic domes are made out of tetrahedrons,* the basic geometric form in nature, according to Fuller.

3. The domes are extremely strong. They can withstand winds up to 200 miles per hour.
4. Geodesic domes could withstand extreme cold and high winds. They could be erected in only a few hours. After extensive testing, the Marine Corps decided to use geodesic domes in the Arctic.
5. Fuller manufactured geodesic domes and sold them successfully all over the world. He could spend his time traveling and lecturing.
6. People came to his lectures not only because his ideas were interesting but also because he was a lively, entertaining speaker.
7. Fuller was a prolific inventor. He held more than 2,000 patents on his inventions. He was the author of twenty-five books, including one called *Operating Manual for Spaceship Earth.*
8. Fuller received more than 2,000 patents. He was one of the most prolific inventors in history.
9. He received thirty-nine honorary doctorates during his lifetime and was awarded the Medal of Freedom by President Reagan.

27.2 Conjunctive Adverbs of Unexpected Result, Contrast, and Contradiction

Unexpected Result

Although the music was wonderful, we left the concert early.

	CONJUNCTIVE ADVERB	
= The music was wonderful.	Nevertheless, Still, However,	we left the concert early. we left early (anyway).

**Tetrahedron:* A pyramid made with four triangles.

I don't like to study.	However,	I (still) have to do it.

Meaning: **Nevertheless, still, however . . . (anyway),** and **however . . . (still)** introduce an unexpected result. They mean *although that (previous sentence) is true, . . .*

Contrast

The first two symphonies were classical, *whereas* the last piece was modern.

= The first two pieces were classical.	On the other hand, In contrast, However,	the last piece was modern.

Meaning: **On the other hand, in contrast,** and **however** introduce a contrast. (Notice that **however** is used both for unexpected result and for contrast.)

Contradiction

A: You like carrots, don't you?

B: On the contrary, I hate carrots. (a)

People say Professor Jones doesn't care about his students. *On the contrary,* he is deeply concerned about them. (a)

I don't dislike grammar (as you might think). *On the contrary,* I find it very interesting. (b)

Meaning: **On the contrary** has two meanings:

a. It emphasizes that another person's idea is wrong.

b. It adds emphasis to the speaker's own negative statement by restating it in the affirmative. In this case, the speaker is contradicting what he or she thinks someone else believes.

Exercise 3. Unexpected Result versus Contrast

Fill in the blanks with one of the following conjunctive adverbs, and add punctuation. Use each expression on the list at least once.

Unexpected Result	*Contrast*
nevertheless	on the other hand
still	in contrast
however	however

1. Buckminster Fuller's critics called him a "naive romanticist . " In contrast, __________ the architect Frank Lloyd Wright praised him as having "more absolute integrity than any man I have ever known."[1]
2. Fuller held more than 2,000 patents __________ few of his inventions were marketed.
3. As early as 1918, he had figured out how to build faster airplanes using turbine engines __________ the industry was not ready for the idea and rejected it.
4. Fuller's first design for a two-bedroom house cost only $600 __________ the house was never produced.
5. His Dymaxion Car could go 120 miles per hour and ran thirty-five miles on one gallon of gas __________ only three of the cars were ever produced.
6. The car was not a success __________ thousands of geodesic domes have been constructed all over the world.
7. Other modern architects altered the appearance of their houses but used traditional building techniques __________ Fuller used completely new principles of building.
8. In 1980, the people of Winooski, Vermont, were considering erecting a plastic geodesic dome over their entire town. Those who favored the dome argued that it would save energy and make winter living more comfortable __________ those who opposed the idea felt that it might harm birds and plants and make people feel closed in.
9. Fuller went to Winooski to speak in favor of the dome, and many of the town's 6,700 residents supported it __________ it was never built.

[1]Albin Krebs, "R. Buckminster Fuller, Futurist Inventor, Dies at 87," *New York Times,* July 3, 1983, Section I, p. 17.

10. Fuller believed that we should "reform the environment instead of trying to reform man ________"[2] ________ many of those who study the world's problems feel that spiritual and psychological change is necessary before human beings can live in peace and harmony. What do you think?

Exercise 4. On the Contrary

Complete the sentences. (Remember that **on the contrary** is followed by the affirmative.)

1. The climate is not hospitable along the northern coast of Alaska and Canada, where the Marine Corps installed geodesic domes.

   On the contrary, *it is very severe.*

   or: *it is very cold and windy there.*

2. Fuller's geodesic domes are not heavy; on the contrary, . . .
3. They do not require weeks or months to construct, like ordinary buildings. On the contrary, . . .
4. **A:** When Fuller invented his geodesic dome, was he mainly interested in making money?

   B: No. On the contrary, . . .
5. **A:** Why didn't Fuller's Dymaxion House become popular? Was it too expensive?

   B: On the contrary, . . .
6. **A:** You think Fuller was some kind of nut,* don't you?

   B: On the contrary, . . .

Exercise 5. Conjunctive Adverbs

The following information is from a 1980 newspaper report. Add a conjunctive adverb of *addition, result, unexpected result,* or *contrast* to the second sentence in each pair to show its logical relationship to the first sentence. Use a different conjunctive adverb each time.

1. Buckminster Fuller spoke this week at a two-day International Dome Symposium in Winooski, Vermont. Many other experts spoke.

   Many other experts *also* spoke.

[2]Ibid.

**Nut:* slang for an odd person whose ideas have no real importance.

2. Winooski is not a large town. It has only 6,700 inhabitants.
3. Many citizens of Winooski favor building a transparent dome over the town. Nobody knows what it would cost.
4. One of Winooski's English teachers felt a song was needed to help publicize the project and win people's support. He wrote the theme song of the symposium: "Dome over Winooski."
5. Winooski is an Indian word for "onion." The organization which is promoting the dome is called the Golden Onion Dome Club.
6. The club has several hundred members. There are many in Winooski who are not in favor of the dome.
7. Some worry that the air under the dome might become polluted. Plants might not receive enough sunlight.
8. One housewife wonders who will clean it. She thinks she would feel closed in under a dome.
9. The dome has not been built yet. Some day, somewhere, such an experiment may be tried.

Exercise 6. Completing Sentences with Conjunctive Adverbs

Complete the sentences in any logical way.

1. Most Americans know that automobile exhaust pollutes our atmosphere; nevertheless, . . .
2. Cars consume more gasoline when they are driven at high speed; moreover, . . .
3. Fuel consumption would be reduced if Americans used public transportation instead of cars; still, . . .
4. Buses save fuel because many people ride together; in contrast, . . .
5. Some smaller cities and towns in the United States have no public transportation; as a result, . . .
6. In heavily congested city traffic, a bicycle is probably the fastest way to travel; however, . . .
7. During the 1970s, gasoline prices rose sharply; in fact, . . .
8. Most Americans drove large gas-guzzling* cars until the price of gas went up; then . . .
9. The large American cars used a lot of gasoline; consequently, . . .

**Gas-guzzling:* using a lot of gasoline.

10. Japanese cars rose in popularity at that time; in addition, . . .
11. One advantage of a small car is that it uses less gas; furthermore, . . .
12. However, small cars are not cheap; on the contrary, . . .

27.3 Review: Adverb Clauses, Coordination, and Prepositions

SUBORDINATING CONJUNCTION (adverb clause)

	Because	he was tired, Peter wanted to stay home.	(a)
Peter wanted to stay home	**because**	he was tired.	(b)
John wanted to see a movie	**, whereas**	Sue preferred to go dancing.	(c)

COORDINATING CONJUNCTION

Peter wanted to stay home	**, for**	he was tired.	(d)
John wanted to see a movie	**, but**	Sue wanted to go dancing.	(d)
John	**and**	Sue wanted to go out.	(e)

CORRELATIVE CONJUNCTION

Not only	were several American films playing	**, but also**	a new Japanese film had just opened.		(d)
Both	John	**and**	Sue wanted to go out.		(e)

CONJUNCTIVE ADVERB

John wanted to see a movie	**; on the other hand,** **. On the other hand,**	Sue wanted to go dancing.	(f)

John wanted to see a movie. Sue wanted to go dancing | , however. (f) |

PREPOSITION

| In contrast to | John, Sue did not want to see a movie. (g)

Mary was absent | because of illness. (h) |

Punctuation: The following rules have exceptions but are good rules of thumb:*

Adverb clauses:

a. Use a comma after the clause.
b. Do not use a comma before the clause.
c. *Exception:* Use a comma before clauses of contrast.

Coordinate structures:

d. Use a comma before a coordinating conjunction or a correlative conjunction if it introduces an independent clause.

e. Do not use commas for two parallel structures (not independent clauses).

Conjunctive adverbs:

f. Use a period or semicolon between the two clauses. Use a comma after the conjunctive adverb (at the beginning of a sentence) and before the adverb (at the end).

Prepositional phrases:

g. Use a comma after the phrase at the beginning of the sentence.

h. Do not use a comma before a prepositional phrase at the end of the sentence.

Vocabulary: The following chart lists most of the conjunctions and conjunctive adverbs that you have studied in Units VII and IX, along with some prepositions which are related in meaning.

**Rule of thumb:* a rule that is useful and generally true, although not exact.

Meaning	Subordinating Conjunction	Coordinating Conjunction/ Correlative Conjunction	Conjunctive Adverb	Preposition
ADDITION		and nor not only . . . but also neither . . . nor both . . . and*	also besides furthermore in addition in fact moreover	besides in addition to
ALTERNATIVES		or either . . . or		
REASON	as because inasmuch as in view of the fact that now that since	for		as a result of because of in view of on account of
RESULT	so . . . that such . . . that	so	as a result consequently therefore thus	
PURPOSE	so that in order that			for
INCONGRUITY *Insufficient reason:*	although even though though in spite of the fact that			
Unexpected result:		but . . . (anyway) (still) yet	however nevertheless still	in spite of despite
CONTRAST	whereas while	but	however in contrast on the other hand	in contrast to unlike
CONTRADICTION			on the contrary	

***Both . . . and** does not join independent clauses.

Meaning	Subordinating Conjunction	Coordinating Conjunction/ Correlative Conjunction	Conjunctive Adverb	Preposition
TIME	after when etc.		after that then etc.	after before etc.
CONDITION	as long as if in case provided that unless whether . . . or not	or (else) either . . . or	otherwise	in case of

Note: Subordinating and coordinating conjunctions are two ways to join sentences. They cannot be used together.

Wrong: Although the sun was shining, but I took my umbrella.

Right: **Although the sun was shining, I took my umbrella.**

The sun was shining, but I took my umbrella.

In contrast, conjunctive adverbs do not join sentences grammatically and are sometimes used with conjunctions in order to add emphasis.

***Although* the sun was shining, I *nevertheless* took my umbrella.**

The sun was shining, *but* I *nevertheless* took my umbrella.

Exercise 7. Cumulative Exercise: Subordination, Coordination, and Conjunctive Adverbs

Below are some predictions that futurists are making about our technological capabilities in the twenty-first century. Fill in a subordinating conjunction, coordinating conjunction, correlative conjunction, or conjunctive adverb from the chart. Pay attention both to the meaning and to the punctuation in making your choice.

1. Soon there will be personal computers that are as powerful as today's main frame computers.* In fact, ______ the technology for such computers already exists.

**Main frame computers:* very large computers.

2. Future computers will be able ______________ to make decisions ______________ to learn from their mistakes.

3. A robot will shovel snow for us, ______________ we won't have to do it.

4. The snow robot will "eat" the snow; ______________ it will park itself in the garage and recharge its batteries.

5. However, people may lose their jobs ______________ robots will do more of the work in factories.

6. There will be more manned stations in space; ______________, there probably won't be factories in space ______________ it is not economical to build them there.

7. In the future, we may be able to shoot garbage and toxic waste into the sun ______________ it doesn't pollute the earth.

8. People will live longer. ______________, we will be able to prevent hereditary diseases.

9. The population of the earth will double between now and the year 2050; ______________, we will need more food. ______________, we won't have to depend on farmland for food, ______________ we will be able to produce food in factories.

Exercise 8. Cumulative Exercise: Conjunctions, Conjunctive Adverbs, and Prepositions (oral or written)

A. Combine the ideas in (a) and (b), using the expressions given.

a. to buy (or not to buy) the car
b. the high (low) price

1. so that

I hope the price is low so that I can buy the car.

2. so
3. so . . . that
4. as a result
5. because of
6. because
7. in spite of
8. nevertheless
9. although
10. but

11. provided that/otherwise
12. or
13. even if
14. only if

B. Now combine the following two ideas:

c. John . . . (not) handsome
d. (not) intelligent

15. also
16. however
17. not only . . . but also
18. nor
19. while
20. but
21. in spite of the fact that
22. in addition to
23. still

C. Add another name: Mike.

24. in contrast to/neither . . . nor

Exercise 9. Completion

Punctuate the sentences and complete them in a logical manner.

1. The world is becoming a (better/worse) place to live for . . .
2. As the population grows, we need not only more food but also . . .
3. Nuclear weapons can destroy the world therefore . . .
4. I never met Buckminster Fuller however . . .
5. I need a personal computer so that . . .
6. Modern computers are very powerful yet . . .
7. Space exploration is exciting moreover . . .
8. I would (not) like to travel in space because . . .
9. Americans are buying smaller cars these days because of . . .
10. We will need to reduce pollution in the future otherwise . . .

Transfer Exercises

1. Interview

Ask a classmate these questions. In answering, add a second sentence with a conjunctive adverb.

A. Give a *result.*

1. Do you want to speak and write English well?

   Yes, I do. *Therefore,* I'm taking this course.

2. Is this course easy or hard for you?
3. Do you speak English outside of class?
4. What kind of job do you want to get after you finish your studies?
5. Is it easy or hard to get a job in that field?

B. Give an *additional fact.*

6. What do you like about your best friend?
7. What do you have in common with him or her?
8. What do you and your best friend disagree about?
9. What do you like to do together?
10. If your friend is in this city, do you see or speak to each other often? If not, how do you keep in touch?

C. Give an *unexpected result* or *contrast.*

11. Do you agree with your parents about most things?
12. Do you like the same kind of music as your parents?
13. Are you living with your parents now?
14. Has the lifestyle in your country changed since your parents were young?
15. Will your parents choose your future wife or husband? (*Or:* Did your parents choose your wife or husband?)

2. The Twenty-first Century

Answer the questions and add a second sentence with a conjunctive adverb. You can either use the conjunctive adverb in parentheses or choose another. After you have answered a question according to the instructions, you may want to discuss the question further.

1. Do you think advances in technology will be able to solve the world's problems? (however)
2. Would you like to have a robot to do your housework? (in addition)
3. How can we prevent war?
4. Do you agree that everyone hates war?
5. Is it really a good idea to shoot toxic waste into the sun? (in fact)
6. Can we eliminate hunger in the world? (nevertheless)
7. Will the world be a good place to live when the population has doubled?
8. Would you like to live in a town that had a plastic dome over it during the winter?

Discussion Topics

A. What is the greatest problem facing the world today? Can that problem be solved, in your opinion? If so, how?

B. Will the twenty-first century be a happy period for human beings? If you believe that it probably will, what do you think will contribute the most to our well-being? If you don't think it will be happy, what will be the biggest problems, and what will cause them?

C. Buckminster Fuller felt that people must learn to live unselfishly if the human race was to survive. He said, "Do we really understand that each of us is here for all the others? If the answer is, 'I am here just for *me*,' then I think humanity is going to fail its exam."[1]

Do you agree that the survival of the human race is in danger? Do you agree that we will have to become less selfish in order to survive? How can human beings learn to be less selfish? Are there other values that we need to adopt in order to create a peaceful world?

Composition Topics

Write a short composition about one of the following topics. Use conjunctive adverbs in some of your sentences to show logical relationships.

1. Argue that technology will be able to solve our problems and create a good life for human beings on earth (or elsewhere). Give examples of how this will be done.

[1]William Marlin, "Buckminster Fuller, 'A Terrific Bundle of Experience,' " *Christian Science Monitor,* September 23, 1983, p. 13.

2. Argue that there are limits to the ways in which technology can help solve our problems. Give examples to support your ideas.
3. Argue that technology is harming the planet more than it is improving it. Give examples, and suggest how we can improve the situation.
4. Write about one technological advance predicted by futurists. Use your imagination to describe how it will work and how it will affect our lives. (See Exercise 7.)
5. Write about one of the questions in Transfer Exercise 2.
6. Write about one of the Discussion Topics.

Appendix 1

Spelling Rules for Adding *-s*, *-es*, *-ing*, and *-ed*

Verbs Ending in a Vowel		-s/-es		-ing		-ed/-d	
Consonant + **-e**	like file	*Add* **-s.**	likes files	*Drop the* **-e** *and add* **-ing.**	liking filing	*Add* **-d.**	liked filed
-ie	tie die	*Add* **-s.**	ties dies	*Change* **-ie** *to* **-y** *and add* **-ing.**	tying dying	*Add* **-d.**	tied died
Vowel + **-y**	play enjoy	*Add* **-s.**	plays enjoys	*Add* **-ing.**	playing enjoying	*Add* **-ed.**	played enjoyed
Consonant + **-y**	study carry	*Change* **-y** *to* **-i** *and add* **-es.**	studies carries	*Add* **-ing.**	studying carrying	*Change* **-y** *to* **-i** *and add* **-ed.**	studied carried
Vowel + **-e**	agree sue	*Add* **-s.**	agrees sues	*Add* **-ing.**	agreeing sueing	*Add* **-d.**	agreed sued
Other vowels	shampoo ski	*Add* **-s.**	shampoos skis	*Add* **-ing.**	shampooing skiing	*Add* **-ed.**	shampooed skied

Verbs Ending in a Consonant		Double the Consonant?						
-s, -z, -x, -sh, -ch	kiss push	no	*Add* **-es.**	kisses pushes	*Add* **-ing.**	kissing pushing	*Add* **-ed.**	kissed pushed
-w	snow	no	*Add* **-s.**	snows	*Add* **-ing.**	snowing	*Add* **-ed.**	snowed
Two consonants	last turn	no	*Add* **-s.**	lasts turns	*Add* **-ing.**	lasting turning	*Add* **-ed.**	lasted turned
Two vowels + one consonant	cool seat	no	*Add* **-s.**	cools seats	*Add* **-ing.**	cooling seating	*Add* **-ed.**	cooled seated
One unstressed vowel + one consonant	ópen śuffer	no	*Add* **-s.**	opens suffers	*Add* **-ing.**	opening suffering	*Add* **-ed.**	opened suffered
One stressed vowel + one consonant	stop refér	yes	*Add* **-s.**	stops refers	*Double the consonant and add* **-ing.**	stopping referring	*Double the consonant and add* **-ed.**	stopped referred
			Irregular: have go do	 has goes does			*Irregular:* See Appendix 2.	

Appendix 2

Irregular Verb Forms

Base Form	*Simple Past*	*Past Participle*	*Base Form*	*Simple Past*	*Past Participle*
arise	arose	arisen	eat	ate	eaten
be	was/were	been	fall	fell	fallen
beat	beat	beaten	feed	fed	fed
become	became	become	feel	felt	felt
begin	began	begun	fight	fought	fought
bend	bent	bent	find	found	found
bet	bet	bet	fit	fit	fit
bind	bound	bound	flee	fled	fled
bite	bit	bitten	fly	flew	flown
bleed	bled	bled	forbid	forbade	forbidden
blow	blew	blown	forget	forgot	forgotten
break	broke	broken	forgive	forgave	forgiven
breed	bred	bred	freeze	froze	frozen
bring	brought	brought			
broadcast	broadcast	broadcast	get	got	got, gotten
build	built	built	give	gave	given
burst	burst	burst	go	went	gone
buy	bought	bought	grind	ground	ground
			grow	grew	grown
catch	caught	caught			
choose	chose	chosen	hang	hung	hung
cling	clung	clung	have	had	had
come	came	come	hear	heard	heard
cost	cost	cost	hide	hid	hidden
creep	crept	crept	hit	hit	hit
cut	cut	cut	hold	held	held
			hurt	hurt	hurt
deal	dealt	dealt			
dig	dug	dug	keep	kept	kept
do	did	done	know	knew	known
draw	drew	drawn			
drink	drank	drunk	lay	laid	laid
drive	drove	driven	lead	led	led

Base Form	*Simple Past*	*Past Participle*	*Base Form*	*Simple Past*	*Past Participle*
leave	left	left	slide	slid	slid
lend	lent	lent	slit	slit	slit
let	let	let	speak	spoke	spoken
lie	lay	lain	speed	sped	sped
light	lit (lighted)	lit (lighted)	spend	spent	spent
lose	lost	lost	spin	spun	spun
			split	split	split
make	made	made	spread	spread	spread
mean	meant	meant	spring	sprang	sprung
meet	met	met	stand	stood	stood
			steal	stole	stolen
pay	paid	paid	stick	stuck	stuck
put	put	put	sting	stung	stung
			stink	stank	stunk
quit	quit	quit	strike	struck	struck
			swear	swore	sworn
read	read	read	sweep	swept	swept
ride	rode	ridden	swim	swam	swum
ring	rang	rung	swing	swung	swung
rise	rose	risen			
run	ran	run	take	took	taken
			teach	taught	taught
say	said	said	tear	tore	torn
see	saw	seen	tell	told	told
seek	sought	sought	think	thought	thought
sell	sold	sold	throw	threw	thrown
send	sent	sent			
set	set	set	understand	understood	understood
shake	shook	shaken	upset	upset	upset
shine	shone	shone			
shoot	shot	shot	wake	woke	woken
show	showed	shown	wear	wore	worn
shrink	shrank	shrunk	weave	wove	woven
shut	shut	shut	weep	wept	wept
sing	sang	sung	win	won	won
sink	sank	sunk	wind	wound	wound
sit	sat	sat	withdraw	withdrew	withdrawn
sleep	slept	slept	write	wrote	written

Appendix 3

Some Categories of Non-count Nouns

A. Substances with no definite units

Solid		*Liquid*	*Gas*
butter	gold	coffee	air
cheese	paper	glue	helium
meat	plastic	honey	oxygen
cement	soap	oil	ozone
chalk	toothpaste	tea	smog
cotton	wood	tomato sauce	smoke
glass		water	steam

B. Substances with units too small to count

corn	hair	spaghetti
grass	rice	wheat
hail	sand	

C. General categories made up of subcategories

General Category	*(Related Count Nouns)*
food	(apples, carrots, cookies, potatoes, etc.)
fruit	(grapes, oranges, pineapples, etc.)
clothing	(shirts, dresses, ties, suits, shoes, etc.)
jewelry	(bracelets, necklaces, rings, etc.)
baggage, luggage	(suitcases, trunks, bags, etc.)
equipment	(tools, machines, pens, typewriters, etc.)
furniture	(chairs, tables, lamps, etc.)
hardware	(hammers, nails, screws, screwdrivers, etc.)
machinery	(machines)
money	(coins, bills, cents, dollars, dimes, etc.)
mail	(letters, postcards, packages, etc.)

General Category	*(Related Count Nouns)*
postage	(stamps)
traffic	(cars, buses, trucks, etc.)
homework	(assignments)
work	(jobs, tasks)
slang	(slang words)
vocabulary	(words)
scenery	(mountains, forests, lakes, etc.)
advice	(suggestions, recommendations)
evidence	(facts)
information	(facts)
news	(news item)
art	(paintings, drawings, statues, works of art, etc.)
music	(songs, symphonies, compositions, pieces, etc.)

D. Conditions

darkness	rain	embarrassment
heat	weather	fatigue
humidity	wind	hunger
light		pain
lightning		war

E. Abstract concepts

affection	happiness	poverty
anger	honesty	time
courage	justice	trouble
communication	luck	wealth
fun	patience	

F. Academic subjects, fields

biology	history	physics
chemistry	linguistics	psychology
economics	mathematics	statistics
English literature		

G. Languages

Chinese German Indonesian
(*But:* the ______ language)

H. Gerunds

fishing	manufacturing	smoking
hiking	over-eating	

I. Plural non-count nouns. Only a few plural nouns are non-count. The most common are

cattle	livestock	shorts
clothes	pants	slacks
eyeglasses	police	

Notes: 1. When a non-count noun is used with the meaning "a kind of," it becomes a count noun.

France produces some excellent *wines.* (= kinds of wine)

Fuller discovered a natural *geometry* in nature. (kind or system of geometry)

2. Many nouns can be either count or non-count but with different meanings. Some examples:

Count	*Non-count*
a glass (= container)	glass (= substance)
a beer (= a can or bottle of beer)	beer (= substance)
a paper (= any paper with writing on it)	paper (= blank paper)
a war (= a period of fighting)	war (= the condition of fighting)

Appendix 4

Noun Plurals

A. REGULAR: Follow the rules for adding **-s** and **-es** in Appendix 1.

B. IRREGULAR

1. Common English words

Ending	Singular	Plural	Notes
-o	echo hero potato	echoes heroes potatoes etc.	*Some exceptions:* pianos, radios, solos
-f	calf half leaf loaf self shelf thief wolf	calves halves leaves loaves selves shelves thieves wolves	*Most nouns which end in* **-f** *are regular:* beliefs, sheriffs, roofs
-fe	knife life wife	knives lives wives	
	caribou deer moose sheep	caribou deer moose sheep	
	child die foot goose louse man mouse ox tooth woman	children dice feet geese lice men mice oxen teeth women	

2. Academic words borrowed from Latin and Greek

Ending	Singular	Plural	Notes
-a	formula vertebra	formulae vertebrae	*or:* formulas
-um	bacterium curriculum datum medium memorandum	bacteria curricula data media memoranda	
-us	alumnus nucleus radius stimulus syllabus	alumni nuclei radii stimuli syllabi	
-ix **-ex**	appendix index matrix vortex	appendices indices matrices vortices	*or:* appendixes *or:* indexes *The ending* **-ces** *is pronounced like the word "sees."*
-is	analysis basis crisis hypothesis oasis parenthesis synopsis	analyses bases crises hypotheses oases parentheses synopses	*The final* **-ses** *is pronounced like "sees."*
-on	criterion phenomenon	criteria phenomena	
-s	means series species	means series species	

Appendix 5

Verbs Followed by Infinitives

A. Verbs followed by infinitives without an infinitive (second) subject

Example: **We *decided to have* dinner at home.**

afford
agree
appear
apply
arrange
ask
attempt
(can't) bear
beg
begin
care
cease
choose
claim
consent
continue
dare
decide
demand
deserve
desire
endeavor
expect
fail
forget
get
guarantee
happen
hate
help
hesitate
hope
intend
learn
like
long
manage
mean
need
neglect
offer
plan
prefer
prepare
pretend
proceed
promise
propose
prove
refuse
remember
resolve
say
seem
(can't) stand
start
struggle
swear
tend
threaten
try
turn out
volunteer
wait
want
wish

B. Verbs followed by infinitives with an infinitive (second) subject

Example: **Mary *asked John to sing* a song.**

advise
allow
appoint
ask
assign
authorize
beg
cause
caution

challenge	help	remind
choose	hire	require
command	implore	schedule
compel	instruct	stimulate
convince	invite	teach
dare	like	tell
direct	motivate	tempt
enable	need	train
encourage	oblige	urge
expect	order	want
forbid	permit	warn
force	persuade	wish
get	prepare	

C. Verbs followed by infinitives with **for** + infinitive subject

Example: **We *arranged for him to stay* at a hotel.**

arrange	intend	wait
(would) hate	mean	

Appendix 6

Verbs Followed by Gerunds

Example: **Sue *enjoys living* in the city.**

admit
advise
anticipate
appreciate
attempt
avoid
(can't) bear
begin
cease
choose
complete
consider
continue
defer
delay
deny
detest
discuss
dislike
dread
enjoy
escape
excuse
finish
forget
give up
hate
(can't) help
imagine
include
intend
keep (on)
like
mean
mention
(don't) mind
miss
neglect
postpone
practice
prefer
propose
put off
quit
recall
recommend
regret
remember
resent
resist
resume
risk
(can't) stand
start
stop
suggest
take up
try
tolerate
understand

Appendix 7

Some Preposition Combinations

A. Some preposition combinations with adjectives and verbs

be accustomed to
accuse . . . of
acquit . . . of
be active in
admire . . . for
adjust to
be afraid of
agree with
allocate . . . to
be annoyed with
arrest . . . for
ask for
attach . . . to

believe in
belong to
blame . . . for

call for
be capable of
care about/for
complain about
concentrate on
be concerned about
be confused about
consist of
convert to
convict . . . of
be convinced of
cope with

date from
depend on
disagree with

be disappointed with something/in somebody
do something about

equip . . . with
be excited about
be exhausted from
expose . . . to

be famous for
be fascinated with/by
fine . . . for
forget about
be frightened of

graduate from

be harmful to
help . . . with
be interested in

listen to
look at/for/through
look forward to

be made of
make . . . of

object to
originate in

participate in
pay for
prescribe . . . for
protect . . . from

react to
be relevant to
rely on
resort to
respond to
be responsible for
return to
be rude to
be satisfied with
search for
sentence . . . to
shout at

be similar to
stop . . . from
suffer from

take care of
thank . . . for
think about/of
transfer from . . . to
try . . . for
turn to

be upset about
use . . . for
be used to

work for/on
be worried about

B. Some preposition combinations with nouns

account of
(in) charge of
controversy over/about
effect on
(the) matter with
reason for
report on
solution to
voice in

Bibliographic Sources

Lesson 1: Rodney Jackson and Darla Hillard, "Tracking the Elusive Snow Leopard," *National Geographic,* Vol. 169, No. 6, (June 1986), pp. 793–809.

Lesson 5: William R. Greer, "Flood in Hills: This Year the Town Had the Dam," *New York Times,* November 7, 1985: Section II, p. 22.

Lesson 6: William Raspberry, "So No One Has to Retire," *Washington Post,* October 20, 1986, p. A13.

Lesson 7: Richard Levine, "Column One, Transport: Many Bridge Fares Are to Rise Again," *New York Times,* January 8, 1987, p. II-1. Richard Levine, "Transit Agency Sets Goals, and Even Meets Some," *New York Times,* January 11, 1987, p. IV-32.

Lesson 8: Jamie Murphy, "Down Into the Deep," *Time,* August 11, 1986, pp. 48–54.

Lesson 12: Tamar Lewin, "Sudden Nurse Shortage Threatens Hospital Care," *New York Times,* July 7, 1987, p. A-1.

Lesson 17: Heather Vogel Frederick, "For Women Athletes, a Rugged Champion from Alaska," *Christian Science Monitor,* September 23, 1985, p. 1. The Reverend Donald Hart, "Huslia," in *Everything I Know About Training and Racing Sled Dogs,* by George Attla, with Bella Levorsen, Rome, New York, Arner Publications, 1974. *The World of Sled Dogs,* by Lorna Coppinger, with the International Sled Dog Racing Association, New York, Howell Book House, 1977, pp. 19–80 *passim.*

Lesson 18: David R. Francis, "How TV Helps Preserve Eskimo Culture in Canada's Far North," *Christian Science Monitor,* November 27, 1985, p. 16. David Lamb, "For Nome, Radio is Strictly Voluntary," *Los Angeles Times,* August 20, 1987, p. 20. Molly Moore, "Eskimo Scouts: Surveillance and Survival in Alaska," *Washington Post,* March 4, 1988, p. A-4. Christopher S. Wren, "Far North Has Militia of Eskimos," *New York Times,* April 1, 1986, p. A-14. Robert J. Flaherty and Frances Hubbard Flaherty, *My Eskimo Friends, "Nanook of the North,"* Garden City, NY, Doubleday Page & Co., 1924.

Lesson 19: Michael deCourcy Hinds, "A Dream Come True," *New York Times Magazine,* April 26, 1987, pp. 32–36. William E. Geist, "One Man's Gift: College for 52 in Harlem," *New York Times,* October 19, 1985, p. 1. William Raspberry, "Special People from P.S. 121," *Washington Post,* October 28, 1985, p. A-20.

Lesson 20: Maria Augusta Trapp, *The Story of the Trapp Family Singers,* Philadelphia, J. B. Lippincott, Co., 1949.

Lesson 21: Conrad Phillip Kottack, "Swimming in Cross-Cultural Currents," *Natural History,* May 1985, pp. 2–11.

Lesson 22: Barbara Bradley, "From Fake Reefs to Diapers—Kids Turn Inventors," *Christian Science Monitor,* June 26, 1987, p. 1. Michael W. Miller, "Is America Short on Bright Ideas? Not at College Class in Inventing," *Wall Street Journal,* June 30, 1986, p. 1.

Lesson 23: "Kids Did It!" in the following issues of *National Geographic World:* May 1985, p. 3, August 1985, p. 5, December 1985, p. 23, May 1986, p. 30, June 1986, p. 12, January 1988, p. 3. Bob Secter, "Cold Facts of the Weather," *Los Angeles Times,* February 9, 1987, p. 1. Michael Kernan, "West Virginia's Youthful Curators of Local History," *Smithsonian,* October 1986, pp. 164–166. "They Dig Dinos," *National Geographic World,* October 1987, pp. 6–9. "Tree-Mendous Fun," *National Geographic World,* January 1988, pp. 11–13.

Lesson 24: David E. Pitt, "$6 Million in Art Stolen From Gallery on the Upper East Side," *New York Times,* February 10, 1988, p. B1. David E. Pitt, "Art Gallery Raid Involved Daring Acrobatics," *New York Times,* February 11, 1988, p. B5. Douglas C. McGill, "The Case of the Purloined Goddess," *New York Times,* October 9, 1986, p. C25. Peter S. Greenberg, "Smuggled Treasures," *Art & Antiques,* Summer 1986, pp. 81–84. Roberto Suro, "Going Undercover for Art's Sake," *New York Times Magazine,* December 13, 1987, pp. 42–52.

Lesson 25: David Bourdon, *Calder: Mobilist/Ringmaster/Innovator,* New York, MacMillan Publishing Co., Inc., 1980. Laurie Lisle, *Portrait of an Artist: A Biography of Georgia O'Keeffe,* New York, Seaview Books, 1980.

Lesson 26: Tony Gray, *Champions of Peace,* London, Paddington Press, Ltd., 1976.

Lesson 27: William Marlin, "Buckminster Fuller, 'A Terrific Bundle of Experience,' " *Christian Science Monitor,* September 23, 1983, p. 13. Albin Krebs, "R. Buckminster Fuller, Futurist Inventor, Dies at 87," *New York Times,* July 3, 1983, Section I, p. 17. "A Town in Vermont is Bursting at a Bubble Idea," *New York Times,* March 30, 1980, Section I, p. 26.

Index